blue
rider
press

THE
OPERATORS

THE WILD AND TERRIFYING
INSIDE STORY OF AMERICA'S WAR
IN AFGHANISTAN

MICHAEL HASTINGS

BLUE RIDER PRESS
a member of Penguin Group (USA) Inc.
New York

blue
rider
press

Published by the Penguin Group

Penguin Group (USA) Inc., 375 Hudson Street, New York, New York 10014,
USA • Penguin Group (Canada), 90 Eglinton Avenue East, Suite 700, Toronto,
Ontario M4P 2Y3, Canada (a division of Pearson Penguin Canada Inc.) • Penguin
Books Ltd, 80 Strand, London WC2R 0RL, England • Penguin Ireland, 25 St Stephen's
Green, Dublin 2, Ireland (a division of Penguin Books Ltd) • Penguin Group (Australia),
250 Camberwell Road, Camberwell, Victoria 3124, Australia (a division of Pearson Australia
Group Pty Ltd) • Penguin Books India Pvt Ltd, 11 Community Centre, Panchsheel Park,
New Delhi–110 017, India • Penguin Group (NZ), 67 Apollo Drive, Rosedale, North Shore
0632, New Zealand (a division of Pearson New Zealand Ltd) • Penguin Books (South
Africa) (Pty) Ltd, 24 Sturdee Avenue, Rosebank, Johannesburg 2196, South Africa

Penguin Books Ltd, Registered Offices: 80 Strand, London WC2R 0RL, England

ISBN 978-0-399-15988-6

Printed in the United States of America
1   3   5   7   9   10   8   6   4   2

Book design by Michelle McMillian

While the author has made every effort to provide accurate telephone numbers and Internet addresses at
the time of publication, neither the publisher nor the author assumes any responsibility for errors, or for
changes that occur after publication. Further, the publisher does not have any control over and does not
assume any responsibility for author or third-party websites or their content.

Penguin is committed to publishing works of quality and integrity.
In that spirit, we are proud to offer this book to our readers;
however, the story, the experiences, and the words are the author's alone.

ALWAYS LEARNING   PEARSON

TO MY FAMILY

I was silenced, said no more to him, and we soon left. I was sadly disappointed, and remember that I broke out on John, damning the politicians generally, saying, "You have got things in a hell of a fix, and you may get them out as you best can."

—FROM MEMOIRS OF GENERAL W. T. SHERMAN, on Sherman's first meeting with President Abraham Lincoln

. . . a certain irresponsibility grew.

—HISTORIAN H.D.F. KITTO, on the decline of leadership in Athens during its twenty-seven-year war with Sparta

The sons-of-bitches with all the fruit salad just sat there nodding, saying it would work.

—PRESIDENT JOHN F. KENNEDY, on the bad advice he received from his generals, remarking on the colorful ribbons on their chests

We are mad, not only individually, but nationally. We check manslaughter and isolated murders; but what of war . . .

—LUCIUS ANNAEUS SENECA, ROMAN PHILOSOPHER

CONTENTS

PART IV. THE GRACEFUL EXIT

PART I
THE PLAN

MEDIA رسانه ها

ISAF

RC-C: 629

Hasting
Michael
lling Stone
4005207
red. 15 APRIL
es.

1 | DELTA BRAVO

APRIL 7, 2010, MILTON, VERMONT

I dialed the strange number with a sequence of digits too long to remember. The tone beeped in a distinctly foreign way. My call went through to Afghanistan.

"Hello, Duncan? This is Michael Hastings from *Rolling Stone*."

I was in a house on Lake Champlain, smoking a cigarette on a screened-in porch with a view of the Adirondacks. I put the smoke out in an empty citronella candle, went inside, and grabbed a notebook from the kitchen counter.

Duncan Boothby was the top civilian press advisor to General Stanley McChrystal, the commanding general of all U.S. and NATO forces in Afghanistan. Duncan and I had been e-mailing back and forth for a month to arrange a magazine profile I was planning to write about the general. I'd missed his call yesterday. He'd left a message. This was the first time I'd spoken to him.

Duncan had a slight British accent, ambiguous, watered down. He told me I should come to Paris, France.

"We're going to discreetly remind the Europeans that we bailed their ass out once," he said. "It's time for them to hold fast."

Duncan explained the plan.

The visual: Normandy. D-day. The Allied forces' greatest triumph. Bodies washed ashore then, rows of white crosses now.

The scene: McChrystal standing on the banks of the English Channel, remembering the fallen, a cold spring wind blowing up from Omaha Beach. He's a "war geek," Duncan said; he spends his vacations at battlefields. A few months ago, on a trip back to DC, on his day off he went to Gettysburg.

The narrative: The trip is part of a yearlong effort for McChrystal to visit all forty-four of the allies involved in the war in Afghanistan. This time, it's Paris, Berlin, Warsaw, and Prague. It's to shore up support among our friends in NATO—to put to rest what Duncan called "those funny European feelings about the Americanization of the war." From my perspective, he told me, there would be something new to write about. No one had ever profiled McChrystal in Europe.

Duncan was a talker. He hinted: I'm in the know. I'm in the loop. I'm in the room.

"What do you make of Karzai's outburst the other day?" I asked. Hamid Karzai, the U.S. ally and Afghan president, had threatened to join the Taliban, the U.S. enemy. He'd done so just days after President Barack Obama had met with him. "That make life difficult for you?"

Duncan blamed the White House.

"The White House is in attack mode," he said. "It took President Obama a long time to get to Kabul. They threw the trip together at the last minute. We had six hours to get it ready. Then they came out of the meeting saying how much they slammed Karzai. That insulted him."

I took notes. This was good stuff.

Duncan spun for McChrystal—the general had invested months of his time to develop a friendship with the Afghan president.

"Karzai is a leader with strengths and weaknesses," he said. "My guy has inherited that relationship. Holbrooke and the U.S. ambassador are leaking things, saying they can't work with him. That undercuts our ability to work with him. For the McCains and the Kerrys to turn up, have a meeting with Karzai, criticize him at the airport press conference, then get back for the Sunday talk shows. Frankly, it's not very helpful."

I was surprised by his candidness. He was giving me his critique over the phone, on an unsecured line.

"This is close-hold," Duncan said, using a military phrase for extremely sensitive information. "We don't like to discuss our movements. But I would suggest getting to Paris next week. Wednesday or Thursday. We'll do the trip to Normandy on Saturday."

"Okay, great, yeah," I said. "So I'll plan to meet up with you guys next week. For travel, the main thing is—"

"You'll probably want to go to an event with us on Friday at the Arc de Triomphe, maybe sit down for an interview with The Boss, then take a train out to Normandy, and meet us there."

"Cool. As much as I can get inside the bubble, I mean, travel inside the bubble."

"I'll let you know on the bubble."

He hung up.

I e-mailed my editor at *Rolling Stone*: "Can I go to Paris?"

2 | IT'S NOT SWITZERLAND

SEPTEMBER TO NOVEMBER 2008, KABUL

A handful of staffers are watching television on the 32-inch flat screen outside the office of General David McKiernan at the International Security Assistance Force (ISAF) headquarters in Kabul. The buildings that house ISAF (pronounced *eye-saf*) used to be home to a sporting club for the wealthiest in Afghanistan, but for the last eight years it's been the headquarters for a succession of American generals who have run the war in this country. It doesn't have the harsh look usually associated with a U.S. military base: There are trees, manicured lawns, and a beer garden with a wooden gazebo. Guard towers overlooking the garden are perched on cobblestone walls, just refurbished by the Turks, with shiny new paneling, like the interior of a Hilton Garden Inn.

It's 7:00 A.M. on September 4 in Afghanistan, 9:30 P.M. on September 3 in St. Paul, Minnesota, and Sarah Palin is on the screen. She's giving her acceptance speech at the Republican National Convention. She's getting cheers from the crowd, the crowd is going nuts, but it's too early in the morning in Kabul for anybody to be excited. The door to McKiernan's office is open—it looks like a headmaster's office at a boarding school, all dark oak and thick carpet—and the general passes in and out, checking early-morning e-mail. He overhears a few lines of Palin's speech as she gushes about her husband, Todd. "Sounds like someone's running for prom queen," McKiernan says with a smile.

McKiernan has more than a passing interest in the 2008 presidential election. The next commander in chief is going to be his boss. He's been on the job since June, planning to stay for a two-year tour. It's what he'd promised the Afghan generals, the diplomats, and his NATO allies.

It's the fifty-seven-year-old general's second chance to run a war. He got screwed in Iraq. He pissed off Don Rumsfeld, and Don Rumsfeld doesn't forget. McKiernan was in charge of invading that country, and his plan called for more troops to prevent an insurgency from springing up. Rumsfeld didn't want to hear it; Rumsfeld wanted to go in as small as possible. (And, by the way, a year earlier, McKiernan had testified to defend the Crusader artillery weapons system, a program Rumsfeld wanted killed.) After seeing McKiernan in Iraq, Rumsfeld judges the general to be "a grouch, resisting the secretary of defense," as one retired admiral who advised the Pentagon puts it.

So after Baghdad falls, McKiernan is supposed to take over. Doesn't happen. He ends up in limbo, or what passes for limbo when your country is at war in two countries—commanding the U.S. Army in Europe. His promotion to fourth star gets held up. He doesn't get it for two more years, and even then over Rumsfeld's objections.

During that time, the military world is changing. Iraq is a mess. Americans blame Bush, they blame Rumsfeld, they blame neoconservatives, oil men, Israel, the media, Dick Cheney, Halliburton, Blackwater, Saddam. The U.S. military, by and large, escapes the blame—they were just following orders. The public gives them a pass.

Not so within the ranks: There's score-settling and finger-pointing going on. The finger points to an entire generation of military commanders. The poster boy is General George Casey—he oversaw Iraq's complete spiral to shit and didn't stop it, didn't adapt, or so the story goes. He's got gray hair. He's old-school. To top it off, Casey gets promoted to Army Chief of Staff—he gets rewarded for the mess.

McKiernan is old-school, too. He's not one of these new-school generals, like a Dave Petraeus or a Stan McChrystal. Petraeus already has a historic reputation, and McChrystal is an up-and-coming star, currently working on the Joint Staff at the Pentagon. McKiernan is part of the old generation, or so they claim. He gets dubbed the Quiet Commander; headlines call him "low-key" during his time in Iraq. Even in the midst of an invasion, "he is rarely known to swear." "In any type of a chaotic situation," another general says of him, "he'll be in the middle of it, directing things without emotion." He's a golfer, shoots in the seventies. He was on the debate team in high school. His best friend growing up says he "tended to be shy." He hates PowerPoint and prefers a "walkabout style" of leadership to long-winded briefings, according to his colleagues.

He doesn't have a deep fan base in the media, either. He doesn't like to get his picture taken, doesn't suck up enough when visitors from Congress come over to check out the front lines. McKiernan wouldn't think to send an autographed picture of himself to a journalist, as David Petraeus once did. That's not McKiernan's style—he doesn't even have a good nickname. At over six feet, with silver hair and a handsome square-jawed face, he could be typecast as the father in a teen movie who scares the hell out of any boy stupid enough to take his daughter to the prom.

He still gets his shot at Afghanistan, though. He's next in line. The old school rules still hold sway on the promotion board.

It's been a bit of an awkward transition, partly because President Bush wants to pass off Afghanistan to the next president. McKiernan says a few things that aren't quite diplomatic: He notes that some of those European allies seem to treat war "like summer camp." Even more awkwardly, in October, Dave Petraeus, once his underling, now becomes his superior. Dave gets the job as CENTCOM commander, which means he has oversight of the wars in Afghanistan and Iraq. Not the worst situation, he thinks, just a bit uncomfortable.

A month after Palin's acceptance speech, the presidential election is on television again at ISAF HQ. This time, the staff gathers to watch the vice presidential debate. It's Senator Joe Biden from Delaware, squaring off against the governor of Alaska, Palin. Afghanistan is a hot topic in the debate, and they're listening to see where the candidates stand, what they can expect. McKiernan has had a troop request on the table at the White House for months, asking for some thirty thousand more soldiers. The White House has resisted—they want NATO to pony up the reserves, and McKiernan is hoping the next administration will give him the soldiers he's asked for.

Palin and Biden agree: more troops and resources to Afghanistan. What they don't agree on is McKiernan's name. Palin keeps calling him "McClellan"; two times she says it. (The staff breaks out laughing, incredulous; a McKiernan advisor pings an e-mail to the general, joking about how Palin got his name wrong.) Biden resists the urge to correct her. Instead, he points out that McCain, her running mate, has said, "The reason we don't read about Afghanistan anymore in the paper [is that] it's succeeded."

Afghanistan: an American success story. The media dub it the Forgotten War. The nightmare in Iraq overshadows the conflict. The United States regularly declares success in Afghanistan, despite mounting evidence to the contrary. A year doesn't pass without public declarations of progress. In 2001, Secretary of Defense Donald Rumsfeld says, "It's not a quagmire." In 2003, the commanding general in Afghanistan says that U.S. forces should be down to 4,500 soldiers by the end of the following summer. After that summer, General John P. Abizaid says the Taliban "is increasingly ineffective." In 2005, the Taliban is "collapsing," says General Dave Barno. In 2007, we are "prevailing against the effects of prolonged war," declares Major General Robert Durbin. In 2008, General Dan McNeill claims that "my successor will find an insurgency here, but it is not spreading." That same year, Defense Secretary Robert Gates assures us we have a "very successful counterinsurgency," and we won't need a "larger western footprint" in the country. The United States is spending every three months in Iraq what they'd spend in an entire year in Afghanistan; there are over thirty thousand troops in Afghanistan, about one quarter of the number deployed in Iraq.

McKiernan recognizes the trend lines aren't great. Since 2006, violence has spiked dramatically, from two thousand annual attacks to over four thousand in 2008. American and NATO soldiers are getting killed at a rate of nearly one per day. Civilian casualties have tripled over the past three years, killing a total of approximately 4,570 people. The more U.S. and NATO troops added, the worse the violence gets. The Taliban has regained control over key provinces, including those surrounding the country's capital. On October 13, a *New York Times* reporter writes a story suggesting we're losing. McKiernan dismisses it; the guy "was only in town for a week." But yes, things aren't good. McKiernan gets a classified report from America's seventeen intelligence agencies saying the prognosis is "grim." McKiernan wants those troops to hold the line—who's going to be the next commander in chief?

A few weeks after the vice presidential debate, Lieutenant General Doug Lute, head of Iraq, Afghanistan, and Pakistan policies at the White House, visits McKiernan in Kabul. A White House staffer nicknames Lute "General White Flag"—he likes to surrender. It's not a nice nickname. He didn't want to surge in Iraq, and he's skeptical on Afghanistan. He tells McKiernan that Obama has it locked up; it's a foregone conclusion, Lute says. Obama is going to be the next president.

Which is fine with McKiernan. During the campaign, Obama announces after he returns from a visit to Kabul that he'd give McKiernan "the troops he needed." McKiernan is impressed when he meets Obama that summer; he speaks to the senator in a phone call again before the election. He wants to build the relationship, quietly. And—let's face it—McCain is an asshole, thinks he's a military genius. Palin can't even get his name right. McKiernan, although he would never say so publicly, is pulling for Obama, a senior military official close to him tells me.

McKiernan is suspicious of McCain, too, because McCain views Petraeus as some kind of godlike figure. Anyone so close to Petraeus can't be good for McKiernan. He's waiting for the full attention to get back to Afghanistan.

On November 4, 2008, Obama wins the election. McKiernan is working up a new strategy to get to the president—three strategic reviews are going on, one at ISAF, one at CENTCOM, and one in the Bush White House. Lots of wacky ideas are being thrown about: The CIA has a plan to just withdraw everyone and go total psyops—like broadcasting horrible atrocities of ISAF soldiers to scare the shit out of the Taliban. McKiernan's plan calls for a comprehensive counterinsurgency strategy. It's heavy on training Afghan security forces—he puts the date of how long it's going to take at 2014, at the earliest. He sees the country's limitations: "There's no way this place is going to be the next Switzerland," he tells me during an interview that fall in Kabul.

3 | LADY GAGA

APRIL 15, 2010, PARIS

The hotel *Rolling Stone* put me up in sucked.

"How can you not have wireless access?" I asked the woman at the front desk of the Hotel SynXis Pavillon Louvre Rivoli. It was a modest/shitty/overpriced tourist ghetto with a do-it-yourself espresso maker in the lobby.

"We have wireless," she said.

"What's the password?"

"There is not a password. You pick up the signal from our neighbors."

"Getting a signal from somebody else doesn't count as wireless access."

"Perhaps it is because you are on the fifth floor."

"Can I move to another room?"

She typed a few things into her computer.

"There are not other rooms."

I was supposed to meet Duncan in twenty minutes at the Hotel Westminster. McChrystal was staying there, too. According to Google Maps, it was a ten-minute walk.

It was April in Paris, a beautiful afternoon. The French citizens were typically hip and metropolitan, walking specimens from Chanel and Christian Dior inserts. I was in basic Brooks Brothers: navy blue blazer, navy tie with gold flowerish-looking things, and gray flannels. It was what I wore when I reported, a habit I started in Baghdad in 2005. I was relatively young then, twenty-five, and a polo shirt, jeans, and sneakers didn't get me very far. It showed disrespect to the Arabs and pinged me as an even bigger asshole American than I actually was. If I dressed nicely, I didn't get searched as often in the dozen or so security checkpoints I would pass through on a typical day. The Iraqis would think I was a VIP, a diplomat, an engineer. The illusion of respectability.

I turned down Rue de la Paix, passing the eight-hundred-euro-a-night Grand Hyatt and a Cartier jewelry boutique, a diamond necklace in the window selling for over ten thousand euros. The Westminster was right next door under a discreet gold-and-black entranceway.

The lobby was four-star: plush red chairs and couches, marble floor, table service. The Ritz Hotel—the one where Princess Di's last security camera footage was taken as she passed through the revolving door—was around the corner. I texted Duncan that I was in the lobby. I ordered an espresso and a Perrier.

In the lobby, there was a glass display for an expensive pen (Blancpain, ballpoint, €150) and a pile of international newspapers: the *Financial Times*, *The Guardian*, *Le Monde*. A wealthy Italian in a Brioni suit was on the phone, yelling loudly enough so whoever he was talking to could hear him, which meant I could hear, too. "I have a meeting with the Kuwaitis now," he screamed. There was a late-middle-aged American couple with matching black Tumi luggage checking in.

I took out my notebook. I started making a numbered list. Memory was unreliable, as they said, and I'd learned that I never really knew what material I was going to need for a story until later. I tried to discipline myself to write down ten details about any scene. I had gotten to number four (1. chandelier, 2. blancpain, 3. montblanc, 4. wedged btw cartier on rue de la paix) when the elevator doors to the lobby opened. I slipped my notebook into my inside blazer pocket. A man in a gray suit and red tie and white shirt walked out.

"Duncan? Michael Hastings."

We shook hands.

I still couldn't place his accent—slightly British, though he was an American. He had doughboyish smooth skin, white with any easy sunburn, cheerful. He was in his late thirties or early forties, one of the new kind of public relations experts the Pentagon had employed: the beneficiary of the government's aggressive push to privatize many functions in the war that had been done by uniformed military in the past.

"We have the Arc de Triomphe ceremony in an hour or so. I'll introduce you to members of the team," he said. "That's Ray." Duncan pointed to a twenty-eight-year-old Hispanic man in jeans and a T-shirt talking to the desk clerk.

Ray told me he set up communications for General McChrystal. He was a staff sergeant, and he'd worked for other generals. All the communications were encrypted, he told me, so they could send and receive top-secret information when they were traveling.

"We have to prevent against attacks," he said. A number of foreign governments—both friendly and enemy—viewed trips like this as opportunities to spy, he explained. "We're always getting attacked."

"No shit?"

"Yeah, you should have seen the look on their faces at the desk when we told them we had to switch all the rooms yesterday. We couldn't get the right satellite reception." The French, or perhaps some other government, Ray suggested, had probably rigged the rooms that the hotel had reserved for them in order to spy on the general. It was an old trick: Book the Americans in the hotel room where the listening devices are set up. The South Koreans, in the eighties, were notorious for it; they'd book journalists on top of one another in the same hotel so the bugging wire just had to run up and down one part of the building. A friend of mine, an American State Department official, had recently traveled to Islamabad, Pakistan. The official had wondered why he always got the same room in the luxury Serena Hotel—he initially thought it was because they liked him.

The doors to the lobby opened. A troop of green uniforms entered. It was jarring—American military uniforms in a European capital, in color, not black-and-white. Although military officials often traveled in civilian clothes when outside a war zone, they put on their most impressive outfits when they had official business to conduct. Dark forest-colored pants and blazers decorated with shiny gold buttons and colorful pins on the lapels, an inscrutable kaleidoscope of middle-aged merit badges—tiny silver parachutes, rifles, a rainbow's worth of ribbons. I recognized McChrystal, with four gold stars on his shoulder.

As advertised from his press clippings, he was gaunt and lean. His slate blue eyes had this eerie capacity to drill down into your brain, especially if you fucked up or said something stupid. He reminded me of Christian Bale in *Rescue Dawn*, if Bale had spent a few more years in Vietcong captivity. McChrystal was unique, the first Special Forces soldier to have taken such a prominent battlefield command. Special Forces guys like him were called "snake-eaters." It was considered a compliment.

For five years, McChrystal was America's top hunter/killer, responsible for the deaths of hundreds of enemies, maybe terrorists, maybe a few civilians. He oversaw a network of prison camps in Iraq where detainees were regularly tortured—kept out in the cold, naked, covered in mud, with the occasional beating. He'd been credited with taking one of the biggest terrorist scalps of them all, Abu Musab al-Zarqawi. Zarqawi was killed in a strike in the summer of 2006 near Baqubah, Iraq. McChrystal's teams had obsessively pursued him. "If we don't get Zarqawi, we will be failures," he had told his men a year earlier. After the attack killed

Zarqawi and seven others, McChrystal showed up at the destroyed safe house to inspect the damage himself. There wasn't much left, just a couple of burnt pages from a copy of the Arabic edition of *Newsweek* and enough of a fingerprint to confirm it was the most wanted man in Iraq. President George W. Bush publicly thanked McChrystal, saying he had done excellent work, marking him as the nation's most respectable assassin. Thanks to McChrystal's dynamic reputation, President Obama had selected him for the top job in Afghanistan a year earlier, despite a number of other controversies in his career.

I got an adrenaline kick from meeting my subject. *Time* magazine's runner-up for Person of the Year. The commanding general of the biggest war currently going on Earth. Stanley McChrystal, aliases Big Stan, the Pope, COMISAF (Commander of the International Security Assistance Force), The Boss, M4, Stan, General McChrystal, Sir. A "rock star," as his staff liked to call him.

Duncan made the introduction.

"Michael is writing the article for *Rolling Stone*," Duncan said.

"Thanks for having me, sir, it's a real privilege," I said.

"I don't care about the article," McChrystal said. "Just put me on the cover."

I paused. He was joking, sort of. I wanted to come back with something funny. Or at least make an attempt at humor. I didn't have a clue who was going to be on the cover, though. A writer rarely has a say in those decisions. The name Bono flashed through my mind. I reached for something a little more current . . .

"It's between you and Lady Gaga, sir."

His top staff stopped the cross talk. The moment had the potential to get awkward. Had I stepped over the line? Was I being disrespectful? What was my deal? Who is this kid? How's The Boss going to respond?

McChrystal looked at me and smiled. "Put me in the heart-shaped bathtub with Lady Gaga," he said. "Maybe some rose petals. I just want to get on the cover so I can finally gain my son's respect." (His son was in a band.)

Everyone laughed.

McChrystal and the other generals headed upstairs to get ready for the ceremony, one hour away.

I stayed in the lobby and ordered another espresso.

4 | "INTIMIDATED BY THE CROWD"

JANUARY TO FEBRUARY 2009, WASHINGTON, DC

It's the first ten days of his presidency, and Obama goes to the Pentagon. He walks into a room on the second floor known as the Tank. The Tank is sacred. The Tank is where the serious matters of state are discussed—"the highly classified conversations," says a U.S. military official. The Tank gets its name from where it started, in the basement, *Dr. Strangelove*–like, but now it's upstairs in the E ring with a blond wood table and big leather armchairs. It's legendary. Secretary of Defense Bob Gates makes sure to go to the Tank once a week. (Rumsfeld didn't; Rumsfeld made the generals come to him. Gates is wiser; he goes to them like he's "coming to kiss the ring of the Godfathers," says a Pentagon official.)

The president works the room, speaking to Joint Chiefs of Staff Admiral Mike Mullen and about ten other senior military officials, including a three-star general named Stan McChrystal. Gates follows behind him. Obama doesn't seem quite right, McChrystal will recall, he isn't acting like a strong leader. He seems "intimidated by the crowd," a senior military official who attended the meeting will tell me. He's acting "like a Democrat who thinks he's walking into a room full of Republicans," the senior military official added. "You could tell he was tentative."

Obama's mistake: Despite being very impressive, he's not comfortable with the military, McChrystal thinks. He made a "bad read," continues the senior military official who attended the meeting. "We wanted to be led; we would have been putty in his hands." (McChrystal would share similiar feelings with his staff, telling them that Obama seemed "intimidated and uncomfortable.")

Obama doesn't get the military culture, military officials will say privately. They don't think he likes them or supports them. They sense weakness. Obama doesn't have the feel. There are questions, from the highest to lowest ranks. He's a wimp, Barack *Hussein* Obama. One Marine unit teaches a local Afghan kid to call an African-American female Marine "raccoon" or "Obama"; I've heard other white soldiers refer to him as a nigger, maybe for shock value. There's that race thing. There's his Nobel Peace Prize. Some soldiers say they love him, of course, that he's the best, that everyone should have voted for him. It's mixed.

In the upper ranks of the brass: Obama is a Democrat, always a question mark. The Pentagon is filled with Republicans—it's been a long eight years, and the last three defense secretaries have all been in the GOP. A popular joke: A soldier walks into an elevator with Nancy Pelosi, Harry Reid, and Osama Bin Laden. Third floor, going up. He has two bullets in his pistol. Doors open: Pelosi is shot twice, Reid and Bin Laden are strangled.

A CBS sports announcer tells that joke back home in a magazine story, and he gets condemned for it. He has to issue a public apology. He tells the joke overseas on a USO tour: The troops think it's hilarious. I tell the joke once on an embed to test it out: The troops laugh hard.

Still, Democrats: easier to push around.

Obama was against the Iraq invasion, calling it a "dumb war." He's correct, of course, and opposing it was the smart decision, the right decision, yet . . . He didn't support Iraq, ergo he doesn't support us. Or something like that. His perceived antimilitary vibe is a political vulnerability; McCain tries to exploit it during the campaign, pushing a story that Obama snubbed wounded veterans on a trip to Germany. The story is false, but maybe there's something there.

As a candidate, Obama visits Afghanistan and Iraq during the summer of 2008. In Kabul, he's greeted as a hero, he goes to the embassy, goes to ISAF; the word at camp gets out that Obama is there, and by the time he gets to ISAF, dozens of soldiers are out to see him. He works the rope line, poses for pictures; he's a big hit, according to a U.S. military official who helped arrange the trip in Kabul. Then he heads to Baghdad, stopping at the U.S. embassy in Saddam's old palace. Embassy officials and military officials in Iraq are wary—they think he's using this as a campaign stop. The Baghdad embassy—this is still Bush country, this is John McCain territory. This isn't, necessarily, Obama's base.

At the embassy, he gives a talk in the main palace hall, where there's a Green Beans Coffee stand. The hall is packed, one of the biggest turnouts State Department officials can remember. After the talk, out of earshot of the soldiers and diplomats, he starts to complain. He starts to act very un-Obama-like, according to a U.S. embassy official who helped organize the trip in Baghdad. He's asked to go out to take a few more pictures with soldiers and embassy staffers. He's asked to sign copies of his book. "He didn't want to take pictures with any more soldiers; he was complaining about it," a State Department official tells me. "Look, I was excited to meet him. I wanted to like him. Let's just say the scales fell from my eyes after I did. These are people over here who've been fighting the war, or working every day for the war effort, and he didn't want to take fucking pictures with them?"

I push back: Look, it's a brutal schedule. I'm sure he was tired, stressed out, venting.

The embassy official isn't buying it: For the one day he's in Baghdad, no matter how tired, how stressed, Obama should suck it up. He shouldn't have bitched about taking a photo. Obama is the "crankiest CODEL"—short for "congressional delegation"—that he's had visit Baghdad, says this State Department official. And he has handled dozens of them. Embassy staffers gather afterward: Is it me, or were you all not impressed with Obama? The staffers agree: I thought I was the only one! The State Department official votes for Obama anyway. On the same trip, Obama meets with General Petraeus, and the presidential candidate tries to pin the general down on how fast he can get the troops out of Iraq.

These are the kinds of stories that fuel the suspicions high-ranking officials in the military have about Obama: He's one of the most talented and natural politicians in a generation, but he doesn't really understand them. Doesn't get their culture, doesn't get their wars. The wars, to Obama, are campaign issues. His primary relationship to the conflicts in Iraq and Afghanistan is how they affect his electoral fortunes—his opposition to the Iraq War gave his candidacy the spark that set it off, allowing him to separate himself from the other two Democratic candidates who had supported Iraq. He wants to firm up his national security credentials, so he says he'll focus on Afghanistan, the "right war." Promising to focus on that war makes a good line on the campaign trail. He didn't serve—so what that Reagan didn't, so what that Bush didn't really? They played the part. They are hooah, and the troops love hooah. Bush gave the generals what they wanted, and the generals like to get what they want.

Obama's aware of the vulnerability, writing in his second memoir how "Republicans increasingly portrayed Democrats as weak on defense." That decades-old problem for Democrats, allegedly soft on national security ever since Truman was accused of "losing China." Bullshit, naturally, and historically self-destructive, but it has had major consequences, as three generations of Democratic leaders have fallen over themselves to prove that they can play tough. Truman can't run for reelection because he's not winning in Korea (Truman had to go into Korea because we couldn't lose Korea!); Kennedy has to out–Cold Warrior Richard Nixon to get the job.

Johnson has to prove he won't "lose Vietnam," so he digs an even deeper hole, destroying his presidency. ("I don't think it's worth fighting and I don't think we can get out. It's the biggest damn mess I ever saw," Johnson says in 1964, a year before he commits hundreds of thousands of troops to Saigon.) Carter—shit! He gets pushed around by the Iranians, while Reagan cuts a secret deal with them, gives them weapons, no less—but forget that. Clinton proves the military's worst fears: He wants to let fags in, dodged the draft, smoked dope, and gets mocked when he tries to kill Bin Laden with missile strikes.

Obama, his advisors believe, has to prove he isn't really antiwar. That he's serious. That he can keep America safe. (Remember Hillary's three A.M. phone call ad?) That he'll play by the bipartisan conventions of the national security community. During the presidential campaign, he stresses that we "took our eye off the ball" in Afghanistan and have to refocus our efforts there. Obama goes out of his way to say he "doesn't oppose all wars."

That January, McKiernan's request for more troops is waiting on Obama's desk. With three reviews just complete, Obama orders up his own review. Bruce Riedel, a terrorism expert, is called in to write up the draft. On February 17, a month after visiting the Pentagon, Obama releases a statement, the first major comment he's made on the war while in office. He says he's sending seventeen thousand troops to Afghanistan, that he's approving a "months-old" troop request, pinning the blame for the delay and increase on the previous administration. Obama expands the war into Pakistan, too, upping the number of drone strikes in the first year of his presidency to fifty-five, almost doubling the number that Bush had ordered in the previous four years.

What Obama and his top advisors don't realize is that the seventeen thousand troops are just the beginning. Seventeen thousand becomes twenty-one thousand a month later. McKiernan still has a request in for nine thousand more, part of his original ask. But he will tell military officials close to him that it's all he needs to do the job. He doesn't think

Afghanistan can support too many more American troops. McKiernan, an ally of the president, is not going to press for another massive troop increase. Inside the Pentagon, other senior military officials don't see it that way. Twenty-one thousand isn't enough, nor is thirty thousand, for the war they have in mind. The Pentagon wants more troops, and sets out to find a way to get them.

5 | ARC DE TRIOMPHE

APRIL 15, 2010, PARIS

McChrystal's entourage waited outside the Westminster. A gray minivan pulled up. The staff poured in, getting seats. A navy blue Peugeot parked behind it. A French general stepped out, wearing a fancy light gray uniform with gold epaulets. McChrystal and his wife, Annie, an outgoing and fit brunette just on the other side of fifty who had joined him in Paris for the weekend, ducked inside.

I walked up to the minivan. There wasn't enough room.

Duncan waved down a taxi. "We'll follow them," he said.

Duncan and I jumped into the cab.

"Arc de Triomphe, s'il vous plaît."

The cabdriver hit the gas and started weaving through traffic, starts and stops.

"It's sort of fun to be following that car, especially when it's filled with American military uniforms," Duncan said.

"Like something out of the Cold War," I said.

Duncan checked his BlackBerry.

"Two French journalists have been kidnapped outside of Kabul," he told me. "They were supposed to have an interview with McChrystal and got kidnapped the day before. It's a bit of a problem. The French are willing to pay ransom, and the Taliban know that."

"Has it come up in discussions?"

"Yes, briefly."

The French's willingness to pay ransom was an irritant to the Americans. By paying off the kidnappers, the Americans believed the Europeans were incentivizing kidnappings, a sin on a par with negotiating with terrorists. The French had lost ten soldiers in one incident in 2008 because they had stopped paying protection money to the Taliban, U.S. officials believed. So the Taliban surrounded them and attacked. It was symptomatic of the long-standing gripe Americans had with their European allies: They just didn't seem like they wanted to fight the war.

Duncan rattled off a list of national "caveats"—the restrictions countries put on their forces operating in Afghanistan. I'd heard it before. NATO originally imposed some eighty-three restrictions on their troops, creating a deep resentment among American and British soldiers. U.S. military officials claimed that most of the NATO allies needed someone back in Brussels to give them approval for the simplest operations, including calling for a medevac flight, Duncan said. The rules had a weird, cultural-stereotype-reinforcing absurdity. The Dutch resisted working more than eight hours a day. The Italians and the Spanish were discouraged from taking part in combat operations. Another country refused to do counternarcotics; yet another would *only* take part in counternarcotics; a few wouldn't fight after a snowfall; the Turks wouldn't leave Kabul; another nation wouldn't allow Afghan soldiers on their helicopters. The Danish troops' tour lasted only six months. The Germans weren't allowed to leave their bases at night, and in Berlin, the leadership refused to call it a war. It was a "humanitarian mission." American soldiers had a list of derogatory nicknames for the International Security Assistance Force acronym ISAF—*I Suck at Fighting, In Sandals and Flip-flops,* and *I Saw Americans Fight.*

"So what's the purpose of this event?"

"It's one of the things that generals have to do," Duncan said. "He's an introvert. This kind of thing makes him very uncomfortable. Honestly, he'd much rather be back in Afghanistan."

Formations of French soldiers were standing in the courtyard in front of the Arc de Triomphe—French navy, marines, army, and police. A French military band started to play when McChrystal stepped out of the car to inspect the formations and lay a wreath at the Tomb of the Unknown Soldier. A crowd of tourists gathered across the street to watch. The band played "La Marseillaise."

Not much happened worth writing about, I thought. Well, there was always Normandy.

Duncan and I started to walk back to the hotel.

"The trip to Normandy is off," Duncan told me.

Fuck. That was the entire reason for me to be there—to get a scene at the beaches of Normandy.

"With the wives here, and the high tempo of operations in Afghanistan, it's been decided that it would be better just to stay in Paris."

"Oh, okay," I said. "That's cool with me."

Normandy was off. It wasn't actually cool with me, but there wasn't anything I could do about it. Par for the course, really. In my experience, reporting trips rarely went according to plan, especially when the military was involved. There was almost always a fuckup, a logistics disaster, a lengthy delay, or an interview that was promised that would never come through. The only option was to roll with it and try to scramble to find material to take its place.

Back at the hotel, Duncan brought me up to the third floor, room 314.

The suite had been converted to an operations center, set up to run the war on the go, and McChrystal's traveling staff of about ten was gathered there. Ray, the communications guy, had set up about fifteen silver

Panasonic Toughbooks across the tables, crisscrossing blue cables over the hotel carpet, hooked into satellite dishes to provide encrypted and classified phone and e-mail communications.

Duncan pointed out the other members of the team.

Major General Mike Flynn was considered within the military as one of the most brilliant intelligence officers of his generation. This was the fourth time he'd worked as McChrystal's number two. He was of Irish descent, wiry, with black hair and a touch of gray, "a rat on acid," as one of the staffers called him, pointing to what his staff jokingly called a severe case of attention deficit disorder. ("You would never want to be his assistant," Duncan warned. "He goes through them very quickly.") He'd partied hard growing up in a family of nine, regularly getting out-of-control drunk while narrowly avoiding serious trouble. He followed in the well-established career path of youthful screwups: He joined the Army, finding his home in the military intelligence branch. He kept his interests varied throughout his career: He took up surfing on a stint in Hawaii and got a master's degree in telecommunications in the mid-eighties. Since the wars in Iraq and Afghanistan had started, he'd become a reservoir of the country's most critical secrets, a walking database of highly sensitive intelligence in the War on Terror—whom we wanted to kill, whom we killed, and what country we killed them in. His colleagues, though, also considered him somewhat indiscreet; he felt that information should be widely shared, a shift from the traditional bureaucratic practices within the intelligence community of hoarding the choicest intelligence morsels. While he worked at the Pentagon, he didn't even bother to lock the doors to his car—"a used, beat-up, crappy car," as his wife described it. He didn't think anyone would bother trying to steal his old cassette tapes, he said. When he talked to me, I could almost see the sparks fly inside his skull from the clash between the classified and unclassified halves of his brain.

Duncan pointed to Mike Flynn's younger brother, Colonel Charlie Flynn, who was leaning over Ray's shoulder, staring at a laptop screen. It was pretty unusual to have two brothers as part of the same general's staff. I started to get the sense that McChrystal viewed his staff as an extension of his family, surrounding himself with men from whom he could expect absolute loyalty. While Charlie looked like a shorter and thicker version of his older brother, their personalities were diametric. Mike came across as flighty and imaginative, a man who could go from point X to Z to Y, outlining the insurgent network of the Pakistani Taliban, then wondering where he placed his ham sandwich. Charlie was a stickler for going from point A to point B, so hurry the fuck up. Charlie joined the infantry rather than military intelligence, choosing the physical over the cerebral, and he was now McChrystal's executive officer, meaning his primary job was keeping The Boss on schedule. Charlie would be the one to tell me when my interview with McChrystal was finished. You'll notice it's over, Duncan told me, when a vein on Charlie's forehead starts to pop.

A middle-aged fellow in a startlingly white Navy uniform was sitting quietly, reading over some papers. Maybe late forties, early fifties. He was Rear Admiral Gregory Smith, director of communications for ISAF. His face reminded me of the cartoon dog Droopy. Duncan explained Smith was his internal rival in determining McChrystal's media strategy. Duncan was a civilian contractor; Smith was military public affairs. They regularly clashed over the best way to handle the press. In recent years, the Pentagon had moved from relying on military public affairs officers toward civilian experts like Duncan who had real-world media experience. (The traditional military style of public relations—a combination of stonewalling, poorly written press releases, and making demonstrably false claims—had become such an embarrassment during the Iraq War that the Pentagon had launched a searching, multibillion-dollar effort to overhaul and reshape its media strategy, which included hiring guys like Duncan, who at one time worked as a producer for CNN. The Pentagon had about twenty-seven thousand people working on public relations, spending $4.7 billion in a single year.) Nowadays, it was normal for each general to have his own personal media handlers—sometimes numbering as many as a half dozen within an entourage—to raise his profile in the press.

I knew Smith's name from newspaper stories—whenever ISAF had to respond on the record to a top media outlet like *The Washington Post* or *The New York Times*, his name would be attached to the typically banal quotes. He'd also just gotten involved in a nasty exchange with a popular freelance journalist named Michael Yon. Yon, considered very military-friendly, had been kicked off an embed. He retaliated by calling Smith and his public affairs staff a bunch of "crazy monkeys" and Smith in particular "another monkey." Yon accused Smith of being part of a "smear campaign" against him. "Next time military generals talk about poor press performance in Afghanistan," Yon wrote on his Facebook page that April, "please remember that McChrystal and crew lacked the dexterity to handle a single, unarmed writer . . . How can McChrystal handle the Taliban?"

The younger staffers on McChrystal's team came in and out of the suite: Major Casey Welch, thirty-two, with a classic Midwestern look, was McChrystal's aide-de-camp. Khosh Sadat was an Afghan Special Forces commando and the other aide-de-camp. He was brought along on the Europe trip to provide good visuals during meetings and photo ops. (McChrystal wanted to show that the Afghans were part of the war, too, so they deserved a high-profile slot on his staff.) Then there was Lieutenant Commander Dave Silverman, a Navy SEAL; he'd worked under McChrystal in Baghdad, running a Special Forces team to capture and kill Al-Qaeda in Iraq.

An older white guy in a suit and tie walked by without saying hello. He had thinning hair and a bitter aura, his wardrobe unfamiliar with an ironing board.

"That's Jake," Duncan said. "He's kind of a dick."

Jake McFerren, a retired Army colonel, was McChrystal's longtime friend and confidant. They'd been roommates at West Point, and McChrystal hired him to be his top political advisor.

McChrystal walked into the room through the connecting door. He'd ditched his uniform and was now wearing a blue shirt and tie—off-the-rack civilian casual. He sat down at the table.

"General, do you have time for Michael to ask a few questions?"

"Let's do it."

I hit record on my tape recorder.

"Is this an open line?" McChrystal asked, pointing to a phone that Ray had installed.

"Ray, is this an open line?" Duncan repeated.

"Yes, sir," he said.

"Do you need it open? I want to make sure we're not talking in front of a telephone."

Duncan hung up the receiver.

I sat down next to him and started fumbling with my questions. I wanted to begin with his career and family life. First, I asked him if he'd gone for a run that morning. One of McChrystal's defining characteristics, according to all the biographical material I'd read about him, was his obsession with fitness. He regularly would go on jogs for six or seven miles. When he briefly lived in New York to work at the Council on Foreign Relations, he'd run to the office from his place in Brooklyn. His running fetish had become a staple in every profile about him—journalists seemed to view it as a measure of his toughness and drive that translated directly into the ability to win a war.

"I actually like touring by running. I went this morning down past the Louvre at the end, then down the river, and came up by Voltaire's old house," he said.

He described his relationship with his father, Herbert, who had fought in Korea, then been a battalion and brigade commander in Vietnam. Herbert had graduated from West Point in 1945; McChrystal had graduated in 1976. He explained his own notion of his career: "We really felt we were a peacetime generation," he said, comparing his father's generation with his own. "I never thought I was going to be a general, and I certainly never thought I'd be fighting a war as a general."

Duncan interjected, cleverly trying to dictate the direction of the interview.

"Michael is going to come to Kabul for a week, the first week in May," Duncan said. "He's going to hang out with us. Some of the piece is in the next few days. We're originally hoping to bring him up to Normandy, but obviously that sort of changed. But your advice: What are the questions he should ask your team in the next few days, because he'll be spending time with them as much as you?"

"I think that's a good idea," McChrystal said. "Try to understand each of them. Who is related to who? Like we do with the Taliban, or Al-Qaeda. Who was at the wedding? It tells you a lot more about organizations than an organizational chart."

We talked for about eight more minutes until, as Duncan predicted, the vein on Charlie Flynn's forehead bulged.

"He has to go," Charlie said. The general had an important dinner to attend.

McChrystal leaned back. Duncan had told me he hated to do these kinds of events—dinners, ceremonies, diplomatic niceties.

"How'd I get screwed into going to this dinner?" McChrystal demanded.

"The dinner comes with the position, sir," Charlie replied.

McChrystal turned sharply in his chair.

"Hey, Charlie, does this come with the position?" He flicked Charlie the middle finger. He stood up.

"What's the update on the Kandahar bombing?" McChrystal asked, shifting back to the war.

"We have two KIAs, but that hasn't been confirmed," Charlie said. (The final result of the attack: three dead civilians and seventeen wounded.)

He took a final look around the suite. "I'd rather have my ass kicked by a roomful of people than go to this dinner," McChrystal said. He paused for a beat. "Unfortunately, no one in this room could do it."

With that, he went out the door.

"Who's he going to dinner with?" I asked Dave, the Navy SEAL.

"Some French minister," said Dave. "It's fucking gay."

I'd spent many weeks around the country's most senior military officials, and I'd never heard them talk like this before. It was the kind of banter I'd heard on the front lines, but not inside headquarters, where blandness and discretion often trumped colorful language and obscene hand gestures, at least in front of reporters. What exactly was I dealing with here?

"Mike, by the way," Dave said to me, "there's no way he could kick my ass."

6 | "A VIOLENT ACT"

JANUARY TO MAY 2009,
KABUL AND WASHINGTON, DC

In January, General David McKiernan receives an e-mail from the White House. They're looking for a new ambassador to take the place of William Wood, a Bush appointee, in Kabul. Chemical Bill—that's what Embassy officials call him; a man obsessed with poppy eradication, as he'd done with coca when he was down in Colombia. Chemical Bill has run the embassy into the ground. Under his watch, private security contractors from AmorGroup North America party hard, engaging in "deviant actions" that "took place over the past year and a half and were not isolated incidents," according to a report from a government watchdog group. The guards' behavior will eventually make headlines when the lewd pictures they've taken of themselves are posted on the Internet. There's a name for the kind of alcohol shots the guards take: vodka butt shots. The world is treated to digital pictures of drunken and overpaid bald men spraying shaving cream on one another's penises.

Wood's own fondness for the occasional cocktail doesn't go over very well in the Islamic culture. American military officials aren't always impressed with him, either. During an hour-and-a-half meeting at the U.S.

embassy in the fall, attended by a congressional delegation, Wood disappears for fifteen minutes. When he comes back, according to a U.S. official who attended the meeting, he's in "high spirits"; he starts interrupting McKiernan, he starts interrupting the congressional delegation. After the meeting, McKiernan tells a staffer that he never wants "to go to the embassy again." None of that, however, has much to do with why Wood is being replaced—he's been in Kabul for two years already.

The White House wants McKiernan's input on who should take Wood's place. What about Karl W. Eikenberry?

Eikenberry is a three-star general. He's done two tours in Afghanistan, with his second in 2005 as the commander of all U.S. forces there. While other military officials were crowing about success in Afghanistan, Eikenberry had been warning that the Taliban was making a comeback.

He'd been in the Pentagon on September 11 when the plane struck—almost killed him, he recalls; he was protected only by the reinforced Mylar glass. He finds a secretary who points to another general's door. It's locked! she screams. He kicks the door down and rescues the general. Hollywood-style shit. He doesn't quite look like a hero, though. Parted hair, nervous, like a door-to-door *Encyclopædia Britannica* salesman in Topeka who knows Wikipedia is about to put him out of business. He has a reputation as an intellectual—brainy, with master's degrees from Harvard and Stanford and an advanced degree in Chinese history from Nanjing University.

McKiernan tells the White House that he doesn't think Eikenberry is a good choice. Eikenberry would have to retire from the military to take the job, and McKiernan doesn't think having two military officers—one active duty, one recently retired—will work. He thinks that might lead to unnecessary clashes and battles of ego. He thinks the U.S. ambassador should be a civilian career diplomat. Karzai, too, doesn't like Eikenberry—they've spent "thousands of hours" working together, according to a U.S. embassy official, and they didn't get along the last time he was in charge there.

On January 27, 2009, the White House announces their choice, leaking the name of the next ambassador to *The New York Times*: Karl W. Eikenberry.

In retrospect, military officials close to McKiernan say overruling him on the choice of Eikenberry was a worrying sign that McKiernan had lost support in Washington. (They ignore it, though, because really, anybody is better than Wood.) McKiernan is shocked by how little time he's gotten with the new president—during the first three months of 2009, while the White House is conducting its first Afghan policy review, McKiernan speaks to Obama only twice.

That spring, McKiernan makes the *Time* 100, a list of the people the magazine believes are the most important and influential in the world. The accompanying article, written by retired NATO commander Wesley Clark, describes him as "extraordinarily calm under stress, a clear thinker, tough, and morally courageous."

It's the last good press McKiernan gets. In the Pentagon, the rumblings to remove him are getting louder. There are those within the Pentagon who aren't satisfied with McKiernan's demand for only thirty thousand troops. The general also doesn't have the right style. In March, McKiernan briefs Admiral Mike Mullen, chairman of the Joint Chiefs of Staff, and Gates in a video teleconference. His responses don't impress them, or so they claim. "He was weak," a Pentagon official close to Gates and Mullen tells me. "He wasn't high-energy. This is a war fighter's game, and McKiernan had some of the right concepts, but he didn't have the creativity and energy."

Mullen's number-one choice to replace McKiernan is Stanley McChrystal. He's known him for years and has personally groomed him, giving him entrée to an elite crowd—Mullen, for instance, introduced McChrystal to New York mayor Mike Bloomberg at a dinner party a few years earlier. (McChrystal would later model his command center in Afghanistan after Bloomberg's office in New York.) For the past year, McChrystal has worked down the hall from Mullen in the Pentagon as the director of his staff, impressing the admiral with his work ethic. "He wasn't strolling in at 0630 with fucking mocha lattes," the Pentagon official tells me. Mullen and Gates agree on McKiernan, and Petraeus, the CENTCOM commander who was once his subordinate, backs the move.

Gates takes the decision to the White House in April. Gates carries a big stick. He's the most important holdover from the Bush administration, the man Obama has come to heavily rely on for advice in foreign affairs. *What does Bob Gates think?* is a question the president often asks. Insiders in the White House call him Yoda, the Pentagon his Dagobah system—squat-looking, round face, finely combed gray hair. Obama defers to Gates's judgment and respects his three decades' worth of experience in the defense and intelligence communities. Obama signs off on McChrystal, taking Mullen's and Gates's word that he's the best choice.

Mullen flies to Kabul to give McKiernan the news in late April. Mullen is another throwback, an officer and a gentleman. He wants McKiernan to save face; just resign, he tells him, that's the way to go. McKiernan tells him no way: You'll have to fire me. McKiernan is stunned— mainly because he hasn't done anything wrong. There's no dereliction of duty, no screwups on the battlefield, no insubordination. Mullen tells him he's just not the right man for the job anymore. The next day, McKiernan goes on what had been a long-scheduled vacation—his first in ten months. He spends the days worried if he's really going to get fired.

On Wednesday, May 6, over a dinner at Camp Eggers, the headquarters for the Afghan training mission, Gates again asks McKiernan for his resignation. McKiernan again refuses to give it. He tells the defense secretary that he made promises to Afghans and his NATO allies that he'd serve with them the full two years. Gates says he'll fire him if he doesn't resign. He doesn't, and Gates fires him. "Firing a four-star general like that," a Pentagon official tells me. "It was a violent act. You couldn't point to some fuckup, like he was negligent in battle, or invaded Pakistan—it was a series of performances in briefs that slowly eroded [Gates's and Mullen's] confidence in him."

At McKiernan's headquarters in Kabul, the word slowly leaks out. On Saturday, May 9, he gathers his staff in a meeting room at the Yellow House—the nickname for the building where he has his office. There are about thirty of his staff in the room. No one knows what's coming; McKiernan has to fly to Pakistan in the morning, so they think maybe it has something to do with that, military officials who attended the meeting tell me.

McKiernan walks into the room. "I'm being relieved from command," he tells the staffers. He speaks for about five minutes. As he thanks his staff for their service, he has to stop. He starts to choke up. He chooses to say a last thanks and leaves the room. "We all sat there shocked," according to a military official who was in the room. "No one said a word. For two minutes."

On Monday, May 11, Gates is asked at a press conference whether this ends McKiernan's career. "Probably," he responds. It's a brutal answer after the general's thirty-seven years of service. Gates piles on with a few more veiled criticisms: Afghanistan needs "fresh eyes" and "fresh thinking," he says. "We have a new strategy, a new mission, and a new ambassador. I believe that new military leadership is needed."

It's the "first sacking of a wartime theater commander," notes *The Washington Post*, since General Douglas MacArthur was fired by Truman at the height of the Korean War.

The media's response to McKiernan's firing is vicious and swift. The man who weeks earlier had been considered one of the hundred most influential people in the world is now a loser, a dud, someone who *doesn't get it*. The meme forms quickly in the press and on blogs: McKiernan is old-school, McKiernan doesn't understand how to be a general these days. McKiernan doesn't comprehend counterinsurgency. This is his greatest crime.

Counterinsurgency (COIN) is a set of tactics for fighting the Taliban that have become very popular within the military's new generation of leaders. The accusation that *he doesn't get COIN* is both damning and false. McKiernan had been employing a counterinsurgency strategy for his entire tenure, setting up local police forces and pushing his soldiers to live among the population. McKiernan, though, doesn't get how to suck up to the media, doesn't pucker up to the senators, doesn't play the bureaucratic game as well as his rivals. McKiernan gives too much of a shit about Europe and NATO. McKiernan isn't shaking things up enough, not taking enough risks. McKiernan is no Dave Petraeus—the father of modern counterinsurgency, who in 2006 oversaw the writing of a new Army manual called FM 3-24, the COIN bible for American officers; McKiernan is no Stan McChrystal, another rising star and COIN acolyte. Both Petraeus and McChrystal are COINdinistas, the nickname given to the faction within the military community that has embraced the counterinsurgency doctrine with an almost evangelical fervor. There's a feeling among these men that McKiernan *isn't a true believer.*

McKiernan is the B-Team, and as Admiral Mullen would later say, McChrystal is "the A-Team." McChrystal had served loyally as a Pentagon spokesperson; he'd been successful at waging a counterterrorism campaign in Iraq; he'd ingratiated himself first with Rumsfeld, Bush, and Cheney and later with Mullen and Gates. Stan McChrystal *gets counterinsurgency*, and he'll soon get his chance in the spotlight.

On June 2, McKiernan boards a plane to leave Kabul. His top staff goes with him, a gesture of loyalty he appreciates. He's given a warm send-off among the soldiers on base, who line up for over an hour to shake his hand and say their good-byes. His supporters in the military firmly believe he's gotten a raw deal. Where the conventional wisdom has suddenly turned to say that McKiernan doesn't get it, doesn't understand, a few military officials see something else. It has very little to do with ability, senior military officials will tell me. It's bureaucratic infighting and office politics. "McKiernan was on the wrong team," a senior military official says. "He isn't on Petraeus's team; McChrystal is. All of these top leaders are dynamic and adaptable—the idea McKiernan didn't understand COIN is laughable." McKiernan went to William & Mary, not West Point, the military academy that had produced the tight-knit clique of powerful generals who had begun to seize control of the Army, which included Petraeus, McChrystal, and General Ray Odierno in Iraq, all West Point graduates. Privately, McKiernan will tell friends that it was Petraeus who was behind getting rid of him. (Petraeus denies to colleagues that he had a hand in McKiernan's dismissal—but "of course that's what Petraeus would say," observes a senior Pentagon official. "Petraeus supported the move.")

There's a little blowback within the ranks, grumbling that Gates hasn't shown McKiernan enough respect and the reasons for letting him go don't really add up. "McChrystal is a Special Forces guy; he's never commanded an army this big. It could be a problem," a senior military official tells me at the time. McKiernan's firing, another U.S. official says, is a "dirty" move to get a public relations bump that comes from the "strong move of switching generals to win the war."

Senior military and Pentagon officials would describe yet another dynamic at work. The Pentagon secretly (and not so secretly; talk to any COINdinistas, and they'll say the same thing) wants more than the twenty-one thousand troops Obama has given McKiernan. They're still well short of the hundred thousand American troop number that COIN supporters within the Pentagon think is the minimum that needs to be in Afghanistan. McKiernan wasn't going to ask for tens of thousands of more soldiers and Marines—he'd already gone to the mat once, and he felt if he was eventually given the additional nine thousand troops he had requested, he'd have enough to win. On the other hand, by firing McKiernan, the Pentagon had a chance to "reset," says one U.S. military official. The COINdinistas felt they couldn't get all the soldiers they had wanted with McKiernan in charge, but a "new mission" and a "new military leadership" would give the Pentagon another shot to escalate. A new general, in other words, presents a new opportunity to ask for more boots on the ground. "Gates was the mastermind behind this whole thing," a military official with knowledge of the events would tell me. (Gates will deny this.) Maybe Obama's Yoda has a bit of Vader in him after all.

7 | ON THE X

Duncan, Dave Silverman, his wife, and I headed to a small Italian restaurant for dinner. Dave's wife was a restaurateur in Washington, DC, and she had chosen the place.

Dave was about five feet eight with a blond crew cut. He was a thirty-three-year-old naval officer trained as a Navy SEAL. The others on the team jokingly called him the Admiral—although he was outranked on the senior staff, his input on larger strategic questions was taken seriously. He arranged logistics for the general's travel and played a key role in shaping McChrystal's communication strategy. He spoke in quick and compact bursts, compressing complex ideas into an insanely efficient militarized syntax. One of his jobs was to handle the Sync Matrix, or as Dave explained it, "to map out what the general is trying to accomplish, then put that on a time chart and functionally organize what we're doing by his end states and objectives at certain dates and times, and then identify what events are missing based on his goals, plug those events in, and then leverage existing events as the forums we use to articulate our message."

The Europe trip was one of those events.

Dave joined the Navy SEALs, he told me, because it was the closest experience to a "high-performing sporting environment" that he could get in the military. He'd been a star water-polo player in San Francisco, where he'd grown up. The camaraderie, the eliteness of it, the chance to serve his country—his father had been a pilot in Vietnam, his grandfather fought in Patton's army.

Dave was hilarious. Dave made gay jokes—everybody in the military made gay jokes all the time, but Dave was a liberal from San Francisco, so it was okay. When Dave talked about one of his friends' toddlers, a real hyperactive kid, he said the only way to deal with the kid was to put him in the pool. Dave described the water in the pool as a "tactical neutralizer." He didn't find that description odd.

We sat down to dinner. I asked if he minded if I took notes. He said it was okay. We started talking.

I felt comfortable around McChrystal and his team. Why was that? I'd been with them only for a few hours.

Maybe it was the war.

Most of Dave's adult life had been dominated by war. The rest of the team had been immersed in it for the past decade—even Duncan had spent a year working in Iraq before going to Afghanistan. War consumed me, too. I thought about it all the time. If Dave was the badass Navy SEAL, Duncan the hired PR gun, I had become the "veteran war correspondent." In 2005, I had started covering Iraq for *Newsweek*. At twenty-five, I was the youngest Baghdad correspondent at the magazine. My younger brother was an infantry platoon leader, fighting in Iraq while I was there covering it. He won a Bronze Star and watched three of his good friends receive life-altering wounds. In 2007 a young woman I loved was killed by Al-Qaeda in Iraq. It was an unbearable experience, and I spent the next year writing a book to honor her memory. I promised myself that I was through with war. Then I covered the U.S. presidential elections, traveling across the country on the campaign trail. Midway through, right after Hillary Clinton dropped out, I left my job at *Newsweek*. Three months later, I went to Afghanistan for the first time.

Dave and I talked strategy. We talked McChrystal. We talked the players: General Jim Jones, the president's national security advisor; Clinton, the secretary of state; Eikenberry; Richard Holbrooke, the U.S. special envoy to Iraq and Afghanistan; and President Obama. Jones, Dave said, was "a clown . . . stuck in 1985." Dave told me McChrystal viewed Holbrooke as a "wounded animal": terrified of losing his job, ready to lash out and screw up the entire plan. Dave confirmed what others on the staff had said about Eikenberry: They didn't like or trust him. Hillary was fine—she had been a big supporter of The Boss. As for Obama? "He's not a leader," Dave said. "He's an orator." Dave said that McChrystal had been disappointed so far with Obama and the distance the White House kept from Kabul. (Obama had made only one trip to Afghanistan— fourteen months after taking office.) It was severe trash-talking about almost all the major civilian players involved in Afghanistan policy, and over the next few weeks, I would learn that Dave's feelings were shared by McChrystal and others on the staff as well.

In Dave's view, McChrystal was "MacArthur without the arrogance." He'd worked with him in Baghdad. Much of what Dave did in Iraq was classified—he was on a Special Forces team that tracked and killed high-value insurgents and terrorists under the Joint Special Operations Command (JSOC). McChrystal had transformed JSOC's culture: He'd linked up the MIT whiz kids with the Special Forces operators, making it the most capable "man-hunting operation on earth," Dave said.

"The operators are the guys on the *X*," Dave riffed. The *X* was the target; the bull's-eye; the spot on the satellite map where the action went down. "Everyone else is supporting the operator. But the operator doesn't get anywhere near the *X* if the other guys aren't doing their job."

Dave told stories, three of which somehow involved strip clubs and waking up smelling like strippers. The stories were all pretty funny, and his wife gamely put up with them. If you've never woken up smelling like a stripper before, perhaps the humor is lost.

We did the date/place swap—I told him when I was in Baghdad, he told me about the times he was there. It was a kind of ritual. The saying: It's a small war. You run into the same people, or people who were part of the same incidents. Bombings, battles, massacres, scandals. Involved in them or observing them. Each adding details to the experience, details neither could possibly have seen at the time—it's always too much, it's always overwhelming, what you see is always just a fraction of the war.

We talked media. There were journalists lining up to write books about McChrystal—they hadn't decided whom to give the best access to yet, preferring to hold it out as a carrot for better coverage, Duncan said. Dave mentioned a TV reporter who flashed her breasts to get an embed with his Navy SEAL team.

"That's bullshit," I said.

"It's not," he said.

"Did you look?"

"Of course," he said.

Dave's wife shook her head in faux exasperation.

"Duncan," Dave said, "tell your story about The Famous Television Anchor."

"Oh, that story," Duncan said.

The Famous Television Anchor, whose name Duncan asked me not to reveal, was a big personality at an American network. She was doing a story on McChrystal. They were in a Blackhawk helicopter. Duncan was sitting next to the anchor. One of McChrystal's things was that his entourage didn't travel in body armor, which played a key role in this story. The anchor kept cupping her breasts. She looked at Duncan, who had a quizzical expression on his face. "It's my implants—they get cold," she told Duncan. "I have to hold up little heat packs to them"—the kind skiers use to warm their gloves. "Here, you can feel them." The anchor grabbed Duncan's hands and pressed them to her breasts.

"That's a crazy story," I said. "It's fucking unbelievable."

My colleagues had a number of creative ways to build trust with the subjects of their reporting, apparently. And to an outsider, perhaps that kind of behavior might seem outrageous. But most correspondents I knew would go to extreme lengths to get a story—they regularly risked their lives, after all—in what was a highly competitive field. I actually sympathized with the two reporters, and I knew it was especially difficult for women journalists in war zones. They were always subjected to a kind of leering chauvinism, while male reporters could more easily play at being a soldier in this theater of macho men.

After a two-hour dinner, we grabbed a taxi and returned to the Westminster. I walked back to the Hotel Rivoli from there.

8 | THE A-TEAM

MAY TO JUNE 2009, WASHINGTON, DC

It's Friday night at the Pentagon, May 8, 2009, and Charlie Flynn is sitting at his desk in the outer office of the Joint Chiefs of Staff. He's McChrystal's executive officer, the closest to the man besides his wife—Charlie has been living with McChrystal at his house in the suburbs for a few months, commuting home on weekends to see his family in Virginia. Charlie is getting ready to leave for the weekend when Stan asks to talk to him.

They're giving me the job in Afghanistan, he tells Charlie.

"You don't have to answer right now," McChrystal says. "But when you go home this weekend, talk to your wife about it."

"Sir, I'm with you; I don't need to talk to my wife," Charlie says. McChrystal tells him okay—but talk to your wife. He'll be in touch on Sunday.

Charlie is like *fuck, yeah*. Charlie can't wait to get out of the Pentagon. He's spent eight of the last ten years deployed in combat. He's known McChrystal since '88, when he was a first lieutenant on assignment in Fort Benning, Georgia, living in the same temporary housing, their wives pregnant around the same time. They strike up a friendship—an up-and-coming lieutenant and a young major. They both like long runs and drinking beer, and they both love the Army.

They cross paths again, living on the same base in Fort Bragg, North Carolina, with the XVIII Airborne. Charlie starts to get command, they part ways—McChrystal goes off to do Harvard, Charlie goes to the Naval College. They both do Iraq—Charlie does two rotations in Iraq, and one in Afghanistan.

Charlie is a battalion commander in Afghanistan in 2002. There's only one American brigade there; he says the rest are Special Forces. "We didn't really know what we were doing in Afghanistan," he says about that time. "We thought we did, but we didn't know."

About halfway through his rotation, the invasion of Iraq begins.

"There was this big sucking sound of resources leaving Afghanistan," he says. "Where is all the fuel going, where is all the aircraft going?" There was no such thing as counterinsurgency then. He was going out in Helmand in rough conditions, living out in the field three weeks at a time, hunting Al-Qaeda or Taliban. After Baghdad, though, Afghanistan gets pushed aside—Charlie doesn't think he'll be back again. He spends the next few years coming in and out of Iraq.

On Sunday, McChrystal calls.

Yeah, I'm in. Who else?

Mike Flynn, of course. Charlie and Mike are two of the nine Flynn children. A military family. Their dad deployed to Korea. They got a taste of what it means when the country doesn't know it's at war. Their mom would be walking down the street in the small town in Rhode Island where they lived, going to Martin's, a neighborhood store. Where's your husband? the storekeeper asked. His mother would say, Oh, he's in Korea. Oh yeah, that's right; tell him I say hello. Charlie remembers thinking: Why don't these people know that the Korean War is going on? (Why don't these people know about Iraq? Afghanistan? Don't they *know*?) "Simple fact," says Charlie. "If you aren't there, you don't understand."

Mike and Charlie—back for another adventure. Growing up, they had wild times. Mike Flynn crashes four—count, four—automobiles. He gets in one wreck with Charlie. Crossing an intersection, a car slams into them, a T-bone. Charlie and Mike climb out of their car—they're okay. The other car—blood. Mike looks at it, sees the dead body. Oh, shit. They tell their dad. Nothing shocks their dad—Korean War vet, father of nine.

Mike Flynn is on board. They just need to work his transfer from his division.

Charlie opens up an office in the basement of the Pentagon. It's down in the National Military Command Center (NMCC), and he finds an empty room kept open for emergencies, like when Russia invaded Georgia. It's supposed to be where the Af/Pak cell is, but Charlie commandeers the space to prepare for Afghanistan. Putting in new phone lines; getting the computers up; getting ready for McChrystal's testimony before Congress; getting McChrystal's vaccinations, making sure he goes to the dentist. Calling the people they trust: gathering the best people and minds, he says.

"People would say, 'What am I going to do?'" Charlie says. "We'd say, don't worry, we'll figure it out."

McChrystal needs an aide-de-camp.

Thirty-two-year-old Major Casey Welch walks into his grandmother's house in Kentucky. "Did you hear that McKiernan or McSomething got fired?" she asks him. On Tuesday, he gets the call—Casey has been recommended by his last battalion commander, who knows McChrystal. On Thursday, Casey is in the Pentagon for an interview with The Boss, which ends up lasting only ten minutes. Casey has spent three of the past five years deployed. He's just returned from Samarra, Iraq, six months ago. He's recently married. Only one caveat: If it's going to be more than a year, tell him now. McChrystal okays the year—he knows Casey would stay longer if he asked, but he's gracious enough not to ask.

Casey gets a seat in the basement, working the phones. He joins Charlie and Lieutenant Commander John Pitta; Pitta is a fighter pilot, twice deployed to Iraq, who'd been doing nights as a watch officer in the NMCC. He's part of the team now, working days in the basement while he's still on the night shift. The phones are ringing off the hook—Mullen gives them carte blanche to pull in anyone, in any branch of the service. It's crazy, says Pitta, a blur. Other guys are arriving and they don't even have badges to get into the Pentagon, so they have to be escorted to the bathroom.

Dave Silverman is thinking of retiring—he's thirty-three, he's done enough. He's thinking of the private sector. He gets the call—for Stan, he'll do it. He'd been under him on a SEAL team in Baghdad and felt it was an opportunity he couldn't turn down. Duncan gets recommended through Lieutenant General William B. Caldwell to do press. Caldwell, once the top military spokesperson in Iraq, had relied on Duncan's advice in Baghdad, becoming known as the general's "Cardinal Richelieu," the influential advisor behind the curtain. Before Iraq, Duncan had worked for a public relations firm in Connecticut, though he'd also tried his hand at the theater, performing onstage in Durham, North Carolina. One reviewer described him as "a gifted young actor." He arrives in the Pentagon, starts working on McChrystal's congressional confirmation. Duncan knows it could be a rough fight. McChrystal's role in the cover-up of the friendly-fire death of Pat Tillman, an NFL star who joined the Army Rangers, is going to come up; Camp Nama, a base in Iraq that McChrystal was linked to after allegations of torture there were reported, is going to come up. These two red flags, seemingly ignored by Gates and Obama when they chose him for the job, wouldn't likely be dismissed by the media. McChrystal, until that point, has only a few Google hits—he is nearly a blank slate, a known unknown, with brief mentions here and there of his JSOC days, his involvement in the Tillman fiasco, and a few cameos in Human Rights Watch reports. It's Duncan's job to guide the reporters as they pick up the chalk to sketch a fuller picture of the man.

Jake McFerren? Hell yes. A retired colonel, and McChrystal's West Point roommate. Jake and Stan would go on double dates with their wives, once taking them to dinner at a Jack in the Box when the ladies were dressed in formal wear for a dance. Jake spent the last few years at NATO in Brussels. He gets named his top civilian political advisor, "responsible for helping foster international relations with the 44 countries that currently make up the coalition forces," his job description will read. He's also "one of the general's old army drinking buddies," another journalist will later note.

McChrystal calls Sir Graeme Lamb himself. Lamb did Iraq with him; Lamb is a Brit, an SAS legend. "I've always seen myself as a bit of a martini, shaken or stirred, type," Lamb says. British Special Forces had been integrated under the JSOC command, working closely with the Americans, and Lamb had been the key British soldier who worked with McChrystal in Iraq. Lamb had just retired—he was planning on heading down to Chile to do a snowboarding course, to get the motorcycle out of the garage and go down to Brunswick "putting some light back in his bones down in the Alps," he says. McChrystal calls him, he comes to DC, and they go out to dinner at a Mexican restaurant. Before the second beer, Lamb is in, and McChrystal doesn't even pay for the dinner, says Lamb. McChrystal rates high in Lamb's world—the kind of friend, "hard-forged," whom you can call in the middle of the night, to whom you can say, "Graeme, I have a problem. I'm in Laos."

Petraeus had three months to put together a staff for Iraq; McChrystal has three weeks for Afghanistan, says Flynn. It's the continuation of a rivalry between the two hotshot generals, both taking credit for the success in Iraq, and a sign of the growing sense among McChrystal's staff that they'll have a much harder task ahead in Afghanistan.

In the basement of the Pentagon, the core group of thirty or so men assemble: a handpicked collection of killers, spies, fighter jocks, patriots, political operatives, counterinsurgency experts, and outright maniacs, the likes of which the American military has never seen. They will soon become the most powerful force shaping U.S. policy in Afghanistan.

9 "BITE ME"

APRIL 16, 2010, PARIS

The next morning, Duncan invited me to sit in on a briefing as McChrystal prepared for a speech he was scheduled to give at the École Militaire, a French military academy. I was trying to get as much reporting done as possible. I planned to leave France on Sunday to head back to Washington, where I had a number of other interviews already scheduled.

In the hotel suite, I picked a spot across from McChrystal to lean against the wall, doing what is called fly-on-the-wall reporting. It is a technique originally pioneered and made popular by Theodore White, an American journalist who wrote the 1960 best seller *The Making of the President*. In the book, White had traveled and re-created scenes from President John F. Kennedy's 1960 campaign—it put the reader, as it were, inside the room, like a fly on the wall. A bug.

Usually when reporting on powerful public figures, the press advisor and I would have had a conversation that established what journalists call "ground rules," placing restrictions on what can and cannot be reported. But, as I'd already seen, McChrystal and his team followed their own freewheeling playbook. When I arrived in Paris, Duncan repeatedly dismissed the idea of ground rules, telling me it wasn't the way the team did things. McChrystal would also tell me he wasn't "going to tell me how to write my story." In fact, McChrystal and his staff requested to go off the record only twice during my entire time with them—requests that I honored when it came time to write my story and that I continue to honor to this day. This was great for me, an incredible opportunity for a journalist, as it gave me the freedom to report what I saw and heard.

The staff gathered in room 314. The wives were out seeing the sights—they were supposed to go check out the palace at Versailles.

"There will be no simultaneous translation of the speech," Duncan said.

"Take care of talking in Coalition English," a French general, also in the room, mentioned, referring to the acronym-laden military-speak.

Casey Welch handed McChrystal a set of index cards with his speech typed on them.

"Let's bring it up to 32 font. I'll need my glasses for this."

Casey started to print out a new set of speech cards on the portable laser printer.

"We've made many mistakes in the past eight years," McChrystal said, trying out an opening line.

He went through the talking points: From 1919 to 1929, the Afghan king tried to modernize the country and failed after his wife was photographed in Europe in a sleeveless dress. The more conservative elements of Afghan society pushed back. ("Do we know if that photo was taken in Paris? Would be good to add that detail if so.") The life expectancy of an Afghan is forty-four years. The country has been at war for thirty years. Most Afghans don't even remember a time before war. Even well-intentioned efforts have met with resistance in Afghanistan. The Soviets "did a lot of things right," McChrystal said, but they also killed a million Afghans and lost. The traditional tribal order had been destroyed. Afghanistan, he said, is so confusing "that even Afghans don't understand it."

McChrystal flipped through the remaining cards.

"Okay. New COIN effort, minimize civilian casualties. Then I'll talk about how it's going," he said. "We're at, what, twenty to twenty-five minutes? Is that too long?"

"We don't want to cut the history," said Jake, his longtime friend and top civilian advisor. "That lays the groundwork for the complexity argument." The complexity argument was a way for McChrystal to explain that the cluster-fuck called Afghanistan defied satisfying analysis. Framing the argument by its unfathomable complexity offered McChrystal protection from those in the audience who wanted to judge whether his plan was failing or succeeding. It was a way to talk about Afghanistan like it was the Bermuda Triangle of geopolitics, an inexplicable spot on Earth where countries simply vanished.

"Casey, cut all of it until 'This is what makes this hard.' I'll start there."

Casey, working on the Toughbook, put the changes into the speech. He started to print out new cards with the correct-size font.

McChrystal didn't want to screw up the talk. Six months earlier, during a speech in London, he'd made public comments that were critical of Vice President Joe Biden. Biden hadn't wanted to put more ground troops into the country, preferring to draw down to a much smaller number of U.S. forces who would focus exclusively on a counterterrorism mission. In shorthand, the strategy was called CT Plus, an alternative to the general's counter-insurgency plan. McChrystal had called the strategy Biden was promoting "shortsighted" and had said that it would lead to "Chaosistan." The comments earned him his first public smackdown from the White House. It was also the first reported instance of the mutual distrust between McChrystal and the White House that would persist throughout the next year.

To prepare for the question-and-answer session, McChrystal's staff started to throw out the possible questions he might be asked.

"I never know what's going to pop out until I'm up there, that's the problem," McChrystal said, flipping through the printouts.

"Neither do we, chief," said Jake.

"The French might ask if you're here for more troops, and how the French are doing," said Duncan.

"Hey, that's too easy. I was just down in Kandahar and I saw the colonel from Task Force Lafayette—didn't expect to see him there. I was like, 'Hello, Pierre,'" McChrystal said, grinning.

"If you're asked about women's rights," Duncan said.

"Women don't have rights," McChrystal answered. The joke fell flat.

"It's true, though," said Jake. "We shouldn't be in there pushing our culture. It's just going to anger the fundamentally conservative culture, like we say—"

McChrystal interrupted before Jake could go on.

"What was the Biden question we got yesterday?" McChrystal asked.

He couldn't resist opening up the room for a few jokes at the vice president's expense.

"Are you asking about Vice President Biden?" McChrystal said with a laugh. "Who's that?"

"Biden?" Jake said. "Did you say: Bite Me??"

Everyone started laughing. Jake finished off the back-and-forth with another jab at the vice president.

"Are you talking about the guy who swears on television?" Jake said.

After the meeting, I waited outside the hotel for Duncan. I noticed an Arab guy, around five-feet-five, walking by in shorts and sneakers. I continued to smoke my cigarette. Duncan and I walked to the Métro to catch a train to the École Militaire. At the top of the Métro steps, I saw the same Arab guy again.

"Hey, man, do people really spy on you guys?"

"Yes, they try," Duncan said.

"I think I just saw a guy I'd seen earlier walking by the hotel."

"He's not doing a very good job then, is he?"

Duncan and I arrived at the military academy, a regally styled, sand-colored complex built by Louis XV. I took a seat at the back of the auditorium. The audience was made up of French academics, military students, and active-duty military officers. I settled in to listen to the speech McChrystal had just rehearsed.

"Afghanistan is hard," he began.

10 | THE PHOTO OP

MAY TO JUNE 2009, WASHINGTON, DC

At four thirty P.M. on May 19, 2009, Stan McChrystal walks into the Oval Office. It's the big time, the spotlight. He's with Bob Gates, and the event is closed to the press, but there's a White House photographer in the room. This is McChrystal's first official meeting with the president, the man who has selected him to run his war. He meets Obama, shakes his hand; they're standing in front of the president's desk. They exchange pleasantries. The White House photographer snaps a shot: Obama, mouth open, right hand held up, frozen mid-gesture; McChrystal in full dress uniform, listening quietly. The photo ends up on McChrystal's fast-growing Wikipedia page.

McChrystal walks out of the Oval Office.

McChrystal is let down. He is disappointed. Obama didn't seem to even know who he was. Obama didn't seem to get that McChrystal was *his commander* in *his war*. His war, McChrystal thinks. Obama's war? No longer, McChrystal realizes: It's going to be *my* war now. When the music stops in Washington, it's McChrystal who's going to be left standing without a chair. He knows this. "They all know it," he says about his team. "It's clear to me, it's clear to us. I'm going into this open-eyed. And of course in good company." He knows he's just taken on a shit-ton of responsibility. Obama just gives him a perfunctory handshake and sends him on his way.

This isn't what McChrystal expected. He's expecting a commander in chief who is more engaged; who is able to express concern; who is willing to give him what he needs to win. That's what he'd told the National Security Council when they offered him the job: "I'm going over there to either win it or lose it," he tells them. Where's Obama's heart in this? His head? Sure, there's health care and the bank bailouts and the recession, but this is his war we're talking about—and I'm his general.

How'd the meeting go?

The staff see the disappointment on The Boss's face. "It was a ten-minute photo op," Dave Silverman tells me. "Obama clearly didn't know anything about him, who he was. Here's the guy who's going to run his fucking war, but he didn't seem very engaged. The Boss was pretty disappointed." Casey and Duncan agree.

At the time, they try to pass it off as an aberration—shit, Obama has got a lot on his mind, probably not worth reading too much into it. Back to work. McChrystal's selection is playing well in the press. Everybody is mentioning the Tillman thing, but everybody is also saying that the confirmation is going to go smoothly. The hearings are scheduled for the first week of June.

McChrystal's team knows that detainee abuse is going to come up. The allegation: He was aware of the "harsh interrogation techniques" at a place called Camp Nama in Iraq. A Human Rights Watch report released in 2006 placed him on the scene, inspecting the prison while the interrogators at the site were torturing prisoners to find out information about men like Abu Musab al-Zarqawi. *The New York Times* reported that soldiers there "beat prisoners with rifle butts, yelled and spit in their faces at a nearby area, and used detainees as target practice in a game of jailer paintball." An investigation by Vice Admiral Lowell Jacoby into the unit, called Task Force 6-26, found that detainees there had "burn marks on their back," and "witnessed officers . . . punching detainees in the face to the point the individual needs medical attention." A 2004 memo describing the abuses was passed on to McChrystal. An interrogator who was there that same year said that "most abusive" interrogation techniques needed written authorization, "indicating that the use of these tactics was approved up the chain of command."

McChrystal's team has a preemptive strike: They prepare a letter stating that McChrystal promises to follow the Geneva Conventions. Good thinking.

The Tillman thing: How best to handle it? Pat Tillman had been killed by friendly fire in Afghanistan in April 2004. McChrystal knew about it almost immediately, but he still went ahead and signed off on a falsified recommendation for Tillman's Silver Star that suggested he was killed by the enemy. A week after Tillman's death, McChrystal sent a memo up the chain of command, specifically warning that President Bush should avoid mentioning the cause of Tillman's death. "If the circumstances of Corporal Tillman's death become public," he wrote, it could cause "public embarrassment" for the president.

Coming from the secretive Special Forces world, he'd been able to avoid most questions on his role. There was an Army review, and McChrystal escaped any reprimand, despite his leadership position. His name was blacked out when the Army report became public. He's refused to answer questions from the Tillman family. Won't be able to dodge it in the hearings, though. Duncan and the team confer: Maybe this time he's going to have to apologize.

Tillman's parents are out there. His mother, Mary Tillman, sends a letter to President Obama, saying McChrystal should be "scrutinized very carefully." Her husband says McChrystal participated in a "falsified homicide investigation." One of the interrogators from Iraq won't shut up, either—he's been talking to Hill staffers, and he's even submitted a list of questions for them to ask McChrystal.

McChrystal's staff is worrying too much. He gets only one question about Camp Nama—from Senator Carl Levin. He admits to Levin that he was "uncomfortable" with the harsh interrogation techniques used to gather intelligence in Iraq, and says that he "reduce[d]" them when he took over in 2003. He's got a line prepared on Tillman: "We failed the family," he says, five years after Pat Tillman's death. "I apologize for it."

Tillman's parents and the interrogator aren't getting much traction in the press. They are more or less ignored. The headlines from the confirmation reflect that McChrystal is preordained—he's Mullen and Gates's handpicked choice; nothing is going to stop him from getting the job. NEW APPROACH TO AFGHANISTAN LIKELY, reads *The Washington Post*; NEW COMMANDER SAYS AFGHAN WAR IS "WINNABLE," says another paper; and MCCHRYSTAL NOT SURE IF MORE U.S. FORCES NEEDED IN AFGHANISTAN, says *U.S. News & World Report*.

McChrystal gets unanimous confirmation from the Senate. On June 9, 2009, he gets his fourth star.

11 | TOTALLY SHIT-FACED

APRIL 16, 2010, PARIS

A man I'll call C. was sitting against the wall in The Duke's Bar, a cushy hotel watering hole with dark lighting and oak panels on the ground floor of the Westminster. The younger members of the team—Dave, Khosh, and Casey—were crushed in the booth around him.

C. was a member of the SAS, the most elite British commando unit, and if I used his real name, I could possibly put his life at risk. He was on leave from Afghanistan, and he'd taken the train from London to Paris to hang out with McChrystal's team. C., in his early thirties, was a veteran of Iraq and Afghanistan. He was flying back to Kabul on Monday.

C., I'm told, is a crazy motherfucker. He liked to drive around Kabul in a Toyota Land Cruiser. He kept a nine-millimeter pistol in the driver's side door compartment, an MP5 submachine gun resting on the driver's side seat, a LAW rocket launcher in the backseat, and a machine gun mounted in the trunk.

C. was in the middle of a story: One of his Afghan soldiers had gotten fucked up in a gunfight, badly burned. He needed to get medical help, so he drove the soldier, who was screaming occasionally when not passed out, to a base where Italian doctors were on staff. The Italians refused to treat the patient—he was an Afghan, and they needed some kind of permission first, and it appeared that permission would take hours to get. C. told them to fuck off and tried the next clinic, run by French military doctors. "The fucking frogs told us the same thing," C. said.

C. was getting really pissed off. His Afghan soldier was getting closer to death. He drove him to another NATO base. The guards phoned up a doctor. C. talked to the doctor—she seemed like a nice lady, he said.

Five minutes later, an American man showed up. Where is the doctor? C. asked him. "I'm the doctor," the man said. "What can I do to help?" He had a really high-pitched voice.

"The guy was a fucking poof," C. said. "I swear to God I was expecting to see a girl." The American doctor treated the Afghan soldier and saved his life. "That American was a good fucking guy," C. recalled.

The team jumped back into a conversation about last night's drama—McChrystal's dinner with the French minister. Khosh, the Afghan aide-de-camp, had gotten snubbed. The American military attaché in Paris, a colonel, realized that he didn't have a seat at the table when McChrystal and his entourage arrived to dine with the minister. Rather than bringing this up to McChrystal or the staff, the American attaché pulled Khosh aside and told him he was taking his seat at the table. He made Khosh wait outside for the entire meal.

This incensed the team.

"Where the fuck was that attaché's last posting? Hawaii, then Paris? I mean, what the fuck?" said Dave.

"It's fine," Khosh said diplomatically.

"It's not fucking fine," Dave said. The move, Dave explained, went against all fairness. It showed that these guys in Paris didn't get it—they were completely disconnected from the war. The point of having Khosh at the dinner was to show that the Afghans were in the fight, that they weren't just worthless shitbags who had to be prodded along by Americans and Europeans. The Afghans were part of the team, too. Khosh's presence was meant to provide a "good visual" for the French government, as Dave put it, representing the importance of actually getting the people who live in the country you're fighting in to fight for you. Stealing Khosh's seat at the last minute undercut the message the team wanted to send.

There was an eagerness to tell McChrystal about it. He'd set the attaché straight.

"That guy is going to get fucking chewed out. I can't wait to see that happen at the airport. His fucking career is over," Dave said. Casey agreed.

C. stared at me. He had intense and hungry eyes, like a coyote on the hunt for a puppy. He had heard I was doing a profile of McChrystal. Unprompted, he decided to give me his input on him. The general, he said, was a living legend in the Special Operations community, a giant leap above the office-bound dipshits who usually had four stars on their shoulders. McChrystal had what C. considered to be the most important attribute for a leader: respect from men like himself.

"The fucking lads love Stan McChrystal," he told me. "You'd be out in Somewhere, Iraq, and someone would take a knee beside you, and a corporal would be like, 'Who the fuck is that?' And it's fucking Stan McChrystal."

McChrystal and the other top staff officers came into the bar. It was McChrystal's thirty-third wedding anniversary. What had originally been planned as a dinner for McChrystal and his wife had now ballooned to include part of his senior staff going out for dinner with the two of them. The younger members of the staff would eat separately at another restaurant. They invited me to join them.

We left the hotel and walked a few blocks. We peeled off at an overpriced tourist restaurant and headed up to the second floor. We ate. Wine was served. I didn't drink.

Midway through the dinner, Dave turned to me.

"Mike, you have to fucking come to Berlin with us, man," he told me. Berlin was the next stop on the NATO tour.

"Ah, shit, I'd love to, but I can't. I have to be back in DC. I'm supposed to interview Holbrooke."

"You can fucking interview him anytime, that's fucking easy. He loves publicity. Come on. Come to Berlin." Dave looked to Duncan. "Duncan?"

Duncan smiled.

"This is beginning to sound like fucking *Almost Famous*," I said. "I'm getting kidnapped."

The movie, directed by Cameron Crowe, was loosely based on his experience as a *Rolling Stone* reporter. His assignment was to write a story about a rock band. His one-day story turned into a lengthy road trip on tour with the band. ("Rock stars have kidnapped my son!" his mother cried.) Crowe befriended the band members, then wrote an extremely revealing story. ("Oh, the enemy. A rock writer," one band member warned in the film.) The band got pissed off about what he'd written, and denied everything that happened. ("I am a golden god.") At the end of the movie, the lead guitarist had an epiphany. He saw the error of his ways and showed up at the reporter's doorstep, apologetic, and believing that the truth should ultimately prevail. Credits rolled. I'd enjoyed the movie, but my experience as a reporter had led me to believe that there wasn't always a happy ending if you wrote about people with brutal honesty.

"You have to fucking come, man," Dave said.

I didn't want to stay with them. My editor, Eric Bates, had warned me about falling into the access trap. By becoming so indebted to them for the access they'd given me, I'd lose my objectivity. I'd e-mailed Eric back: If I start getting Stockholm syndrome, I'm sure we can knock it out of me. I could already start to feel the pull. I was starting to like them, and they seemed to like me. They were cool. They had a reckless, who-gives-a-fuck attitude. I was getting inside the bubble—an imaginary barrier that popped up around the inner sanctums of the most powerful institutions to keep reality at bay. I'd seen the bubble in White Houses, on the campaign trail, inside embassies, at the highest levels of large corporations. The bubble had a reality-distorting effect on those inside it, while perversely convincing those within the bubble that their view of reality was the absolute truth. ("Establishment reporters undoubtedly know a lot of things I don't," legendary outsider journalist I. F. Stone once observed. "But a lot of what they know isn't true.") The bubble compensated for its false impressions by giving bubble dwellers feelings of prestige from their proximity to power. The bubble was incredibly seductive, the ultimate expression of insiderness. If I succumbed to the logic of the bubble, I could lose the desire to write with a critical eye.

After dinner, the gang headed to Kitty O'Shea's Irish pub, right around the corner from the hotel. Kitty O'Shea's was a touristy-looking bar, not exactly the hippest spot in Paris.

Drinking began in earnest.

Around ten thirty P.M., I ran into Duncan outside. He hung up his cell phone. The McChrystals, the Flynns, and the rest were on their way over, he told me. They'd finished up the anniversary dinner.

By midnight, the team was totally shit-faced.

Except for me.

"Why aren't you drinking?" Jake asked me. It was the third time he'd asked me that. Each time, he tried to push a beer on me while I was talking to him and McChrystal.

"I haven't really drank in ten years," I said. "Last time I got drunk, I ended up in a county jail with only boxers on, a navy blue blazer, a pair of Nike sneakers, and a restraining order against me. I was in there for, like, four days. My father said: A good scare is worth more than good advice. So I stopped drinking."

"Shit. That stopped you?" Jake said. "That's where we started!"

Jake and McChrystal and I laughed. There was a bit of the awkward moment. I had overshared.

Casey broke the silence. He pulled McChrystal aside. He started to drunkenly apologize for fucking up the index cards—he was sorry he didn't get the right font size.

The team took over half the bar. They locked arms in a big circle and started giving toasts. They toasted to Afghanistan. They toasted to one another. They toasted to Big Stan. They toasted to *Rolling Stone*. They started singing songs.

"On the cover of the *Rolling Stone*," Flynn and his brother Charlie belted out, singing the lyrics to the hit song performed by Dr. Hook and the Medicine Show. "On the COOOOVER of the *Rolling Stone*!"

In honor of Khosh, they started to do an Afghan wedding dance. The Flynns and C. added their Irish heritage to it. The bar quieted as C. started singing an old Irish ballad. I couldn't make out the words; it just sounded sad. Lost love, ghosts, and famine.

"ERRRRRyyyyyEEEEooooHHH . . ." C. howled.

The Flynns made up their own song. The words were unintelligible, but the chorus was clear: "AFGHANISTAN!" they yelled. "AFGHANISTAN!"

I was standing outside the circle.

Dave came up to me. "You're not going to fuck us, are you?"

I answered what I always answer: "I'm going to write a story; some of the stuff you'll like, some of the stuff you probably won't like."

Jake came up to me. "We'll hunt you down and kill you if we don't like what you write," he said. "C. will hunt you down and kill you."

I looked at Jake. He had what I'd heard people in the military call retired colonel syndrome. A certain inferiority complex and bitterness about not rising to the rank of general.

"Well, I get death threats like that about once a year, so no worries."

I wasn't that disturbed by the claim. Whenever I'd been reporting around groups of dudes whose job it was to kill people, one of them would usually mention that they were going to kill me. I went outside to have a cigarette. Duncan joined me.

"How's things, old chap?"

"Pretty good; this is really cool. By the way, Jake just threatened to kill me."

Duncan's face dropped. "What?"

"No, no worries, dude, I took it as a joke, and it's not the first time."

"He should not have said that," Duncan said. "That's not how to deal with the press."

"You warned me; you said he was a dick."

I could tell Duncan was pissed off by the development.

Back inside the bar, the toasts were still going on. McChrystal was standing outside the circle.

"It's a great group of guys you've got. I mean, the team is very impressive," I said.

"You see, they don't care about Afghanistan," he said.

I waited. They don't care about Afghanistan? I didn't think that was what he wanted to say, exactly, though it was true. It could be Iraq or Fiji or Canada. The country didn't matter. The mission mattered.

"No, let me take that back. They care about Afghanistan. It's each other. That's what it's about. All these men," he told me, "I'd die for them. And they'd die for me."

Jake staggered up to us.

"This is a dangerous man," he said, pointing to me. "Watch what you say to him."

McChrystal took his advice. Our conversation ended.

At two A.M., we exited the bar. Casey took care of the bill—about three hundred euros' worth of whiskey and beer, he said. Mike Flynn came out the door, still singing what sounded like "Suspicious Minds." McChrystal tripped over the curb, nearly face-planting in the street. The manager of the bar ran out behind us, telling us to be quiet and not to wake the neighbors. The boozy foot patrol continued down the street, back into the Westminster lobby.

Jake wobbled up the stairs in the lobby, a glass of beer he'd taken from the bar still in his hand. Charlie collapsed in a chair in the lobby, checking his BlackBerry.

"That's dangerous to do while drunk, sir," I said to him.

"C. is coming back down," he said.

"Are you guys still going out?" I asked. He nodded yes.

Casey grabbed my arm and pulled me aside.

"Mike," he said. "You have to understand. I'd do anything for General McChrystal. We'd do anything for him. You're privileged to be here."

I agreed.

"Remember the end of *Saving Private Ryan*?" Casey asked. "Remember what Tom Hanks said to Matt Damon?"

"Yeah, yeah," I said.

"What Tom Hanks said to Private Ryan. He saved his life. He said 'Earn it.'" Casey paused. "With your story. Earn it."

I started to walk back to my hotel. Before falling asleep, I typed up what happened that night, down to the last detail.

The team woke at seven A.M. the next day. McChrystal allegedly got his seven miles of running in. The staff went up the Eiffel Tower. The generals were worried that other tourists in the elevator car could smell the beer on them.

12 | "DEAD SILENCE"

On June 12, Charlie Flynn takes a bus from the Pentagon to Andrews Air Force Base. There are twelve people on the bus. They're taking off for Kabul.

Thank God, Charlie thinks—the hiring is done, the confirmation is complete, and no more desk job at the Pentagon. What a relief to get back to the war, he thinks.

After a twenty-hour flight, Casey is at the headquarters to meet the two Flynns and McChrystal. (Casey and Pitta went out a few days before.) He hands them the keys to their hooches. He takes them on the grand ISAF tour.

They walk into the Joint Operations Center in the headquarters. It's the room where McKiernan had commanded from only ten days before. It's dead silent. It is the tactical and operations focal point for the entire country, and there is nothing going on there, says Casey. The Flynns flank McChrystal, who doesn't say much, just observing. The Flynns are horrified by the lack of activity—in total disbelief—and they start machine-gunning questions. They are wired to shake things up, says Casey. They start looking for walls to knock down—literally.

There's some Italian guy with an office—the chief of staff of ISAF. He gets kicked out. Dave knocks down the wall and makes it a COMISAF planning room. The Dutch have a DSOC room—Division Support Operations Center—and they're out, too. Command Sergeant Major Michael Hall, McChrystal's choice for top enlisted man in the country, will get an office on the second floor.

There's friction. You're talking territory on the base, and the whole thing becomes emotional. If you're taking space away from a foreign country, well, they take it as a national slight, says Casey.

The welcome party for McChrystal is at the Milano, which used to be called Club 24. It's an on-base club and restaurant next to the Destille Garden, also known as the beer garden. To get to the party, McChrystal passes through the beer garden. There's a bunch of dudes in uniform sitting around, sipping coffee, a whole civilized affair.

Casey is watching The Boss for his reaction—it's just a glance, but he knows that McChrystal is fired up. He's not showing it—no burst blood vessels, he's not yelling and screaming. That's not his style. He is just profoundly unimpressed. He doesn't say much directly—he just asks questions, Socratic style, says Casey.

How many resources are used to bring that coffee in? How many planes per latte? How many man-hours are lost by the drinking of alcohol? How do these people have jobs where they can come down here and sit for an hour? How would you feel if you're out there fighting the war and the headquarters staff is taking a leisurely morning sipping espresso? How often is this place filled up? How many hangovers equal mission failure?

McChrystal wants to tear down the beer garden. He says he wants to put in a firing range instead.

The beer garden represents something much larger—a countrywide phenomenon. A complacency, as McChrystal sees it. It's been eight years.

These motherfuckers are acting like the war started yesterday. Plenty of time to go. The complacency is represented in the sprawling military bases, with street sign names like Disney Drive. (It's not named after the cartoon wonderland, but after a specialist named Jason A. Disney who'd lost his life at Bagram in a heavy-equipment accident in 2002.) Entire American towns transplanted to Afghanistan, complete with Baskin Robbins Ice Cream, NFL football on flat-screen TVs, and lobster dinners on Sundays. There's the Burger King and Taco Bell and a T.G.I. Friday's in Kandahar.

What that means to McChrystal: Flights that could be bringing in supplies to support those out in the field are getting wasted shipping in burgers and ice cream and Xboxes. There are Marines in Helmand getting blown up every day, living on MREs, while fobbits (like a hobbit who lives on a forward operation base, or FOB) are whining that the marinara sauce for their cheese sticks is too salty. It's a waste of critical resources.

Then there's the booze. It's especially bad on Thursday nights. In the first few weeks in Kabul, McChrystal's staff will leave the office at four A.M. and come across drunk and stumbling Europeans (and American civilians) who've been partying all night. American soldiers aren't allowed to drink—they have to follow General Order Number One, which prohibits both booze and pornography—but that rule doesn't apply to all of our NATO allies. The booze has got to go, McChrystal thinks; he just needs an excuse.

He'll get it in September. A NATO bomb kills seventy Afghan civilians in Kunduz. Headquarters doesn't hear about it until the afternoon— the people who are supposed to tell them about it were hungover and didn't make it into the office on time. McChrystal bans alcohol from the base, and later, he bans Burger King and tries to close T.G.I. Friday's, too.

The European allies don't appreciate the alcohol ban. It goes over "like a fart in church," says Dave.

McChrystal then tackles the identity of the American military itself. Not only does he want to change the culture of NATO, of Afghanistan, but of his own U.S. Army. He extols the virtues of counterinsurgency. He questions what he sees as the outdated culture of shoot-first-and-blow-shit-up soldiering, the default attitude of most infantry personnel. He shifts the emphasis away from killing the enemy and toward "protecting the civilian population." He issues a series of new directives. "We must avoid the trap of winning tactical victories—but suffering strategic defeats—by causing civilian casualties or excessive damage and thus alienating the people," he writes. "I expect leaders at all levels to scrutinize and limit the use of force like close air support against residential compounds and other locations likely to produce civilian casualties in accordance with this guidance." He writes that "air-to-ground munitions" and "indirect fires" against homes are "only authorized under very limited and prescribed conditions." Other orders: Fly less recklessly and shoot less recklessly. He is praised in the media and among COINdinistas for "curtailing convoys' reckless driving." "Following this intent," he writes, "requires a cultural shift within our forces—and complete understanding at every level—down to the most junior soldiers."

He doesn't stop there. He offers a not-so-subtle rebuke of every general who'd come before him. "We need to think and act *very* differently to be successful," he writes (the italics are his). He implores his troops to focus "95 percent" of their energy on helping the people of Afghanistan build schools and roads and solve land disputes. "Empower those [Afghans] who display competence, care, and commitment to their people," he says.

The new guidance is greeted as a revelation. No one, his supporters claim, has ever done this before. "McChrystal Really Gets It," gushes one blogger on *The Huffington Post*.

This isn't quite true: The previous general, David McKiernan, had a set of tactical directives that are remarkably similar. He had also called on commanders to apply "the utmost discrimination in our application of firepower." "Respect for the Afghan people, their culture, their religion, and their customs is essential," he wrote. He, too, had cracked down on reckless driving. "On the road and in vehicles, ISAF personnel will demonstrate respect and consideration for Afghan traffic and pedestrians," he said.

What is different is that McChrystal and his team are committed to selling the idea that what he's doing is a radical departure from what had been done. Taking his cues from General Petraeus's wildly successful cultivation of the press corps to craft a narrative of victory in Iraq, McChrystal and his team will try to do the same in Afghanistan. He is, so the story goes, finally bringing counterinsurgency to Kabul. This conveniently ignores the fact that every general for the past five years has claimed to be doing a counterinsurgency strategy. (General Barno in 2004: "What we're doing is moving to a more classic counterinsurgency strategy.") The media play along, mistaking style for substance: McChrystal is the savior, and he's doing what no one else has done before. When McChrystal speaks of the principles of COIN, his words are not empty, as his predecessors' were. He really means it. (One stat reveals what a senior military official calls McChrystal's "smoke and mirrors": After McChrystal takes over, there's actually an overall jump in civilian casulaties.) McChrystal makes for a good story; he feeds the desire among the public to have a hero arrive to save the day in a war that looks increasingly hero-less.

13 | THE HORROR, THE HORROR

APRIL 17, 2010, PARIS

I woke up Saturday morning to find the world in crisis.

The details had been out there, a low hum of media noise that follows any major natural disaster. They had been peppering television screens I'd glanced at. I'd caught the gist of it from the headlines on newsstands, radio snippets in taxi rides, the papers on the table in the lobby. Scrolling headlines or brief glances on the Internet. I'd overheard a few conversations, mentions of some nasty ash cloud. Like any normal citizen in the developed world, warmly wrapped in my own beautiful life, the disaster didn't break through my consciousness. I viewed it as I would an earthquake in Peru, a forest fire in Santa Barbara, a flood in Pakistan, a cyclone in Bangladesh: It sucked, but it didn't have much to do with me.

A volcano in Iceland had erupted. Then Western civilization came to a standstill.

Downstairs in the lobby of my shitty hotel, five people crowded the front desk. They were stranded, they said. They'd gone to the airport and come back.

"The airport is closed," the desk clerk told me.

"When will it be opened?"

"Tomorrow at noon."

This natural disaster had taken on a decidedly personal dimension. I had a flight back to DC tomorrow. It looked like the flight would be canceled.

It still seemed a little odd, and I couldn't quite believe it. How could an ash cloud in Iceland stop all flights to and from Europe?

I called Continental Airlines. I was on hold for forty-five minutes before I hung up. I accessed the bad wireless from the lobby. Continental's website didn't allow me to change my ticket, either. I read up on the volcano on the web. One hundred thousand flights were canceled. The airlines were estimated to lose $1.7 billion. Seven hundred fifty tons of ash had spewed into the air. It was the first time the volcano had erupted since 1821.

The eruption had happened on April 14—I was flying from New York to Paris while the eruption was taking place. By the time I landed, European countries had already started to close their airspace. I'd gotten out on one of the last flights from America without knowing it. And now I was stuck in Paris.

I improvised.

The evening before, Dave made an offer: Come to Berlin with us. After last night's drunken spectacle, I was starting to get pretty psyched about the assignment. I couldn't quite believe how the story was playing out. I was getting the perfect material for a profile, beyond all my expectations. For the past few years, I'd wanted to write an in-depth profile of a general. Now I was waiting for someone to tap me on the shoulder and say, "Hey, asshole, wake up, this isn't what you think."

Over the past year, journalists had regularly been given intimate access to McChrystal and his staff. A reporter for *The New York Times* spent a few days in Kabul with him, producing a profile that found McChrystal's only fault was that he worked so hard, "he sometimes affords little tolerance for those who do not." He described his running habits: "eight miles a clip, usually with an audiobook at his ears." A writer from *The Atlantic* had enjoyed a good stay, writing an article titled "Man Versus Afghanistan." He asked if McChrystal was Afghanistan's only hope. He found reason to believe: McChrystal's "eight miles a day, eating one meal a day, and sleeping four hours a night—itself expresses an unyielding, almost cultic, determination." *Time* magazine had put him as runner-up for Person of the Year, opening with an anecdote about a competitive "eight to ten mile" run he had with General Petraeus. *60 Minutes* spent the most personal time with him: He allowed them to film him while he was jogging around the base. They'd all told the same story: McChrystal as a modern combination of saint and ninja, a "Jedi Knight," as *Newsweek* called him. The stories, to me, rang false.

I'd seen another side of his personality. I didn't quite know why they had shown it to me. Perhaps, I thought, because I was with *Rolling Stone* and they wanted to play the part of rock stars? ("On the cover of the *Rolling Stone!*" the Flynns had yelled.) Or maybe the side I'd been shown was there all along, and no one else had decided to write about it?

We'd grown accustomed to seeing the general as a superman—and the press rarely challenged this narrative in their coverage. We'd been bombarded with hagiographic profiles and heroic narratives of almost all our military leaders. When there were criticisms of generals, it usually came too late: after they'd left command, in score-settling books, sanitized magazine stories, and agenda-driven tell-alls.

Here, I realized, was a chance to tell a different story, to capture what the men running the war actually said and did. What I'd been seeing and hearing was distinctly human: frustration, arrogance, getting smashed, letting off stress. The wars had been going on for nearly ten years, and it had clearly taken its toll. I'd interviewed dozens of top military officials— including General David McKiernan, General Ray Odierno, General Peter Chiarelli, General George Casey. But McChrystal appeared to represent a new kind of military elite, a member of a warrior class that had lost touch with the civilian world. He'd spent much of the last decade overseas consumed by the conflict, preferring war zones to Washington. He'd seen his wife, Annie, fewer than thirty days a year since 2003. When he and his men did have to deal with civilians, they were accustomed to the ritual genuflections of awe. As one State Department official who worked with McChrystal had told me, "First, I wondered why McChrystal was so hard on his military staff, but not on his civilian staff. I figured it out . . . He doesn't really understand civilians—he doesn't truly understand what their purpose is, doesn't see how they are useful."

The military itself was an isolated society—less than 1 percent of the U.S. population served or had any connection to the ongoing wars. It had its own culture and moral code. A recent survey of over four thousand active-duty military officers found that 38 percent believed civilians shouldn't have control over military decisions during wartime. The American public—with an overwhelming apathy—had lost touch with the military, too. We started to mistake putting "Support Our Troops" bumper stickers on our cars and watching F-16s doing flyovers at the Super Bowl for civic participation. The guilt that many felt for not serving was covered up by an uncritical attitude toward those who did. No one wanted a repeat of the hatred shown toward veterans after Vietnam—a fear that had been regularly exploited to the government's advantage as a way to shut down all criticism of its military adventures.

As a country, we'd changed since Vietnam—the ghost McChrystal and his generation of military leaders desperately wanted to exorcize. The fear that their wars, too, could end in disgrace: "It's not going to look like a win, smell like a win, or taste like a win," Major General Bill Mayville, McChrystal's director of operations, would tell me. "This is going to end in an argument." An argument they were determined to win. One of the first books McChrystal read after arriving in Kabul was Stanley Karnow's *Vietnam: A History*. McChrystal called the author to ask if there were any lessons he could apply to Afghanistan. "The main thing I learned is that we never should have been there in the first place," Karnow reportedly told him. It wasn't what the general wanted to hear. In the Vietnam

War, McChrystal's story would have been told as one of a deadly killer, devoid of the heartwarming tales of sacrifice and dedication and jogging that politicians and journalists had wrapped him in. In our cultural memory, he would have landed the role of Colonel Walter E. Kurtz in *Apocalypse Now*, the true killer in self-imposed exile, a reminder of the hypocritical morality of the nation, hiding along the banks of the river fighting an illegal war in Cambodia.

"Every man has a breaking point," the general explains to Captain Willard in Francis Ford Coppola's movie, briefing him on his mission to exterminate Kurtz. "You and I have one. Walter Kurtz has obviously reached his. And very obviously, he has gone insane." Willard pauses, hungover. "Yes, sir, very much so, sir. Obviously insane."

The lesson our leaders took from Vietnam was not, it turns out, how to avoid another Vietnam. It was how to seal off the horror: to ensure that only a small group felt and saw it. An all-volunteer military, and a further reliance on the most elite, specialized soldiers to do the nation's work we prefer to ignore. Entering houses at midnight and shooting un-armed men while they sleep. A widespread acceptance of drone strikes, killings committed by remote control—McChrystal watched a man on a video feed in his headquarters for seventeen days before he ordered the strike on a compound to kill Abu Musab al-Zarqawi. He went to see the dead man's body; the pictures of the corpse were displayed at a press con-ference, a modern-day version of putting a man's head on a spike. Com-partmentalize the horror, then embrace it. No need to leave Kurtz on the riverbank when you can give him the job running the war.

"He's a poet-warrior in the classic sense," says the photojournalist, played by Dennis Hopper. "I mean, sometimes he'll, uh, well, you'll say hello to him, right? And he'll just walk right by you, and he won't even notice you . . . If you can keep your head when all about you are losing theirs and blaming it on you, if you can trust yourself when all men doubt you—I mean, I'm no—I can't—I'm a little man, I'm a little man, he's, he's a great man. I should have been a pair of ragged claws scuttling across floors of silent seas—I mean . . ."

So far, I'd sensed an aura of recklessness around McChrystal and his men. From my conversations with them, it seemed they were sure that McChrystal was fighting the war on his own. They had convinced themselves that only he truly understood the stakes—stakes civilians like the vice president, who had dared to question the wisdom of McChrystal's plan, didn't get. Or the president himself, who had visited the front only once, couldn't comprehend. And if McChrystal and his men believed they were indispensable to the war, then those who could be easily replaced— ambassadors, special envoys, presidents, civilians, journalists—could be dismissed with casual disdain and contempt. McChrystal, on the contrary, deserved only reverence for his sacrifices—which he regularly received from the press and his subordinates, among others—giving them a feel of the untouchable. "McChrystal," as a State Department official would tell me at the time, reflecting on this attitude, "can't be fired."

I'd put enough time in Baghdad and Kabul to gain the credibility to be there, in Paris, with them—and a strange twist of fate might keep me in place.

Every reporting instinct I had said, "Don't blow it." Hold tight. Stay with them as long as possible. Go to Berlin. Forget Washington.

I texted Duncan at noon.

Hey man, can I join you all in Berlin? Fucking volcano!

14 | WE'RE ACTUALLY LOSING

JUNE TO AUGUST 2009, KABUL AND BRUSSELS

On June 26, Gates asks McChrystal to write a strategic assessment of the war. McChrystal gets sixty days to do it, starting July 1. He decides to bring in a group of outside military experts to help write it.

The thinking is twofold: to get ideas so they're not "drinking our own bathwater," as McChrystal tells me, and, more important, to bring in influential Washington voices who'll be able to help sell the plan back home.

About a dozen civilians get the invite, including Catherine Dale, Andrew Exum, Fred Kagan, Kimberly Kagan, Jeremy Shapiro, Stephen Biddle, Terence Kelly, and Anthony Cordesman. They are all well-known inside the Beltway's foreign policy community.

It's short notice. They want them in Afghanistan by the first week of July. Exum is the youngest member of the team at thirty-one. Exum did two tours in Afghanistan, the first when he was twenty-two. "I was back to save the war," he tells me. Cordesman is the oldest, at seventy-one. Biddle, based at the Council on Foreign Relations, is perhaps the most influential: He's planned a vacation at the Basin Harbor Club in Vermont, and he has to reschedule the two weeks he's supposed to teach in July.

They're looking for problems, and they find them. The team gets ferried around the country—Kabul and Khost and Kandahar. They get briefs from intel officers. The intel people tell them about the Quetta Shura—the name for the Taliban's leadership council hiding in the city of Quetta, Pakistan. They show them PowerPoint slides with key leaders and map out insurgent networks with aplomb.

But those aren't the answers the team wants. In one meeting, Exum drills down on the briefers. Who controls the water? Who are the local power brokers? Tell me how they are related to the insurgency.

The intel officers shrug. The questions "scare the hell out of them," says Exum.

Another member of the team grills a Special Forces commander: Who owns this land? What are the disputes? What tribes do they belong to? More shrugs: We don't know.

The assessment team raises another big question: Why are we fighting in Helmand? It's a question McChrystal has as well. Helmand is a province in southern Afghanistan. The ongoing offensive in Helmand is costing an American or allied life every four days. What's it getting us? Helmand has no major population centers. Its primary source of agricultural income is poppy plants. The people are not educated. Helmand is Pashtun, so inclined to support the Taliban. The priorities should be Khost in the east and Kandahar down south, the assessment team determines.

Helmand represents the warped logic of the war: We're there because we're there. And because we're there, we're there some more. It's too late to abandon Helmand—McNeill started it, McKiernan put resources there, and McChrystal has to finish it. It's the momentum; the military has a "fetish for completion," says one member of the assessment team. It is against every martial instinct to withdraw, to retreat, to leave land where blood has been spilled. Even when that land has very little strategic significance, leaving is traumatic. The least significant places like the Korengal and Wagyal valleys will be abandoned to concentrate forces elsewhere in the upcoming year. It's painful to do so. "It hurt," one soldier lamented. "We all lost men. We all sacrificed." Another soldier: "It confuses me why it took so long to make them realize that we weren't making progress up there." A U.S. military official will tell me: "What were we doing there, anyway?" It's almost more painful to realize that leaving those valleys is as meaningless as staying in those valleys—no impact on our national security or the stability in Afghanistan whatsoever.

(McChrystal doesn't think fighting in Helmand is a good idea, he tells U.S. military and civilian officials. No one seems to think fighting in Helmand is a good idea yet . . . They keep fighting in Helmand, and within nine months McChrystal launches another major operation there.)

Back at ISAF, the assessment team gets put into a small office room, next to the headquarters. There's a midsize table, with computers along the wall and computers in the middle. The text of the paper is blasted up on a small screen, like a movie theater. The computer processors are making heat. It's hot as fuck outside. The air-conditioning doesn't work. It's a miserable place to work.

There's a clash of political perspectives. The Kagans are neoconservatives, a husband-and-wife team, a dual-headed beast. The Kagans like to take credit for the Iraq surge and are the most hawkish in the group. The Kagans are close to General Petraeus. Kim Kagan runs a joint in Washington called the Institute for the Study of War.

Exum, on the other hand, is part of the Center for a New American Security, or CNAS—the differences in name reflect the difference in political style. Not so much a difference in substance—they're all for the war—just the pose they take while endorsing it.

CNAS is for the Democrats—reluctant warriors, "middle of the road," cerebral pride, lots of hemming and hawing. You'd never catch a Democrat opening up a place called the Institute for the Study of War.

It's too direct, it's too obvious; it suggests a politically incorrect passion for conflict. The Center for a New American Security is just the kind of serious-sounding name to appeal to the liberal hawks. It's the hottest think tank in town, and they've stocked up on influential reporters—one journalist, David Cloud, joined CNAS, went to advise Ambassador Eikenberry, then returned to cover the Pentagon for the *Los Angeles Times*. Tom Ricks is on the payroll, Robert Kaplan is on the payroll, joined by a rotating cast of other prominent national security journalists, including *New York Times* Pentagon correspondent Thom Shanker.

The sticking point is how to deal with corruption in Afghanistan. McChrystal doesn't really care either way on corruption. He doesn't view it as a pressing issue and thinks it can be tolerated. The Kagans are passionate about fighting it; Shapiro doesn't think it should be a high priority.

Stephen Biddle notices a distinct absence. He's been on these kinds of teams before, helped Petraeus write up an assessment in Iraq in 2007. In Iraq, the State Department was well represented, foreign service officers providing their input. In Kabul, they're not around.

Where's the U.S. embassy in Kabul? Where is Ambassador Eikenberry? Biddle takes his concerns to McChrystal's staff: He thinks it's a problem that Eikenberry isn't involved. If the diplomatic and military sides aren't getting along, "it jeopardizes the mission," Biddle says.

Eikenberry doesn't want to be involved, a senior U.S. official tells me. He doesn't want Stan coming in there and taking over the whole thing. It's an "out of my sandbox" kind of attitude, this official tells me. Worse, the embassy scraps a civil-military program that ISAF has set up. (McKiernan set up the program, so there's also an "anything but McKiernan" attitude among McChrystal's planners.) So although counterinsurgency depends on a hand-and-glove civilian-military partnership, and the strategy will call for that, from the beginning that relationship barely exists.

The biggest question for the assessment team, though, is: Can we win? Is this even worth doing? On this question, the assessment team is split. "There were several of my colleagues who weren't persuaded," says Biddle.

"I thought it was a close call, and on balance, the right thing to do." Others on the team think the whole exercise has been a public relations stunt—"McChrystal knew about 80 percent of the strategy he wanted," says one member of the team. "We were just for show."

The assessment team stays for three weeks. They write eight drafts, according to members of the assessment team. Four times, McChrystal comes in and goes over it with them. He vets each line in the paper. The paper the civilians write gets tossed to another staff member, Colonel Chris Kolenda, to finish; he'll work with McChrystal to finalize the draft.

While working on the assessment, McChrystal gets a visitor from the White House. General Jim Jones, the national security advisor, comes over to Kabul, with *Washington Post* journalist Bob Woodward along to cover the trip. Jones has a message from the White House: If you're thinking of asking for more troops, don't. Jones tells another general at Camp Leatherneck the same thing: Hold the line. Jones explains that the White House already is feeling a bit singed—they'd given them seventeen thousand. Then they came back for four thousand more. And now the generals are going to come back to the bar yet again? If more troops are asked for, Jones tells a briefing room full of colonels and generals, Obama is likely to have a Whiskey Tango Foxtrot moment, or WTF, or *What the fuck?* Jones insists that unlike Bush, President Obama isn't just going to give the generals anything they ask for. It's what Obama has said publicly: "My strong view is that we are not going to succeed simply by piling on more and more troops."

There's not much respect for Jones in Kabul. He doesn't have much clout in DC, either—he's been the victim of a series of leaks attempting to undermine him. He is a safe pick for the NSA job, a way for Obama to signal he was serious and bipartisan about his national security. Jones is chosen because he still gets respect on the Hill from the likes of John McCain—Jones and McCain are close friends.

The White House isn't too impressed with him, either. The rap against Jones inside the White House: He's not pulling the fourteen-hour days with the rest of the staff. He's on "retired general time," a White House insider will tell journalist Richard Wolffe. In truth, people on his staff think he's a joke, too. He starts one of his first all-hands-on-deck NSC meetings by reading a poem. Not some "rah-rah" poem, "some doggerel bullshit about fairies or something," says a White House official who was at the meeting when the poem was read. "He's like Ron Burgundy in *Anchorman*—you put anything on his cards before a briefing, and he'd read it. You could put 'I'm a fucking asshole' on his briefing cards and he'd say that." At another meeting, he took out a diary from a relative who had served in World War II and started reading it out loud. "It was pretty weird," says another U.S. official.

For McChrystal, not asking for more troops is a problem.

By early August, the assessment is close to being complete.

McChrystal flies to Chièvres in Belgium, a NATO airbase, for a secret meeting with Gates, Mullen, and Petraeus. He stops in Brussels and takes his close staff out to dinner. Casey has to pick a restaurant. He chooses a pizza place. It's the most low-rent place he can find, but there are candles on the table. McChrystal isn't pleased; it's "too Gucci," he tells Casey. Sir, it's Brussels, Casey says. It's either pizza or some taco stand on the street.

Over the unfortunately candlelit dinner, McChrystal asks his staff questions, the big questions. Why are we here? He doesn't mean Belgium. He means the war. Why are you fighting? he asks Casey. For the next three hours, they go over every angle. "Is this a modern Crusade?" McChrystal asks his team. "Are we fighting an ideology, a fanatical extremism? Is this really something we should invest our time in? Is it going to hurt or help the region? Can we win?"

The next day, McChrystal meets with Gates, Mullen, and Petraeus. Casey calls it a "mini-Yalta." He goes over the draft with them, wants to get everyone on the same page. He doesn't want to get "steamrolled in case things go haywire," says a U.S. official who was at the meeting. He tells them his stark assessment, tells them the situation is deteriorating, tells them he's going to ask for more troops. The senior brass isn't surprised. It's what they were expecting. This is a chance for them "to look face-to-face before taking the serious next step of putting the assessment out," says a military official who was at the meeting. The serious next step means asking for more troops. The serious next step is what the assessment concludes: We're losing.

The White House, as Jones made clear, isn't ready for the assessment, doesn't want to hear about any more troops. They've already sent twenty-one thousand. Let those get over there, and see what impact they have. This assessment isn't going to be well received, McChrystal is told. Hold on to it.

He doesn't.

15 | PETRAEUS CAN'T DO AFGHANISTAN, AND WE AREN'T GOING TO GET BIN LADEN

APRIL 18, 2010, PARIS

Ocean 11 wasn't allowed to leave France. Neither was Ocean 12.

Those were the call signs for the planes the Air Force supplied McChrystal. Ocean 11—named after the George Clooney heist movie with a star-studded cast about a high-speed team of supercool thieves who pull off the biggest caper in Las Vegas history—was a Learjet. Ocean 12 was the plane for the staff.

McChrystal's plan to fly to Berlin on Monday was in jeopardy.

Dave worked the contingencies. Helicopters? It would be a twelve-hour ride. They'd have to stop and refuel multiple times. It sounded brutal. Did they want to put their wives on a twelve-hour Blackhawk ride? Nope, bad idea. Commercial flights? Not moving yet. Train? That would take too long and they wouldn't have communication capabilities.

Check back again with Ocean 11: Come on, Air Force, have some balls, take off.

McChrystal wasn't the only one stranded. The German defense

minister was trapped in Uzbekistan. The German chancellor was stuck in Italy. McChrystal might have to cancel the entire trip to Berlin.

I was stuck, too. Even if McChrystal could get Ocean 11 to take off, I wouldn't be able to get on the military flight. I could spend another night in Paris, but then I'd risk getting left behind if they finally got clearance. I decided to gamble: Take a train to Berlin to get ahead of them.

I was at the Gare de l'Est at five thirty A.M. There was travel chaos across the continent. Riotous lines of stranded tourists at the Air France office stretched down the block. Rental car agencies ran out of stock. Taxi drivers were price-gouging, charging thousands of euros for cross-country trips. Trains were somewhat fucked as well, their websites overloaded as everyone scrambled to snag the few remaining tickets.

With no way to book a ticket online, I waited for three hours at the station. The only ticket available was an overnight train in coach. I bought it, checked out of my shitty hotel, then went back to the Westminster.

I spent the day hanging out in the Westminster lobby, doing interviews with other members of the staff. At around three P.M., McChrystal came downstairs. He took a seat across from me at The Duke's Bar. He checked his BlackBerry.

"Oh, not another e-mail from Holbrooke," he said.

"Did you read it?" Charlie asked.

"I don't even want to open it," McChrystal said.

"Make sure you don't get any of that on your leg," Charlie said, pretending to wipe his pants as if the mail had popped open and splattered him.

I jotted down notes—Holbrooke, the legendary statesman. Another civilian they couldn't stand.

The team was going out to grab an early dinner at a Mexican restaurant, about a ten-minute walk from the hotel. They asked me if I wanted to go with them. I said okay. I could only stay for an hour or so. My train was leaving that evening. The entire crew fell out of the hotel, and we started to walk.

We went down the street and stopped in front of the Paris Opera House.

"Hey, we should get a picture of this," McChrystal said.

"I'll take it," I said.

McChrystal, Flynn, Dave, Duncan, the other officers and staff posed with their wives. I took a few steps back, clicked lightly on the button to focus it, then snapped a photo of them. Just another group of tourists in Paris.

We started walking again, and Duncan told me that it would be a good time for another interview with McChrystal and Mike Flynn.

"Once we're back in Kabul there won't be much time," he said.

We sat outside at the Mexican restaurant. The waiter pushed two plastic tables together, and the half-dozen members of Team McChrystal and their wives grabbed seats. I sat between McChrystal and Mike Flynn. Jake sat next to McChrystal, at the end of the first table.

I started to interview McChrystal. The rest of the table started talking about an incident on Saturday night: a naked man in a window at a restaurant.

"There was a guy with no clothes on, and everyone was looking up at him," said General Flynn's wife, Lori.

"He was really naked, leaning against the window," Jake said, shaking his head.

The waiter came over to take our order.

"Start with Jake," Lori said.

"Beer," Jake said. *"Grande."*

"Grande beer," Annie said, laughing.

"You can't have two until you have one," Jake said.

Annie and Jackie ordered sauvignon blanc.

"I'll take a large beer," said Mike Flynn.

"That's Mike's French," McChrystal said. *"Large beer."*

"My favorite French teacher growing up said there are only three things you need to know in any language: Where's the bathroom, thank you, and can I have a beer," I said.

"Yeah, can't survive without that," McChrystal said, then looked at his wife. "Did you bring my jacket?"

"You don't need a jacket," Annie answered.

"Paris in the springtime," McChrystal said.

The waiter came back to the table.

"Neun Bier," Jake said, in German.

"He's coming back to Kabul with us," said Charlie Flynn, pointing to the waiter, imagining putting a dude who'll serve beer on demand on the staff.

"Only if he gets this round right," said Mike Flynn.

"He's only got to get one right," said Major General Bill Mayville, meaning McChrystal's drink. "He's got my vote."

We started talking about the volcano.

"What happens if you have hotel reservations, and all that?" McChrystal said.

"If it's a natural disaster, and you don't have travel insurance—"

"*Vous êtes* screwed," said Jake. "That's French."

A few minutes later, McChrystal and I started talking again. Jake interrupted.

"Sorry about threatening to kill you," Jake said.

It was the first time anyone in the group had acknowledged the blowout on Friday night.

"Yeah, geez, the guy is just trying to do his job," McChrystal said.

"No worries. Like I said, it happens all the time, but yeah, you're probably the highest rank to do so," I said. I laughed, and they didn't.

I wanted to ask McChrystal about the other incidents that his staff had told me about over the past few days. We started with his career and time at the Council on Foreign Relations and moved on to Karzai and the past year of the war.

I asked him about the memos Ambassador Karl Eikenberry had

written, criticizing his strategy. They had been leaked to *The New York Times*, and published in full on its website. The ambassador had offered a brutal critique of McChrystal's plan, dismissing President Hamid Karzai as "not an adequate strategic partner" and casting doubt on whether the counterinsurgency plan would be "sufficient" to deal with Al-Qaeda. "We will become more deeply engaged here with no way to extricate ourselves," Eikenberry warned, "short of allowing the country to descend again into lawlessness and chaos."

"I like Karl, I've known him for years, but they'd never said anything like that to us before," McChrystal said, adding that he felt "betrayed" by the leak. "Here's one that covers his flank for the history books. Now if we fail, they can say, 'I told you so.'" McChrystal speculated that it wasn't even Eikenberry who wrote the memo, but two members of his staff.

I asked him about Petraeus. He said his relationship with Petraeus was "complex." He'd replaced Dave three times in five years in jobs. "You know, I've been one step behind him."

Petraeus had uncharacteristically kept a low profile over the past year. He didn't seem to want to get publicly attached to the war in Afghanistan. He'd had his triumph in Iraq, and military officials speculated that he knew there was no way the Afghanistan war was going to turn out well. That it was a loser, and he was happy enough to let McChrystal be left holding the bag.

"He couldn't command this," McChrystal said. "Plus, he's one and 'oh.' This one is very questionable."

Petraeus had been "wonderfully supportive," though, despite the competition between the two. Within military circles, there was a long-standing debate over who should get more credit for what was considered the success in Iraq—McChrystal running JSOC in the shadows, or Petraeus for instituting the overall counterinsurgency strategy. After Obama took office, the White House had told Petraeus to stay out of the spotlight—they were worried about the general's presidential ambitions and they were afraid he would overshadow the young president, McChrystal explained.

The White House told McChrystal, "'We don't want a man on horseback.' I said I don't even have a horse. They are very worried about Petraeus. They certainly don't have to be worried about me," McChrystal said. "But Petraeus, if he wanted to run, he's had a lot of offers. He says he doesn't want to, and I believe him."

"I think he seems like a smart enough guy that in 2012, as a journalist, as someone who covered the campaign—" I started to say.

"Do you think he could win?" McChrystal asked me.

"Not in 2012," I said. "I think in 2016 it would be a no-brainer. But I've seen it happen to these guys who get built up, built up, built up . . . If he steps into it in 2012, the narrative is 'Oh, he shouldn't have done that. Is that a dishonorable thing to do for an honorable general?' And that is the narrative. That's the first cover of *Time*."

The narrative, I thought: General Betray-Us, a slur he'd been tagged with years earlier.

I brought up a recent profile of Petraeus in another magazine.

"I thought that, well—excuse my language—that it was a blow job," I said.

"But the data backs it up," McChrystal said.

"It's hard to get at the truth," I said.

"Hardcore," Jake interjected. "You guys talking about porn?"

"Hell, I want to be part of that conversation," McChrystal said.

We started talking about larger issues within the media, which I felt he was in a unique position to discuss. McChrystal was a spokesperson at the Pentagon during the invasion of Iraq in March of 2003, his first national exposure to the public.

"We co-opted the media on that one," he said. "You could see it coming. There were a lot of us who didn't think Iraq was a good idea."

Co-opted the media. I almost laughed. Even the military's former Pentagon spokesperson realized—at the time, no less—how massively they were manipulating the press. The ex–White House spokesperson, Scott McClellan, had said the same thing: The press had been "complicit enablers" before the Iraq invasion, failing in their "watchdog role, focusing less on truth and accuracy and more on whether the campaign [to sell the war] was succeeding."

I rattled off a few names of other journalists. I named the writer who'd just done the profile on him for *The Atlantic*, Robert Kaplan.

"Totally co-opted by the military," he said.

I mentioned the journalist Tom Ricks, who'd written two bestselling accounts of the Iraq War.

"Screw Ricks," McChrystal said. Ricks, he said, was the "kind of guy who'd stick a knife in your back."

Duncan had also told me Ricks wasn't to be trusted. One officer who was quoted in Ricks's 2006 book, *Fiasco*, had told Ricks not to use his name, and had asked him to clear all the background quotes he would use from him. Ricks used the officer's name and didn't clear the quotes, hurting the officer's career. (A charge Ricks strongly denies, calling the allegations "junk.") Another officer had inexplicably gone from a hero in Ricks's first Iraq book to a failure in his second, *The Gamble*—all from observations that Ricks had garnered from the same reporting trip.

Woodward?

"I'd never talk to Woodward," McChrystal said. "He came over here with Jones—what was that, last summer? He seems to just be out for the next story."

"Woodward," Jake said with disgust. "Whose leg is Woodward humping now? Jones? So Jones can say he won the war?"

I wondered: Shit, if they didn't like journalists Kaplan, Ricks, and Woodward, they probably weren't going to be big fans of my work, either.

I apologized for taking up McChrystal's time while he was in Paris. I turned to speak with Mike Flynn.

I asked him about a report he had authored in January. The report, which he published on a think tank's website rather than go through the normal chain of command, had declared that your military intelligence was "clueless" about Afghanistan.

"If I would have written that report and been living in Washington, I probably would have been fired," he said. "But I could do it because I was in Kabul."

Living up to his scatterbrained reputation, Flynn accidentally left his e-mail address on the report. He received, he said, "thousands of e-mails" commenting on it.

"But that's good, you know. You just want people out there hammering away, whether it's good or bad, you just want to shock the system. It's the same with you in the media—for your stories, you don't care if people are hating it or loving it; it's the shock to the system, it's about getting people to fucking hammer away on it," he said.

"Whatever the reporting is, think the opposite," he segued, on advice he gives to intelligence gatherers. "Counterintuitive."

"It's interesting, the parallels between the professions," I said. "Norman Mailer said 'journalists are like spies.' We have it even easier in some ways, though, because there's no bureaucracy—I mean, I want to go somewhere, I ask one person, he says okay, and then I'm on my own. My job is to share that collected information to the public, while the spy's job is obviously different. I don't need to get all the permission spies need to get to do shit."

"I try to let my people out there," Flynn said.

I asked him a question that had always perplexed me. As the highest-ranking intelligence officer in the Afghanistan and Pakistan theater, Flynn had access to the most sensitive and detailed intelligence reports; I didn't want to miss an opportunity to get his take.

"Why haven't we gotten Bin Laden?" I asked.

"I don't think we're going to get Bin Laden," he told me. "I think we'll get a call one day from the Paks: Bin Laden's dead, we captured al-Zawahiri. But we need closure on that issue."

We're not going to get Bin Laden? Of everything I had heard so far, this stunned me the most. One of the top intelligence officers in the military telling me that we're not going to get Bin Laden? Bin Laden was our whole raison d'être in Afghanistan. He brought us there, he's what kept us there, and if it's true that we're not going to get him . . . What the fuck?

I didn't want to miss my train. The conversation drifted back to public images and profiles.

"Everyone has a dark side," Flynn said, seemingly referring to McChrystal.

"Mike, don't tell him that," said Flynn's wife, Lori, sitting across the table.

"Like Tiger Woods," I said. "His whole image was built up and torn down overnight."

"Exactly, like Tiger Woods."

I put my notebook and tape recorder away. I finished my Diet Coke and said good-bye.

"See you guys in Berlin," I said.

"See you there, Mike."

I went back to the hotel, picked up my checked luggage, and headed to the train station.

16 | THE ELECTIONS, PART I

APRIL TO AUGUST 2009,
ZABUL, KABUL, AND WASHINGTON, DC

President Hamid Karzai is running for reelection. He's up against two other high-profile contenders: Dr. Abdullah Abdullah and Ashraf Ghani. Abdullah is from the Northern Alliance, the militia that fought the Taliban during the civil war. After Ahmad Shah Massoud was assassinated, it was the Northern Alliance—with their warlord commanders—who teamed up with the Americans to bring the Taliban down. Ethnically, it's a group made up of mainly Tajiks, Uzbeks, Hazaras, and Turkmen. Statistically speaking, about 40 percent of the Afghan population. Abdullah was a friend to Massoud, and the Alliance's foreign minister. He's become the most visible political figure opposing Karzai, and he's running as an independent.

Ashraf Ghani is the intellectual—he's written a book called *Fixing Failed States*. Naturally, he's the West's favorite. He's that gem, a moderate, a technocrat, beloved by American journalists and think-tankers and diplomats. He's lived almost half his life outside Afghanistan: He's studied at Columbia, at Harvard, at Stanford. He's worked for the World

Bank. He's been a commentator for the BBC. Political consultant James Carville helps him on his campaign.

Ashraf Ghani is thoroughly Westernized, which means he doesn't have popular support. Which means he doesn't have a militia. Which means he doesn't have power. Which means he doesn't have a chance. But he's the kind of candidate the Americans love because he makes them feel good. He makes them believe democracy has taken root in Afghanistan—look at Ashraf Ghani.

Karzai won the presidency in 2004. He had a huge advantage—he'd been appointed president in 2001 by the Afghans and the international community. His advantage hasn't waned. Though he's hated by almost everyone but his relatives—Americans and Afghans alike—he also controls the election commission. He has sway over the security forces. He runs the state media. It's clear, months before the first vote is cast, that Karzai is likely to win. One U.S. official who works on the election wonders about the point of it. "I don't know how much sense it makes to have an election in the middle of a war," he tells me. "It makes the elections look illegitimate."

That's a minority view. A swarm of United Nations officials, State Department officials, U.S. military officials, and any NGO that can scam a contract have flocked to Kabul to make sure the election goes off. The election will cost about $300 million, most of which is coming from the United States. For international organizations with a mandate for democracy promotion, it's time to get a cut. Whether the Afghans want an election or not, they're going to get one. Whether an election is going to cause more stability or less stability is up for debate. Whether the election is going to be free and fair in a country where 70 percent can't read the ballot, that's nit-picking. Whether the candidates running are totally corrupt, human rights violators, drug-running thugs—that doesn't matter, either. Elections usually make for a good visual—elections are almost always used to demonstrate progress. The election gives the United

States government a chance to say, "See? It's working, there's an election."

The election is the top priority for the State Department—Hillary Clinton pledges $40 million to support it.

Matthew Hoh works for the State Department. He isn't supposed to be at the polling station on election day, but he finds himself at one anyway. The Americans aren't supposed to influence the outcome. They are supposed to stay away from the election sites.

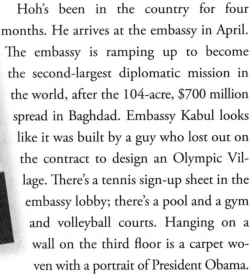

The Obama Carpet

Hoh's been in the country for four months. He arrives at the embassy in April. The embassy is ramping up to become the second-largest diplomatic mission in the world, after the 104-acre, $700 million spread in Baghdad. Embassy Kabul looks like it was built by a guy who lost out on the contract to design an Olympic Village. There's a tennis sign-up sheet in the embassy lobby; there's a pool and a gym and volleyball courts. Hanging on a wall on the third floor is a carpet woven with a portrait of President Obama. It's overcrowded. There are too many people and too few rooms, the excess numbers spilling out into prefabricated trailers. You aren't really allowed to go out in Kabul without security, so most of the time, everyone at the embassy stays and lives at the embassy, their version of Kabul.

The embassy has requested 180 new positions. DC grants it the 180 new jobs. Hoh is there to take one of them. He served two tours in Iraq, once as a civilian advisor and once as a Marine. He'd been at the Pentagon working for the secretary of the Navy during the invasion of Iraq, worked on the Iraq desk at the State Department, and the whole State thing was an eye-opener—interagency meetings with CIA, NSC, Treasury, DoD, USAID . . . meeting after meeting, nothing getting done, so few at the senior level wanting to work together because, God forbid, somebody gets credit and somebody else doesn't.

He's working Iraq, been on the ground there, but in Washington his experience doesn't count—forget what you think about Iraq, it's what you know about DC that matters. Hoh jumps at the chance to leave—he gets a job to run a Provincial Reconstruction Team, or PRT, for the State Department. Or so they told him before he left DC.

Embassy Kabul requested the 180 slots without knowing what it was going to do with the 180 slots. The embassy, Hoh says, is "completely dysfunctional," disorganized, with no leadership. He's standing in the PRT office and everyone is freaking out because they have no idea what to do with him. They submitted a request six months before, and in that time they failed to figure out how to use the 180 new slots. They tell him he's going to work on a brigade staff in Jalalabad—only temporary, to fill in for two months. That's not what he signed up for, but he goes anyway.

In Jalalabad, near the Pakistan border, he gets an overview of the war. He learns: The Taliban is not a monolithic organization. He learns: U.S. forces are not fighting and dying to combat terrorists, but are fighting and dying in local political disputes. In Asadabad, the neighboring capital, the governor doesn't want Americans and the Afghan army going up to a certain area of the province because he's got an illicit opium operation there. Another time, the governor tries to fly to Dubai during a crisis. The governor doesn't give a shit; the Americans have to stop him at the airport and send him back to Asadabad.

Hoh flies over hundreds of valleys; he looks down at one, asks his friend from Special Forces, Ever been to that valley? No. Never will go to it, either.

He learns: Every valley has its own dynamic. "The Taliban" is a catch-all phrase for local people who don't want foreigners in their valley. Even if we wanted to put troops in every valley, it would require hundreds of thousands—at least four hundred thousand, according to standard estimates.

His team gets approached by members of an insurgent group called Hizb-I-Islami, or HIG—they are open to negotiating with the government they've been fighting for years. Hoh tells the embassy, Let's talk to them.

He learns: The embassy says stay out of it, not to interfere, not to negotiate. Despite the constant American refrain that there's "no military solution" to the war, there is very little momentum in finding a political solution. Low-level entreaties are regularly ignored. If negotiations start, it has to start with Washington's approval, then Kabul's approval, and then, maybe, Hoh could start talking to the people he thought he was supposed to be talking to.

In June, he's back in Kabul. He has a two-hour conversation with his boss and her deputy. He tells them he's thinking about leaving. Everything he's seen points toward a damning conclusion: What the Americans are doing is futile and has very little to do with protecting the United States from terrorists.

His bosses agree with him—they're at the end of their tours—but tell him to give it a chance. A new group of people is coming in. Eikenberry just arrived. McChrystal just arrived. The elections are coming up. Why don't you take a job at a Provincial Reconstruction Team down in the southeast, in Zabul province?

American officials consider the presidential election as the year's key political event. It has been almost the entire focus of the U.S. diplomatic mission there over the past year. It will establish national leadership for at least the next five years. It is a major step, U.S. officials say, in finding that political solution.

The State Department official in charge of the elections leaves Afghanistan in June. The other State Department official who's supposed to be running the election takes three and a half weeks of vacation in July, says Hoh. We're not picking favorites, but Eikenberry holds press conferences with two of Karzai's opponents. Holbrooke talks to them as well. Karzai doesn't like it.

Zabul isn't much better than J-Bad. Same problems. No interest in reconciliation. Our policy is fueling the insurgency, not stopping it, Hoh thinks. Over-the-top corruption.

Two of Hoh's Afghan friends call it the "golden era," as in, it's the era to get the gold.

On election day, August 20, 2009, Hoh isn't supposed to go near a polling site. Luckily, the Afghans have set up an illegal polling site on the Afghan army base. Good for Hoh, because he has access to it. He recognizes a familiar face, the Afghan army colonel who runs the base is running the site. He's in slacks and a button-down shirt today. He's on his mobile phone, telling his men what candidate to vote for. About two or three hundred people show up at the polling site; the final tally of the day is twelve hundred votes cast.

Across the country, the reports of fraud flood in. Rumors abound about entire ballot boxes filled out in Pakistan and shipped in across the border. Some voters are using disappearing ink, voting ten or twenty times a person. Thousands of votes are counted where only hundreds of Afghans cast ballots. Turnout in the south of the country is an estimated 8 or 9 percent, yet the vote tally indicates that at least 40 percent of the population voted. All in all, an estimated 1.5 million fraudulent votes. That's probably a low estimate. In Kandahar, Karzai's power base, three hundred fifty thousand votes come in, though only twenty-five thousand people went to the polls. There are eight hundred fake polling sites like the one where Hoh is.

Hoh wonders if the $300 million spent to hold the election was a wise use of resources.

17 | TEXTS TO BERLIN

APRIL 18–19, 2010, FRENCH–GERMAN BORDER

FROM: D BOOTHBY

Sun, April 18, 10:03 P.M.

How is your trip progressing. You missed the worst meal in paris. Flynn wore a sparkly hat.

FROM: M HASTINGS

Sun, April 18, 10:16 P.M.

Good. On way to berlin. In compartment with two hot French chicks and gypsy family. Flynn is mad genius. How are things?

FROM: D BOOTHBY

Mon, April 19, 1:53 P.M.

Not as good as with 2 hot French chicks. New eta afternoon. Totally right on mad genius.

FROM: D. BOOTHBY

Mon, April 19, 1:54 P.M.

Germans won't let us in german chief of defense who is escorting 4
bodies has been prohibited from flying—stuck in Uzebsiktan.
Commander has
Therefore cancelled rest of europe trip and we are trying to get home
as soon. As possible. Might have to drive to southern Italy. Most likely
cancelled but we are trying one more trick for germany should know by
this evening. There is a bus load of Japanese ladies camping out in the
lobby. This is getting wierd. Waiting for a swarm of bees next. How
are you?

FROM: M HASTINGS
Mon, April 19, 8:56 P.M.
That sucks. Hoping you all make it. Hanging at Ritz.

FROM: D BOOTHBY
Tues, April 20, 5:37 A.M.
still trying an on outside pull to get in to germ. Requires special
permissions from French and Germans and some expert flying and a
quick diversion to Iceland to extinguish volcano. More in the AM.

FROM: D BOOTHBY
Were comming.

18 | THE ELECTIONS, PART II

AUGUST TO OCTOBER 2009, KABUL

In Kabul, the election becomes a political crisis.

Peter Galbraith is the number-two man at the United Nations mission in Afghanistan. He's Holbrooke's guy—they'd run into each other in Pakistan earlier in the year, and Holbrooke offers him a job. He's the former U.S. ambassador to Croatia, negotiated a treaty in East Timor in 2001, and wrote two bestselling books on Iraq. He'd been in the thick of it with the Kurds when Saddam launched a genocidal campaign against them in the eighties. He had great relationships with the Pakistanis—Benazir Bhutto was a childhood friend—and his gig in Kabul would allow him to participate in what were likely going to be very difficult and lengthy negotiations with the Pakistanis, "shuttle diplomacy," as Galbraith calls it. Before he can get to that, though, he's got the job of supporting the Afghan elections.

Galbraith is living in Palace 7, a former royal estate where the UN headquarters staff lives. There's a filled-in swimming pool that the Taliban allegedly used for executions. There's an enormous dining area with a "ten-mile-long table," Galbraith says, and a sweeping staircase leading up to the second-floor suites, where Galbraith has his room. It's palatial and surreal, and the Romanian security guards have pet peacocks that roam around the grounds to the sound track of the loud diesel generator. At the other end of the hall lives Kai Eide, his boss. Eide has a nicer room. Eide is Norwegian. Galbraith and Eide have a history—Eide introduced Galbraith to his wife back in the early '90s in Zagreb, Croatia. She's Norwegian, too. More important, Galbraith wasn't Eide's choice for the job—the Americans forced Galbraith on him, Eide will tell me. "I was under tremendous pressure to appoint him," Eide says. "He was Dick Holbrooke's arm into the UN mission."

Galbraith arrives in Kabul in June. He starts to travel around the country, inquiring about the polling sites. He asks to visit a number of them, and isn't given permission to do so. He finds what he describes as an "election process in chaos." When Eide has to leave the country to travel during the summer, Galbraith is in charge. It's Galbraith who realizes that twelve hundred of the polling stations exist "only on paper." He'll call them "ghost polling sites." While Eide is out, Galbraith brings his concerns up to the Afghan minister of defense and the Afghan minister of interior. The Afghan ministers aren't too interested in hearing about fake polling centers, and neither is Eide. Galbraith thinks Eide is close to Karzai and is worried about upsetting him. When Eide returns after one of his trips, he tells Galbraith to knock it off—the Afghan government has complained about his questions. Don't bring up the ghost polling centers again, Eide warns him.

On the night of August 20, 2009, it's clear to those UN officials gathered in the twenty-four-hour election-monitoring center that the fraud Galbraith warned about is happening. One province, Paktika, was reporting a 200 percent turnout. Other counts, in the country's most dangerous areas, are wildly overblown as well. The election center collects more than eighty pages of complaints about fraud and voting irregularities. Other problems: 91 percent of the election coverage from the state-run radio focused on Karzai, and he got six times more play from the state-run TV station than his closest opponent. (According to Galbraith, Eide later deletes this paragraph about media bias from an official report.) Eide is briefed on the fraud, but doesn't want his staff to say anything to anyone about it. "Galbraith wanted me to come out with a strong statement indicating the amount of fraud," Eide explains. "How could I possibly do that? I had no indication of whether it was ten or fifteen or twenty percent."

At Palace 7 the next morning, Eide has a breakfast meeting with Holbrooke. They sit around the ten-mile-long table. Eide looks tired, stressed out. Holbrooke mentions that it looks like there are "a bunch of fraudulent results."

"These results aren't fraudulent," Eide says.

"Talk to your deputy," Holbrooke says, looking at Galbraith.

Galbraith thinks: Gee, thanks, Richard.

Eide starts to get angry, agitated. Because of the massive fraud, Holbrooke suggests that they have a second-round runoff. Eide is opposed to the idea. Eide wants to avoid a runoff, which means Karzai has to get over 50 percent of the vote. Eide wants to count the fraudulent votes to get Karzai over the top, says Galbraith. Eide, on the other hand, is worried that the country is on the brink of serious unrest, "violence in the streets," he'll later recall in an interview.

"I'm warning you, be very careful, this is very dangerous," Eide tells Holbrooke. "You should not tell Karzai that."

Holbrooke and Galbraith believe that the entire credibility of the mission is at stake. Counterinsurgency requires a legitimate partner, and a fraudulently elected leader is, by definition, illegitimate. It's too big to ignore, Holbrooke tells Eide; we have to say something. Holbrooke leaves the breakfast—he's got a meeting with Karzai in a few hours.

Eide gets on the phone to Karzai right after Holbrooke leaves. Holbrooke doesn't want to declare you the winner, Eide tells Karzai. Holbrooke wants a runoff. But you can ignore Holbrooke, Eide explains, because he doesn't represent the Obama administration. (It's a sentiment he repeats to Galbraith: Holbrooke doesn't have the backing of the White House, so screw Holbrooke.) According to Galbraith, Eide would later tell Karzai that he was "biased" toward the Afghan president because "those who are out to get you are out to get me"—meaning Holbrooke. "Holbrooke's first objective was to get rid of Karzai, which I thought was completely unacceptable interference in Afghanistan's internal affairs," says Eide.

When Holbrooke shows up at Karzai's palace, the president is "loaded for bear," says Galbraith. Karzai is furious. The sixty-eight-year-old Holbrooke is an experienced statesman—he's in his element when he's confronting heads of state head-on, as he did with Slobodan Milošević in Serbia. He treats conflict like "it's jazz music," says a State Department official close to him, improvisational and exciting, the sounds of the clashing motives and voices and agendas and intrigues that make life worth living. He's also got a sizable personality, which has rubbed the Afghans (and Eide and the White House) the wrong way.

This day, Holbrooke doesn't even have a chance to bring up having a second-round runoff. Eide's tip-off pays dividends—Karzai is apoplectic. Karzai ends the meeting "acrimoniously," according to a U.S. official familiar with the encounter. Eide's gambit works: He keeps his relationship with Karzai tight while undermining the American special envoy, explains Galbraith. Later that night, Eikenberry has to go to the palace and smooth things over with Karzai.

On August 24, Galbraith meets up again with Holbrooke, in Istanbul. He tells Holbrooke what the UN position is going to be: Ignore the fraud. At the same time, *The Guardian* writes a story quoting an unnamed UN official saying there is fraud. Eide hears from Afghan officials that Galbraith had criticized him at a visit to the elections commission before he'd left for Istanbul.

At two thirty A.M., Galbraith gets a text message from Eide saying that an Afghan minister had told him Galbraith criticized him. Galbraith gets another text message from Eide about the *Guardian* story.

Eide is starting to lose his shit, says Galbraith. The two thirty A.M. text messages are followed by an e-mail to a UN political officer threatening to fire him over the anonymous quote. Eide's evidence? *The Guardian* is a British newspaper, and the UN political officer is also British. It must have been from him, Eide concludes, out of a staff of hundreds. The tension between Galbraith and Eide is about to become very public; Eide blames Galbraith for bringing the fraud to light too quickly, while Galbraith blames Eide for what he sees as legitimizing a fraudulent election.

The American response to the election is, in general, confused.

The U.S. military trumpets the success of the election as the most significant operation the Afghans have organized and pulled off to date. NATO is encouraged by how the Afghans have handled the complexities of democracy.

The White House doesn't know how to play it. They seem to want a runoff election between Karzai and Abdullah. This pisses off Karzai. Karzai is going to win a runoff election anyway, so why piss off Karzai?

Obama doesn't back Holbrooke. Holbrooke is a longtime Clinton loyalist—he'd supported Hillary rather than Obama during the campaign and, after Hillary Clinton was selected as secretary of state, making him the special envoy was her idea. But on the election issue, it doesn't look like Hillary is going to stand behind Holbrooke, either. Karzai, reading the political signs, doesn't think Holbrooke has much clout. National Security Advisor Jim Jones tells Holbrooke: You might as well resign; you've lost the faith of the president. And so Holbrooke—considered America's überdiplomat, forty years of experience—is no longer in the game in Afghanistan. He can't get a meeting alone with President Obama. ("Richard Holbrooke expected everyone in the White House to treat him like Richard Holbrooke," says a White House official. "But they didn't care who he was. It was his fault, too, for not recognizing that.") This leaves Galbraith exposed in Kabul—if Dick Holbrooke doesn't have the juice, then neither does Peter Galbraith. At a meeting in September, Hillary Clinton will tell Eide that the U.S. isn't going to get involved in a

United Nations dispute—a signal to Eide that Galbraith doesn't have her support.

On October 28, armed gunmen storm a guesthouse in Kabul where UN election workers are living. The workers have been brought to Kabul specifically to work on the runoff vote. Six UN employees are killed. An American guarding the compound is also killed by an Afghan army soldier. It's an odd coincidence that the attackers happened to target those particular UN staff.

Dr. Abdullah Abdullah is the second-highest vote-getter. The campaign against him is starting to get bizarre and dirty—there's an e-mail getting bounced around among Afghan elites, called "The Truth About Abdullah Abdullah." It's a wild e-mail from the Karl Rove school of campaigning: It calls Abdullah a bisexual, accuses him of sleeping with prostitutes in Dubai, calls him an Iranian agent, lists the cost of his "designer suits." The e-mail lists Abdullah's supposed "allies," many who just happen to be opponents of Hamid Karzai.

Dr. Abdullah Abdullah drops out of the election. The runoff vote is canceled.

Ashraf Ghani, America's favorite, gets 3 percent of the vote.

Holbrooke gets sidelined—he ends up looking weak, which translates to the Americans as ending up looking weak in Karzai's eyes. The White House doesn't force Karzai to do anything.

Karzai wins by fraud.

Karzai's half brother Ahmed Wali Karzai, the provincial council chief in Kandahar, tells one of Eikenberry's deputies not to worry about it. In a State Department cable headlined "Elections: What's the Point?" the president's half brother explains to the Americans that "the people in this region don't understand having one election, let alone two.

"The people do not want change," says Ahmed Wali Karzai. "They think the president is alive, and everything is fine. Why have an election?"

19 | TEAM AMERICA ROLLS THE RITZ

APRIL 20, 2010, BERLIN

The lobby of the Ritz-Carlton was packed with Germans and Israelis. A tight security perimeter was in place outside. A legion of cops dressed in black—a few with shaved heads—stood guard under the glass awning that jutted out from the towering gray facade of the ten-story hotel. Police vehicles with flashing lights parked diagonally at the end of Potsdamer Platz alongside metal barricades to block off the street. A red carpet was laid out for the arriving dignitaries—Israeli embassy officials, German military officers and diplomats, wealthy businessmen with their wives—leading into a receiving line to a reception on the mezzanine.

The purpose of the gala was to promote friendship between the two countries. That explained the tight security—the German government's paranoia to avoid not-so-random acts of anti-Jewish violence, fearful of a new generation of skinheads who hadn't gotten the memo that the Nazis lost.

The spectacle fit with my experience of Berlin so far: an entire city where the brutal history of the twentieth century couldn't be avoided. Even its übermodern, globalized, cosmopolitan hipness failed to disguise the most savage century on record. Remnants of war acted like the city's second skyline: memorials to dead Germans in World War I, memorials to remember the Holocaust, a memorial to the Soviets who died fighting them, government buildings identified by whether they were leveled in massive bombing runs or rebuilt later, and a partial chunk of the Berlin Wall, a Cold War memento less than a block away from the Ritz. The city of three million appeared to have taken on the responsibility to remember the approximately one hundred twenty million, both victims and perpetrators alike, who'd perished in the world wars of the past hundred years.

This was the task McChrystal would confront: to convince the German political elite that they should continue to send troops to fight in Afghanistan, no matter how unpopular the war had become. Polling showed that some 80 percent of Germans opposed involvement in Afghanistan. Absurdly, the country's leaders tried to convince their public that they weren't *really* in a war, anyway—they were involved in "networked security" and "humanitarian action." Germany's president was forced to resign after he implied that the forty-five hundred German troops in northern Afghanistan *were actually at war*. A series of incidents had brought the absurdity of the government's claim to the forefront: After the air strike in Kunduz that killed seventy civilians, the German defense minister took responsibility and resigned—something that would have been unheard of in the United States. The German officer who had called in the air strike was subjected to a highly publicized hearing within months—again, something Americans would never do. (In the past ten years, no high-ranking American officer has ever been severely punished for killing civilians.) In the past few weeks, the country had suffered seven combat deaths in Afghanistan, one of its worst losses of life in fighting since 1945. McChrystal had recently ordered an American brigade to join the German contingent in the north of the country, an escalation that was undoubtedly going to mean more deaths for the Germans.

It was around seven P.M. I sat in the corner of the lobby drinking espresso, occasionally popping outside to smoke a cigarette. I wanted to capture the scene of McChrystal and his staff rolling into the Ritz. Team America—the name McChrystal's staff called themselves, referring to the comedic film about U.S. cluelessness—arrives in Berlin. A four-star general arrives at the five-star hotel.

I hadn't heard from Duncan or anyone else on the team all day. I worried that they'd hit a snag. In the past twenty-four hours, I'd started to get a strange kind of separation anxiety, a fear that I wouldn't be able to continue the story. I'd scrapped my plan to go back to DC. My plan now was to push on to Kabul. My trip was originally going to be about two or three days. Now it looked like it might last a month.

I had downtime to digest the reporting. A question persisted: What was the motivation behind McChrystal's decision to have me tag along? Was it that *Rolling Stone* would reach a demographic of young officers and recruits whom they wanted to impress? Would it confirm the view that the team held of McChrystal—that he was "a rock star," as they regularly called him? Dave explained that Special Forces operators had a healthy disrespect for authority; *Rolling Stone* fit this self-styled image perfectly. They were building Brand McChrystal—ballsy, envelope-pushing, risk-taking. *New York Times Magazine* cover? Done. *Time* cover? Check. *Atlantic* cover? Too easy. *60 Minutes* profile? No worries. *Rolling Stone?* Boom. It was a natural evolution of a very aggressive media strategy to establish McChrystal as a contender for the greatest general of his generation, on a par with Petraeus.

My presence with them was a physical, real-time manifestation of their entire attitude. How do you jump out of an airplane at thirty thousand feet, or sneak into an enemy compound in the middle of the night, or swim in hypothermic ocean waters, without a willingness to take risks? McChrystal's team lived for risk. Up the risk; tell risk to go fuck itself. What General Mike Flynn had told me kept going through my head: Shock the system. Get as much attention as possible. Love it or hate it.

Sir Graeme Lamb once said, to roughly paraphrase: You have a pond and you keep throwing rocks in the pond, and you keep throwing big rocks in, and you keep making bigger waves, and eventually you see what you're looking for. Eventually you can see the bottom of the pond—the ecosystem has been unsettled, and everything becomes clear.

I didn't quite get it, but then no one quite got what Graeme Lamb was saying. Wisdom is like that. It all fit, though—whether the pond was in Kabul or Washington, just start tossing in rocks, increase the size of the rocks, decrease the size of the rocks. Make an improvised explosive device with the rocks.

Perhaps I was a rock to throw, part of some larger strategy I didn't see.

I noticed another smaller group of American and German officers in uniform. They didn't look like they were part of the Israel–Germany gala. They stood to the left of the stairs, near the open entrance to the bar. I assumed they were there to welcome McChrystal. That was a good sign.

After forty-five minutes of waiting, a large bus pulled up outside. It had purple lettering on the side.

Dave came through the door, followed by Ray and a few others. They were carrying American military gear in camouflage bags along with trash bags filled with top secret material. Due to security regulations, the classified material that was printed on the trip needed to be disposed of in the appropriate manner and place, which meant burning it back in Kabul. Even their trash was top secret.

Dave went up to the front desk with Ray and Master Sergeant Rudy Valentine, McChrystal's personal cook and body man. Rudy was a gentle, quiet soul—he'd served twenty-plus years in the Army. He'd grown up poor in a town in Michigan. ("Ask him about the rabbits," Dave told me. I did: He raised and killed rabbits to feed his younger siblings.) He didn't drink or swear. The repeated deployments over the past decade had put a heavy burden on his marriage. He was devoted to McChrystal—each trip, he'd make sure the general's luggage was in his room, and prepare his uniforms for the day.

They started the check-in process. Rudy got the thirty or so plastic room keys made up. Dave made contact with the welcoming party, telling them McChrystal was on his way in. A few moments later, McChrystal entered with Mike, Charlie, and Jake.

"Hope this isn't all for me," McChrystal said, acknowledging the gala. It wasn't.

The welcoming party of German and American defense attachés swept McChrystal and the other generals into the Ritz's bar area. Waitresses started passing out small appetizers and beer.

Dave and Casey conferred.

"We need to get The Boss out of there," Dave said.

"We'll bring him up to his room and let him and Annie do their thing," Casey said.

The team was frazzled from the trip. They'd spent fourteen hours on the bus, commandeered from a company that usually took Japanese tourists around France. There were two bus drivers. Originally, the drivers were under the impression they would be driving to Italy. Dave told them that morning in Paris they were mistaken. The plan had changed. Get with the program. The two drivers resisted—they had been told Italy, and they were adamantly opposed to going to Berlin. After a few minutes of argument, they conceded to Dave. Not happily—they remained French and surly, taking their revenge through a daylong exercise in passive resistance. European Union labor regulations allowed the bus drivers to take a break every two and a half hours to smoke a cigarette, the drivers claimed.

"We were going sixteen miles an hour, I swear to God," Dave said. "Guderian made it to Paris faster than we made it to Berlin." A reference to the German general who led the invasion of France in World War II, who developed a strategy of deploying fast-moving and heavily armored tanks to overwhelm the enemy—a strategy infamously known as blitzkrieg.

The bus crawled. The team started drinking. Beers were opened. They cracked a bottle of schnapps. For lunch, they stopped on the side of the road at a gas station. Mike Flynn ate his meal on top of a trash can. At each stop, as the bus drivers sucked down Gauloises, Ray set up the communications equipment to download the e-mails and other materials that had arrived during the two hours they were out of contact. The Japanese tourist bus wasn't equipped for mobile telecom.

I saw Duncan.

"Delta Bravo, what's up, man?" I said. "I was worried you guys weren't going to make it."

The ash cloud, at this very moment, was hovering over Germany. No one yet knew if or when flights would resume. Days, weeks, a month. I asked Duncan what tipped the balance for them to come here. It would have been safer to fly out of Italy, cut their losses, and return to Kabul early.

"The implicit risk is it gets worse, and we get stuck," Duncan said. "But this is very much the attitude of our General McChrystal—into the ash cloud."

The bar at the Ritz was in the back corner of the lobby. It had three open-air entranceways divided by three stubby rectangular walls, the marble floor changing to carpet; there were lounge seats, tables, and a counter against the back wall where a bartender stood serving eleven-euro drinks.

I mingled in the crowd around the bar for a few minutes. Mike Flynn and Jake pounded a few beers. Flynn had received word over e-mail that the top insurgent leader in Iraq had been killed. He was satisfied. "He was a guy we'd been looking for for a while," he said.

A tall blond woman in a green sweater tightly covering a sizable chest walked by. I took note.

I went upstairs to room 915. I wanted to capture the scene of Ray, the communications specialist, setting up the operations center.

In room 915, Ray was rolling out the cables, organizing the Tough-books, and setting up the printer. Even though they'd only been there fifteen minutes, they were almost done.

Admiral Smith, McChrystal's communications director, was sitting down, looking over notes. He and Duncan started discussing talking points, what McChrystal needed to say to convince the Germans that they could return to their more comfortable role—away from fighting. The Germans had a number of restrictions placed on their forces, including not being allowed to go out at night. ("With the Germans, though, it's like my British friend told me," said Dave. "Maybe it's good that they aren't allowed to go out at night, if you know what I mean.")

"National agendas . . . And the public polling. Low support . . . And adopt the strategy over time to start a security effort to support more of a government development role," Smith said.

They discussed the think-tank event scheduled for tomorrow.

"We have a small change. We have sixteen RSVPs for the think tank down from twenty late adds. A lot of these folks are based in Berlin," Duncan said.

Casey worked on the speech, printing it out this time in 32-point font.

Rudy brought up the bags. Annie McChrystal entered the room.

"We ate junk food the whole way," she told me about the bus trip. She looked happy, keeping the upbeat public attitude that was a job requirement for being the wife of a four-star general. She carried her responsibilities well, though her demanding partnership of stress and solitude had left its visible scars, like an attractive middle-aged woman from Florida who'd spent too much time in the sun. "I was waiting for the Ranger songs. We were having too much fun. I can't remember the last time I spent fourteen hours with him awake! I loved every minute of it. He was stuck on the bus and he couldn't go anywhere."

Mike Flynn walked in. "Shit, they had all kinds of nice chow as soon as we walked in," Flynn said, looking around the room. "Jesus Christ, what the hell did you guys do? You missed it—"

"We had to get the bags—"

McChrystal blasted in.

"Hey, don't bitch about how working for me is a tough time," he announced. He saw me and froze for a second. He continued. "They had a little party. They were pouring beer down there. I was going to come up here, they grabbed me, gave me beer, more beer, then they gave me pizza. I'm like, 'Hey, I'm here. I'm German. Screw the French.'" He winked at me. "I'll tell you one thing," he said. "I'm glad we came. It's a good call. As long as I don't screw it up. I'm prepared to take that risk."

I went back downstairs. A defense attaché's wife was in a heated discussion with the French colonel over *le seduction*. The French colonel was convinced the Americans didn't understand seduction. She agreed. She was wasted and loud, wearing a blue raincoat. She was about ten years younger than her husband. She swung her martini glass back and forth at high velocity without spilling a drop.

She cornered me outside while I was smoking a cigarette. She told me she and her husband got invited to sex parties all the time in Berlin. "Daz boom, boom," she said. Her husband came up to her and pried the martini glass from her hand. They left the party.

20 | ON PRINCIPLE

SEPTEMBER TO OCTOBER 2009, ZABUL, KABUL, NEW YORK, WASHINGTON, DC, AND VERMONT

Matt Hoh has seen enough. He's living in Zabul in a run-down building with twelve guys and one shower. He likes the job, but no longer believes in the mission. He's in a small room with a makeshift wooden bed on the second floor. The Provincial Reconstruction Team, or PRT, is across from the governor's office. He takes out a Panasonic Toughbook. He starts to write his letter of resignation. He writes it over three days. He sends a draft to two of his friends: What do you think? He sends the final version to Frank Ruggiero, the senior civilian representative in southern Afghanistan. I'm quitting, he tells Frank. He goes to Kandahar to talk to Frank. Frank tells him to think it over. Hoh goes back to Zabul, finalizes the letter on September 11, 2009, but changes the date to September 10, because he thinks the other date is too dramatic. He sits tight in Zabul.

In Kabul at the embassy, Holbrooke comes into the meeting Monday morning with Hoh's letter. It's all Holbrooke talks about for the hour. Holbrooke passes the letter to Hillary and to Obama.

Hoh gets an e-mail from the assistant to the ambassador: Come to Kabul to discuss it. He meets with Eikenberry three times. Eikenberry suggests he work as his personal representative over at ISAF with Stan McChrystal. Hoh crosses the street, meets with Dave and Charlie, has pizza with them. Good guys, he thinks, but he doesn't want the job. Before he leaves, he talks to Eikenberry again. Eikenberry is sympathetic, Eikenberry agrees with his letter, and Eikenberry doesn't want to lose any staff if he can help it. He offers Hoh a job in the embassy, and tells him that at the end of his tour, Hoh can publish his letter and he'd even publicly endorse it. Eikenberry tells him it's one of the clearest analyses he's read of the war. Another diplomat at the embassy confides to Hoh that if he had children of military age, he wouldn't want them serving in Afghanistan. As the letter is forwarded around, Hoh receives messages of support from his counterparts in six other provinces.

Hoh leaves Kabul, stops overnight in Dubai.

Holbrooke is back in New York for a UN General Assembly meeting. Holbrooke is staying at the Waldorf; he asks Hoh to meet with him. He goes into the Waldorf, and Holbrooke's staff is there, along with a douche bag from the CIA. Matt is friendly, introduces himself; the CIA dude is cold, says, "I work for another agency," playing the spy card, wanting to show off his covertness.

Holbrooke comes into the Waldorf, packing up. He's got a meeting with the Egyptian foreign minister. Holbrooke and Hoh talk for an hour and a half.

"I agree with you," Holbrooke tells him, "but I'm not going to tell you how much."

Holbrooke agrees with the letter about 95 percent, another diplomat tells Hoh. He speaks to others on Holbrooke's staff—they seem to be talking about a completely different war from the one he sees. How can you say they don't want freedom, if we just get the right ingredients, the right mixture of counterinsurgency and the right amount of time? one staffer asks Hoh. It reminds him of the talk in Iraq back in the day, the disconnect between reality and what the believers believed. Holbrooke asks him to join his team; Hoh thinks about it for a few days, then declines.

Hoh gets back to DC. He's living in an apartment in Arlington, on an air mattress, not really settled. It takes the State Department six weeks to process his resignation. He's back home, feeling a little paranoid, a little dark, typical PTSD stuff, wanting to avoid crowds. It'll last a couple of weeks. He skips a U2 concert. He's in a bar on Monday night, watching *Monday Night Football.* Broncos versus Chargers. He's sitting next to a guy who turns out to be an editor at *The Washington Post.* They talk Afghanistan: He tells the editor that he's just resigned. What's your problem? Are you some kind of malcontent? You have a drug problem or something? the editor asks him. Are you not credible? The editor tells him to call the *Post* the next day. He does. Forty-five minutes later, a *Post* reporter calls back. Over the next two days, they do six hours' worth of interviews. Hoh provides the reporter with his Marine fitness reports: This is no malcontent, this guy is a fucking hero, this guy risked his life to try to save another Marine from drowning during a helicopter crash, this guy was singled out for his reconstruction work in Iraq . . .

Next Monday, he's in the bar again, Eagles versus Redskins. The *Post* reporter e-mails: Here's the story. Hoh's Facebook page starts to light up. He wakes up Tuesday at eight A.M. There are fifteen voicemails on his phone. There are seventy-five media requests. There are television crews waiting outside his apartment. CNN, ABC, CBS.

His letter of resignation is published in full on the *Post*'s website. It reads, in part:

"To put [it] simply: I fail to see the value or the worth in continued U.S. casualties or expenditures of resources in support of the Afghan government in what is, truly, a 35-year old civil war . . . If the history of Afghanistan is one great stage play, the United States is no more than a supporting actor, among several previously, in a tragedy that not only pits tribes, valleys, clans, villages and families against one another, but, from at least the end of King Zahir Shah's reign, has violently and savagely pitted the urban, secular, educated and modern of Afghanistan against the rural, religious, illiterate and traditional . . . I have observed that the bulk of the insurgency fights not for the white banner of the Taliban, but rather against the presence of foreign soldiers . . . Our support for [the Afghan] government, coupled with a misunderstanding of the insurgency's true nature, reminds me horribly of our involvement with South Vietnam; an unpopular and corrupt government we backed at the expense of our Nation's own internal peace, against an insurgency whose nationalism we arrogantly and ignorantly mistook as a rival to our own Cold War ideology . . . If honest, our stated strategy of securing Afghanistan to prevent al-Qaeda resurgence or regrouping would require us to additionally invade and occupy western Pakistan, Somalia, Sudan, Yemen, etc. Our presence in Afghanistan has only increased destabilization and insurgency in Pakistan . . . More so, the September 11th attacks, as well as the Madrid and London bombings, were primarily planned and organized in Western Europe; a point that highlights the threat is not one tied to traditional geographic or political boundaries . . . I realize the emotion and tone of my letter and ask you [to] excuse any ill temper . . . Thousands of our men and women have returned home with physical and mental wounds, some that will never heal or will only worsen with time. The dead return only in bodily form to be received by families who must be reassured their dead have sacrificed for a purpose worthy of futures lost, love vanished, and promised dreams unkept. I have lost confidence such assurances can anymore be made. As such, I submit my resignation."

After a decade's worth of failed policy in both Iraq and Afghanistan, Matthew Hoh is only the third senior American government official to have resigned for reasons of conscience.

Three weeks after Hoh's resignation, Peter Galbraith will be back home in Vermont. He'll get a call from a journalist, asking him if he has a response to the fact that he's been fired. Fired? It's news to him. He'd agreed to leave the mission temporarily over the differences in view on the election fraud. But Kai Eide couldn't stand being embarrassed, so he made sure he got the boot, Galbraith believes. Eide, on the other hand, says that he could no longer "trust" Galbraith. ("Kai and Peter had different philosophies," says a senior UN official who worked with both men. "Imposing on Kai a man with a bad history with Kai had to end in disaster. They were irreconcilable.") Galbraith gets another call from Afghan expert Michael Semple.

"Peter," says Semple, a former UN official and an Irishman who's considered the leading Taliban expert. "It gave me joy to hear that you got fired when I read it in the papers."

"Fuck you," Galbraith says.

"No, you don't understand," Semple continues. "Had you embezzled money, it would have taken the UN eighteen months to fire you. Had you sexually harassed an employee, it would have taken them a year. But take a stand on principle? The UN fires you overnight."

Over the next few months, Galbraith will be the victim of a vicious smear campaign, accusing him of unethically profiting from his work with the Kurds in Iraq. The story is broken by *The New York Times*, carrying a dateline of Oslo, Norway, Eide's home country. "I was shocked when I read about it," Eide tells me. "I hand no knowledge of it." A month after that, Eide will publicly accuse Galbraith of trying to persuade the Americans to overthrow Karzai and replace him with Ashraf Ghani—a charge Galbraith vehemently denies. Galbraith will continue to return fire in the media, warning that the troop surge "makes no sense," and filing a suit against the United Nations for his improper termination. Eide steps down from his post early in the next year.

21 | SPIES LIKE US

APRIL 20, 2010, BERLIN, AROUND MIDNIGHT

The blonde with the very pronounced upper body took a seat at the bar.

I sat in one of the comfortable lounge chairs, about thirty feet away from her. Duncan was to my left. Charlie Flynn leaned back in his seat across the table.

Flynn and I eyed the blonde.

Duncan twisted in his seat to look where we were staring.

"What do you make of her?" I asked Duncan and Charlie.

Charlie tilted his head to one side.

Duncan turned back around. "She's either a high-class prostitute or a spy," he said.

"Are you kidding?"

"No, she was working Dave earlier pretty hard."

"Now that you mention it, the first time I saw her was when you guys all arrived. She was hanging out around the bar during the welcoming party."

"She's either an operative or a lobby worker," Duncan repeated.

Charlie nodded. I sipped my Perrier.

The woman got up. She said something to the bartender that we couldn't hear.

To leave the bar, she had to pass our table.

Twenty feet away. Fifteen feet. Ten feet. Five feet. Three feet.

"Hey, how are you?" Charlie said to her.

She stopped.

"I'm very good, thank you," she said.

Botoxed, maybe collagen implants, breasts certainly augmented. I thought: prostitute.

"Want to join us for a drink?" Charlie asked her.

I was surprised. The woman whom Duncan and Charlie had identified as either (a) a prostitute or (b) a spy now sat down at the table with us after receiving an invitation from General McChrystal's executive officer.

She said her name was Kerina. She gave her last name as well. She explained why she was in the lobby bar of the Berlin Ritz: She'd been in Stockholm visiting a boyfriend, who happened to be married to someone else. The boyfriend was in the oil and mineral business. She and the boyfriend had some kind of falling-out. Then the volcano hit, and she didn't want to stay in Stockholm. She couldn't leave yet to go to Morocco, where she'd planned a ten-day trip. She lost her credit card, somehow, her AmEx. She also may or may not have misplaced her passport.

She slipped off the gray jacket she was wearing.

"So what do you do?" Charlie asked.

"I'm a travel writer."

She claimed she was a columnist and had a blog. She said she'd written for travel magazines and a sex column for a men's fashion magazine. She said she lived in Canada but had German citizenship. She kept talking, explaining, maybe a little drunk. She said she'd taken helicopter lessons and jumped out of airplanes at high altitude.

It all sounded like an elaborate ruse. None of it sounded credible.

Her phone rang.

"Excuse me, I have to take this call."

She got up and stepped outside the edge of the bar, which merged with the lobby.

When she got out of earshot, Duncan nodded to the jacket she left behind.

"Might not be secure to talk," he said, indicating that her jacket could be bugged. He leaned forward.

"I have been Googling what she said," Duncan whispered, Black-Berry in hand. "None of the things she said is true. Her story doesn't check out."

"I did see her earlier," I said. "I've worked for that magazine she claims to write for, and she didn't know any of the editors' names. So that's strange."

"Holy shit, this is great," Charlie said. "Like having my own ops center right here, just feeding me information."

Duncan continued. "I'm not buying her rich story. A girl like that would have a five-hundred-dollar haircut," he said. "That's not a five-hundred-dollar haircut."

"What do you make of the helicopter lessons?" I asked.

"She's had cockpit time," Charlie said, gesturing to his groin. "Thousands of hours on the stick."

We stopped talking. She walked back into view, hanging up. She said good-bye in what sounded like a foreign language.

Suspicious. She'd done most of the talking up to this point. Now she asked the questions and Duncan and Charlie tried not to answer them. They didn't want to tell her who they were with or what they were doing in Berlin.

"Business," Charlie said. He wasn't wearing his uniform, which was typical for the downtime when he traveled.

Duncan concurred. "Business," he said.

She turned to me. "What are you doing?"

"I'm a journalist," I said. "I'm writing for *Rolling Stone*. I'm going to Afghanistan in a couple of days."

Duncan's eyes flashed. I had fucked up, apparently. Operational security.

"Are you all going to Afghanistan?"

They shook their heads.

I stopped talking about Afghanistan.

Duncan and Charlie's paranoia had rubbed off. Already paranoid by nature, the idea that this woman might be a spy—sent by a foreign intelligence agency to snoop on General McChrystal—seemed both dangerous and hilarious.

I threw out a story to test the spy thesis. I had a cursory John le Carré–based knowledge of covert operations and spycraft during the Cold War. Two words came to mind: honey trap.

"A friend of mine has this great story about the Cold War," I said. "This French diplomat was in Moscow in the early eighties. The KGB chief summons him to his office. The chief throws down a folder of black-and-white photos. It's the French diplomat banging these two Russian chicks he's had a threesome with. Blackmail. The KGB chief stares across the desk: 'We are going to send copies of these photos to your wife.' The French diplomat nods. 'Then you don't mind if I keep these for myself?'"

I laughed the loudest at my own joke. Kerina laughed, too. Charlie nodded.

"I'm going for a cigarette," I said.

Duncan joined me, leaving Kerina and Charlie alone.

"You broke operational security," Duncan scolded. "You shouldn't have said we were going to Afghanistan."

"Yeah, okay," I said. "Sorry."

I was actually thinking: You guys can come up with your own cover stories if you're so worried. I'm not going to lie. What the fuck—Charlie was the one who asked her to sit with us in the first place. That didn't seem like such an operationally secure move, either.

"We have to get Charlie out of there," he said. Duncan was worried Charlie might get seduced. "We shouldn't leave the two of them alone."

"This is crazy, though," I said. "That she's a spy."

"That's the lobby scene, you know? Spies, high-class prostitutes, that's what it is."

We walked back to the table. I said good night. Duncan said good night. Charlie said good night.

I went outside for one more cigarette.

Through the glass doors, I watched Kerina walk through the lobby. She turned—and came outside.

"You know there is a smoking lounge in the back," she said.

"Oh, really?"

We went back to the smoking lounge. My mouth was dry. I was nervous. I waited for her to pop the question: How much? Or was she going to try to pump me for information?

She took a different tack. She asked me life questions.

"Are you happy?" she said. "What do you want to accomplish?"

I was thrown off guard. Are we having a moment? Is the moment serious? These were odd questions for a prostitute to ask. Not so odd if she's a spy—to get my guard down. And she didn't have that dead-eyed coldness in her eyes, either.

"I should go to bed," I said.

She walked to the elevator with me.

"What floor?" I asked.

"Ninth," she says. "Are you on the ninth floor, too?"

The ninth floor. That was the floor the operations center was on. That was the floor McChrystal was staying on.

Holy shit, maybe she was a spy.

"I'm on the fifth," I said.

The door to the fifth floor opened. I stepped out.

I texted Duncan immediately.

Gathered more info—she is staying on 9th floor! I think she's a spy.

Duncan responded:

Poor tradecraft. But at least they are learning and that is healthy.

Duncan texted me again and asked if I wanted to get a final drink in his room.

I waited a few minutes, then went to his room on the ninth floor.

He opened the door in a white hotel robe. I took a seat on the chair next to the bed. We started to talk. I was excited at the possibility that she was a spy. It was an unusual chance to witness a foreign agent trying to infiltrate one of the military's most sensitive commands.

Duncan sipped a beer. I took a bitter lemon seltzer from the minibar.

It was late enough to discuss those big ideas that couldn't be mentioned during the day.

Duncan started talking about the team. Their love for McChrystal. The brotherhood. Why did they make the sacrifice? The war for them was more about the man than the conflict. They were there for him. Each on a search for meaning, naturally—and McChrystal was meaning. McChrystal was historic. McChrystal was MacArthur and Grant and Patton, and yet he lived and breathed and walked among them. They gave McChrystal their loyalty, and McChrystal gave shape to their identities. The wars gave McChrystal his own. He was the ultimate operator, his decisions felt in Kabul and Washington and Islamabad and Baghdad and Sana'a and elsewhere, in still-classified hideouts, playing at changing the world. The other operators out there, the politicians, the pundits, the soldiers, the diplomats, the spies, the insurgents, the hacks, and the flacks, swarming him, loving him, hating him, working against him, all playing the game.

I could live like this forever, I said. The Ritz, the Hotel Rivoli, the bullet trains, the first-class lounges, the wars. Drinking bitter lemon and asking fucked-up questions until dawn. Who is the spy? Who is Duncan? What the fuck are we doing here at two A.M.?

Duncan talked about himself—rootless, wandering, the kind of person war zones tend to attract. Why do we do what we do? A tremendous loneliness? Trying to fit in? It was a version of life that kept life at bay. It was a fantasy. Who wants the real world? Who can operate there after this, here?

Duncan: a collection of stories and vague origins. A naturalized American citizen who was born in England. Once a Shakespearean stage actor. Once a producer for a television network. Once a hotel manager off an interstate. Duncan found the war, first in Baghdad in 2006, where he worked as a communications consultant. Duncan spent time as a spokesperson at Fort Leavenworth. The timeline was always fuzzy. Not married, no kids. When exactly he was there, when exactly he was here.

Duncan had worked as a manager at a large chain hotel in Connecticut—the lost and found at that hotel was filled with dildos, he said. It was amazing how many people left dildos behind at hotels, like cell phone chargers and laptop cords. There was a whole box in the lost and found filled with dildos, multicolored, different sizes. The dildos were held for thirty days, per lost-and-found policy, before being thrown out. But no one ever came back to collect a forgotten dildo.

We're all here to fill the void, I offered, poorly explaining my favorite passage from *A Scanner Darkly*, a novel written by Philip K. Dick. Working stiff police officer Bob Arctor has the wife, the two kids, the power mower, the house. One day, he hits his head in the kitchen—the cobwebs cleared, he wanted out. "Nothing new could ever be expected. It was like . . . a little plastic boat that would sail on forever without incident, until it finally sank, which would be a secret relief to all." Arctor immersed himself in drugs and paranoia and a cause—he goes undercover as an agent to find his truer self in a "dark world where ugly things and surprising things and once in a while tiny wondrous things spilled out at him constantly." Knowing, all the while, that the cause itself is a lie. I quoted Portuguese writer Fernando Pessoa, who'd spent a life assuming dozens of different identities, writing under fake names and bylines. In one passage, Pessoa describes the secret to living a boring, middle-class life: "To resign oneself to monotony is to experience everything as forever new . . . He, of course, would say none of this. Were he capable of saying it, he wouldn't be capable of being happy."

I bungled the quotations, but I thought I'd gotten the meaning across.

Duncan brought up my story. I'd been waiting for this conversation, some kind of official push back to address what I had seen and heard.

"These guys, the team, they are enamored with him," he said, speaking of the general. "They are excited, excited to talk to you."

"They're impressive. I mean, I'd like to do a story that looks at the whole team, you know, that would be great."

"There is some concern about Friday night."

The night in Paris.

"Friday night, well, you know, I'm going to put it in the proper context—I can make sure of that."

He had another drink, and I finished my bitter lemon.

"Keep our interest in mind when you're writing the story," he said. "We're naive, haven't really done this stuff before."

"Okay," I said, thinking of the half-dozen other profiles they'd done.

"I'll be leaving in two days," Duncan said. "Hopefully my plane doesn't crash."

"Fuck, that would really screw up my story," I joked.

"I don't think so. Then you could write what you wanted without worrying about me losing my job."

I left. It was around three A.M.

22 | "I'M PRESIDENT. I DON'T GIVE A SHIT WHAT THEY SAY"

SEPTEMBER TO DECEMBER 2009, WASHINGTON, DC

There's a funny thing about these wars in Iraq and Afghanistan: What drives the policy debate and media coverage is rarely what's actually happening on the ground. Baghdad burns for years until Washington really pays attention to it. The reason Washington pays attention to Iraq is because the Democrats use the war as a political issue to hammer Bush on a daily basis. Baghdad is nearly as fucked-up in the fall of 2004 as it is in the fall of 2005 and the fall of 2006, but Washington cares about it only in '04 and '06, because there's a presidential and then a congressional election coming up. Iraq today is unraveling—terrorist attacks and civilian casualties continue, and the Iraqi government is repressive and authoritarian—but there's no political advantage for either Democrats or Republicans to point that out.

The same dynamic is at play in Afghanistan. The country is just slightly more fucked-up in the fall of 2009 than in the fall of 2008. However, Afghanistan isn't the kind of divisive issue that anyone in DC really gets much mileage out of, so it's ignored.

That changes on September 21, 2009. *Washington Post* reporter Bob Woodward publishes McChrystal's confidential assessment of the war. The report's conclusion is that we are on the verge of "mission failure." The implication: McChrystal wants more troops.

Overnight, Afghanistan starts to matter in Washington.

There's a lot of leakology about the document. Who leaked it? Who benefits? Whom does it hurt? It leaks four days after Michèle Flournoy, undersecretary of defense for policy, brought copies to members of Congress—maybe Congress leaked it, maybe Flournoy herself. If you're giving it to Congress you have to figure it's going to leak, right? Maybe Jim Jones leaked it—he's close to Woodward, so that makes sense. Maybe McChrystal leaked it, or Gates, or Mullen, so they could put pressure on Obama. Maybe it's just one of those random things—maybe there isn't a very thoughtful motive and it's just that Woodward, sitting across the desk, is such an amazing reporter (and he is that, no doubt) that he persuades his source to give it to him after an hour of conversation.

In Kabul, McChrystal learns that the assessment leaked. He's pissed for about thirty minutes, but then he says, "Hey, maybe it's better that it's out there."

The White House disagrees. The White House is furious.

For one, they're pissed at McChrystal. Is McChrystal trying to fuck them, or is McChrystal politically naive? A White House official tells me the leak undercuts the strategic impact of the twenty-one thousand troops already sent. They didn't even give the new troops a chance to turn things around.

On September 27, six days after the leak, a McChrystal interview airs on *60 Minutes*. During the interview, McChrystal lets it slip that Obama has spoken to him only once since he took over the war. That's a headline. (What prompts the *60 Minutes* correspondent to ask that question? Could it be that McChrystal's staff happens to mention it to the *60 Minutes* correspondent when the camera is off? McChrystal doesn't think Obama is talking to him enough. Maybe putting a little calculated pressure on him through the media, they'll get the face time they want with the commander in chief. Maybe not so naive . . .)

The White House doesn't like what happens in London, either. Four days after the *60 Minutes* interview, McChrystal gives a talk at the Institute for Strategic Studies. He's asked about a policy option to draw down U.S. troops to focus on counterterrorism operations, an option that Vice President Joe Biden has been advocating. "The short answer is: no," he tells the audience. He then says if Obama adopts that policy, it would lead to "Chaosistan." He tells the audience he's been encouraged to speak bluntly, though "they may change their minds and crush me someday." (Chaosistan, it turns out, is also a name given to a classified CIA analysis.) He'll tell a magazine that Biden's plan is akin to fighting a fire by "letting just half the building burn down."

This time, Obama summons him to a face-to-face meeting aboard Air Force One. Obama is in Copenhagen. They meet for less than an hour. McChrystal isn't impressed. Another photo op—a direct response to the *60 Minutes* story. They believe it's a photo op to convey the idea that "Hey, look, Obama does talk to his generals," members of his team will tell me. The White House, says Duncan, is still in "campaign mode." The incident, though, reveals that McChrystal can use the media to get what he wants—just fire up that Washington media! Soon after the *60 Minutes* story, McChrystal starts speaking to the president twice a month.

The leak, though, is the big one. The leak brings unwanted attention to the brand-new strategy review the Obama administration had quietly begun on September 13. It's at least the fifth review of the Afghanistan war policy in just over a year for the United States government. It's Obama's second review of the strategy. The urgency behind the review, though, is not due to the existence of McChrystal's strategic assessment. It's because McChrystal's strategic assessment *goes* public.

The Pentagon uses the media to force Obama's hand. Before the review even begins, Petraeus calls a *Washington Post* columnist and tells him that the only viable option is a "fully resourced, comprehensive counterinsurgency campaign." McChrystal's allies in the press rally to push his plan—inviting influential thinkers to the assessment team pays dividends. Stephen Biddle writes an essay supporting the strategy he helped devise. The Kagans do the same. As does Anthony Cordesman. For *The Washington Post*, Andrew Exum reviews a new book about Pat Tillman by Jon Krakauer—*Where Men Win Glory*. The book is hard on McChrystal, accuses him of being involved in the Tillman cover-up. Exum pans the book. He doesn't mention McChrystal's role in the cover-up, or mention him by name. Exum fails to disclose the fact he worked for McChrystal as an advisor. (The deception is egregious enough that the *Washington Post* ombudsman is forced to apologize for the oversight.) The same book is also reviewed in *The New York Times*—the reporter trashes the book as well. The review, rather strangely, doesn't mention McChrystal's role in the Tillman cover-up, either. This reporter, Dexter Filkins, publishes a glowing *New York Times Magazine* cover story on McChrystal the next month.

There are two camps in the debate over the Afghanistan policy: Team Biden and Team Pentagon. Biden wants a small footprint, Pentagon wants a big footprint. For guidance, the guys in the White House are reading *Lessons in Disaster*, a book about the Johnson administration's disastrous decision to escalate in Vietnam. The guys in the Pentagon are flipping through *A Better War*, a book that argues that the military could have won Vietnam if the politicians in Washington had just given them more time. McChrystal presents three options to the president—80,000 more troops, 40,000 more troops, and 25,000 more troops. By shooting high, he's hoping to get the middle number, what he truly wants.

The battle lines are drawn: Petraeus, Mullen, Gates, Hillary, and McChrystal are all pushing for at least forty thousand more troops. Biden, Eikenberry, Holbrooke, and Lute think that's a mistake. They are ignored; all Eikenberry does is "whine," according to a White House official. The White House claims the conclusion of the review isn't preordained, but outside the White House bubble it's clear from early on that Obama is going to cave. "If he approves anything less than General McChrystal's 40,000-troop option," *The New York Times* points out, "Mr. Obama could face criticism from Republicans and some moderate Democrats." Obama isn't going to stand up to all that shiny brass. He doesn't want to look weak. He's intimidated by the crowd.

There's another massive leak. On November 11, *The New York Times* runs a story about the memos Ambassador Eikenberry wrote. The two memos are devastating and scathing critiques of McChrystal's strategy. They are also the most prescient. The cables explain, point by point, why the McChrystal strategy is doomed to fail. They say Hamid Karzai is "not an adequate strategic partner." The memos say that sending more troops is likely to intensify "overall violence and instability" and leave the U.S. without an exit strategy. They call the projected transition to Afghan control "imprecise and optimistic" and the costs of the effort "astronomical." Eikenberry points out that there is no Afghan civilian government to take over after the military operation, and that any such government would take "years to build." He writes that "more troops won't end the insurgency." He also points out that Karzai has "explicitly rejected" the counterinsurgency proposal since being briefed on it. The memos, actually, read a lot like Matt Hoh's resignation letter.

When McChrystal learns about the Eikenberry cables, he is incensed. His feelings infect his staff. "When was the last time Eikenberry even commanded troops?" Casey Welch tells me. All in all, it's a bad sign— McChrystal's own strategy calls for a civilian and military partnership, and now it's public record that the top diplomat and top general in Afghanistan have radically different views of the war. More to the point, Karzai, the man who the United States will be relying on, doesn't want any part of the strategy, either.

The White House credits itself for what it calls the most comprehensive foreign policy review ever conducted.

The first detailed account of this fall review appears a few months later in a book called *The Promise*, written by Jonathan Alter. Alter is a veteran journalist and a Democratic insider in the White House. He's got the sources and lays it out from President Obama's perspective.

In page after page, Alter recounts the administration's best efforts to get a handle on Afghanistan. Obama wakes up to the fact that Gates and Mullen and Petraeus might not have his best interests at heart. In the first week of October, Obama calls Gates and Mullen to the Oval Office. With a "cold fury," according to the account of the meeting, Obama tells Gates and Mullen never to "box him in" again. He tells them the leaks are "disrespectful of the process" and harmful to the men and women deployed in Afghanistan. Mullen is "chagrined" by the meeting; Gates will go on to say in a speech that the generals and diplomats should give their advice "candidly but privately." The White House believes they made their point, though an insider will tell journalist Richard Wolffe that Obama was "frustrated by the length of time to elicit everything he needed from the military." The White House convinces itself that it is in control of the policy. The White House thinks McChrystal is "naive" and "in over his head" as far as the media.

During the review, Vice President Biden repeatedly suggests another plan. Rather than send a hundred forty thousand troops, why not do CT Plus, or counterterrorism plus? Rather than a comprehensive counterinsurgency plan, this would call for a smaller troop presence augmented by U.S. Special Forces and Predator drones, focused on hunting and killing Al-Qaeda. The glaring logical gap the Biden plan tries to address: There are "less than one hundred" Al-Qaeda fighters in Afghanistan, according to Jim Jones. So why do we need a hundred fifty thousand NATO troops to protect us from less than one hundred Al-Qaeda fighters? We know that the soldiers in Afghanistan won't be fighting Al-Qaeda in the vast majority of the cases. They'll be fighting local insurgents who are fighting (a) because they are in a civil war or (b) because there are foreigners on their land. McChrystal's strategy has so little to do with Al-Qaeda that Senator Lindsey Graham has to remind McChrystal and Petraeus that they need to include more Al-Qaeda in their "message" to sell the war.

Obama will repeatedly ask his military commanders to outline the Biden option, but they never send Obama the plan.

The political pressure on Obama to act builds. There's an outcry from the press that he's dragging his feet. The White House responds by saying they are taking their time, they are making a mature policy decision—something that Bush never did in Iraq and Lyndon Johnson never did in Vietnam. The White House fears Petraeus could resign in protest if Obama doesn't commit to the troop surge. Press reports quote other unnamed military officials saying McChrystal will resign, too. McCain and Senator Joseph Lieberman start to lobby for Obama to send more troops. Jones starts to come around to the idea of sending more troops—he doesn't want "to sandbag his old colleagues," he thinks. Gates claims he struggled to reach his decision about sending more troops—he waits to endorse whatever decision best defends the interests of his generals. Another insider tells Wolffe: "The Afghan review went in the direction of Gates's position."

At the ninth meeting, on November 23, Obama is given a plan that he thinks is an improvement. Not, he thinks, the Biden plan, and not the McChrystal plan. The generals want forty thousand troops to surge over twenty-one months. In this plan, the forty thousand troops would surge over nine months. A "significant number of troops" would begin to come home by July 2011—with the caveat that the plan is based on "conditions on the ground," a stipulation Gates and Mullen insist on. On November 26, the White House staffers work on an eight-page single-spaced consensus memo to fashion a policy, according to Alter. On November 29, Obama and Biden speak to the top military brass alone—walking into the meeting, Obama assures Biden that the July 2011 deadline would not be "countermanded" by the military.

In the end, Obama attempts to split the difference—he gives the military the troops they want, but tells them they need to leave sooner than they'd like to. He thinks this asserts his authority and proves that he hasn't caved. The Pentagon reads it another way: He gave us what we wanted, and he dragged his feet for months, which confirms their suspicions that he isn't truly committed to the war.

Obama insists that we won't embark on a decade-long nation-building campaign. That troops need to start coming home sooner rather than later. Otherwise, he fears he'll lose his liberal base. Within days of the policy announcement, Gates, Clinton, and others at the Pentagon make statements that describe what sounds like a decade-long nation-building campaign.

Obama gives McChrystal what he wants, warning him over a VTC: "Do not occupy what you cannot transfer." Sure. McChrystal tells me the review is "painful," and he calls the politics behind it "foolishness." He describes the force of the opposition as "wicked." McChrystal tells me things start to get better for him once Obama "took control of the process" and "stopped listening to his political advisors." In other words, Obama starts to do well once he starts to do what McChrystal wants him to do. The White House, though, thinks it has the upper hand, as one advisor says about Obama's attitude: "I'm president. I don't give a shit what they say. I'm drawing down those troops."

23 | THE STRATEGY

APRIL 21, 2010, BERLIN

On the mezzanine level of the Ritz-Carlton, twenty German military and foreign policy experts gathered in a conference room to listen to McChrystal speak. The goal of the meeting was to shape the views of the country's "opinion makers." McChrystal believed he had a better chance of getting them on his side if he could look them in the eye.

"Let me start by introducing myself. I'm Stan McChrystal. I command ISAF right now," he said. "We arrived in Berlin last night after a fourteen-hour bus ride from Paris. We got lost for the last hour or so. We're a little bit like a rock band, except with no talent."

The experts laughed.

"Afghanistan is so confusing that even the Afghans don't understand Afghanistan," McChrystal said. "If you think about Afghanistan—"

McChrystal turned to four whiteboards set up for the conference. He drew Afghanistan.

"That's supposed to be Afghanistan. Sometimes I put legs on it and it's a small dog."

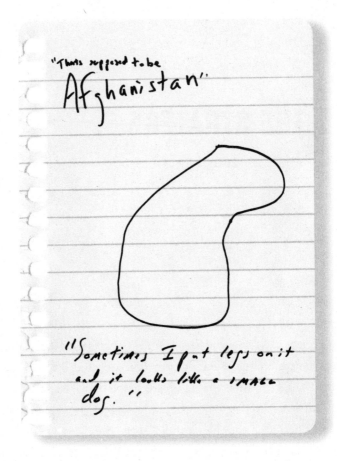

I made copies of his sketches in my notebook, adding a few notes of my own.

He summarized, layering fact upon fact. Afghanistan has a population of thirty million. Historically it was a buffer state between great powers. There is one major road in the country. There are Pashtuns in the south, Tajiks, Hazaras, and Uzbeks in the north. It's really more complicated than that, he says; in the twenties, the Pashtuns were relocated everywhere, so there are Pashtun populations mixed in.

"You can get confused real quick," he said. A single person can identify as a Popalzai, a Durrani, a Kandahari, and an Afghan. Ethnic divides weren't that big a deal until after the Soviets left in 1989. There's a tremendous cultural aversion to change. It's not Islam, it's not Taliban, it's not Al-Qaeda. It's Afghan culture. It's cultural conservatism, he explained.

"So when we come in and start talking about women's rights," he said diplomatically, "they might not see it that way."

The Soviets came, McChrystal said, and "they did a lot of things right. The Soviets did a lot of things correctly." They modernized. They created an Afghan army and police force. They built roads. They promoted a strong central government. They promoted education for both boys and girls. They did things "differently," too, he says. He means the Soviets carpet bombed and killed an "unimaginable" number of people. Death toll: 1.5 million. Then the nineties: The warlords took over. The warlords fought one another, killing tens of thousands. Then the Taliban fought the warlords, killing tens of thousands more. The warlords lost. Then, in 2001, the Americans came in. The Taliban went out. The warlords, "those same characters," McChrystal said, are now back in power.

The economy is torn to pieces. Seventy percent less irrigation than Afghanistan had in 1975. Other facts: GDP is around $15.6 billion, with close to 97 percent coming from foreign aid. That's not sustainable. The literacy rate is about 28 percent. It's a culture made up of fighters, McChrystal said, an entire class of professional fighters who know only how to fight. We want to get them to put their arms down and take up other, peaceful jobs. But there are no jobs. Ergo, we have to create new jobs and get them to put their weapons down.

Corruption: $3 billion has flown out of Kabul Airport, in cash, over the last three years. The corruption is at a level that "Afghans have never seen," McChrystal said. It is the fifth poorest country in the world.

The country has been at war for thirty-one years. The average life span of an Afghan is forty-five years. Sixty-eight percent of the population is under twenty-five years old. No one remembers what peace looks like, McChrystal said. Karzai thinks he does, said McChrystal—when Karzai talked to McChrystal, he often got nostalgic about how things were when he was a kid. So the goal is to try to re-create Afghanistan in the 1970s:

Forget the two coups and the Soviet invasion. To find the "brief period of solace," as it's been described, between the fifties and the seventies, when American backpackers and hippies traveled safely through the country. The goal is to turn the clock back to 1979.

"The people are tired, they're frustrated. They had great expectations. Now, their expectations might have been unrealistic. They don't see what they were promised. They don't have confidence. People don't know the future. They don't have confidence the government will win. They don't have confidence that the international community will stay. They fear the Taliban. The insurgency is extensive around the country."

McChrystal drew another diagram.

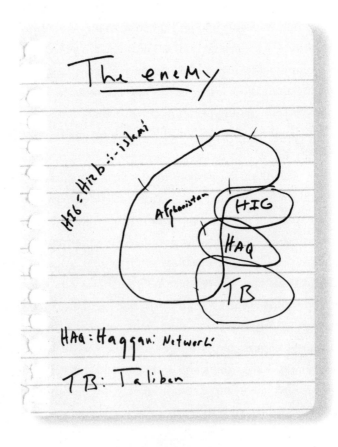

Insurgents are Afghans. What is essential for success is not to kill the insurgents, because they are the Afghan people. If you kill the insurgency, you kill the Afghan people you came to protect, and there's nobody left to win over.

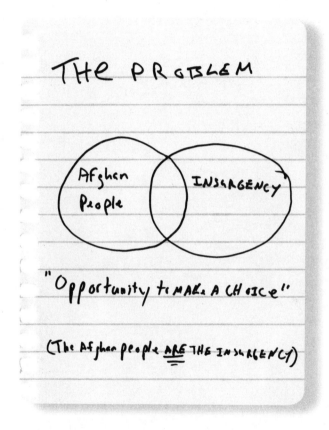

If you kill two out of ten insurgents, you don't end up with eight insurgents. You might end up multiplying the number of fighters aligned against you. McChrystal called it "insurgent math."

If you kill two, he said, "more likely, you're going to have something like twenty. Those two that were killed, their relatives don't understand that they're doing bad things. Okay, [they think,] a foreigner killed my brother, I got to fight them."

However, you have to kill sometimes, too, he noted.

"You can't win a COIN by killing people," McChrystal said. "But you do have to kill people when you have no other choice."

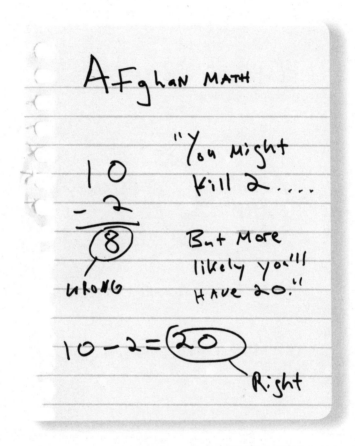

He added an arrow to his whiteboard diagram. This was the strategy.

"If you push the insurgents like a rat in the corner, they will fight," he said. "We all would. The way out is to come back into society. With honor. In five years or ten years, the problem will be right back again. A lot of people in Afghanistan have blood on their hands. If we spend

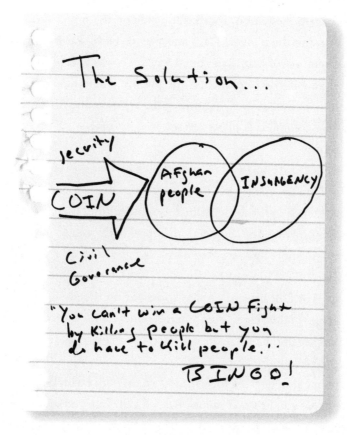

our time worrying about that, there won't be anyone to have peace talks with."

He finished: "We've made more mistakes than you can imagine since we've been there."

There was a ten-minute question-and-answer period.

A German foreign affairs expert noted: I noticed you spent forty-five minutes talking about the war and mentioned Al-Qaeda only once. He'd nailed the gaping flaw in the entire premise of the war—if it was supposed to be about terrorism, how was it that the vast majority of our resources and energy were directed at insurgent networks that posed no threat to Western Europe or the United States?

After the presentation, I walked outside on the mezzanine. Dave was there, working the phones. Dave was pissed. Dave was trying to get the general back to Afghanistan, but Ocean 11 was still grounded. Dave spoke to an Air Force colonel on the phone. He pointed out that commercial pilots were now flying out of the airport. The Air Force colonel told him: Commercial pilots are allowed to take more risks than Air Force pilots.

"One of Dave's jobs is to remind the USAF that they're worse than the French," Duncan said.

Dave looked over the mezzanine into the lobby. He spoke in compact bursts—acronym-laden language that packed as much information as possible into short sentence fragments. He arranged things, fixed things, did the logistics. I listened in.

"Yeah, Jeff. The attaché's office. I just got off the phone with your attaché again. I said, 'Hey, listen, there's some confusion from both sides. The pilots are in the middle.' I said, 'Do me a favor, please call the AMD at 603, USAV, and give them the no-kidding situation here in Berlin.' That's happening now. As for the waivers, do me a favor. Give me a point of contact. If you just text me it, then I'll call. Can you hold on one second, Jeff? [Answers the other line.] This is Dave. Yeah, this is Dave Silverman. Yeah. Yeah. With the German MOD here in Berlin. We leave right now to depart there for a 1230 meeting with the minister of defense. Okay, bye. [He switches back.] Hey, Jeff? Hey, Jeff, you there? Jeff, hello? Motherfucker. One second . . ."

Next on the schedule was a ceremony at the Ministry of Defense. Dave, Duncan, and I jumped into a taxi.

"This fucking volcano is the bane of my existence," Dave said.

Dave got an e-mail forwarded to him: In March, McChrystal had gone on patrol with a unit in southern Afghanistan. One of the soldiers in the unit had been killed—one of the guys McChrystal had met. Another member of the unit e-mailed McChrystal the news. Dave started to read out loud what the soldier, Staff Sergeant Israel Arroyo, had written to McChrystal:

"'It comes from the battlefield. It is not about the loss of the soldier, but the preservation of that soldier's will to give it all knowing they were willing to sacrifice for their country . . . comrades, friends, and family. That's why we soldiers still stay in the fight. I've lost three soldiers on this squad this year. Still stay in the fight. Not for me, but for my fallen heroes. For their memories and families. The bond between soldiers is stronger than anything in the world. Even when one dies, the other will live to tell about a great comrade or friend. This bond no soldier has ever lost, always. Amen.'"

"So this sergeant who wrote to him . . ." Duncan said.

"Not exactly sure, but definitely one of the guys on patrol with him was killed," Dave said.

"Man, the guys he went down to explain firsthand . . ." I said.

Dave's attention switched back to the event at the Ministry of Defense. "Where are we standing in the road . . ." Dave said.

"Are the press not allowed in? Do they have to do their shots from outside? I see they are doing their shots," Duncan said as we pulled up to the back of the Ministry of Defense.

Dave looked back down at his BlackBerry and continued reading Arroyo's account of what had killed his friend.

"'Sir, we were doing an RNS patrol three hundred meters from the COP. The ANA saw lights in because they know us and the villagers. Three to four steps back, Corporal Ingram entered and stepped on an AP mine that day, killing him and wounding two others: the medic, PFC Carlson, and PFC Hill. I was lucky because nothing happened to me, but my bell rung pretty hard. Ingram made it to . . . KAF, but didn't make it. Corporal Ingram's last words to me before he loaded on the bird that day was to write to you. With sadness in my heart, I do so.'"

"Jesus Christ," I said.

"What did he write back?" Duncan said.

Dave started reading out part of McChrystal's response.

" 'Israel, there is not much I can say to a soldier's leader who has felt the reality of this in a way that many others will find difficult to understand. I hope you understand and accept my thoughts and prayers to you and your entire squad. After a month meeting and walking with you, the bombs were . . .' "

We got out of the car and were met by a U.S. military official from the Berlin embassy. Dave and Duncan inspected the grounds. The ceremony was to take place behind the Ministry of Defense building. There was a smooth stone courtyard with a pathway leading into the new war memorial. During World War II, the building was the headquarters for the German military; it was also the spot where the coup against Hitler was attempted in 1944. The conspirators were executed in the courtyard, and there was a memorial to German Resistance fighters placed inside the compound to remember them. The ceremony for McChrystal, though, was at a newer memorial, built the year before and dedicated to the 3,100 soldiers and civilians who died in military operations after World War II.

Duncan and Dave did the advance work to make sure where McChrystal was arriving from, how many steps he was going to take, how long the ceremony would last. What if it rains? Where's the umbrella? Who hands him the wreath? Where are the German media going to stand?

They counted off the paces and the path McChrystal would walk.

"Just stop right there," said the U.S. defense attaché. "And yeah, you right there."

"Where is everybody else standing?" Duncan asked. "Where are we standing?"

"Along this line. The impression I had was it was just going to be four . . . COMISAF, minister of defense. . . . That's the impression I had," the attaché said. "All the press—behind the red line there." He pointed to a red line marked on the ground adjacent to the memorial.

We walked into the monument. In Germany, even having a monument recognizing the war in Afghanistan was controversial. German chancellor Angela Merkel had made headlines when she decided to go to a memorial service for German soldiers killed in action at the beginning of the month—it was the first time after four years in office that she'd gone to the funeral of a soldier who'd been killed. The structure had a Vietnam Veterans Memorial Wall feel to it, with the names of those who had been killed projected up on granite stone. Each dead was marked with a German dog tag, and an oath spelled out in Morse code.

"A German dog tag, they break it in half and keep the other half on the body," the attaché explained.

"This is all Afghanistan?" I asked, pointing to the new additions.

"They've lost thirty or forty," the attaché said. "I'd have to get the exact number."

McChrystal showed up with a German police escort—a black leather motorcycle squad that looked like something out of *The Matrix*. The German media stood behind the red line. I'd never seen a press corps so quickly quiet down.

The skies were gray. The rain started. The music started. McChrystal walked into the memorial and laid down the wreath. The cameras clicked rapid-fire.

We had lunch inside the ministry. I sat at a table with a high-ranking German officer who was in charge of media affairs. He was a large man with broad shoulders and silver hair and an intimidatingly wide forehead. He explained the context for the upcoming event. Local residents near a base in northern Germany were pissed about the sound of helicopters flying overhead. Recently, a few of those helicopter pilots had been in a helicopter crash, and the next ceremony was to award them medals. The German officer wanted to use the event to make the point that the Germans shouldn't be complaining about noisy helicopter traffic.

"It's a good opportunity to orchestrate the media," he said.

Those at the lunch looked at me. I was a member of the media. Would I take offense that the military viewed me as a target for orchestration? Nope. We shared an awkward chuckle.

The ceremony for the pilots was at the other end of the building. A lectern had been set up next to a glass case displaying the medals. The German defense minister spoke. He was at the high point of his career—a smooth-looking thirty-eight-year-old, considered an up-and-coming star in German politics. (The shine wouldn't last the year: Ten months later, he was forced to resign after he was outed for plagiarizing sections of his doctoral thesis.)

I wandered around the room. McChrystal and the defense minister both delivered brief remarks. I started examining the glass case, taking pictures of the medals with my phone. I noticed I was the only American left in the room: Team McChrystal had blown out of there. I tried to catch up with them, but a German police officer wouldn't let me go through the back door to get to the motorcade.

I received a text from Duncan: The convoy had rolled. I missed it. I was left behind.

24 | "LET ME BE CLEAR"

DECEMBER 2009, WEST POINT, KABUL, AND WASHINGTON, DC

Obama chooses West Point to deliver his speech on his new strategy. Or, more accurately, McChrystal and Petraeus's strategy. He tells the audience of cadets all the reasons why fighting Afghanistan is a bad idea. He tells them that we're going to do it anyway. He uses his favorite catchphrase, "Let me be clear"—a signal that he's not going to be clear at all. The president will pay a price for his ambiguity.

There are three audiences for the speech: Obama's liberal base, the Pentagon, and the Afghans. Obama adds in a line: The United States will begin to withdraw troops in July 2011. He adds the line so the military won't "jam him," as they jammed him with the McChrystal assessment, according to a senior U.S. official. Put a public benchmark out there, put the Pentagon on notice.

To make the case for escalation, Obama reaches back to the specter of September 11. He morphs, as Bush did before him, the Taliban into Al-Qaeda. He blames the failure in Afghanistan on the Iraq War, which he points out he was against. He says that he's not interested in a "nation-building project of up to a decade," saying it's too costly to be there. He claims this year it will cost $30 billion for the military (it ends up costing $59.5 billion). He acknowledges that the real issue isn't even Afghanistan, it's Pakistan—a conclusion his advisors had come to during the three-month-long review. (So if the problem is Pakistan, why are we sending a hundred thousand troops to Afghanistan?) Obama also says that he'll close the prison at Guantánamo Bay (he doesn't) and that all troops will be out of Iraq by the end of 2011 (maybe they'll be gone).

He goes on at length about how Afghanistan is not Vietnam. In Vietnam, he says, the United States didn't have a broad-based coalition of allies. (There were only New Zealanders, Filipinos, Australians, Thais, South Vietnamese, and South Koreans fighting alongside the Americans. In Afghanistan, only nine of the forty-three nations Obama cites are supplying over one thousand troops.) He says that in Vietnam we were fighting a popular insurgency and in Afghanistan we aren't. (At the time, U.S. officials also claimed the Vietcong weren't that popular and blamed journalists for exaggerating their presence. In Afghanistan, the Karzai government is about as popular as the Taliban—Karzai even calls the Taliban his "brothers.")

The July 2011 line about beginning to withdraw from Afghanistan is supposed to be heard by the antiwar left, too. It's not. They hear the other message: that Obama is going to triple the scope of the war, an unprecedented escalation that will create an almost entirely new conflict. (The surge in Iraq was only a one-sixth increase in the number of troops; Obama has, in under a year, tripled the number of Americans in Afghanistan, while doubling the total number of NATO troops.)

The Afghans are supposed to take another message from Obama's speech: that we're going to be in with them for the long haul. The Afghans don't hear that, though. They hear that the United States is getting the fuck out in July 2011.

The Pentagon hears July 2011 and its response is: Hmmm, how about 2014? Even the choice of July 2011 is suspicious. "It was clearly a political decision," says one Pentagon official. "Anyone who knows anything about Afghanistan knows that it doesn't make sense to start withdrawing troops in the middle of the fighting season." (The summer is traditionally when fighting spikes in Afghanistan.)

In Kabul, McChrystal's staff reacts negatively to the speech.

"It was a terrible speech," says Dave Silverman. "It was written by a fucking twenty-five-year-old." (Actually, a thirty-two-year-old.) Dave's feelings are echoed through McChrystal's command and throughout the military at large. Doesn't Obama understand that this isn't one of those issues where you can split the difference? By putting July 2011 in there, Obama is making it harder to get support among the Afghans for the strategy, Pentagon officials complain. In a way, Obama is getting the worst of both worlds. He's paying the domestic political costs for escalating, but he's not gaining the confidence of the Afghans, which the strategy is supposed to rely on. The Afghans sense we're just looking for the exit. This sense is reinforced by lines like "If I did not think that the security of the United States and the safety of the American people were at stake in Afghanistan, I would gladly order every single one of our troops home tomorrow," and "That's why our troop commitment in Afghanistan cannot be open-ended—because the nation that I'm most interested in building is our own," and "America will have to show our strength in the way that we end wars."

The speech isn't well received, really anywhere. The West Point audience is relatively subdued. The press trashes it. To tell a group of cadets that the war they are fighting is a huge waste of resources doesn't engender confidence. And what Obama is saying—that he doesn't want to nation-build—is exactly the opposite of what the counterinsurgency doctrine he's adopting calls for.

McChrystal gets almost all of his forty thousand troops. He's due back in DC to testify before Congress in December. He flies back with Eikenberry, and they don't talk much. Bad blood over the leaked cables.

McChrystal prepares for his testimony. McChrystal's lawyer, Colonel Richard Gross, plays the role of the affable southern senator; Mike Flynn plays the role of the hard-questioning liberal type. When McChrystal arrives in Washington, he'll confide to a few reporters that he never once questioned his own strategy during the three months of the review. A senior U.S. official talks to Pakistan's ambassador in Washington: I need to know, the ambassador says, is this July 2011 deadline legitimate? Don't worry about the deadline, the official says.

Afghan officials are already complaining to McChrystal: Are you leaving or not?

During his December testimony to Congress, McChrystal makes sure to keep mentioning Al-Qaeda—even though in the original briefings on his strategy Al-Qaeda was barely mentioned. McChrystal gives shout-outs to most of the members of his team, including their names in the *Congressional Record*: Dave, Jake, Casey, Charlie, and the others. One congressman, Representative Ted Poe from Texas, characterizes Obama's plan as "the surge and retreat policy."

The congressman continues: "So we will start bringing troops home, but we won't necessarily bring them all home, then. Is that what you understand?"

"Exactly, Congressman. There will be some slope, some pace that is determined by conditions."

"And if the conditions are worse, what happens then?"

"Sir, the president can always make decisions based upon conditions on the ground."

The loophole for an indefinite stay is kept wide open.

25 | WORSHIPPING THE GODS OF BEER

APRIL 21, 2010, BERLIN

I walked back to the Ritz. I was bummed. I would have liked to have seen McChrystal address the German parliament. But I figured I'd take the downtime to go back to my room and write up some of my notes from the morning.

I entered my room on the sixth floor. There was a note under the door. It was in a Ritz-Carlton envelope. I opened it. It was written on the hotel's letterhead. It read:

Hello Michael:

Was too lazy and still drunk at 6 am so decided to take the train this afternoon. If you would like to have a drink, give me a call. (Shall be here until about 5 pm.)

Kerina

The spy. She'd left her number. Was this the behavior of a high-class prostitute? I hesitated. I was on dangerous ground here. Should I call? If she really was a spy, could I confirm she was a spy? That would be useful for my story. But if anyone on McChrystal's team saw me talking to her, they would not be pleased that I was hanging out with a possible secret agent.

To be continued.

A few hours later, I went down to the lobby. Duncan, Khosh, Dave, and his wife were waiting. We had reservations at a Japanese restaurant in East Berlin. Two German reporters were going to join us for the meal.

Khosh and I started chatting.

I looked over to the front desk. Kerina was checking out of the hotel. She looked at me and smiled.

"Dude, that's the woman Duncan and Charlie think is a spy," Khosh said. "Weird."

"Yes," I said.

We arrived at the trendy Japanese restaurant. The two German reporters were jet-lagged and zonked out and mildly traumatized. They'd just returned from Afghanistan a few hours earlier, accompanying the German defense minister and four dead German soldiers. The trip had taken three days longer because of the volcano.

I spoke to one of the reporters, a young man named Julian. He was in his early thirties and a star in German media. The experience of traveling with the caskets had affected him. He told me he'd been one of the more outspoken voices in the German press supporting the war, putting him in a small minority. That's funny, I said. In the United States, only a minority in the media were opposed to escalating in Afghanistan.

"I supported this, and what if it doesn't work?" he asked. "I know these soldiers; I have spent time with them in combat. So to have it be a waste . . . What would that mean?"

It was interesting: Julian was prepared to take ownership of the position he took and the consequences of it. I'd rarely heard an American journalist express any such regrets or take responsibility for the policies they had promoted. Maybe it was a European thing.

Maybe Julian's trip home with the four caskets had given him doubts, perhaps revealing the acute German sensitivity to war. Over the past decade, the United States liked to mock Europeans for their unwillingness to get involved in armed conflict—Rumsfeld famously decried them as "Old Europe," expressing a widespread feeling across the media and foreign policy establishment. Rather than respect from America's elite, the hesitancy to avoid bloodshed brought derision.

Most media types, though, hadn't spent a few days stuck with dead soldiers in Uzbekistan.

The sake and beer kept flowing.

At the other end of the table, Dave and Duncan were talking about Fred and Kimberly Kagan, the two neoconservative experts who'd been on the assessment team last summer. The Kagans, Duncan explained, wanted to come over to Kabul to do another tour of the war zone. Duncan had been putting them off, much to the Kagans' displeasure. Duncan was worried that if he didn't give the Kagans access—shuttling them around to bases, setting up interviews with military officials—they would write a critical op-ed of McChrystal's strategy.

"The Kagans are making threats," Duncan said.

"Fuck the Kagans," Dave said.

After dinner, we headed to meet up with McChrystal and the senior staff. I was in a cab with Dave and Duncan and Dave's wife. We were driving through East Berlin.

"This place does have a communist feel to it," Dave said. "Is that a statue of Hitler—"

"Dave. Stop talking," his wife said.

"It's a statue of Frederick the Great," said the cabdriver.

Dave looked at the cabdriver. "I want to tell you that Germany has a proud military history from the Prussians to von Clausewitz," he said. "You guys should be proud of it. Prussians. Rommel."

From the backseat, I asked the cabdriver what he thought of the war in Afghanistan.

"Afghanistan is in a civil war," the cabdriver said. "Germany shouldn't be a part of it. It's very unpopular here."

Dave went silent. He looked hard at the driver. "Sir, as a representative of the American government, I want to tell you. We're here to convince Germany that we can win."

We pulled up outside a Mexican restaurant, a few blocks from the Ritz. McChrystal, the Flynns, Jake, Admiral Smith, Khosh, Lori, and Annie were sitting at a large table in a corner of the restaurant. A couple of massive pitchers of beer—held in a strange upside-down pyramidal contraption with a tap at the bottom, a unique specialty of the restaurant—were in the middle of the table.

We took our seats around the table.

McChrystal was nursing his glass of beer. He wanted to take it easy tonight, he said. His favorite beer was Bud Light Lime, but the bar didn't serve it.

General Flynn had other ideas. "I worship the god of beer," he said, laughing as he pretended to prostrate himself across the table when the waitress brought another pitcher.

"How the hell did you ever get your security clearance?" Jake asked.

"I lied," Flynn said.

The guys around the table greeted his answer with an uproarious laugh.

Security clearances were an important status symbol in Washington. The clearances went from secret to beyond top secret. To get a top-secret clearance, it usually took three to six months, which entailed intensive interviews with your friends and family. Contracting companies had made tens of millions of dollars providing employees with clearances to the government—and keeping a clearance once you were out of the government meant you could make more money in the private sector. Over the past ten years, the government had acquired a secrecy fetish, classifying over 2.6 million new secrets. Analysts had pointed out that one of the main reasons the government tried to hold on so tightly to its documents wasn't that their release would hurt national security, the catchall justification to classify, but that the government wanted to prevent embarrassment. An unspoken reality in Washington—which Flynn had hit on with his gibe—was that if people actually told the truth during interviews for their security clearances, they probably wouldn't get them. Everybody lied about drug use, but more bizarrely, if you spent time in dodgy places around the world and lived abroad for any length of time—Iraq, Afghanistan, Gaza, Pakistan—that often ended up being used against you, which ensured keeping out most people who actually had intimate knowledge of these places. "The more you know, the greater the risk you are to national security," as one former U.S. official put it, ironically.

I stepped outside with Duncan and Julian to smoke a cigarette. Julian asked me how the story was going so far.

"Have you ever seen the Werner Herzog movie *Grizzly Man*?" I asked them.

They neither confirmed nor denied, so I continued. The movie, I explained, was about a radical environmentalist named Timothy Treadwell. Treadwell was obsessed with grizzly bears. He made it his life's work to study them. He studied them in a way that wasn't really academic. He lived with them in the wilderness in Alaska and videotaped them constantly. He stuck his hand in bear shit and believed he was communing with the animals. His stand-ups before the camera had a hypomanic feel. He was convinced he was the savior for the bears. He viewed park rangers and hunters as his sworn enemies.

It quickly became clear to the audience that Timothy Treadwell was insane.

There was one person, though, who didn't recognize Treadwell's insanity: the director and narrator, Werner Herzog. This is because Herzog is insane, too. It's what makes the movie work. Crazy recognizes crazy.

"So yeah, I kind of feel like Herzog around these guys," I told them. "Especially since we're in Germany."

An hour later, Team McChrystal left the bar. Highly buzzed, they walked back to the Ritz. I followed.

26 | WHO IS STANLEY McCHRYSTAL? PART I, 1954–1976

Right from his first days at West Point, McChrystal exhibits the mixture of brilliance and contempt for authority that would follow him throughout his career. He gets over one hundred demerits, earning the title of a "century man," wearing it as a badge of honor. He parties hard. He writes a series of provocative articles and stories for the school's literary magazine, including one piece of fiction where he imagines assassinating the president of the United States. He learns to thrive in a very rigid environment while still pushing the envelope every chance he gets.

Born on August 14, 1954, he grows up in a military family. He moves around to different bases. He's a very good athlete. Baseball is his sport, and even in Little League he would call out strikes to the crowd before whipping a fastball down the middle. He has five siblings, one sister and four brothers. All would be involved in the military, either joining it or marrying into it. His brother Scott is an Army chaplain in the Assemblies of God Church; his eldest brother, Herbert J. McChrystal III, also a chaplain, writes a book called *Spiritual Fitness: An Imperative for the Army Chaplaincy*. McChrystal's mother dies when he is fourteen. His father,

Herbert, a West Point grad of '45, would retire as a two-star general, having fought in Korea and Vietnam.

McChrystal enters West Point in 1972, while the Vietnam War is still going on. The U.S. military is close to its all-time low in popularity at the time—there is "tremendous anti-military sentiment" throughout the country, according to General David Barno, one of McChrystal's classmates. On trips to the outside world, the cadets are briefed on what to do if riots break out and they get attacked. Barno recalls having eggs thrown at him on a trip to Syracuse, New York, for a football game.

It's a wild time at West Point, a mix of testosterone, hooliganism, and reactionary patriotism—the class of '76 is the last class to have graduated before the institution becomes coed. The all-male academy is known as the Prison on the Hudson. One football season, there's a mess hall rally where ten tables are stacked atop one another during a massive, balls to the wall food fight, which happens three or four times that year. Paintings are ruined, chairs and tables destroyed. On training trips to Camp Buckner, where Vietnam-like conditions are simulated (living in Quonset huts, for instance), one cadet is notorious for lighting his jacket on fire with lighter fluid and throwing himself into a lake. Birthdays are celebrated by a tradition called "rat fucking"—a gang of cadets rush into a room, grab the birthday boy, and fuck him up. Tie him, tape him, drag him through snow or mud, covered in shaving cream. "It was pretty out-of-control," says Barno, who would later serve as commander in Afghanistan from 2003 to 2005. The class, filled with "huge talent" and wide-

The Pointer's *editorial board,*
featuring McFerren and McChrystal

OH, SURE LET THE WOMEN COME.

But let's make things fair. All women admitted to West Point should be required to wear their hair in some ultra conservative style — a style equivalent to the one West Point men wear, one that could not be quickly brushed out (to look normal) during leaves. It would only be fair, I think, for all women admitted to West Point to be required to wear their hair in buns.

PIG FAT BUNS

An editorial in The Pointer *from the class of '76*

eyed teenagers with a strong sense of idealism," says Barno, goes on to produce the top generals of the wars in Iraq and Afghanistan, including Barno and General Ray Odierno, who would command all U.S. forces in Iraq for two years.

McChrystal is a dissident ringleader on campus. One classmate, who asked not to be named, describes finding McChrystal passed out in the shower after he drank a case of beer he'd hidden under the sink. He views the tactical officers, sort of like glorified residential advisors at West Point, as the enemy.

The troublemaking puts a serious crimp on his social life: In 1973 he starts to date Annie, whom he'd met at Fort Hood, Texas, but usually when she visits she barely gets a chance to see him. "I'd come visit and I'd end up spending most of my time in the library, while Stan was in the Area," she tells me. McChrystal's roommate, Jake McFerren, remembers having to keep Annie company in the library while Stan marched away his Saturday afternoons. "I remember going down to the Area, all the cadets were marching one way, back and forth. Stan sees me and Annie, and he breaks away, marches completely perpendicular to the formation, comes up and says, 'This is bullshit.'"

McChrystal's most notorious achievement—immortalized in a description underneath his yearbook photo—is the raid on Grant Hall, a gray stone building that was used for social engagements, a place for females visiting the all-male school to hang out.

McChrystal and five others borrow old weapons from the campus museum, including a French MAT-49 submachine gun and dummy hand grenades made from socks. At 2215 hours, dressed in full commando gear and with painted faces, they storm Grant Hall. The main intent, says Barno (who didn't participate in the raid) was to "create chaos." McChrystal writes a satirical piece about his experience for *The Pointer*, the West Point literary magazine where he serves as managing editor. He describes the scene: "We moved swiftly to the . . . heavy brown doorway. Our hearts beating wildly . . . there were five of them blissfully unaware of the anger which lurked so near. . . . [L]ed by the sergeant, we burst out firing rapidly, dashed down the ramp, the light of Grant Hall cast a pallid glow on all of us. The rest is history." A postscript to the story, which is accompanied by a cartoon of the raid with a soldier sneaking up on a busty coed and a photo of the five cadets in commando gear, says: "Delinquency: Extremely poor judgment, i.e. horse play with weapons in public at 2215 hours, frightening female visitors, and causing MP's to be summoned 10 May 1974." McChrystal headlined the article: "Where Goats Dare."

McChrystal the Goat. The Goat is the name for the cadet who graduates last in the class. There are famous Goats—like George Armstrong Custer and George E. Pickett. The Goat excels in "mischief," as one historian puts it, in fraternization, in extracurricular escapades along Flirtation Walk down by the Hudson. There is a two-century-long tradition of Goatism. Custer graduates last—726 demerit points!—yet is known as one of the most "dynamic" commanders in the Civil War. He becomes the Union's youngest general. He earns his place in history, though, eleven years after the Civil War ends: His career spectacularly flames out in the massacre at

Part of a photo spread from The Pointer

Little Bighorn, a misstep in the U.S. government's campaign to wipe out America's native population. Other Goats went on to win silver stars, great victories, and rise to the highest ranks. It is General Dwight D. Eisenhower who will later say, "If anybody recognized greatness in me at West Point, he surely kept it to himself."

McChrystal embodies the Goat ethos, though he's far from last in the class. McChrystal ranks 298 out of a class of 855, according to an official at West Point, a serious underachievement for a man widely regarded as brilliant. This puts him in the league with Sherman and Grant and Eisenhower and Patton—not quite scholars, but destined for history. His more compelling work is his writing, the seven short stories he produces for *The Pointer*. They are works of fiction and satire, which read like a cross between *The Naked and the Dead*–like war fiction and the amusingly subversive writings of a college student. The stories reveal a creative imagination that is obsessed with war, conflict, terrorism, and bucking authority.

One story, written in November 1975, titled "Brinkman's Note," is a piece of suspense fiction. The main character, an unnamed narrator, first appears to be trying to stop a plot to assassinate the president. It turns out, however, that the narrator himself is the assassin. He's able to infiltrate the White House. "I had coordinated these plans routinely the day before with another member of the president's staff, and everything was set. The main door to the plant opened. The president strode in smiling. From the right coat pocket of the raincoat I carried, I slowly drew forth my .32 caliber pistol. In Brinkman's failure, I had succeeded."

Other stories eerily foreshadow the issues he'd have to deal with thirty years later in Afghanistan and Iraq, including the difficulties training the Afghan security forces and the civilian casualties during insurgencies. In a story called "The Journal of Captain Litton," the main character is a British officer in the Middle East who writes, "commanding these North Africans is a noxious prospect at best . . . I'm hopeful that once they are out and moving amongst the enemy troops they will steady somewhat and we will have reasonable chance of success." The story hinges on the captain's aide, an Arab named Abu, who eventually betrays all of the captain's secrets to the enemy. Another story, "In the Line of Duty," also set in the Middle East, is about a unit of Americans that accidentally opens fire on a local boy. With Vietnam looming in the backdrop, McChrystal the cadet confronted the issues of getting dragged into an open-ended counterinsurgency in a foreign land. His fictional character, a young lieutenant named Gewissen, would oppose a policy that the real McChrystal, later as a general, would have to embrace. "The troops, on constant alert for expected guerilla activity, had apparently mistaken the boy for a terrorist approaching the wire and had opened fire with a .50 caliber machine," the story reads. Gewissen visits the scene of the incident and the following exchange with his commander occurs:

> "I was told what happened, LT, don't worry too much about it and tell the guard he can rest easy, too. We'll put in a report that it was strictly in the line of duty. After all, what can the country expect when they put a nineteen-year-old kid over here on such an important mission?"
>
> "Duty sir? Just what the hell is our duty? Wouldn't you say we had a duty to that kid?"
>
> Harris hardened, his voice growing colder. "Your duty is to the country, LT."
>
> "Which country, sir, this one or the one that sent us?" Gewissen was shouting now. "What about our duty to ourselves?"

One of McChrystal's last pieces for *The Pointer* best gets at the psyche of the young cadet—chafing at bureaucracy, a dry sense of humor, and the willingness to flip the giant bird to his superiors. It's about a student who sneaks into the registrar's office to destroy Honeywell 635, a computer that has kept track of all the cadet's "1,672 demerit hours in two months" and his poor academic performance. "The bombs are in place and in minutes vengeance will be mine," the story opens. "At first I attributed my constant bad fortune to some sadistic captain in the tactical department who, probably for some very good reason, bore a grudge against the family. Later, I thought that the CIA, FBI, SLA, or PTA might have sent a killer agent out to cause my slow, painful death, and at one point I even started attending chapel three times a day to cover all possibilities."

27 | "THE JERK IN GREEN"

APRIL 22, 2010, BERLIN

The next morning, I checked out the local papers to see the kind of coverage they gave McChrystal's visit. He was on the front page of the three major German dailies. I bought copies of all three newspapers from the newsstand in the lobby. I headed up to the ops center on the ninth floor, the papers folded under my arm.

Charlie, Jake, and Admiral Smith were in the room. They were discussing McChrystal's next speech.

"You're going to talk about Marja, so that's a major military operation. Obviously you have to lead toward Kandahar," Jake said. "I like him saying it's already going on. It's not going to be D-Day, not a big assault. He used the term yesterday. It's a *process*."

The Marja offensive had started two months earlier, dispatching some ten thousand NATO soldiers and five thousand Afghan security forces to regain control over a town of about fifty thousand Afghans. Marja was located in Helmand province—the very place McChrystal had been concerned about committing forces to when he took over a year earlier. But now McChrystal had hyped it as the most important battle to date. It had not gone well. McChrystal claimed that expectations for a clean and neat resolution were unrealistic. There were also no results to show. To deflect the criticism, the military used a variety of phrases to indicate the distinct lack of resolution in counterinsurgency operations—"rising tide of security" was one of them, "process" another. What was happening in Marja didn't bode well for the next major offensive planned for Kandahar. Marja was supposed to be a "proof of concept," as military officials put it, for Kandahar, and the concept looked like a failure.

While the team worked on the speech, they continued to game-plan a way back to Kabul. There was a NATO conference for foreign ministers in Tallinn, Estonia. NATO and State Department officials had suggested McChrystal put in an appearance there. Charlie tried to figure out why.

"They're fucked up," Charlie said. "They want him to go talk to the foreign ministers, but they don't know if the foreign ministers are going to be there?" Charlie shook his head. "They're fucked up," he said again.

McChrystal walked in the room. "Hey," he said.

"Sir."

"This is our recommendation for the five-to-seven-minute intervention," Jake said. (Intervention: what NATO ministers call speeches.)

Admiral Smith handed him an outline of notes. They wanted McChrystal to focus on "the training mission," as it sounded less like "war." They suggested he use phrases like "mentoring the Afghans." Any questions about Kandahar should also be spun back to the larger point about the training mission, his advisors said.

"Five to seven minutes?" McChrystal said, skeptically, after looking over the speech.

"Is it more?"

"Oh, yeah."

Dave sketched possible travel scenarios out on a whiteboard.

"Hey, Mike, how are you this morning?" McChrystal asked.

"Great, sir," I said. "You see the papers?"

I took the three papers that were under my arm and put them on the desk. "You're all over them, man," said Jake.

"None of us speak German, do we?" McChrystal asked. "They could be going, 'This asshole, look at the jerk in green.'"

"How was your run this morning?" I asked.

"We lifted. Getting a touch of plantar fasciitis. I've had it for ten years. Just a touch."

Jake, who was stationed in Berlin in the eighties during the Cold War, remembered a little bit of German. He started to translate the papers.

Dave in Berlin

"You're here, you're the commander, and you were giving the overall strategy in the north," Jake said.

Charlie was getting pissed about the small talk. He wanted to get the Estonia trip straightened out. He tried to interrupt.

"This FM and the agenda for it is completely fucked up," he told McChrystal. "No one has got control of it. They don't know what foreign ministers are going to be there."

"We just talked to Tallinn," Jake said, referring to an advisor who was currently in the Estonian capital. "He's walking into the meeting, he says, 'I don't even know who is in this meeting.'"

"Here's the option—" Charlie tried interrupting again.

McChrystal was still looking at the papers. "This says essentially I am handsome and well hung," McChrystal said.

"In German," said Dave, looking up from his scribbling on the whiteboard.

"This one, too," said Jake, laughing.

"That's our story," McChrystal said.

"We're sticking to it," said Jake.

They wanted McChrystal to either go to Estonia or sit in on a meeting via video teleconference. The possible plan: to leave at 0530, arrive at 0830, stay on the ground for four hours, back on Ocean 11 at 1345, and 1445 on to Kabul. The wives were going to the train station tomorrow. They would just tell them good-bye.

"Where's my body double?" McChrystal said about the video teleconference. He'd have to sit for two hundred forty minutes in front of a camera to broadcast his image onto a screen in a meeting room in Estonia.

"We'll just have to get a sock-puppet cutout of you," said Jake.

"If they come back and say they want you for three hours, an option would be, leave here at five in the morning. Five thirty is takeoff," Charlie said. "The pilots can make this."

"I think so," said Dave, laughing—the fucking Air Force.

"What's your recommendation?" McChrystal asked.

"I recommend: One, we don't know on the agenda," Charlie said, predicting the Estonians would react in the same positive way as the Germans. McChrystal, though, was concerned his presence might overshadow other NATO delegates.

"He would be beside himself if you showed up," Jake said, not as concerned, referring to the Estonian foreign minister.

"Like, 'Wow, the guy has actually made the effort to get here,'" Charlie said.

"We know Clinton is there," Jake said. "But they don't know who else." Getting possible facetime with Clinton, an ally in his policy battles with the White House, was an incentive.

"Do they have a seat for me?" McChrystal asked.

"We'll make sure they do. I told them we're looking at timing and would brief you," Jake said. "They got kind of, 'Okay, please keep us informed.'"

"If it's three hours, I'd rather do it in person," McChrystal said, rejecting the VTC option.

Okay. The room went silent. McChrystal gave his orders.

"Course of action: One, we need to get there an hour ahead of time—"

"We don't have badges, we don't have shit," Charlie said.

"Can you give me a place to shower and change?" McChrystal said. "I'd rather not ride in uniform."

"Or you want to do it in ACUs," said Charlie. The ACU, or Army Combat Uniform, was the style of outfit McChrystal wore while in Afghanistan. It wasn't a dress uniform; it was like a camouflaged jumpsuit with sand-colored boots.

"Good idea," said Jake on the ACUs. "All the way back to the fight." It would remind the civilians at the foreign minister conference, Jake explained, that McChrystal was a combatant commander from a live war zone.

"Oh hell yeah," McChrystal said. "Just find me a shred of reason to do it."

"That would take away the shower part," said Dave.

"Here's my guidance," McChrystal said. "I want to go. I'll do that as the primary, assuming that's what they want. I want to make sure. I don't want to show up here and people say, 'Why'd you do this?'"

"They're all VTCing in now," Jake said.

"Why couldn't they fly out?"

"They got diverted. One of them got as far as Dubai and flew back." The volcano, again ruining plans.

"Okay, so that'd be course of action two," McChrystal said. "It's easier to go there. I can have a bigger impact face-to-face."

"You'd have a big impact on Rasmussen," said Jake, referring to NATO secretary-general Anders Fogh Rasmussen.

"That's the point. He's the one I'm really worried about. But I just want to make sure—"

"You'd made the effort to see him going back into Kabul, and made the gigantic fucking effort with the meeting in Tallinn—" said Jake.

"Of course, last time I went to the foreign minister, I got an ugly note from Colin Powell," McChrystal said.

"Really?" said Jake." He's not even there."

"He's not even in government," McChrystal said.

"What was his point?" Jake said.

"What were you doing in Clinton's territory? I sent him a note right back, I said, 'The secretary-general directed me to be there.' I got a chain of command."

"Which [FM] was that, sir?" Dave asked.

"The one in December [2009]. It was at the height of all the foolishness," McChrystal said. McChrystal had gotten the note at the end of Obama's strategic review, and he didn't appreciate the unsolicited advice from Powell.

"He thought I was fighting our government, which I wasn't," McChrystal said. "What are you doing going there? I was fucking ordered there."

"Like we want to get on a plane," Dave said.

"Like you're just looking for reasons to get there," said Jake.

"I didn't know if you knew him well," Dave said.

"I think his thinking was DC thinking," McChrystal said. "That was early December, prior to my testimony. Everybody was accusing us of trying to do the political thing."

McChrystal tabled the decision on Estonia for later in the day. I left the control room. I had an appointment at the Afghan embassy to get an entry visa to Afghanistan.

28 | WHO IS STANLEY MCCHRYSTAL? PART II, 1976-PRESENT DAY

Lieutenant Stanley McChrystal enters an army in the late seventies that is broken, riddled with drugs and race problems. The soldiers aren't very good: a collection of drunks, dirtbags, junkies, and scammers. He graduates from Special Forces school in 1979, eventually becoming the regimental commander of the elite 3rd Battalion, 75th Ranger regiment, in 1986—a dangerous position, even in peacetime, as nearly two dozen Rangers are killed in training accidents during the eighties. It is also an unorthodox career path—most soldiers who want to climb the ranks to general don't go into the Special Forces.

He revolutionizes the training regime for the Rangers—a habit he would develop, trying to transform systems in place that he felt were outdated. According to Command Sergeant Major Michael Hall, a long-time friend who would serve with him as the highest noncommissioned officer in Afghanistan, McChrystal introduces mixed martial arts, like jujitsu, to the hand-to-hand combat training and changes the drills on the rifle range (requiring everyone to qualify with night-vision goggles), and forces soldiers not just to run, but to build up their endurance with weekly marches carrying heavy backpacks. He checks a few more boxes on his career in the late nineties, spending a year at Harvard's Kennedy School of Government and then the Council on Foreign Relations in New York City, where he coauthors a treatise on the merits and drawbacks of humanitarian interventionism. ("I didn't want to write anything at first," he says, playing the anti-intellectual card. "But I ended up enjoying it.")

What McChrystal learns at West Point—and reinforces as he climbs the ranks in the Special Ops world—is how to walk a very fine line in the rigid military hierarchy and yet still succeed. He sees exactly how far he can go without getting tossed out. Being a highly intelligent badass can get you ahead. He was, after all, managing editor of *The Pointer*, and graduating two hundred ninety-eighth isn't really that bad. His behavior demonstrates his capacity for risk and his willingness to put his views out there, consequences be damned. "He was very focused," says his wife, Annie. "Even as a young officer he seemed to know what he wanted to do. I don't think his personality has changed in all these years." His personality is perfect for the "Rules be damned" ethos that takes hold after September 11. He does his first tour in Afghanistan as the chief of staff of the XVIII Airborne Corps. In 2003, he serves as a Pentagon spokesperson alongside Victoria Clarke at the start of the Iraq War. The stint is memorable for quotes that would have acted as albatrosses to most others, like backing up Donald Rumsfeld's infamous remark about looting in Baghdad—"Stuff happens." As Pentagon spokesperson, McChrystal gave his take on the chaos: "Looting is a problem, but it is not a major threat. People are not being killed in looting." He also, rather unfortunately, mentions that major combat operations in Iraq are over, a week before Bush's "Mission Accomplished" speech.

At the end of 2003, he takes over as commander of the Joint Special Operations Command, running the most elite units in the military, including Delta Force, Navy SEALs, and the Rangers. He's extremely successful as head of JSOC: During the Iraq surge, McChrystal's team killed and captured "thousands, I don't even know how many," says General Flynn. McChrystal is credited with helping to stabilize Iraq, almost in equal measure to Petraeus's surge.

It's during this time that McChrystal, along with Flynn, develops what was for the U.S. military a fairly radical view on information, all in the goal of searching out terrorist networks. They map out networks, picking off various scumbags and insurgents and hunting them down. They take this worldview—networks, information sharing, the impossibility of controlling information, when to apply lethal force, when to kill, when to capture—with them on the next big assignment to Afghanistan in 2009. They even, in a way, have brought it to how they view all their enemies, both foreign and domestic: Find who is linked to whom, find who's at the wedding, and be faster, smarter, ballsier than everybody else. Then take the fuckers out. "The Boss would find the twenty-four-year-old kid with a nose ring, with some fucking brilliant degree from MIT, sitting in the corner with sixteen computer monitors humming," says a Special Forces commando who worked with McChrystal in Iraq. "He'd say, 'Hey—you fucking muscleheads couldn't find lunch without help. You got to work together with these guys.'" Military experts will later describe McChrystal's JSOC as "industrial-strength counterterrorism."

Controversy is never far behind: McChrystal's career should have been over at least two times by now. He is tainted by one of the most controversial scandals of the previous administration: detainee abuse and torture at prisons in Iraq, and the cover-up of Pat Tillman's death. The behavior surrounding Tillman's death will continue to haunt him, though. "We didn't want to give [the family] a half-baked finding," McChrystal said, yet Tillman's family felt McChrystal had done exactly that. He would apologize to the family in public during his testimony, but he never personally calls Pat Tillman's mother, Mary—a slight which she agonizes over to this day.

At the time, Tillman's death also revealed how savvy McChrystal could be when he was inclined to serve his political masters. The football player's death is being spun as a heroic, good-news story during the contested 2004 election cycle. Bush is being overrun with bad news, including the Abu Ghraib prison scandal and the disastrous first attack on Fallujah. McChrystal is trying to help President Bush out, according to members of Tillman's family. (Though personally a Democrat, McChrystal felt great loyalty to Rumsfeld, Cheney, and Bush.)

Tillman's family would later accuse McChrystal of a "cover-up" and trying to "cover his ass." "The false narrative, which McChrystal clearly helped construct, diminished Pat's true actions," wrote Mary Tillman in her 2008 book, *Boots on the Ground by Dusk*. Mary Tillman believes that McChrystal got away with it because he was Dick Cheney's and Donald Rumsfeld's "golden boy," she writes. He's close to Cheney—according to U.S. military officials, a number of times throughout the Bush administration McChrystal got orders directly from Cheney. McChrystal even goes so far as to send a message to Cheney that the JSOC "guys all really love him," according to Pentagon insiders. Rumsfeld and Cheney embrace McChrystal's willingness to get things done, even if it includes bending the rules or skipping the chain of command. Author Jon Krakauer, who's written the most definitive account of Tillman's death, will accuse McChrystal of having a "credibility problem."

Certainly, having friends in high places helps him skate. Cheney, in his memoir, will personally thank McChrystal, and reminisce about a dinner he had with America's Special Operations Forces in 2008 that opened with this blessing: "We are soldiers, God, agents of correction." Rumsfeld, in his 2011 memoir, praises the general, writing dramatically of McChrystal watching "the mortally wounded Zarqawi pulled out of the rubble before he died a short time later." But on a more fundamental level, McChrystal's charm, his candor, and his sheer intelligence—he is an avid reader, gets briefings on his iPod, and is constantly listening to audiobooks—are compelling to journalists, and they also help him in policy debates. If there's a vacuum, he's not afraid to fill it with his own ideas. Where General David Petraeus—who also is beloved in the press—

is a teacher's pet with a Ranger's tab, McChrystal is a snake-eating rebel. He's cool—he didn't care when his teenage son came home with blue hair and a Mohawk. He's a liberal. He asks for opinions and seems genuinely interested in the answer. He's irreverently driven, and the same characteristics that endeared him to Rummy and Cheney endear him to some in the press corps.

It's hard for McChrystal to leave his terrorist-hunter image behind, despite the fact that the media have tried to give him a total makeover as a counterinsurgency evangelical. He's not a killer anymore—he's an intellectual and a philosopher who reads Winston Churchill's 1898 account of the Boer War, looking for similarities between then and now. The killer attitude exists within him, though, just below the surface. After taking over in Afghanistan, McChrystal's team ups the number of Special Forces units in the country from four to nineteen and puts the Taliban and insurgent networks "under extraordinary pressure," says Mike Flynn. That comes with considerable controversy: A Special Forces night raid ends in the deaths of two pregnant Afghan women and allegations of a cover-up. McChrystal publicly apologizes for these kinds of events—"We've shot an amazing number of people," he's said—but old habits die hard. He'll tell a Navy SEAL in the hallway of the ISAF headquarters: "You better be out there hitting four or five targets tonight," then adding, "I'm going to have to scold you in the morning for it, though." As Dave Silverman will tell me: "Deep down, he still . . ." Dave lets his thoughts trail off. "He really remembers the time before fondly."

29 | REALITY CHECKS IN

APRIL 22–23, 2010, BERLIN

The Afghan embassy was in an upscale neighborhood on the city's west side. The two-floor house, with a serene garden pathway, didn't stand out. Only a small sign marked its existence.

I went upstairs to the second floor. An Afghan man sitting at a wooden desk opened a drawer filled with passports. He found mine. He stamped it and handed it to me.

"You are a journalist," he said.

"Yes," I said.

He motioned for me to walk with him. He led me down the steps and outside to the garden. He said he had a few things he wanted to tell me. He wanted, he told me, to get his voice out there. He asked that I didn't use his name.

The Afghan official told me he'd been in Germany eight years. He'd left Kabul in 2001, after the invasion. He went first to Russia, then moved to Berlin. He told me he was depressed when he looked at his country.

I asked him what he thought of General McChrystal's plan to make Karzai a credible leader.

"Inside Afghanistan, the politicians listen. They promise. Then, when they go back to Kabul, everything is forgotten," he said. "Afghan people have mistrust about their politicians because they have promised so much and they have given so little. Nothing is as Karzai says. No one listens to it or cares about it. No one takes it seriously. They just consider it as another promise that will never be fulfilled."

Did he see any chance of the Americans' winning?

"There are people who are free from corruption, but their voices are not heard. Winning is a credible government that can enforce the law. A government that cares about the common people. How can they steal a million from this poor country? Empire collapses under the weight of corruption," he said.

It was a dismal assessment of the prospects for any kind of success. The most important question, though, was if he would ever go back. He was one of the at least three million Afghan refugees who had fled the country over the past few decades. He was a liberal intellectual, a member of the brain trust that our strategy rested on.

"It is hard for me to imagine going back," he said.

I thanked him and left the embassy. In Europe, so distant from the conflict, McChrystal's confident talk of strategy and success could at times seem almost plausible. But I'd stepped outside the bubble only for an afternoon and, in only one interview, the actual reality of the war had started to seep back in.

I returned to the hotel. Later that evening, I joined Khosh and Duncan at the Ritz bar. It was going to be my last night with them in Berlin. I was heading to Dubai tomorrow.

"Did you get your visa?" Khosh asked. "How much did you pay?"

"Thirty euros," I said.

"How many for the bribe?"

"No bribe," I said.

"That's impressive," Duncan said. "It's about $120 in the States."

"No bribe?" Khosh said, surprised. "That's good."

"They were actually all really, really cool," I said. "The embassy guy said, 'Do you have time to talk?' He was like, 'I want to get my voice out there.' He says the corruption they see now is worse than they've ever seen before. Do you think that's true?"

"Who said that?" Duncan asked.

"The Afghan embassy guy," I said.

"The Boss talks about hypercorruption," Duncan said. "Like there's dynamics between the international money flowing in is part of it. Also the drug money. It's so out of control. The people who take, who benefit from corruption, are not just subsidized. It's their main income. So it's not even bribe money that's getting recycled into the economy. It's capital flight."

"Like property in Dubai, right?"

"It's not just that," Khosh said. "When an Afghan thinks he is not going to be secure, he thinks about getting enough money so he can get out of the country."

Khosh paused. He was in his early thirties. He spoke perfect English with a British accent. He'd studied at the Royal Military Academy Sandhurst. He'd been in the Afghan army since 2002. He was married, and he lived in Kabul. He did not walk to work in his uniform—it was too risky. He'd fought in secret operations and battles and trained with Afghanistan's most elite commando unit. The images of the war stuck with him. Everyone has lost someone in Afghanistan, he told me, and there was no time to grieve.

One image in particular stayed with him. He told me about the dogs Special Forces soldiers took with them on raids. They'd put a video camera on the dog's head. The dog would run in the compound first. The fighters inside would freak out—they would be expecting a human, and as a general rule, Muslims abhor dogs. The commandos would get to see the video feed from the dog. During one raid, Khosh and the commandos threw a grenade into the house first. After the explosion, they sent the dog in to see who was inside. The dog came out, a bloody hand gripped in its teeth.

Khosh described his Kabul to me. He lived in a strange world straddling two cultures. He traveled with McChrystal, which meant he was seen on Afghan television. This was a great risk. He knew it was safer to be invisible, he said. Like the spies. Like the informants. Like those who could hide their loyalties, or whose loyalties were flexible. The spies and the informants and the collaborators all came to Kabul. He described where they met: outside a stadium, an old British fort, where the Taliban once performed their executions. Now it was spook central. You couldn't just go to a village to meet the source, he said. If a man is seen in the village jumping in a car and meeting with you, he's done. He's beheaded. Khosh was in Helmand in 2006. He went to a village and spoke to the doctor. The doctor told him nothing, he just talked. The next day he was beheaded, his head put in a bag and left in the bazaar in front of his shop. He was the only doctor in the village. Experience says you don't even go and speak to the guy, Khosh tells me. They'll just say he is a spy and kill him. You've got to call them to come to a major city where it doesn't look odd.

"Everyone tells me, don't worry about this fight," Khosh told me. "Don't worry about this country. Make your money and make your life. Go to India. Go to Tajikistan. Go buy a house. Because these people are not going to be here forever."

"You could do that, Khosh," Duncan said. "You could make a lot of money as a contractor. You could buy your own apartment in Dubai. Why not?"

"Because I know. I know the international community is going to be here for longer. I know we are going to get better. No matter what. Because I know."

Khosh believed. He had risked it all to be part of McChrystal's team. A future without the Americans wasn't a possibility he could entertain.

"It's hard to imagine [the Americans] pulling out and leaving this country with bloodshed," he said.

"Really?" I said. "Because we have a history of doing that."

"Well, exactly, but not just like this. I'll know when that time comes. I'll pull out. I wouldn't really even go . . . I know when . . . because I can go anywhere and I can work. I've got a university degree . . . I've got a Sandhurst degree . . ."

"And you've got friends," Duncan said.

"I've got friends, exactly," Khosh said. "I can go to any country in the West. I'll just say, 'Hey, suicide bombers are trying to come into your country. I'll serve your fucking country.'"

Even Khosh, one of the most dedicated to NATO's cause, had his own exit strategy. He'd have to deal with some racism, sure, he knew, but it would be worth it.

"It's funny. When I was going to the UK once and I got stopped at customs, 'You got a visa?' the customs guy asked. We were coming in for the anniversary [party] with C.'s [the British Special Forces commando] friends. They stopped us. 'Where are you people going?' 'Well, we came over to see our friends. We are coming to visit the Ministry of Defence.' 'What exactly do you do?' 'Well, we can't tell you exactly what we do. I can't tell you what I do. I'm not going to tell you where I am going. I have a Ministry of Defence letter from this country telling me I'm invited. Let me in.' The guy who was asking the questions wasn't even fucking British. He was some Pakistani or something. I shit you not. He fucking came in on an ice container on a cruise ship."

Khosh and the embassy official were the two Afghans I'd spoken to on this trip so far, two people whose country the war was actually being fought in. The embassy official would never return, and Khosh wondered if he'd be there for longer than the next five years.

Friday, I was ready to leave. I'd meet up with them in Kabul next week. I'd spend a few days in Dubai, waiting for Duncan's call. I went upstairs to the operations center to say my good-byes.

I saw McChrystal. I thanked him for allowing me to spend time with his team.

"I'd join up myself," I joked. "But there's no way I could pass the security clearance."

"Hey, I'm here," Jake replied.

McChrystal laughed.

I checked out and got on a train to Frankfurt.

PART II

INTERLUDE: DUBAI

"There is danger here! A dry brown vibrating hum or frequency in the air, like insect wings rubbing together. . . . There is a nightmare feeling in Interzone with its glut of nylon shirts, cameras, watches, sex, and opiates sold across the counter. Something profoundly menacing in the completely laissez-faire . . . The whole Zone is a trap, and someday it will close . . ."—William S. Burroughs, *Interzone*

I arrived Saturday morning at the Dubai International Airport, DXB, a giant duty-free shopping mall disguised as three airplane terminals. DXB was the entry point to the city that had become a central hub for the American war effort in both Iraq and Afghanistan. American government officials, Afghan government officials, Iraqi government officials, spies, aid workers, mercenaries, and journalists usually passed through Dubai on the way to the war. Mixed in were Russian mobsters, radical Islamists, Saudi sheikhs, Israeli hit squads, and wealthy businessmen from across the globe looking for a tax shelter, a blow job, or a place to launder money. Situated on the Persian Gulf, it had high-quality beaches with the year-round water temperature of a warm bath. Dubai was the

GPS point where the hypocritical and corrupt West met the corrupt and hypocritical East, ensuring that hypocrisy and cash were the only two reliable lubricants in the clash of civilizations.

The customs check were manned by young twentysomething Emiratis in white robes and red sashes stamping passports, lazily, disinterested, all slightly overweight and lethargic. Once I passed through customs, there was a good chance I wouldn't come in contact with another Emirati for the next three days. The entire service economy of the city was based on low-skilled workers who'd been shipped in from Pakistan, India, Thailand, and the Philippines, among other places in Central Asia. The Emiratis, it seemed, were always out of sight, hiding out in air-conditioned towers, leaving the dirty work to others.

A chubby man-child in a white robe stamped my passport. He didn't ask any questions. I got on an escalator heading down, passing underneath a big banner advertisement displayed in bright blue colors: COME SWIM WITH THE DOLPHINS AT ATLANTIS: THE PALM.

It was seven A.M., and the humid eighty-five-degree weather hovered between the floor of the parking garage and the arrivals gate. Men in robes and women in tight T-shirts and jangling gold earrings pushed luggage carts and lit cigarettes. There were two rows of taxis, one line of black sedans, and another line of pink cars with all women drivers, a special program to encourage women in business. I headed off to my hotel in the city. I'd booked two nights at the a place called the Royal Meridien, and one night at the Atlantis: The Palm.

As I left the airport in the cab, Dubai revealed itself as a maze of futuristic skylines that came in endless layers. The tallest building in the world, the Burj Khalifa; the indoor ski slope at the Snowdome; the seven-star hotel, the Burj Al Arab. Tunneling down the highway, I passed skyscraper after skyscraper, interspersed with massive cranes for construction. The city once boasted of having thirty thousand cranes, the most of any city in the world. At the height of the boom the Emirates had a gross domestic product of some $261 billion, incredible for a country of 1.5

million people. The boom had exploded, the bubble burst. Now Dubai alone was facing a debt crisis of $88 billion. The skyscrapers were empty, and the cranes no longer in use. Dubai was collapsing and the corruption that brought it to life had come to the surface. There was a smell to it, like a marina at low tide littered with luxury yachts run aground.

Atlantis: The Palm would become the focal point of my weekend, and the most fitting spot for a pilgrimage. Few other pieces of architectural excess had come to represent the city of Dubai like the Palm. It was built on a man-made island in the shape of a palm tree, visible from space, constructed at the height of the economic boom. It cost $1.5 billion to build, with another $20 million spent for a party celebrating its grand opening in 2008.

Out on the Palm Island, Afghan government officials, using embezzled funds, had purchased luxury condos for their weekend- and month-long getaways. As I crossed over the bridge, the island looked deserted. It was as if someone had given the design team a library full of J. G. Ballard novels for inspiration, and then told them to make it a bit more family friendly. The sand-colored condos, like the high-rises on the mainland, looked abandoned, only the occasional beach towel hanging off a balcony.

This was the role model we'd been pushing on the world. If only Baghdad and Kabul and Kandahar could be like Dubai! If they could all be tax havens and resort towns and business friendly. How beautiful it would be, to remake the entire "arc of instability," as American war planners called the area stretching from the Middle East to Central Asia, into an archipelago of city-states like Dubai, which boasted the largest shopping mall in the world, the Mall of the Emirates, with boutiques for terrorists and tyrants and businessmen alike. What a model it was! Just ask the Uzbek who had brought up my luggage and the Paki who drove me to the Palm. The world was flat, the edges of the empire jagged and bloody, but we could smooth it all over, eventually.

The Palm appeared in stark contrast to the emptiness of the rest of the island. It was bustling. I entered underneath the grossly oversize archway, like entering a monarch's palace. It looked like there were five or six different kinds of conventions going on, above-the-board trade organizations as well as cash-and-carry industries. There were families, too, from Europe and the neighboring Middle Eastern states. I was welcomed exuberantly at the front desk—I'd called ahead, and though I had rarely done so in the past, gotten the media rate. I was handed a map to the facility—a water fun park, the dolphin pool, seven restaurants (including Nobu), and a massive aquarium in the lobby. I got upgraded to a corner suite on the seventeenth floor. There was a balcony, about a twelve-hundred-square-foot living room, and a four-hundred-square-foot bathroom. It was the largest hotel room I'd ever stayed in, with a decadent bathroom including a hot tub, a chaise lounge in the room, and a separate room with only sinks.

In such luxury, I spent the three days doing what I almost never do—I could count the number of drinks I've had in the past ten years on one hand. I comforted myself knowing that I wasn't interviewing anyone, nor was anyone writing a profile of me. With the war now seventy-two hours away, I decided to get drunk.

The war correspondent: romantic, addicted, deranged. He first appeared in the Crimean War in 1854. In his epitaph at St. Paul's Cathedral in London, William Howard Russell was named the "first and greatest" of the bunch. Russell, who was detested by the generals, accused of being unpatriotic and of aiding the enemy, was once booted out of the head-quarters to pitch a tent among the soldiers during a cholera epidemic. Russell called himself the "miserable parent of a luckless tribe." In the Civil War, American journalists found out that conflict makes good copy: Circulation boomed, newspapers in New York sent over a hundred correspondents to cover it, and *The New York Herald* shelled out $1 million to be there. "Exaggeration, outright lies, puffery, slander," wrote one historian on the quality of Civil War coverage. General William T. Sherman complained of reporters "picking up dropped expressions, inciting jeal-

ousy and discontent, and doing infinite mischief." Sherman said he'd prefer to pay journalists half his salary to *not* write about him.

World War I dampened the thrill for the journalists: "The most colos-
sal, murderous, mismanaged butchery that has ever taken place on earth.
Any writer who said otherwise lied. So writers either wrote propaganda,
shut up, or fought," wrote Ernest Hemingway. The correspondent, too,
would soon become a character in the war story. He was the rogue, the
adventurer, the suspected womanizer, the kind of fellow who didn't get
out of bed until noon. Evelyn Waugh sent the luckless tribe up in his
novel *Scoop*: "Why, once Jakes went out to cover a revolution in one of
the Balkan capitals. He overslept in his carriage, woke up in the wrong
station, didn't know any different, got out, went straight to a hotel, and
cabled off a thousand words about barricades in the streets, flaming
churches, machine guns answering the rattle of his typewriter as he wrote,
a dead child, like a broken doll, spread-eagled in the deserted railway, you
know? Well, they were surprised at his office, getting a story from the
wrong country, but they trusted Jakes and splashed it on six international
newspapers. That day every special in Europe got orders to rush to the
new revolution. They arrived in shoals. Everything seemed quiet enough,
but it was as much as their jobs were worth to say so, with Jakes filing a
thousand words of blood and thunder a day. So they chimed in, too.
Government stocks dropped, financial panic, a state of emergency declared, army mobilized, famine, mutiny, and in less than two weeks there
was an honest to God revolution under way, just as Jakes had said. That's
the power of the press for you. They gave Jakes the Nobel Peace Prize for
his harrowing description of the carnage, but that was color stuff."

By World War II, legendary correspondent Ernie Pyle made the cover
of *Time* magazine for his reporting on American soldiers. "Fuck my shit,"
he said privately, using a dropped expression picked up from GIs. "Fuck
my shit. That's what war adds up to." Pyle was killed by a Japanese sniper
in 1944. The news of his death reached war photographer Robert Capa
in a cramped Army press headquarters in Leipzig, Germany, where he

slept in the middle of the night. "Ernie got it," he heard, as the whisper of the news passed through the room. "We all got up and drank ourselves stupid," Capa remembered.

The war, though, had given a purpose to Capa's life. "There's absolutely no reason for me to get up in the morning anymore," Capa wrote about the summer of 1942, living alone in a New York apartment. Overdue bills, a summons from the Justice Department, a nickel to his name. Another envelope pushed through the door: Ah, an assignment! Fifteen hundred bucks from *Collier's* magazine to go to England to cover the war. The war got him out of bed. He has an affair with a woman in England the week before D-day. He couldn't commit to her. He was always grieving for the dead woman he once loved—she got crushed by a tank covering the Spanish Civil War with him in 1937. She was twenty-six years old. Capa landed with the first wave of Allied forces on Normandy—he spent ninety minutes ashore, taking one hundred six photos. Only eight survived, an error by a photo assistant in London while the photos were developed. The pictures were blurry, a fact he captured in the title of his autobiography, *Slightly Out of Focus*. He was the first celebrity war photographer and he embodied the romance of the profession—he dated Hollywood stars and hung out in Parisian cafés with other artists and writers. "I would say the war correspondent gets more drinks, more girls, better pay, and greater freedom to choose his spot, and being allowed to be a coward and not be executed is his torture. The war correspondent has his stake—his life—in his own hands, and he can put it on this horse or that, or he can put it back in his pocket at the very last minute. I am a gambler."

Capa kept gambling. In 1954, he was asked to go to Indochina. He didn't really want to go, but he went. He was on a patrol with French soldiers. He walked ahead of them down the road to get the picture. He stepped on a landmine. He was forty years old. "Is this the first American correspondent killed in Indochina?" asked the Vietnamese doctor who pronounced him dead. "It is a harsh way for American to learn."

In the Vietnam War, the correspondents openly questioned the government—as critics of not just policy, but of war itself. Explicit accounts and photos seemed to jeopardize the entire war-making enterprise. Careers were made: Halberstam, Arnett, Sheehan, Herr, Rather, Apple, Hersh, and the list goes on. My Lai, for the first time, was an account of an American atrocity as news. There was an honor roll of dead correspondents: Larry Burrows and three others lost in a helicopter crash over Laos. A twenty-three-year-old *Newsweek* photographer killed in Khe Sanh. Sean Flynn and a friend disappeared in Cambodia. Eighty-three journalists total. The war ended, leaving its mark on journalism. The skeptical coverage was supposed to be the model for the next generation. War had been exposed as the Giant Lying Machine, in Halberstam's words. It was all, it seemed, a scam.

In the nineties, the conflicts were bloody and didn't usually involve American boys. A new phrase was popularized in the lexicon of journalism: the war junkie. It was rare to find a reporter to admit to being one, at least in public. There was more honor in self-identifying as an alcoholic. It was not appropriate to speak of the perverse fun of war. It must be buried under other motives. The war correspondent had to wrap himself in the language of human rights. He must *bear witness*, performing some kind of pseudo-religious rite. He was forced, in public, to talk about war as damning, ignoble, awful, tragic. Yet he kept going back for more. The irony had slowly crept in. A British journalist's account of his time in the Balkans twins his heroin addiction with his compulsion to cover the conflict. He kicked the heroin. The book became an instant classic. I saw him in Baghdad a few years later. Pulitzer Prize–winning journalist Chris Hedges summed it all up: "The rush of battle is one of the most potent and lethal addictions, for war is a drug, one I have ingested many times."

At twenty-two, I landed an internship at *Newsweek* magazine. Three years later, the magazine sent me to Baghdad, a war started with the full support of many in the press. I'd learned from all the literature that I had read that war always ended in violence, pain, self-destruction, madness, and tragedy. I confirmed this well-proven thesis for myself.

Here's what else I learned: The correspondent's identity becomes inseparable from war. His essence, his habits, his worldview, prestige, personal life. A former colleague at *Newsweek* explained: "They," he told me, "are invested in being war correspondents. They are invested in the myth of it. They wake up every day and they buff their armor. They make it nice and shiny." Advice got passed down to me, one war correspondent to another: If you're young and willing to die, there are lots of career opportunities. Never follow photographers. Photographers will get you killed. There are not old war photographers; there are dead war photographers. If you ain't being shot at, it ain't reporting. Women don't really understand it. You have an excuse for failed marriages and failed relationships. A bureau chief for a major American newspaper sat in his office in Baghdad, watching Italian porn beamed in on the satellite television, listening to the lulls between booming car bombs. My wife just doesn't understand what I'm going through, the veteran war correspondent told the twentysomething girl while putting his hand on her leg. In another memoir, a reporter used the acknowledgment section to blame the war for his unfaithfulness. He lost the woman he loved, dick caught in the vice of robust American interventionism in the Middle East. A friend of mine wrote a draft of a novel mocking the war junkies. In real life, he got kidnapped once by the Taliban for three months. The FBI agent who helped secured his release told him, "You know this means you're going to get a lot of pussy." The opening line of the novel that will never be published: *Baghdad. Bullet. Brains. Splatter.* Full stop. *War is beautiful.* His wife divorced him, too. He was doing eight balls at the pub. Don't you know what he's been through? the lawyer asked her during the divorce—he was in Fallujah. Hah, she laughed. Fuck Fallujah, and fuck you. More advice: Your editors pretend to care about your well-being, but they actually don't. Don't get kidnapped. Don't fuck up. Don't believe the lies. You're not one of them. There was a simple truth, my colleague explained: War corrodes and kills everything it touches. It destroys what's inside you. War makes you sad.

In Dubai, in room 1725 of the Palm, I closed my eyes but I didn't sleep. If I did, I wouldn't think of what happened last time. I was now less than twelve hours away from returning.

In October of 2008, I'm in Afghanistan for the first time. The sun is out and the soldiers at a small outpost near the Pakistani border are preparing their trucks for a two-day mission. The outpost looks like a ski lodge. Mountains surround it. They're fueling up vehicles and loading supplies onto their trucks—citrus-flavored Rip It energy drinks, PowerBars, MREs, crates of water bottles. I'm making phone calls on my T-Mobile, pacing in the gravel yard. I hang up. There is a huge blast right outside the guard tower, about seventy-five feet away. A funnel of smoke shoots to the sky.

The private in the guard tower screams over the radio: "Oh, God, we've been hit by a suicide bomber!" and everyone starts to move, throwing their body armor and helmets on and sprinting toward the tower. There is gunfire from an AK-47, though it's impossible to see who it's directed at.

The Afghan guards come stumbling through the gate, carrying a teenager who looks like he's dying. Blood runs down the face of an older Afghan police officer. Doc Allen, the unit's medic, tells them to put the two men down and he starts working on them, taking off their clothes, trying to find where all the blood is coming from. The kid has about forty or fifty small holes in him, made by the ball bearings that exploded out of the suicide vest. Doc Allen takes off the kid's pants to make sure he hasn't been hit in the groin, and the kid's lying there naked and bleeding on a slab of concrete outside the motor pool, a white bandage pressed over his penis. One of his friends is kneeling by him and holding his hand.

Outside the gate, Sergeant Joseph Biggs is making sure no one else is hit. Biggs is a twenty-four-year-old from Florida. He has over a dozen tattoos, including one on his left arm that says *WAR* and one on his right that says *KILL*, and another on his bicep that spells out the Arabic word for *INFIDEL*. Biggs has been blown up twice before, two Purple Hearts. He has silver hair and his head sometimes starts bleeding randomly. He dates a waitress from Hooters. In Afghanistan, he's sleeping with a female helicopter pilot, referred to by her made-up radio call sign Sexy-Six. He points to a live grenade on the ground, near one of the severed legs of the bomber. "He was about to throw that," he says.

For forty-five minutes, Doc Allen keeps the kid alive. A Blackhawk helicopter comes in, stirring up a dust storm, and the two men are loaded on. Doc Allen saves their lives. Doc Allen mutters that he's touched way too much Haji cock in his lifetime. His best friend was killed in Fallujah, his fiancée was later hit by a car. He thinks reporters are bad luck.

The unit meets in the tactical operations center, where Captain Terry Hilt is trying to piece together what happened. Hilt says that the suicide bomber approached through the valley between the two hills, a group of five or six boys running up and surrounding him as he got close. The children are eight or nine years old and are regulars at the base. They come over most days after school and the Americans give them chores to do, like filling sandbags or gathering up golf balls that have been hit into the valley. Most of the guys here like having them around.

The base's security cameras capture the attack. On the footage, we see the bomber get close to the gate (the kids, at this point, have run away, taking a seat on the Hesco barriers near the burn pit that have been set up as backstops out on the firing range). The bomber stops outside the barbed-wire fence, and the young guard stands up and calls to him to stand where he is and wait to be searched. On camera, the guard moves across the screen from right to left, and offscreen the suicide bomber pulls out a grenade. The guard stops and backs up, cocking his AK-47 and lifting it up to fire, and that's when the suicide vest explodes. Smoke fills the screen and the guard disappears, then reappears, staggering backward and screaming before falling to the ground.

"We're going to need to clean that whole yard," Hilt says. "Once everyone is inside, I'll talk to everyone real quick. We're going to try to HIIDE him [identify using a retinal or fingerprint scan], if we can find the head. Hey, Sergeant Biggs."

"Hooah," Biggs says.

"You said the head was out there?"

"No, just the scalp, just the hair."

"The flesh out there," another soldier adds, "it's everywhere."

"I guess we don't bring them kids back no more," Biggs says. "I always said with the kids around, there's going to be some shit like that. The kids are the ones who brought him over here, the little terrorist bastards."

The rest of the soldiers gather in the living room (or the morale welfare and recreation area, MWR, as it's called), where at night they watch DVDs and play the video game Rockstar.

"Everyone knows what just happened," Hilt says to the group. "A suicide bomber at the front gate blew himself up. A couple things are going to happen: The kids that typically hang around were walking with the guy prior to detonating. They won't be coming back here. The mission is going to be off. Hey, what typically happens after one bomber?"

"Another one," the soldiers answer in chorus.

"There are body parts all over the place, all through the district center," Hilt says. "Doc, we got plenty of rubber gloves? We're going to get some and do a police crawl across the DC. If you find fingers, any of that stuff, don't touch it. Call for one of the HIIDE guys. We might be able to get it to hit on the HIIDE system."

Hilt pauses and then adds, "Pictures. Do not be taking pictures of friggin' body parts. You'll get in a lot of trouble if you try to take pictures of body parts home. We got really lucky. Stay vigilant."

The soldiers pull on rubber gloves and go outside and begin walking slowly over the gravel, looking for pieces of the bomber. One soldier scrapes up a chunk of flesh with a shovel.

"Mmm, pancakes," he says. "Why the fuck couldn't they have used a car bomb? I don't mind cleaning up after car bombs. Everything's burned up."

They dump the body parts in a clear plastic garbage bag. The bomber's legs are still there near the gate, intact from the knee down. His legs are hairy. He was wearing white high-tops with a yellow stripe. The scalp is on the ground next to a Hesco barrier, a blood-wet mop of black hair.

Staff Sergeant Daniel Smith spots a blackened finger hanging off the concertina wire, and Sergeant Aaron Smelley, who's in charge of identification, takes it and places it on the portable HIIDE machine and presses hard to get a scan. After a few tries, he gets a reading, but the fingerprint doesn't match any known terrorist in the database. Smelley carries these memories with him, like last month, when they had to pile the bodies of seven dead insurgents into a truck. The insurgents had been killed by an attack helicopter. The troops take pictures. There's one of Smelley kneeling down over a body. The face of the body is pale. There's a bloodstain behind the head, making the grass red. Smelley takes the picture home with him—his friend texts me it years later. This is what fucked Smelley up, he writes in the text.

The Afghan police bury the leftover body parts a few hundred meters away from the base in a small cemetery. They place a pile of rocks on top to mark the grave, then lay the bomber's yellow-striped high-tops next to the rocks. This is shrugged off as some kind of Muslim tradition, but who knows. Later that afternoon, two Afghan men from one of the nearby villages come to look at the gravesite. As they start to walk away, one of them turns back, picks up the high-tops, and takes them for himself.

That night, wild dogs bark and fight over the bits of flesh that flew so far from the base they were missed during the cleanup. The soldiers are under orders to kill the dogs.

I called room service at the Palm at four thirty A.M. I ordered a pack of Marlboro Reds, whole-grain cereal, a grapefruit, eggs, a bread basket, and an iced coffee. I turned off most of the lights and I turned on the television. I found a music channel, some version of MTV, and I turned up the volume. Lady Gaga's song "Telephone" came on.

Two hours later, I stumbled through airport security back at DXB. I looked up at the departures monitor. The monitor listed names of unfamiliar capitals, places where slim guidebooks devoted a warning to something called "civil unrest." Mashhad, Dhaka, Shiraz, Erbil, Kabul, Baghdad, Bishkek, Kandahar, Karachi, Khartoum . . . I found the Kabul flight leaving at noon. The airport lounge was filled with mostly Americans and Europeans. The smaller smoking lounge, just outside the gate, overflowed, cigarette fumes escaping from the disgusting Plexiglas cell. The Americans lined up at the desk with Harley-Davidson jackets, North Face fleeces, military-issued rucksacks in digital green camouflage or tan, mustaches and tattoos and buzz cuts, a few with a U.S.-issue government ID hanging around their necks in canvas badge holders with inscriptions like OPERATION ENDURING FREEDOM and U.S. EMBASSY BAGHDAD. The Europeans wore suits and skinny jeans. The Afghans, too, had a few seats on the flight.

PART III

AFGHANISTAN

Safi Airways
شركت هوائی صافی
LOUNGE INVITATION
دعوة إلى الصالة

Safi Airways would like to welcome
هوائی صافی" بدعوة
Mr/Mrs/Ms Hastings / Michael MR.
دة/الأنسة
to enjoy the comforts of the
SAFI AIRWAYS / MARHABA LOUNGE next to
حة والاستجمام فی
prior to your flight gate #12-3
ركت هوائی صافی" /مرحبا
Flight No: 4G204 Date: 27APR10
Issued by: _____ _____ STD: _____
وعد المغادرة الجدد
موعد المغادرة الجدد
كم _____ التاريخ _____
رة من قبل:

30 | A SHORT HISTORY OF A HORRIBLE IDEA

1950–2010, ALGIERS, SAIGON, WASHINGTON, DC, BAGHDAD, AND KABUL

In the mid-1950s, a thirty-seven-year-old French officer named David Galula spends two years fighting rebels in Algeria. The rebels are trying to overthrow the colonial government that has ruled the country since the 1840s. The French will lose to the rebels in 1962.

Galula learns a few valuable lessons, though: that Arabs have a "notorious inability to organize," an observation which he apologizes for ("I sound no doubt terribly colonialist, but it's a fact"); that there isn't a good doctrine for him to follow to fight the insurgents; and, by the time the French get around to figuring out how to fight them, the war has already been lost. ("Too little too late," he'll write. "France was always several steps behind the demands of the situation on the military front.") He writes two books about his experience, one called *Pacification in Algeria, 1956–1958*, written in 1962, and another called *Counterinsurgency Warfare: Theory and Practice*, written in 1964.

If America hadn't entered Vietnam, Galula's work would have been left in the dustbin of history. Galula is part of the school of French military officers associated with *guerre revolutionnaire*. The school's ideas are

completely discredited in France. Losing three consecutive wars will do
that to the military class: getting steamrolled in World War II, then getting decimated at Dien Bien Phu in Vietnam, and, finally, losing Algeria
in a massively humiliating defeat, ending with the exodus of one million
Frenchmen from North Africa.

Rather than accepting defeat, Galula's contemporaries in the military
blame the French government for wimping out. A group of French officers form a secret terrorist organization, called the Organisation de
l'Armée Secrète, or OAS, which is linked to a number of fascist groups,
like Franco's Falangists in Spain. An OAS sympathizer tries to assassinate
French president Charles de Gaulle and fails. The fascists in OAS promote the same kinds of theories Galula likes to write about. They're also
implicated in the brutal torture regime France conducted in Algiers,
which makes their counterinsurgency ideas "tainted," according to one
writer.

Unable to find work in France, the French counterinsurgency
gang discovers a receptive audience in America. Under President John
Kennedy—concerned with figuring out ways to counter communist
revolutions—the United States foreign policy and military establishment
catches their first bout of counterinsurgency fever. From 1960 to 1963,
there's an "explosion of interest" in COIN, writes Ann Marlowe, an analyst who's written the most definitive account of Galula's life. In 1960,
Galula attends the Armed Forces Staff College in Norfolk, Virginia. In
1962, Vietnam War architect General William Westmoreland gets him
a research position at Harvard, where he becomes friends with Henry
Kissinger. Galula lasts a year in Cambridge before another American
counterinsurgency expert—General Edward Lansdale, a man darkly par-
odied in Graham Greene's novel *The Quiet American*—tries to help him
get a job at Mobil Oil company. Galula's career never quite takes off
in Washington, though there's evidence of his thinking in some of the
Vietnam War's biggest debacles and boondoggles, including the Civil
Operations and Revolutionary Development Support program (CORDS;

his book *Pacification in Algeria* will be cited in a previously classified USAID study laying out the principles for the program) and the controversial Phoenix Program, which assassinates more than twenty thousand suspected Vietcong sympathizers. (One of the American minds behind the Phoenix operation, Nelson Brickham, would carry Galula's other book around Vietnam, pushing it on his friends.) Galula returns to Paris in 1964.

Over the next eight years, the United States military adopts a variety of counterinsurgency tactics in Vietnam, such as physically separating the local population from the insurgency in the strategic hamlet program, which required the forcible removal of peasants from their villages. After leaving over three million Vietnamese dead and 58,195 American soldiers killed, the United States withdraws from Southeast Asia, failing to accomplish its goals of defeating the Vietcong and the North Vietnamese. After the war ends, counterinsurgency becomes anathema in American military circles. The backlash, according to historian Andrew Birtle, was due to the fact that COIN had been "overblown and oversold." In 1984, Secretary of Defense Caspar Weinberger pens what is seen as official repudiation of the U.S. strategy in Vietnam. The doctrine states the U.S. should only get involved in conflicts with limited engagements, clear exit strategies, and use overwhelming force. A decade later, Weinberger's policy is updated and enshrined by General Colin Powell—himself a Vietnam veteran—in what becomes known as the Powell Doctrine.

By the 1990s, counterinsurgency has been definitively replaced by a new fad of the moment, Revolution in Military Affairs, or RMA. RMA calls for using technology, not troops, to fight our future wars. Even General David Petraeus—the father of the modern counterinsurgency movement, which will find inspiration in Galula's theories—promotes technology over boots on the ground, writing a paper in 1997 called "Never Send a Man When You Can Send a Bullet." During the 2000 election, avoiding sending American troops to perform nation-building missions is conservative dogma, leading then-candidate George W. Bush to say that he wouldn't do "nation-building." His national security advisor Condoleezza Rice would say that "We don't need to have the 82nd Airborne escorting kids to kindergarten." When both the wars in Afghansitan and Iraq begin, they are premised on this idea of high technology, low risk—quick, deadly, and as few American troops on the ground as possible, as was the case in the first Gulf War.

It's the decision in 2003 to invade Iraq that eventually leads to the revival of counterinsurgency within the U.S. military. A number of the military officers and advisors associated with COIN—those COINdinistas—would later say they had serious reservations about the invasion. McChrystal tells me he didn't think Iraq was a "good idea" because the country didn't really pose a terrorist threat; Petraeus would famously ask during the invasion, "Tell me how this ends?" hinting at his own suspicions. Military officials in Baghdad claim in April 2003 that there will only be a few thousand Marines in Iraq by the end of the summer, and plan to start bringing the troops home. On the ground, an insurgency is quickly taking root, though few commanders will admit it—and it takes three more years before units begin to uniformly apply principles to counter it.

As in the early sixties, the Americans find another foreigner to help them craft their theories. This time, it's an Australian by the name of David Kilcullen. Kilcullen gets flattered in a series of media profiles and becomes a top advisor to General Petraeus. Like Galula, he'll write two books (*The Accidental Guerrilla* and another just called *Counterinsurgency*) making the case not just for counterinsurgency in Iraq, but COIN in Afghanistan, Pakistan, and number of other possible countries over the decades to come. (Kilcullen, too, views the decision to invade Iraq as "fucking stupid.") Kilcullen's most formative experience, he writes, is from a few months he spent in West Java in the 1996. Armed with time in Indonesia, he's embraced by a cadre of American officers who want counterinsurgency to become the dominant force shaping U.S. military policy. One of these officers, John Nagl, writes another book that fuels the COINdinista revolution, called *Learning to Eat Soup with a Knife*, about the British colonial war in Malaya.

What happens next is now part of the movement's legend. Horrified by the disaster in Iraq, a group of savvy young colonels and generals spends a year in Fort Leavenworth in 2006 under the tutelage of David Petraeus, writing a brand-new counterinsurgency field manual, *FM 3-24*. The book is downloaded 1.5 million times in a month. It references David Galula's experience in Algeria forty-two times. Galula's experience—a French captain who commanded only 120 men in a lightly populated rural area in a North African country sixty years ago—becomes the model for America's new war planners.

The manual performs a rather impressive sleight of hand: tying counterinsurgency to the War on Terror. The vast majority of the fighting in Iraq and Afghanistan is not against any combatant who poses a threat to the United States homeland. But to justify the tremendous outlay of resources and lives it requires to enact a counterinsurgency plan, the theorists claim that COIN, somehow, is an effective way to deal with transnational terrorist groups like Al-Qaeda. That this is patently false does not give the movement much pause. A RAND study, "How Terrorist Groups End," commissioned in 2008, explicitly points out that the best way to defeat terrorist networks is not through military force, but through law enforcement. The authors looked at 648 terrorist groups that were active from 1968 to 2006. In 40 percent of the cases, policing is "the most effective strategy," with local intelligence and police agencies able to able to penetrate and disrupt the terror groups, while 43 percent reached a political accommodation with the government. The study states: "Military force led to the end of terrorist groups in 7 percent of the cases," and that military force has not "significantly undermined [Al-Qaeda's] capabilities."

After completing the new manual, Petraeus gets picked to return to Iraq to put his revamped theory to the test. He asks for twenty thousand more troops and gets them, increasing the overall number of forces in

Iraq to a hundred fifty thousand, or a 15 percent increase. What follows is eighteen months of brutal fighting, at the cost of over one thousand American lives, and over ten thousand Iraqis killed. Behind the scenes, McChrystal, operating his own Phoenix-like Special Ops program, wipes out "thousands," according to McChrystal's deputy, Major General Bill Mayville, noting that "JSOC was a killing machine." Violence does, however, eventually decline, and Petraeus—and counterinsurgency—is able to take credit for creating the conditions for a face-saving withdrawal. COIN, it appears, is finally vindicated. The surge becomes a modern military myth, one eagerly embraced in Washington by those in the media and political world who'd been complicit in starting the Iraq War.

A closer inspection of the surge myth reveals a murkier set of factors. One of the major turning points in the war is in Anbar province, when local tribal leaders decide to turn against Al-Qaeda. This starts happening a year before Petraeus returns to command and has little to do with American military strategy. Analysis crediting the turnaround in Anbar usually ignores the reason why Al-Qaeda in Iraq (AQI) was able to establish a foothold there in the first place: American bungling for the first three years of the war. The tribal leaders welcomed Al-Qaeda to fight the American occupiers, but then realized they'd made a significant tactical error. Al-Qaeda in Iraq eclipsed the American occupation in brutality and stupidity—as one tribal leader would say, he would have "worked with the devil" to beat Al-Qaeda. The tribal leaders realized that they weren't just fighting the Americans—the new Shiite-led government in Baghdad was also keen to wipe them out. Faced with the brutality of AQI, coupled with a sectarian cleansing campaign originating from the highest levels of the new government in Baghdad, the tribal leaders, mainly Sunnis, make a desperate play: They tell the Americans that for the right price, they'd partner with them. American soldiers start to hand out bags of cash to insurgents—about $360 million spent in just one year. Overnight, former enemies who had killed Americans for three straight years became "freedom fighters." ("They are true Iraqi patriots," as one American general will describe his former enemies.) We find a way to buy off the enemies we'd created by invading—the strategy is akin to digging a hole in the desert, then filling the hole with cash and dead bodies and calling it a victory.

In Baghdad, the sectarian cleansing campaign had already taken its toll. Over 1.5 million refugees flee the country, and neighborhoods that were once ethnically mixed have been almost entirely cleansed. The COINdinistas strive to prove the surge strategy is an enlightened form of combat—"graduate level of war," as *FM 3-24* calls COIN—but the reality on the ground is dark and not very reminiscent of graduate school. Petraeus and his allies decide to team up with a Shiite Islamist government, picking the majority's side in a civil war. The Americans themselves round up tens of thousands of young Iraqi males. The Iraqi army and police, fully funded and trained by the U.S. military, conduct a campaign of torture and killing, assassinating suspected enemies and abusing Sunnis with electric shocks and power drills, with entire units being used as death squads. The Sunnis respond in kind. The American response to this campaign, as *The New York Times* would later note, was an "institutional shrug."

In the end, the surge proved extremely flawed: Its justification, to allow the Iraqis breathing room to set up a multiethnic government, doesn't work. The Shiite government, even after violence drops to only three hundred Iraqi civilians getting killed a month in 2009—as opposed to three thousand a month in 2006—continues to go after the Sunnis. The Shiites now have an even greater edge: The names and biometrics of Sunni insurgents who had temporarily allied themselves with the Americans are easily accessible to the new Iraqi government.

None of this really matters, though, in Washington, DC, a reality of which Petraeus is acutely aware. As he'd written earlier in his career, it's not what happens that matters; it's what policy makers think happens— the key is "perception," he writes And the perception in Washington is that the surge is a triumph. Though a political failure in Iraq, it proves a political success in Washington.

If the COINdinistas had stopped at Iraq, perhaps the charade would have held up over time. But they couldn't help themselves. With careers made by the prestige and money that can be achieved only through continuing their campaign elsewhere, the COINdinistas start talking about GCOIN, or global counterinsurgency, a worldwide fight to perform nation-building under the rubric of the War on Terror. Petraeus and the COINdinistas, with a new leading figure in the guise of General Stanley McChrystal, would soon push their theories on Afghanistan in full force. Iraq becomes the blueprint for success. The COINdinistas would, in other words, make the time-honored mistake of trying to fight the last war. "The entire COIN strategy is a fraud perpetuated on the American people," says Douglas Macgregor, a retired colonel and leading critic of counterinsurgency who attended West Point with McChrystal. "The idea that we are going to spend a trillion dollars to reshape the culture of the Islamic world is utter nonsense."

Counterinsurgency, its proponents in Afghanistan claim, is the only way to prevent "terrorist safe havens." Like "weapons of mass destruction" in Iraq, the "terrorist safe haven" phrase becomes the buzz-worthy and fear-inducing phrase to justify their plans. Though this doesn't make sense—a terrorist safe haven can be anywhere, as the September 11 attacks were planned in Hamburg, Florida, and San Diego, among other places—in order to sell COIN to the broader public and foreign policy community, terrorist safe havens become another necessary fiction. ("It's all very cynical, politically," says Marc Sageman, a former CIA case officer who has extensive experience in the region. "Afghanistan is not in our vital interest—there's nothing for us there.") Only counterinsurgency can win the War on Terror, the COIN supporters testify. "Losing wars is really expensive," John Nagl will say, adding, "And sons of bitches flying airplanes into buildings is really fucking expensive." Petraeus links the two ideas: "The intellectual construct for the War on Terror . . .

needs to be a counterinsurgency construct, not a narrow counterterrorism construct."

The escalation in Afghanistan is on an entirely different scale from the escalation in Iraq, however—it creates a new war. The surge in Afghanistan triples the number of forces and more than quadruples the cost of the conflict. Its chances of success are low, almost nonexistent. Another RAND study, "How Insurgencies End," examined eighty-nine insurgencies and pointed out that the success rate for counterinsurgencies where the government is an "anocracy"—that is, a democracy in name only, as we have in Afghanistan—has only a 15 percent success rate. "External sponsors," like Washington is to Kabul, "sometimes back winning causes but rarely emerge with a clear victory." The average counterinsurgency campaign lasts ten years—the mark this war hit in October 2011. We are now left with an entire strategic framework inspired by French failures in Algeria, an imperial war in the Philippines, a British colonial war in Malaysia, and the humiliation of Vietnam. Its proponents remain undeterred—they think it works. As General McChrystal would remind an audience in Europe, "I keep Galula by my bedside."

31 | BAD ROMANCE

APRIL 27, 2010, KABUL

The flight attendant informed me that they didn't serve alcohol. It was an Islamic restriction. I knew this, but asked again anyway.

"Not even beer? Wine?"

"No, sir, we don't have beer," the flight attendant whispered. "Or wine."

He was in his early thirties, dark skin and gelled hair. He looked very clean and perfumed. He spoke quietly as a courtesy, not wanting me to embarrass myself in front of the other passengers if they heard I'd asked for alcohol. I felt rough and brain-dead, the booze from the three days in Dubai seeping out through my blue blazer, teeth caked in nicotine, stomach queasy. I remembered why I swore off drinking ten years ago—a poison, I thought.

I sat in the front of the plane. It gave me extra space to pass out in semiprivacy. The ticket cost around $700 round-trip.

Safi Airways was one of the four commercial airlines that flew into Afghanistan. It was the only one worth flying. The other three—Pamir, Ariana, and Kam Air—had slightly frightening track records. Ariana—

the national government-funded airline for Afghanistan—had planes that looked like they were hijacked from Pan Am in the early eighties. Pamir always seemed on the verge of a catastrophic crash—in May, a Pamir flight slammed into a mountain, killing forty-four. Safi, on the other hand, leased its planes from Lufthansa and had a team of German mechanics to service them. Since Safi flew to Frankfurt and had upgraded to a new terminal in Dubai, it had to meet European safety standards, and to keep its space at the terminals, it meant the flights had to be consistently on time. American officials flying commercial into Kabul weren't allowed on either Pamir or Ariana. Not safe enough.

I looked back to the coach cabin, separated from business class by a flimsy red curtain. The passengers were packed in tight, six to a row, each overhead compartment jammed shut and the space underneath the seats crammed with enough carry-ons to cause a half-dozen blood clots. There was a different look to the passengers from when I last flew to Kabul, eighteen months earlier. At that time, the war still hadn't become entirely Americanized. The travelers had looked like they were going to a night-

Serial No: 01534

Safi Airways

دعوة إلى صالة "شركت هوائى صافى"
LOUNGE INVITATION

Safi Airways would like to welcome   تتشرف "شركت هوائى صافى" بدعوة
Mr/Mrs/Ms Hastings / michael MR.   السيد/السيدة/الأنسة
to enjoy the comforts of the   للتمتع بالراحة والاسترخاء فى
SAFI AIRWAYS / MARHABA LOUNGE next to   صالة "شركت هوائى صافى" / مرحبا
prior to your flight   gate #123   قبل رحلتكم
Flight No: 462704 Date: 27APR10 STD: موعد المغادرة المحدد التاريخ رقم الرحلة
Issued by: صادرة من قبل

club in London or a reggae festival in southern Vermont—European metrosexuals, most likely diplomats or aid workers, Canadian humanitarians in polo shirts, and American aid workers with a backpacker feel to them. The Westerners were a minority on that flight—it was mostly made up of Afghan businessmen in surprisingly nice suits.

The demographics had changed completely since McChrystal's escalation. Americans were the majority of passengers now, many with the hardened and sunburned look of private contractors, as if they'd just been pulled off a sales lot in Midland, Texas, before putting a new John Deere tractor on layaway—blue jeans, guts for men, muffin tops for women, baseball caps. The younger Americans on the flight now had one-week-old buzz cuts and no fashion sense—camouflage, combat boots, tan badge holders swinging around their necks. These men and women were the beneficiaries of the $206 billion in private contracts that the military had handed out to companies like Kellog, Brown, Root, known simply as KBR, a well-connected all-purpose government contractor, and Dyn-Corp. They wore what passed as a uniform for contractors in a war zone: martial regalia bought in PXs, Harley-Davidson and NFL logos, and names of American military facilities plastered on T-shirts and patches on backpacks (*BALAD, CAMP VICTORY, FOB SALERNO, ROCKET CITY*). It was a style easily transferable to any of the 813 American military installations that pockmarked the globe, whether in Baghdad, Kabul, Kuwait, Djibouti, or Manas.

Security contractors hired to protect all the new arrivals were another noticeable addition to the flight. PSDs, as they were called, for private security detail, better known simply as mercenaries. Almost all of them wore scruffy desert beards with steroid physiques. Over the past decade, mercenaries had become the easy villain in war zones. Criticizing the troops was off-limits; mercenaries were a more convenient target for the Afghan and the U.S. government to hammer. They got paid three or four times more than an average soldier and were regularly involved in debauchery and scandal—most recently, throwing wild parties in Kunduz where they had hired Afghan boys to dance for them. One private security contractor from Blackwater had punched a photographer friend of mine in the nose at the last party I'd gone to at the BBC bureau—he had it coming, but still. The Karzai government accused the mercenaries of corruption, drug running, and taking the best recruits away from the Afghan army and police—the security companies offered more cash to Afghans working for them as hired guns than the government did, the AK-47 equivalent of a brain drain. A number of the security companies had connections to the insurgency, with an estimated 10 percent of the hundreds of millions in cash paid to contractors that ended up being used as payoffs to insurgent groups, fueling the very insurgency the United States had vowed to stop. An audit by the special inspector general's office of the $70 billion given to Afghanistan in aid money from 2002 to 2009 found at least $18 billion unaccounted for.

Karzai had talked about banning the mercenaries entirely from the country, which terrified the Americans and Europeans who knew they couldn't operate there without them. It was too dangerous to move or build without heavily armed bodyguards. It was a fact they didn't like to publicly acknowledge. The mercenaries laid the underlying dynamics of the war bare—it was all about money and violence for them. That made policy makers uneasy as they tried to push the user-friendly, humanitarian aspect of the conflict.

The mercenaries deserved much of the criticism they got, but there was a definite hypocrisy to how they were officially looked down upon. They'd become an essential part of the war effort, necessary for both the government and nongovernmental organizations to do their jobs, as critical to American plans as any combat soldier. Yet policy makers and politicians and journalists did not hesitate to use them as scapegoats in a way they'd never do to soldiers or aid workers. They pretended the mercenary behavior, and all it represented, was an aberration and not the norm.

A planeload of contractors and mercenaries and other assorted sketchballs.

Afghanistan was losing its cool, I thought.

The war there was once much hipper than the war in Iraq. Iraq was brutal and negative and always too hot, a country we'd turned into an ugly nationwide construction site filled with righteously ignorant Americans and pissed-off Iraqis, a force field of resentment guarding every interaction. In Iraq, the United States had clumsily and savagely imposed its will on an unwilling host, and the signs were visible everywhere, from the seven security checkpoints needed to get into the Green Zone to the hateful stares in Baghdad neighborhoods, both rich and poor. Afghanistan had been the Good War—a boutique conflict with an internationalized flavor, a capital city where Westerners were welcome to smoke hash and drink booze freely. The locals, at least in relatively cosmopolitan Kabul, were a more colorful, wacky, and stylish bunch—young men listened to Jay-Z cassette tapes, watched an *American Idol*–like rip-off on Afghan television, and pieced together outfits of Levi's jeans, flowing orange and red scarves, and knockoff Ray-Bans. The fighters painted their assault rifles with flowers. The landscape was beautiful: scenic, snowcapped mountains and romantic red sands in the desert, travel magazine–quality images. As the war grew, so did the mechanisms of occupation required to sustain it. Megabases, mercenaries, KBR, and a degenerate class of expatriate war junkies who'd been gone from home for way too long. The cool had worn thin, replaced by a darker and grim absurdity that was impossible to ignore.

I took Safi's in-flight magazine out of the seat-back pocket. Two stories were noted on the cover: "Fighting Dogs: Warriors for the Masses," and "Art Dubai: It Smells like Blood." Inside there was another story headlined HEROIN HELL KABUL AND THE WAY OUT and a picture of an Afghan man who lost his arm in a NATO air strike.

This wasn't typical in-flight magazine material. There were no advertisements about frequent flier miles or profiles of B-list celebrities or recommendations for an up-and-coming chef's new restaurant in Chicago. Reading it, I had to stop myself from laughing—the magazine was clearly insane. Whoever published it must be insane, whoever's reading it must be insane, and whoever didn't take the next flight back to Dubai must be totally fucking nuts. It read like a guidebook about a war zone theme park, something the Mad Hatter would give Alice to speed-read on her journey down a Central Asian rabbit hole.

I turned to page fifteen. *Live Entertainment in Kabul,* read the slug at the top. The dogs "are usually pulled apart before they can inflict serious damage on each other." Any nation's airline with an in-flight magazine that extolled the virtues of dogfighting, smelling blood, and an exhibit on civilian casualties in Kunduz was clearly a nation that any rational human being would limit their involvement with. We'd done the exact opposite. According to the magazine, Safi Airways online ticket sales had grown 43 percent since September 2009, thanks to the escalation. Next month, Safi planned to open a new route to Doha, Qatar, three times a week.

I stood up to stretch my legs. The young flight attendant was preparing meals in the area behind the cockpit. We started talking.

He told me his name was Hekmatullah Rahimi, and that he was thirty years old. He worked for a company that ran a catering service for the flights. I asked him, as a young, motivated Afghan—the kind of Afghan whom America and its allies, in theory, needed to make the strategy successful—how he felt about McChrystal's plan and Obama's policy.

"It's not going to work," he said. "We learned from the election that if you are a good man, like Abdullah Abdullah, and you stick your head up, you will get it chopped off. There are thousands of young Abdullah Abdullahs out there, but they all want to leave."

Hekmatullah told me he was planning just that: to make enough money to move to Canada where he could join his family, who already lived there. He didn't know how long it would take. He didn't know if he'd get a visa. He said he knew the Americans would leave—and he wanted to leave before the bailout. It was the same feeling that Khosh had described and that the Afghan immigration official in Berlin had acted on. Getting out, joining the Afghan diaspora that now numbered close to

50,000 in Canada alone. There was no place in Afghanistan for him, he said. He was honest, he felt, at least more honest than the criminals running the government. His catering business was doing well, but he wasn't sure how long that would last. He lived in a strange world, a house in Kabul, shuttling back and forth to Dubai. Every day, he'd look at the Afghan government officials and businessmen who bought business-class tickets, stuffing their faces with pita bread and couscous, making their fortunes in Kabul, then taking their fortunes with them as soon as they could. Working on a commercial jet, the Dubai–Kabul line, the possibility of escape was always in front of his eyes, yet just out of sight.

I sat back down in my seat and looked out the window. We were flying over Iran, then across the border into western Afghanistan. Kipling and other noteworthy imperialists had fallen in love with this spectacular terrain. They'd fallen in love with the country and its aura—what it represented as a proving ground for glory and greatness for the empire, an arena for men, an exciting adventure among the savage little fuckers with turbans and flashy swords. It's barely worth pointing out that, with the hindsight of history, the civilized imperialists matched the uncivilized natives in savageness, pound for pound. The side with the technology would continue to convince themselves of the nobility and moral superiority of their efforts—if it wasn't love, it bordered on regularly scheduled enchantment. During the eighties, Americans romanticized the Islamic extremists as freedom fighters: pure, Allah-fearing people fighting the scourge of Godless communism. We gave the Islamic radicals weapons to kill Soviet boys, and cheered when they did so. Now a new generation of closeted Orientalists had popped up since the war began in 2001, penning memoirs about the beauty of the place, the generosity of the people, the intoxicating flavor of the food, the harmonious bleating of goats, and the untapped potential hidden beneath the rubble. *Three Cups of Tea*, *The Bookseller of Kabul*, *Kabul Beauty School*, *The Punishment of Virtue*. A kind of politically correct imperialism. Explaining why, for the sake of the Afghan people, brute force from the Americans was required—just not so brutally, if possible, please. All determined that Afghanistan, too, could one day be another outpost of progress. All describing how they were seduced and fell in love with the nation's simpleminded otherness. I wasn't there—I'd much sooner fall in love with a landfill in East Lansing than a minaret in Kandahar. For me, Afghanistan wasn't the stuff of romance, but a country of nightmarish fantasy.

Maybe I just had a bad attitude. My experience with the country had been one, so far, of extreme violence. On my last trip, within a period of a month, I'd witnessed a suicide bombing and a rocket attack followed by a forty-five-minute gunfight along the Pakistani border. A few days later, two more suicide bombers entered the ministry of culture office next to my hotel in Kabul. The bombers killed five people. The hotel I was staying at, called the Serena, was designed as a luxury property, five stars. It was a distinctly post-Taliban landmark in the city, opened in 2005. It was a hangout for Afghan elites and Westerners—with the added irony that regular Afghan citizens weren't allowed inside the building for security reasons. It cost $356 a night and boasted three restaurants, none of which served alcohol. It was a frequent target of attack—most devastatingly in January 2008, when Taliban fighters linked to the Haqqani network ran into the hotel, detonated a suicide bomb, and killed seven. They shot one hotel worker in the health club; a Norwegian journalist was killed in the lobby. The vicious attack on the Serena was the reason that I'd actually chosen to stay there—I figured the hotel would have pretty tight security after having a few of their guests slaughtered. I was correct: The new layers of security were worth the $356 a night.

That autumn in 2008 was a violent time in Afghanistan, with some of the worst violence the war had seen up to that point. I'd gone there to do a story on the Forgotten War. Afghanistan had not been getting regular media attention for years, overshadowed by Iraq. The soldiers I spoke to would go on leave and tell their friends they were fighting in Afghanistan, and would be told: I didn't even know we were in Afghanistan anymore. Kabul at that time had the sense of a city under siege, with the Taliban operating a shadow government in districts surrounding it. After spending a month in the country, the contours of the impending disaster became fairly clear: With Obama's election and Iraq winding down, the war was about to take center stage in the foreign policy world, the grumblings on the ground for more troops would get louder, and the Forgotten War would soon be remembered with tragic consequences.

Within the surreal confines of the Safi Airways cabin, the question I'd left with the last time I was there returned to me. Why are we here?

Spending over a week with McChrystal and his team in Western Europe had caused me, briefly, to rethink my answers. The excitement and the feeling of being on the inside made me give them the benefit of the doubt. Sure, the war had become morally dubious, ridiculously expensive, and would likely fuel anti-American terrorism for years to come—but they were such cool guys, and they were nice to me . . . Why not just give them a chance, like a number of my colleagues always did? Part of me wished I could just take what they said and be done with it—there's hope, it's getting better, it makes perfect sense to be there, sort of. Their confidence and expertise was persuasive. If they believed in the mission, then why couldn't I?

Perhaps the problem was me, not the war. Maybe I had some kind of character flaw or mental defect that prevented me from going along with the military's line. The war is going to be difficult, hard, probably will fail, but McChrystal gets it because he reads books about Winston Churchill and Vietnam and has an iPod and is really good at killing people. Why couldn't I ignore the doubts even his staff had about the war? McChrystal himself had serious reservations, it seemed, telling me he thought the war was "questionable." Another senior advisor told me: "If Americans pulled back and started paying attention to this war, it would become even less popular." McChrytsal regularly said that even Afghans couldn't understand Afghanistan—what chance did we have, then?

The more time that I spent outside the bubble—and it had only been a matter of days now—and the closer I got to landing in Kabul, I couldn't shake my own skepticism. It returned, in full force. No matter how professional or competent or dynamic McChrystal and his team were, the task they had set out for themselves was so obviously doomed.

A loud noise pinged over the flight's intercom. The fasten-your-seatbelt light went on. The German pilot announced we would begin our descent.

The plane looped down over the Kabul International Airport, passing over the city surrounded by sunbaked and craggy mountains that looked reddish brown from above. A few thousand feet below us, American helicopters sliced across the sky, looking like expensive windup toys, the first signs of the war. The airport was divided into two halves, one side for the civilians, the other for the military. On the military side, large cargo planes rested idle, while American Blackhawks and Chinooks touched down alongside jets with United Nations markings. On the civilian side, antique-looking Russian helicopters and out-of-service commercial jets parked abandoned on the far side of the runway.

Our plane touched down. I was the third one off, stepping down onto the tarmac. In the news magazine world—when there was a newsmagazine world of *Time* and *Newsweek* and *U.S. News & World Report*—there used to be something called a tarmac opener, or "tarmacer," as I heard editors call it. It was the name given to the first scene of a story that opened with a dignitary or president getting off an airplane in whatever strange country the magazine was writing about that week. *President Dipshit Dumbshit stepped off the plane onto the tarmac at the Xanadu International Airport into ninety-degree heat, looked around at the handful of paid supporters there to meet him, and said, "We'll get the rebels this time . . ."*

A tarmac opener for my arrival went through my head: *The hungover correspondent held the handrail as he descended the steps of the plane, greeted only by baggage carriers in blue jumpsuits and a bus driver waiting to take the new arrivals on the three-minute drive, standing room only, to the terminal. It'd been eighteen months since he'd last set foot in Kabul, and in that time the situation in Afghanistan had gone from horrible to really horrible.*

After getting his passport stamped and visa declared valid, he waited by the luggage carousel. The correspondent reached for a cigarette, then noticed newly plastered No Smoking signs. The Americans have really fucked up this country, he thought. Last time I was here, at least I was allowed to smoke inside the airport.

I picked up my one checked bag. An Afghan man waited at the exit to check the baggage tickets, making sure no one stole the incoming luggage. I'd hired a security company to pick me up from the airport. The security company specialized in providing protection for media organizations. I'd worked with them off and on for five years. As a twenty-five-year-old, I'd gone to their media hostile environment course in Virginia, where I learned how to not get kidnapped and the best way to put on a tourniquet—wrap it really tight. On my last two trips to Iraq, I'd stayed at their compound in Baghdad. It worked out well, and I decided I'd stay in their Kabul media center this time. It was where CNN had its bureau—renting out an entire floor—and visiting journalists could reserve rooms. The company did airport pickups and drop-offs, included in the price for a room.

I switched on my T-Mobile and texted my contact at the security company.

Hi, this is Michael. Arrived.

Got it. Our guy is on the other side of security.

I placed my bag through an X-ray machine and walked out into the airport lobby. I'd made it inside the country. I looked around and spotted a young Afghan man wearing a knit tuque, cargo pants, and hiking boots. He looked like the guy. I made eye contact and he nodded. He introduced himself as Raheem. He grabbed my black wheeled luggage and we headed outside.

The security company relied on Afghans to operate within the airport.

Raheem was hooked in to the scene—every third person we passed on the sidewalk in front of the airport, he knew. I had a question I'd been wanting to ask. There were always stories about the airports, how money and drugs were regularly flown out of the country on a daily basis. Yet there were always four or five security checkpoints. I asked Raheem how they did it.

"I mean, how do you smuggle bags of cash or drugs or whatever out of here?"

He laughed, as if I'd asked one of the more obvious and apparent questions.

"Baksheesh," he said. "Bribes. You just give one of these guys cash, and they escort you around all the security."

I nodded. Made sense.

We passed a green guardhouse. On the other side was the parking lot. Rickety trolleys, wheels missing and banged up, littered the lot. Men selling Afghan currency from cigar boxes had small stands up to sell money to the new arrivals. I lit a cigarette.

"Mike?"

A British guard dressed in tan fatigues extended his hand. We shook.

"Thanks for picking me up," I said.

"Jimmy," he said.

We got into a beat-up white SUV. In the backseat there were two bottles of water, a medical kit, and a set of body armor. It was Kabul, not Baghdad, so there was no need to wear the armor, or even have armed guards. Still, out of habit, I sat in the backseat, slouching down.

Jimmy was talkative, and as we rolled out of the airport, he gave me the rundown on the latest security developments. In most countries, you ask about the weather; in Afghanistan, it was the latest kidnapping or roadside bomb. There were reports that a Canadian journalist had been snatched in Kabul. The city had been quiet the last week, though there were persistent reports that five car bombs had snuck into the city.

"Sunny with a chance of shrapnel," Jimmy said.

Jimmy was former Special Forces. He was now hustling a couple of contracts. Besides occasionally freelancing for the media company, he'd done high-profile personal security details for A-list Hollywood celebrities while they traveled in the Middle East. He had another contract to help the Americans train Afghan security forces at a base not far from Kabul.

I told Jimmy I'd been hanging out with McChrystal—that they'd been telling me about the progress the new strategy was making.

He turned around in his seat, looking at me, eyebrows raised.

"It's all pretty fucking hopeless," he said. "You need a thousand McChrystals. I don't have the heart to tell the Americans that. I don't want to hurt their morale."

The car wound through Kabul traffic. The government had set up the Ring of Steel, a circle of military checkpoints around the city, focused to prevent insurgents from penetrating deep into the capital. Raheem drove us through a maze of knee-deep potholes, dirt roads, and anything-goes traffic circles. Every few blocks, we passed groups of men with AK-47s, checking cars, smoking, waiting outside heavily fortified compounds or on the streets waving down vehicles.

Our car got stopped. An Afghan police officer asked to go through my bag. Raheem told him to go fuck himself. The cop persisted. I opened my bag. He tossed through my clothes, then waved us on.

"He's looking for alcohol," Raheem explained.

It was a new racket, which had been pioneered by ambitious guards at the airport. The main concern of the security forces manning the X-ray machines wasn't weapons or explosives—it was booze. The airport cops would take the alcohol, sell it to another contact who would then sell the booze back to foreigners on the city's black market. So foreigners who tried to smuggle in whiskey, if they were caught, could end up buying back their whiskey (or someone else's whiskey) days or weeks later. The cop was looking for a piece of the action. I didn't have any booze, and Raheem wasn't going to give him any bribes. The cop closed the car door and we drove on.

Jimmy explained there were fears among the expat community that Kabul would soon go dry. Karzai had launched one of his periodic crackdowns against Western vice. He'd ordered a raid on a popular restaurant, taking the waitresses into custody—four women from Kyrgyzstan. He had their vaginas examined by a medical professional to see if the women were prostitutes. He'd also issued an edict that alcohol would not be tolerated in Kabul any longer. There were two schools of thought as to why he did this: One was that it was a politically popular and easy way for him to burnish his fundamentalist credentials. Targeting intoxicated Westerners was a convenient and low-cost way to do so, sure to get local media attention. The other blamed a recent story in *Time* magazine about the city's famous nightlife. The story was one of those evergreen pieces of journalism that would pop up every six months or so—descriptions of the Kabul party scene, the Mexican and Indian restaurants, the afterhours bars. The Westerners who lived in Kabul hated those stories—it brought unwanted attention to their lifestyles, making it harder for them to get high and drunk without harassment.

We stopped in front of the media compound. Raheem hit the radio. A reinforced steel door protecting the driveway swung open, and we pulled inside. The compound was set up in an imposing house, four floors and a roof deck with a small courtyard out front. It was located in a wealthy neighborhood, surrounded by lavish mansions built with drug money, including one pink monstrosity for rent just down the street, a style known as "narcotecture." Most of the homes looked like beachfront palaces in Miami if designed by coke fiends. Dried palm leaves and barbed wire extended up from the courtyard wall to give more privacy. The add-ons also prevented anyone from tossing explosives into the courtyard or trying to overrun the place. Four or five Afghan security guards milled about, AK-47s swung over their shoulders. On the roof, makeshift plywood television studios for CNN and European networks peered out over the city, perfect for live shots with a backdrop of Kabul. Raheem grabbed my bag and put it in my room in the basement.

I sat down at the desk and opened my laptop. There was some paperwork to fill out: blood type, emergency contact back home, and a section on what questions I should be asked to confirm I was me in case I got kidnapped. Name of dog. Name of first elementary school. Name of favorite hip-hop star. I hooked up to the house's wireless network and checked my e-mail. A friend had forwarded me a link to a YouTube video that had something to do with Lady Gaga.

I clicked on the link.

An Army platoon stationed in western Afghanistan had produced a remake of Lady Gaga's "Telephone" video. The video had gone viral. It slowly uploaded on my computer. I sat back and watched.

A title flashed across the screen: TELEPHONE: THE AFGHANISTAN RE-MAKE. A slightly overweight white soldier with red hair stood next to another with blond hair, staring into each other's eyes. They were both dressed in olive T-shirts and camouflage Army pants, the usual lounge-wear on base. The music begins, the soldiers mimicking a lover's quarrel in a cramped plywood headquarters hut. They start acting out the lyrics. *Hello hello baby, you call and I don't hear a thing . . .* The blonde touches the red-haired soldier on the nose—he collapses. The Gaga dance beat starts—the soldiers begin a frenzy of movement, jumping jack–style dances moves, lip-synching the entire time. It cuts to just the red-haired soldier dancing alone. A dartboard hung on the plywood garage wall is to his left, an M-4 assault rifle leaning against the wall. The scene changes to a garage on base—Beyoncé, a guest singer on the track, breaks in. An African-American soldier lip-synchs to her rhyme. The rest of the squad dances in the background—the red-haired kid has taken his shirt off and wrapped himself up in duct tape. Another has on tight black briefs with a sign attached to his head that says STEAM. Two cardboard cutouts of telephones hang on the garage door. *I should have left my phone at home because this is a disaster . . .* The video goes on for three minutes and forty-six seconds. The credits roll, promising more videos to come—apologizing for the delay because of the frequency of missions.

The Washington Post would describe the video's "powerful poignancy."

During the Vietnam War, the number-one hit song in 1967 was Buffalo Springfield's "For What It's Worth," opening with the lyrics, *"There's something happening here."* It was an antiwar ballad that captured the erosion of public support for the war. Pop culture had turned against Vietnam. There'd been no equivalent song over the past decade. No hit song had ever addressed either the conflict in Afghanistan or Iraq. We lived in Imaginationland, as the *South Park* creators dubbed it (as they also created Team America, the name McChrystal and his team had jokingly appropriated to describe themselves). Our culture was a cocoon against unpleasant realities. The soldiers in the video had weighed in, lip-synching a song about a jealous boyfriend who couldn't reach his girlfriend in the club. The song had nothing to do with Afghanistan and nothing to do with war or peace. That was the point. The disconnect between Afghanistan and the United States was total.

I should have left my phone at home because this is a disaster.

I closed my e-mail and texted Duncan.

Hey dude, I'm in Kabul.

32 | PRESIDENT KARZAI HAS A COLD

FEBRUARY 2010, KABUL

General Stanley McChrystal is preparing to launch the largest operation he's ever commanded. The plan calls for fifteen thousand troops to descend on the town of Marja. Marja is a rural area in Helmand province in southern Afghanistan. Not much to see, more a collection of mud huts and houses. Marja doesn't seem very important—there are only fifty thousand residents, not exactly a population center. In fact, the previous summer, McChrystal looked down upon wasting troops in Helmand. A justification is, of course, offered. Marja must be controlled in order to eventually control Kandahar. Kandahar must be controlled to control Afghanistan. Afghanistan must be controlled to control Pakistan. Pakistan must be controlled to prevent Saudi Arabian terrorists from getting on a flight at John F. Kennedy International Airport in Jamaica, Queens.

Marja is crucial because it's a "proof of concept" for the larger operation to come this summer, McChrystal says. We must push out the insurgents with a "rising tide of security," then install a "government in a box." The White House and the media will be watching closely. Marja would remind Obama advisor David Axelrod of Vietnam, prompting him to caution: "We have to be careful not to believe our own bullshit."

McChrystal wants to give the Marja operation legitimacy—he wants to put an Afghan face on it. For this, he believes, he needs to get President Hamid Karzai's sign-off. McChrystal thinks that Karzai has not embraced his role as "commander in chief," he says. Over the past few months, the general's goal has been to get Karzai to accept more responsibility for his country by bringing him into the loop on military decisions and by personally informing him about civilian casualty incidents. Getting Karzai to step up, U.S. military officials think, is the only way for their strategy to succeed. As every counterinsurgency plan makes clear, a legitimate government is necessary to win. It's critical to have a legitimate leader atop that government.

If there is one thing that Karzai is not, it's a legitimate leader. To make him appear legitimate, McChrystal has dragged him around the country over the past year, bringing him to parts he rarely visits. Trying to get him out of the palace, where McChrystal's staff believes he wallows in a haze of paranoia and delusion. He is, as a State Department cable will describe him, a "lonely and alone man who suspects his inner circle is leading him in the wrong direction, but does not know who else to trust. The president pays significant attention to the mostly negative media coverage of his government—behavior that reinforces his suspicions that enemies are 'out to get him.'" Karzai is particularly frustrating to the Americans because he doesn't even bother acting like a leader, they think. Like the shit he's pulling right now.

It's Friday, there's a ninety-minute window to make the decision to launch Operation Mostarak in Marja. The stakes are as high as they've been. Over ten thousand Afghan and American troops are already out there in the field, motors running, fuel trucks and complex lines of logistics prepared. Reporters are embedded, ready to write about an operation that had been getting hyped for weeks. The operation was supposed to have gone off Thursday night. The sun comes up on Friday, and the operation still hasn't happened.

Afghan defense minister Rahim Wardak assures the Americans that Karzai's permission is coming—we'll get it, we'll get it, we'll get it.

McChrystal asks to get Karzai on the line.

A McChrystal staffer makes the call to the director of protocol at Karzai's palace. General McChrystal wants to speak with President Karzai, the staffer explains.

"He can't," answers the Karzai aide. "President Karzai is taking a nap. He has a cold."

You don't understand, the McChrystal staffer insists. It's about the operation in Marja. It's the largest operation that has been launched in years in Afghanistan. It's important to speak with Karzai now.

"No, that's not possible. He has a cold."

No one wants to wake Karzai up, says Charlie Flynn.

"They are like 'Inshallah,'" says Flynn, using the Arabic phrase for "God willing." Meaning it may or may not happen.

What is this cold? What is this cold? Is Karzai actually sick? Or is he high as a kite? One veteran Kabul journalist believes Karzai is a "two pipe a day man." U.S. officials who work with Karzai think he's a manic depressive and the dope may fuel his paranoia. How is it that when there's a massive military operation about to be launched in his country, the largest since the U.S. invasion, he's spending the day in bed?

McChrystal's team refers to Karzai as "the man with a funny hat." Karzai is known in the West for his stylish tribal outfits, specifically his collection of headgear. His most notable accessory is the karakul—a V-shaped hat made from the pelts of newborn sheep. His getups have earned him plaudits from American fashion designers—Tom Ford once called him the "chicest man on the planet." McChrystal's staff have a different view of his style. They come up with a nickname for his favorite cap: "the Gray Wolf's Vagina."

Karzai is a strange dude with a long history with the Americans. In the eighties, he was one of America's allies in aiding the mujahideen to fight against the Soviets. He's from a wealthy Pashtun family, the Popalzai tribe. He has deep roots in the United States as well: His half brother, Ahmed Wali Karzai, ran an Afghan restaurant in Chicago during the early nineties before returning to Kandahar to become a key player in the nationwide drug ring, according to U.S. officials. His other cousins and uncles have U.S. business interests as well; they own a restaurant in Baltimore called Helmand. Another brother is a biochemistry professor in New York. Karzai, though, never lived in the United States. He spends his time in Pakistan during the Taliban regime. After the attacks on September 11, the Americans turn to Karzai to liberate Kandahar. He's almost killed, and it's an officer in the CIA (who is currently the CIA's station chief in Kabul, a rough-and-tumble redneck nicknamed Spider) whom Karzai credits with saving his life. (It's Spider who will have the best relationship with Karzai during Obama's tenure, not Eikenberry or the generals.) Karzai is chosen at the Bonn conference in Germany in 2001 to become Afghan's interim president—he wins the first election in 2005, then the second in 2009, both with massive amounts of fraud.

During the Bush years—which Eikenberry says Karzai looks back on fondly as the "Golden Age"—Karzai develops a personal relationship with the American president. That changes when Obama takes over. Eikenberry and Holbrooke think that if Karzai can circumvent the regular diplomatic process and go directly to the president, then they won't be able to do their jobs. Obama agrees—and Karzai takes it as an insult. Relations further deteriorate after the fraudulent election, and Karzai starts to behave increasingly erratically, from an American perspective at least. He starts to make not so subtle threats. He appears with Iranian president (and current American enemy number one) Mahmoud Ahmadinejad in March. He takes cash by the bagful from the Iranians, too, delivered to his innermost circle of advisors. He makes a public threat to join the Taliban, a threat he'll make repeatedly over the year ahead. He wants to ban security companies from Afghanistan.

More important: He doesn't agree with McChrystal's counterinsurgency plan. He doesn't want more foreign troops in the country. Never has, and never will. He makes that point explicitly to Ambassador Eikenberry in September 2009. His half brother, Ahmed Wali Karzai, will take the critique even further: Not only is COIN a bad idea, but Afghans don't even care about democracy, Ahmed Wali Karzai says. Those two views, joined together, essentially undermine any rationale for much of what the Americans are planning to do—which is set up some kind of democracy through a comprehensive counterinsurgency strategy. U.S. officials will eventually acknowledge that Karzai doesn't want to do counterinsurgency and therefore makes a bad partner.

One would think this would give the United States pause. It doesn't.

McChrystal's strategy, of course, relies on a credible Afghan government and credible Afghan leadership. It relies on getting Karzai on board. He is clearly not on board. If he's not behaving the way we want him to behave, U.S. military officials tell me, we'll figure out a way to gently force him to behave in the way we want him to behave. We'll turn Karzai into a war president. Today that means getting Karzai to wake up.

On Friday, February 12, McChrystal sees a moment to make this happen. Let Karzai give the order to charge. But he's napping. This does not sit well with McChrystal.

McChrystal decides to go over to the palace to wake up Karzai himself. He convoys over, joined by Minister Wardak and other Afghan officials. He goes into the parlor of the president's residence. They wait for thirty minutes. Karzai finally appears.

"He looked like he'd been in bed all day," Charlie Flynn says.

McChrystal explains to Karzai: Mr. President, we need your permission to do this. This is your insurgency, he tells him, but I'm your general.

Karzai responds: This is the first time in eight years anyone has asked me for my permission to launch a military operation.

They meet for forty-five minutes.

McChrystal leaves the meeting excited, seeing it as a triumph, a "watershed moment," according to Charlie Flynn, that "history will look back on."

Karzai "goes back to bed," says Flynn. "But he's got to be kind of thinking in bed, I'm kind of responsible for this."

McChrystal is asked to check in with his own commander in chief. President Obama wants to talk to him before the Marja invasion. A video teleconference is arranged.

After the call with Obama, McChrystal isn't impressed—what he thought was going to be a man-to-man phone call ends up having dozens of other officials along to listen in. McChrystal finds the move somewhat cynical—something, he tells me, Obama's political advisors must have cooked up to make it seem like he's engaged in the war. Someone must have reminded him that "hey, this is the biggest military operation you've ever launched as president," as one of his staffers tells me. Casey reads his boss closely: "I think he still wished it was a little more candid," he tells me, wanting Obama to have spoken more directly about the importance of the mission.

The operation in Marja goes off. Twenty-five Americans are killed in the first three months. In May, McChrystal will describe it as "a bleeding ulcer." The White House will view it as a failure. The phrase "government in a box" is roundly mocked. Says Afghan expert Andrew Wilder from Tufts University, "We've been there nine years and the best they can come up with is 'government in a box'?" A joke goes around: Yes, Afghanistan does have a government in a box. That box is Kabul.

33 | AN E-MAIL EXCHANGE: COME WALK IN OUR BOOTS

FEBRUARY TO MARCH 2010, ZHARI AND KABUL

On February 27, 2010, at 6:27 P.M., twenty-five-year-old Staff Sergeant Israel Arroyo sends an e-mail to General Stanley McChrystal.

SUBJECT: SOLDIER'S CONCERN

Dear Sir,

. . . I am in TF 1-12, down in the zhari district and would like to ask you to come down and visit and if possible to go out on mission/patrol with us but without your PSD [private security detail]. I am writing because it was said you don't care about the troops and have made it harder to defend ourselves . . .

I also understand your restraint tactic. But if you look at the light infantry soldiers of today [we] have no place here. We have lost many soldiers in this area and don't want to lose any more. With the new R.O.E. [rules of engagement] it is telling the men that they should not shoot even if they are threatened with death. Sir, it may not be the way you intended it to be, but that is how all of the soldiers here took it. Knowing that you get things sugarcoated I am not one to do so. I

have the most respect for you, and do not mean to cause trouble
but I told my soldiers that there is more to this and just to go with
the flow.
SSG Arroyo

Four hours later, Staff Sergeant Israel Arroyo receives a response from General Stanley McChrystal.

SUBJECT: RE: SOLDIER'S CONCERN
SSG Arroyo,
I will come to your location and go out with you. Will work my
schedule to make it as soon as practical. I'm saddened by the
accusation that I don't care about soldiers as it is something I suspect
any soldier takes both personally and professionally—at least I do. But
I know perceptions depend upon your perspective at the time, and I
respect that every soldier's view is his own.
   We haven't changed the ROE—they still absolutely protect the
right and responsibility of every soldier to defend themselves—and
their comrades with whatever means is necessary.
   But I do ask all of us to also view the fight in its wider context. In
its widest sense, the reality of this effort is that the outcome will not be
decided by conventional military math where killing the enemy
accumulates until they are defeated. This fight will be won by the side
who convinces the Afghan people to support them. That sounds less
military than we might like—but it's the stark reality of this situation.
If we want to win, the path is thru winning the support of the
population—there's no other route.
V/R
Stan

Within forty-eight hours of the e-mail exchange, McChrystal descends on a small combat outpost called JFM. He goes on a four-kilometer patrol in the most dangerous area of the country. It is an unprecedented risk for a four-star general to take. He forgets his cap behind at the base. An officer at the nearby forward operating base wonders if he should give it back. The officer ends up keeping it as a memento.

34 | A BOY BORN IN 1987

On April 13, 2010, Corporal Michael Ingram Jr. logs onto his Facebook account. Like his friend SSG Arroyo, he's at combat outpost JFM in Zhari, near Kandahar. He writes this line on his wall:

"Come on fellas hold it together . . . Almost home."

A few weeks earlier, he calls home to speak with his father, Michael Ingram Sr. He calls him Pops. Pops calls him Mikie. He has to pay for the long distance call. It annoys him—why should soldiers have to pay for long distance calls home? It's what he ends up spending his combat pay on. He mostly communicates with his family on Facebook. He talks to his dad every few weeks or so. In the last couple of days he's called him three or four times. He feels the fighting is heating up.

Mikie tells his dad that he can't wait to get home. He has one month left. The tour started badly last summer. They lost two guys in an attack in August. Mikie carried one of the bodies, just a torso, onto the stretcher. Last month, he pulled a muscle working out in the gym. It's a serious enough injury that they want to send him off the front lines for treatment. He refuses—he doesn't want to leave his squad.

Mikie doesn't mention this tonight. He talks life. He's dating a girl, and it's getting serious. He wants to start a family. He wants to get married. He's ready to take life more seriously. He's going to Las Vegas and Graceland when he gets home. But he swears he's going to try to save his money, too. They talk for twenty minutes. He tells his father before hanging up, "It's getting pretty bad over here." His father says, "You'll be home soon." Mikie says, "I don't know."

Mikie posts another message on Facebook. "I love my family . . . lil bro . . . lil sis . . . can't wait until I'm out of the army."

On the evening of Saturday, April 17, Michael Ingram Sr., a self-employed painting contractor, and his wife, Julie, are hanging out with friends in Britton, Michigan. It's about an hour from their home in Newport. They've got the barbecue going and are having fun riding four-wheelers. It's been a nice afternoon.

Julie's phone rings at six thirty P.M. It's her son, Kyle, twenty-one years old. He's screaming.

"The guys in green are here for Pops, the guys in green are here for Pops!"

She doesn't believe it. No, you're wrong. Her son says they won't tell him anything. She tells her son to tell the men that they'll be home around nine thirty. She hangs up.

Julie looks down at her Motorola phone. It's new. She just got it that morning. She has no contacts saved in it. She has no numbers to text or call. She looks around the yard and sees her husband. She doesn't say anything. She thinks: He has three hours of happiness left. She can't tell him. She can't believe it. She doesn't say anything.

At around eight P.M., they leave their friends' place and drive back to their home on Pointe aux Peaux Road. It's a three-bedroom, two-bathroom ranch with a porch out back. They get back at nine fifteen. Julie puts the grandbaby to bed. Julie follows her husband into the backyard. They want to make a bonfire.

Fifteen minutes left.

Julie goes up on the porch. It's nine thirty.

Julie sees a turquoise Ford F-150 parked at the end of the street. Her son said they were driving that car. That was the color: turquoise. Her son isn't home—he didn't want to be there.

Two figures step out of the F-150. She sees them coming. Her husband hasn't noticed them yet.

"Hello, hello," a man calls out.

Julie and Michael walk out to the front of the house. The two figures walk onto the driveway.

The sensor light goes on. The light illuminates the driveway. Her husband sees one man and one woman wearing green.

"We're here to speak with Mr. Michael Ingram Senior," the man says.

Julie starts screaming. Michael Ingram Sr. tries to stay calm. The two officers try to keep them calm. The rest of the night: text messages to friends and family. Come over to the house. They don't sleep, and when they do sleep it's blackness—too tired for nightmares. It begins again in the morning when their eyes open.

On Monday, the front-page story of the local newspaper: NEWPORT MAN KILLED IN AFGHANISTAN. The headline makes it more real—it's in print, it's now fact. The newspaper runs seven or eight more stories about Michael Ingram Jr. He wanted to become a police officer, he never gave his stepmom any trouble, he joined the Army in 2007. His friends remember him.

Mikie likes music—Elvis, Buddy Holly, Sinatra. His favorite song is "Suspicious Minds." If you heard Elvis in the gym, you knew Mikie was working out.

He made the ultimate sacrifice and he would make the ultimate sacrifice again, his father says.

The town erects a billboard with his picture on it: HEAVEN NEEDED A HERO, it reads.

The obituary reads: "Sgt. Michael Keith Ingram, Jr. 'Pookie' born March 6, 1987–April 17, 2010. He died fighting for his country on April 17, 2010, in Afghanistan. Michael is survived by his mother, Patricia

Kitts (Ronald C. Kitts); father, Michael Ingram (Julie Ingram); brothers Jason R. Ingram and Kyle Ingram and sister, Chelsea A. Ingram; grand-mother, Annie Ingram of Newport, MI; numerous aunts, uncles, and cousins. He was preceded in death by his grandfather, James Ingram."

Michael Ingram Sr. is looking through the couch for some reason. He finds a memory card for a computer. He gives it to Julie. Julie pops it in—it's pictures and videos of Mikie in Afghanistan. The card must have fallen out of his pocket when he was home last. She watches and she can hear his voice again and that makes her cry.

His father opens the safe in the house and takes out Mikie's last letter. He wrote it before he deployed. He detailed what should happen when he dies. He wants lots of flowers at his funeral. He wants a nice tomb-stone. At home on leave for Christmas, Mikie opened the safe and revised it. He revised what should be written on his tombstone. He wants it to say *Limitless*. It's the saying he has up in his room at JFM. His stepmom doesn't really understand what it means, but she is going to put it on his headstone because that's what he wanted. The headstone costs $16,000 and the funeral costs $40,000. We don't care about the fucking money, says Julie, we want our boy back.

It takes seven days for his body to arrive in Dover, Delaware. The flight is held up because of an ash cloud from a volcanic explosion in Iceland.

From Dover, his casket is flown to Selfridge Air National Guard Base in Michigan. The casket is unloaded on April 24. It's a cold and rainy day. An honor guard of sixty Vietnam veterans on motorcycles and the Michi-gan State Police escort a white hearse down I-75 South, a left onto M-125, a right onto Santure Road, pulling up to Merkle Funeral Service. Visiting hours twelve to eight P.M.

He's buried on April 30, 2010. It's a beautiful day this time. His casket is placed in a black horse-drawn carriage. His sister sits next to the car-riage driver. The procession from the church to St. Joseph Cemetery goes off without a hitch. The train tracks and a street are shut down for the procession. His father and stepmom sit side by side as the casket is lowered into the ground. His father is holding an American flag, folded up into a triangle. His father keeps clutching it to his chest, moving it around in his hands, his fingers digging into the flag.

Back in Afghanistan, Sergeant Israel Arroyo logs into his e-mail account. He sends a message to McChrystal.

Dear Sir,

On 17 April 2010, I was asked to see if you would attend a memorial of a great soldier, CPL Michael Ingram. after he and I wrote to you last, he started to look up to you. So, I understand you busy. but if you can make it? It would mean alot to his family and I. I am not sure if you remember us but you when on a dismounted patrol with he and I, in the Zhari distric. It will be on or around 21 22 april. thank you for your time in reading this.

Michael Ingram

McChrystal agrees to visit again, as soon as he gets back from Europe.

35 | WHERE IS ISRAEL ARROYO?

APRIL 28, 2010, KABUL, KANDAHAR AIRFIELD, AND FORWARD OPERATING BASE WILSON

My Afghan security guard dropped me off about three blocks away from the entrance to the International Security Assistance Force headquarters. I walked down the street parallel to the compound's garden wall, then took a right on the main street to get to the gate. It was a different path from the one I'd taken on earlier visits. I could still see the effects of the suicide bombing that had hit the base a year and a half earlier. Chunks of concrete missing from the sidewalks with newer and bigger concrete blast walls providing shade for the street. The road in front of the gate had been closed to almost all nonmilitary traffic. Trash filled up cracked and mud-covered gutters—potato chip bags, soda cans, empty cigarette packs. The entrance was infused with the feeling of run-down wariness that often marks the site of bombings with the potential for a repeat performance—an intuition that it would be a waste to spend too much time beautifying a target.

Four Afghan army soldiers sat around a pillbox guard hut, leaning against a traffic gate. I showed my media identification, and they waved me up to a metal door. It was an unenviable job, and perhaps explained their laissez-faire attitude—if there was another bombing, these Afghans would boost the death toll by at least four. A Macedonian guard opened the metal door, didn't bother looking at my ID too closely, and waved me down a path with chain-link fences, tarps, and plywood. It was like a cattle lane to a slaughterhouse, ending in another guardhouse with a full body scanner. Another Macedonian stood behind a dirty plastic window and slipped a visitor badge under the screen. Macedonia was a member of the NATO coalition, sending seventy-nine troops to take turns guarding a door.

Duncan came out to meet me. He wore a suit and red tie, unperturbed by the change in scene. Kabul, Paris, Berlin—Duncan was Duncan, a smooth operator.

We walked through the body scanner. Duncan flashed his badge at a security camera, and we were buzzed through.

"I hope there's not too much radiation in these things," he joked. "I go through them a few times a day."

We walked onto the grounds of the ISAF HQ. Duncan did seem slightly more caffeinated, speed-walking ahead of me, a reflection of the higher operational tempo they kept in Afghanistan.

"You have to keep up," Duncan told me. "We move very, very fast."

We went into the Yellow House, the main building on the base where I had last interviewed General McKiernan in October 2008. A third Macedonian sat at a large wooden desk in the building's lobby. I had to trade in my first visitor badge for a second visitor badge to enter. There was a sign on the wall warning soldiers to drive safely—reckless driving, the sign warned, didn't win the love of the Afghan people.

The plan for the day: I would sit in on the morning briefing, and then I would travel with McChrystal to Kandahar. In Kandahar, we would split up—McChrystal and Flynn would visit a Special Forces detachment somewhere in the south while Duncan and I would meet up with Task

Force 1-12, the infantry unit that McChrystal had gone on patrol with in February. I'd read parts of the e-mails that kid named Staff Sergeant Israel Arroyo had sent. I wanted to interview him if I had the chance.

Duncan sat me down to wait in the operations center. The briefing would start at 0730. Whiteboards lined the wall, scribbled with notes about McChrystal's travel plans. Next to a whiteboard were a few pages printed out of Bruce Lee quotes.

McChrystal's team included a Bruce Lee quote on almost all the daily schedules they printed out. Some of the quotes up on the wall were crossed out—they'd been used already.

I scanned the quotes. There were fifteen listed, some marked as used, with a date next to them.

> *A goal is not always meant to be reached; it often serves as some-thing to aim at. Used 4/11*
>
> *A quick temper will make a fool of you soon enough.*
>
> *A wise man can learn more from a foolish question than a fool can learn from a wise answer.*
>
> *Always be yourself. Express yourself, have faith in yourself. Do not go out for a successful personality and duplicate it.*
>
> *I'm not in this world to live up to your expectations, and you're not in this world to live up to mine.*

The philosopher warrior. It was an image McChrystal's team culti-vated. His men liked to think there was something of Bruce Lee in McChrystal—lean, wise, and deadly.

I drank a cup of coffee.

Duncan popped back into the room to get me for the briefing.

I walked into the situational awareness room, or SAR. I wasn't allowed to record the briefing, but I could take notes on background, he ex-plained. I'd sit in on two briefings over the next week, and this is what I saw and heard.

The room was the cerebral cortex for the war. There were ten television monitors set up across the front of the room, a podium, and three rows of tables with workstations and phones. There was a third row of chairs against the wall. The screens broadcast live updates about the war, distilled down to color-coded data, all the violence broken down in up-to-the-hour statistical analysis. Casualties over the past twenty-four hours were on one screen: yellow for Coalition troops, blue for Afghan security forces, and red for civilians who were killed or injured. Another screen carried information about the latest security incidents: an IED in Kandahar, a political assassination in Jalalabad, serious reporting inaccuracies in ANA recordkeeping, Iran providing an unknown antiaircraft weapon to Helmand. Two more screens had on television news broadcasts, Al Jazeera and CNN. (McChrystal had banned Fox News from the TV screens because of its political slant.) About forty military officers crowded into the room, while across Afghanistan three thousand more officers and enlisted personnel in their own headquarters linked in to watch the briefing. I was the only journalist there.

The briefers went up to the podium, one after the other. A deputy head of the Special Forces command updated McChrystal on the latest operations. He talked about the "jackpots" from last night—the code word given for the killing or capturing of a high-profile target. They had a mission called Operation Euphoria in Spin Boldak. A briefer from the CIA stood up and gave his intelligence update—the latest intel said the Taliban were claiming "they want to shut down Highway One, and they're going to start attacking civilian convoys." He gave a little talk about how all the players in the region were jamming everyone's cell phone signals—the Taliban would shut the network down at night while the "Chinese are jamming illegally, and the Paks are jamming the Chinese." Other major commands across the country got their chance to brief through the video uplink, including a screen beaming back to the Pentagon a lone man sitting at a desk in the bowels of the building, where it was almost midnight.

An officer gave an update on a reconstruction project in Spin Boldak. Another talked about seventeen checkpoints in Wardak province that the Afghan army and police were taking over. Most of the room seemed to have tuned out at this point. McChrystal wanted to know where the exact coordinates for the checkpoints were.

"Let's ask that question now," McChrystal said.

"Uh, not sure what the question is," the officer replied.

"Pay attention, please," McChrystal reprimanded. The officer fumbled around over the video uplink. "Uh, okay, I can send up the grid coordinates."

They moved on to the Casualty Events Update. There had been seven in the last twenty-four hours. The chart broke down like this:

	A ISAF	A ANSF	A CIV
KIA	0	3	1
WIA	24	2	12

"There was a, uh, fifty cal through the windshield," one officer told McChrystal, talking about an incident that wounded an American soldier. McChrystal nodded, taking a sip of coffee from his Styrofoam cup.

Another slide noted the 310 percent increase in Coalition casualties. The briefer attributed the rise in violence to "COIN and the surge."

The officer reported on the latest numbers of IED (improvised explosive device) attacks. The IEDs were bombs, often made out of fertilizer, old munitions, and wood. In Iraq, the Pentagon had spent billions on figuring out how to stop them from detonating, using fourteen different advanced systems to interfere with the remote-controlled detonation device. In Afghanistan, the insurgents had figured out a way around the jammers: to go so low-tech that American technology wouldn't help. The most popular method was called a pressure plate, which resembled the trigger mechanism on an old-fashioned landmine. The bombs were getting even bigger, the average size being close to forty pounds. IEDs were responsible for more than 60 percent of American casualties, and the data predicted that by the end of 2010 approximately eighteen thousand IEDs would be set in Afghanistan, a "vast increase in IED activity," the briefer noted.

McChrystal nodded. "It's a sobering number, to be sure," he said. "This data shows we have a rising challenge here. We have to avoid and defeat IEDs. We need to be more agile, less sluggish."

The rest of the briefings included an update on regional affairs (Mumbai attack conviction: Message to Islamabad Not to Export Terrorism) and other key events (Reports of Assassination in Kunduz) and a discussion about a new award the military was considering handing out for "Courageous Restraint." It was an award to soldiers for not shooting at civilians who they mistakenly believed posed a threat. The idea was to incentivize the new rules of engagement McChrystal had issued, though the general wasn't quite sold on the idea.

"We ask courage of them every day," he said. Whether or not they should get an award for it was a "philosophical question," McChrystal said.

The briefing that morning concluded. Duncan came up beside me.

"We move very, very fast," he said again.

McChrystal and his entourage burst out the door of the headquarters, a convoy of black sport-utility vehicles, heavily armored Suburbans, idled. I jumped in one SUV—in it were a pair of nunchuks.

The nunchuks had been custom-made for McChrystal. On one handle, it said the general's name; on the other, there were four stars. It started as a joke, continuing the Bruce Lee theme: A few months earlier, McChrystal had been going through his checklist with an aide. You have my briefing book? Check. My backpack? Check. My glasses? Check. Nunchuks? McChrystal had said.

The joke stuck.

The convoy rolled across the street to a nearby helicopter landing field. We jumped out; the helicopters arrived; we jumped in the heli-

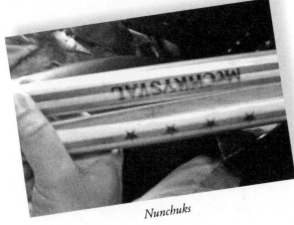

Nunchuks

copters; the helicopters swooped up, flying low over the city, back out to the military side of the Kabul Airport. We jumped out of the helicopters; two jets were waiting for us. Ocean 11 and Ocean 12. We ran across the tarmac and up into the private jet.

The jet had the look of the typical plane for an executive. It had dark blue leather seats and three coffee tables, with plastic cups embossed with the United States government seal. The main difference was the luggage: The seats were stacked with radio equipment, rucksacks, and body armor.

McChrystal walked on the plane and looked around. He bumped into his chief security officer and personal bodyguard, who everyone called Chief. Chief was responsible for getting the nunchuks and the nunchuks holder made.

"You're the same guys I went to the gym this morning with," McChrystal said.

"Yes, sir," Chief answered.

"Everywhere I go, I keep seeing the same people," he said.

McChrystal sat down in the front of the plane.

"It's him surrounding my world," Chief said.

"I must be cloning myself," McChrystal shot back.

Nunchuks holder

This was going to be my last sit-down interview with General McChrystal. Duncan called me up to the front of the plane. I took out my tape recorder and sat across from the general. We started talking as the plane took off. I set my coffee in the cup holder on the fake wood paneling, watching it spill as the jet shot upward.

McChrystal described the war in Afghanistan as "raising a child." It would be messy, and you only had so much control over the outcome. "You might want them to be a rock star, or a heavyweight wrestler or whatever, but at the end of the day, you have to provide the environment, and they have to be what's best for them."

He told me his biggest fear wasn't physical—it was letting down the people who had put faith in him. "They've made a big bet on me," he said. I asked him about the Special Forces missions he went on in Iraq. Did any stand out as particularly crazy? "The funniest," he said, "though not all of them were funny." He went out on a mission in 2006 when Baghdad was "pretty grim." When the Special Forces team entered the house, a fire started. They yelled out the code word *Lancelot*—which meant the house was wired to detonate, something they'd seen before. "That's when, if you're a Monty Python fan, that's the runaway call. 'Runaway!' We ran for the appropriate distance, then at the end we felt like Monty Python characters. I just ran away from the objective. How do I recover my dignity?" he laughed.

I asked what he had on his Kindle. "I'm in the last chapter of *The River War*, by Winston Churchill. That's an account of an operation in the Sudan. Annie just gave me two: *Game Change*, the political story of the campaign, and the Edwards political memoir," written by a former aide to John Edwards, about how he'd helped the former presidential candidate cover up an affair.

"Who's going to write your biography?" I said. "Have you thought about how you're going to be remembered in history?"

"No," he said. "We joke about it, but I've never sat down and thought about it. I'm not sure thinking about what the sportswriters are going to write about the game afterward makes you play better. And I can't control it."

Duncan jumped in. "You're coming up on June 13; it's going to be a year [you've been in command]. How would you grade yourself?"

A good question.

"Wow," McChrystal said. "Thanks, Duncan, I thought you worked for me.

"I would grade the team very well," McChrystal said. "I give us high marks for most of what we've done accumulatively. That said, that doesn't predict the future necessarily. That doesn't mean we won or are on the verge of winning."

Did he believe in the great man theory of history?

"I read about Julius Caesar—and I'm not comparing any of us to Julius Caesar—but he was very fixated on the leadership aspect. We think of him as a tactician, but in reality, he had the ability to identify other leaders and make them effective."

We'd been talking for thirty-five minutes. I only had a few minutes left. I stumbled forward with a question about the reality on the ground versus the reality in Washington—how, I felt, the reality of Washington often trumped what was actually happening in Afghanistan.

"It's reality at every level. It goes back to the young soldier who is in position to accept risk or not. His reality is, it may or may not make sense to accept risk in a situation because it's his personal risk. As you raise it multiple levels, it's more strategic. America sends soldiers here knowing there was risk and making the decisions it was worth the risk. We didn't decide to lose that particular soldier, but we knew there was the risk. What is a reality at one level, tactical, is very different at another level. It doesn't make either wrong. The DC reality is informed by the politics there."

And what did he think of DC politics?

"Politics are informative," he deadpanned. "And sometimes entertaining."

The interview was over—Duncan jumped in with a last question.

"What *Rolling Stone* really wants to know is how you put Dave Silverman in charge of so much," Duncan said.

We shared a laugh.

"It makes great copy," I said. "It's like six chapters in my memoir already."

We landed at the Kandahar Airfield. Known as KAF, it had the distinction of being the busiest airport in the world, with five thousand flights a week, transporting two hundred shipping containers a day. It stretched for ten miles, housed some thirty thousand personnel, and included a T.G.I. Friday's knockoff and a floor hockey rink the Canadians built. One portion of the base was called the Boardwalk, a pavilion where soldiers could sit and drink lattes and get wireless access to the Internet.

Duncan and I got out of the plane—we weren't here to stay. We grabbed our bags and ran to another helicopter that was waiting for us, splitting up from McChrystal and his team. We took off over the southern Afghanistan desert. Twenty minutes later, we touched down at Forward Operating Base Wilson.

FOB Wilson was originally a Canadian and Afghan base. The Afghans had lived in a dilapidated concrete building without electricity or phones. The Americans had revamped everything over the past year, putting Uncle Sugar's stamp of approval on the base. It didn't look much different from other FOBs I'd been at in Iraq or Afghanistan—military architecture had the unique ability to obliterate geography in the same way staying in one Holiday Inn was more or less the same as any other. Gravel, cement walls, rows of Porta-Johns, the rumbling of generators, tents with leaky air-conditioning, plywood huts constructed with nails sticking out, the wafting scents of raw sewage and chlorine, a mess hall reeking of cleaning fluids and cabbage. All had buildings where the tour guide, usually a low-ranking officer, would show you where a rocket landed just last week.

We were met by Lieutenant Colonel Reik Andersen, commander of

1st Battalion, 12th Infantry Regiment, or Task Force 1-12. He didn't look thrilled to see us—a reporter and a guy from headquarters. He'd just had a negative experience with another journalist, he said, *Time*'s Joe Klein, and his relationship with Kabul had been rocky.

"We rolled out the red carpet for him," Andersen said of Klein. "And he repaid us with a bad story."

The story was about a soldier from Task Force 1-12 struggling to get a school built. I'd read it, thought it was a great story, and it seemed fair. But Klein had questioned McChrystal's counterinsurgency strategy, later noting "the level of optimism emanating from General Stanley McChrystal's headquarters stands in near delusional contrast to the situation in Kandahar." The real problem for Andersen, though, wasn't just the content of the story—it was who had read it. High-ranking figures in Washington, mainly, proving that both shit and bad publicity roll downhill. National Security Advisor Jim Jones personally called McChrystal after reading the story. McChrystal was in Paris at the time—he told me he wasn't pleased with Klein, either. McChrystal passed the word to Andersen: You fucked up.

Duncan asked him when we could get out to the combat outpost JFM. That's where Israel Arroyo was stationed.

"I don't think it's a very good idea to go out there," Andersen said.

Andersen had deep lines under his eyes, a face like a well-worn canvas punching bag. It'd been a long tour, he explained. The latest death was Sergeant Michael Ingram Jr., and he handed me a printout sheet showing the pictures of the fifteen soldiers the battalion had lost during the tour. The *Time* magazine story wasn't the first time he'd caught McChrystal's attention. In fact, it was the third time Andersen had been reprimanded from Kabul—his unit had been involved in two high-profile civilian casualty incidents that got him chewed out. Then Arroyo sent the e-mail to McChrystal. When Andersen learned McChrystal was coming down to visit TF 1-12, he thought he was going to be fired. He didn't get fired, but the message was clear: Get on board with counterinsurgency and follow the rules of engagement. Andersen told me that he didn't quite get the whole counterinsurgency thing—"I mean, we're infantry, we're knuckle-draggers, it's not something we can just switch off overnight, you know," he said. He said he didn't quite understand the rules of engagement, either—but to be safe, he made it clear to his soldiers that they should rarely use force, which seemed to confuse everyone even more.

"No, we'd like to go," Duncan said.

Andersen looked resigned to a thankless fate. Like he knew either decision he made would lead him to the same place: face-first into a shit-stained blast wall. Tell the headquarters guy to fuck off, and he risked the wrath of headquarters. Give Duncan what he wanted—and allow him to bring a reporter, shit—and he knew the result would almost certainly be bad, too.

"It's pretty raw out there," Andersen insisted. "You're likely to get a lot of rants about how they don't like rules of engagement."

"Hey, Duncan, it's cool with me if we just stay here," I said. I knew the unit had just lost a soldier the week before. They had only a month left in their tours. I'd been in a similar situation in Baghdad a few years earlier. I figured they were going to be angry and depressed. I knew they wouldn't welcome a reporter. I didn't know if I wanted to see it—my story didn't need it, I thought. I had the very antijournalist instinct of not wanting to immerse myself in someone else's trauma. I did want to meet Israel Arroyo, but I'd be able to do that tomorrow, when McChrystal was scheduled to pay them a visit.

But Duncan wasn't going to be deterred. "No, we'd like to get out there for the night."

"Okay, whatever you want," Andersen said.

We spent an hour or so hanging out at Andersen's office. I stood under a concrete bunker smoking cigarettes. We walked over to Charlie Company's headquarters—Charlie Company was in charge of JFM, and they were supposed to give us a ride over there.

The Charlie Company captain came out. He introduced himself as Duke Reim. We knew each other, sort of. He'd been a lieutenant in Iraq in the 172nd Stryker Brigade, a unit I'd spent a month embedded with in Baghdad in the summer of 2006. My photographer friend Lucian Read—who'd also been there in 2006—had just left Duke and his guys after another long embed. We laughed—it was a small war.

Charlie Company had three large MRAPs parked outside the headquarters tent. A dozen soldiers milled around, checking out Duncan and me. We didn't pass the test.

I started bullshitting with one of the soldiers. I asked him if Israel Arroyo was out there.

He told me no.

"Arroyo left fucking today, man," he said. "He had to escort another soldier back to Germany. That fucking guy had been going around saying he was going to kill an Afghan or kill a fucking interpreter. He was acting fucking nuts, so they let him go home. Arroyo went with him to make sure he didn't do anything fucking stupid."

Arroyo was gone. Very weird. He was the guy I wanted to see. I changed the subject.

"I'm sorry about Sergeant Ingram," I said.

"He's fucking Corporal Ingram to us," the soldier answered. "Rank you get after you die don't count."

It was a point of pride, he said. Ingram wouldn't want to be known as a sergeant.

I pulled opened the MRAP door. Pronounced *em-rap*, the Mine Resistant Ambush Protected vehicle entered the war to replace the High Mobility Multipurpose Wheeled Vehicle, or Humvee. The bombs got bigger, and the three thousand pounds of armor on the Humvee was too easily shredded. The MRAP, though, was about the worst kind of vehicle one could have imagined for the terrain in Afghanistan: mountainous, wadi-filled, and roadless. It was slow, easily got stuck in the mud, and required paved roads to be most effective. The entire country had only one major highway. It also fell far short as the primary ride in a military campaign dedicated to swaying a local population. The twenty-two-ton vehicles were intimidating and loud and frightening and difficult to drive without regularly causing severe property damage. The MRAP underscored the alien nature of our presence. Add a life support system pumping oxygen into the metallic caverns and you might as well be cruising around in a tank on occupied Mars. Rather than project strength, the MRAP perversely sent another message: the complete fear and hatred the Americans had for the people they were supposedly there to protect. The MRAP was there to save us, not them. (It did so: There was an 80 percent better chance of surviving an attack in an MRAP compared to a Humvee.) The network of roads we were building in the country—the humanitarian projects of approximately 720 miles of asphalt over ten years, at the staggering cost of about $600,000 per mile—had a dual purpose in making it easier for us to drive around the country to kill the disgruntled peasants.

I climbed up in the MRAP, and Duncan squeezed in next to me. The door looked extremely heavy—the hatch on the tanklike MRAP weighed at least 120 pounds. There was a warning on the locking mechanism that said it could cause serious injury or death if you weren't careful.

We were heading into a very intense situation. One soldier evacuated for going crazy, another killed ten days ago. Of the twenty-five original members of the platoon at JFM, only seven were still left—the rest had been killed, wounded, or lost their minds.

The MRAP door slammed shut.

36 | INGRAM'S HOUSE

APRIL 28–29, 2010, COMBAT OUTPOST JFM, ZHARI, AND KANDAHAR AIRFIELD

The twenty-two-ton MRAP bounced up and down along a narrow dirt road, crawling at a speed of around ten miles an hour. It was like riding in the back of a garbage truck.

I looked out the window. Combat Outpost JFM was only a few kilometers outside the wire from FOB Wilson. It was startling to see just how close the war was being fought to the large American base. JFM had seen some of the heaviest fighting so far—a NATO operation launched a few years earlier had killed hundreds of Taliban and dozens of NATO troops. What was left behind resembled the Biblical past or a postapocalyptic vision of a distant future, dust storms and gray clouds overhead, signs of colonization in splashes of gravel and barbed wire, Jawa-like figures making strange sounds scavenging about the rubble, every few miles marked with a handful of armed men huddled for survival in cold stone bunkers.

The outpost appeared before us, a concrete citadel, a moat of Hesco barriers filled with dirt and blast walls. A soldier swung open the gates. We moved down the driveway, passing a pit of burning trash, smoldering with black smoke and ash. It was getting close to dusk.

Combat outpost JFM

There was an edgy, animalistic feel to the place. A group of about ten soldiers gathered around a mortar pit like it was a campfire, the focal point of the small base. There were two large guard watchtowers, a sandbagged headquarters made from plywood, a few trailers for bunk beds, and a line of Porta-Johns. One soldier was sitting in a foldout chair next to the mortar tube, getting his head shaved; the others talked among themselves. No one made eye contact.

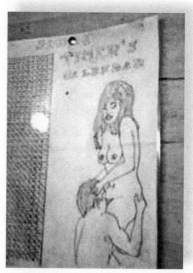

Duncan and I were more or less ignored. We threw our bags into one of the trailers, which looked like a shipping container. They were called CHUs (pronounced *choos*), for containable housing units.

Lieutenant Graham Williams commanded the platoon at JFM. He wasn't impressed by our presence, either. He

A Short Timer's calender inside JFM

gave me a tour of the base. I climbed up one of the guard towers behind him. He pointed off to a small house in the distance.

"That's where Ingram got hit," he said.

I wasn't making much progress in my conversations with the soldiers. They clearly didn't trust us, didn't appreciate our being there. They were still reeling from the trauma of Ingram's death ten days earlier and the frustration of a year at war. I felt I had to do something to gain their trust. I asked Williams if they were going on a patrol tonight. The lieutenant said yes. I asked if I could join them. He said I could if I wanted. He said he didn't give a shit.

It was a strange reaction. Most of the time, a reporter on a patrol is welcomed, or at least the soldiers pretend to welcome him. But by this point in the tour, a reporter had just become a hassle, something else to worry about. They didn't even bother worrying.

It got dark.

Staff Sergeant Kennith Hicks and Lieutenant Williams were going to lead the patrol. I slipped on my body armor and helmet and borrowed a pair of eye protection with clear lenses from one of the soldiers who was staying behind.

The soldiers gathered around Hicks for the pre-patrol briefing. Hicks stood about five feet nine and had close-cropped blond hair. He spoke in a language where *um*s and *uh*s were replaced by *fuck*s and *fucking*s.

"Obviously fucking threats are out there, dismounted," he said. He mentioned Ingram without mentioning Ingram. "You all know what happened. You know what's out there. You know what you're coming up against. Be extremely fucking careful, look for markings on the ground."

Lieutenant Williams added, "There's no hurry. Scan the surface, look for hot spots. Make slow fucking movements. Don't feel like you got to rush through there."

"We should give out diseased blankets to them, like we did to the fucking Indians," said one soldier.

"Fucking give them immunization but instead make it AIDS," said another.

Leaving the patrol base, we crept along the Hesco barriers on a small footpath with a deep drop-off down to a muddy drainage ditch. We started walking down the road. The moon backlit the patrol through the overcast sky. I could make out each soldier clearly as they staggered themselves out, S-shaped, keeping enough distance between themselves so if one stepped on a mine, maybe only one would die.

We got about two hundred meters away when the soldiers took up position in the ruins of an abandoned house. I crawled up the wall and kneeled down on the second floor. It was white and gray, all crumbling rock, like an empty housing project from the world of the Flintstones. All the houses had the appearance of bunkers and combat positions, not homes—meant to kill or hide, not to live in.

Lieutenant Williams saw something move a hundred meters away at another house. Cars had been driving up and pulling away over the last hour, more activity at the house than they'd seen in weeks.

Across the field and down the road, a flashlight flicked on and off.

The light flashed again.

"There's somebody in there," Lieutenant Williams said. "In Ingram's house."

He crawled down from where we were kneeling on the second floor. He waved Hicks and another soldier over to him.

They started to walk down the road.

They disappeared.

THWUMP, THWUMP.

The sound of illumination mortar rounds fired from the base.

The sky lit up.

I looked to my left and right, checking who was next to me. Four silhouettes outlined: three soldiers and an Afghan interpreter, standing and kneeling on the second floor and staring out to where Williams and Hicks had vanished.

The wind started to pick up. There was lightning in the distance. A bad storm was moving in and the dust mixed with the darkness. It was hard to see.

There was no sound coming from Ingram's house.

I waited for the explosion. For the automatic rifle fire to follow. For the adrenaline to dump and the yelling to start. For our entire universe, three hundred meters of limited visibility, to stop all motion, then hit warp speed, the rhythm of violence and death.

There was just silence.

Three figures came back down the road. Williams waved us down from the second floor. We climbed down. They hadn't found anything in Ingram's house.

"We have no medevac support because of the weather, so we're going back," Williams said.

We walked back to the base, slowly, watching our step. The patrol lasted one hour and ten minutes.

The soldiers threw off their gear. The tension eased. The patrol was over and nobody was dead. They gathered around the mortar pit. I started to talk to them.

Twenty-one-year-old Private Jared Pautsch told me his story. His brother Jason had been killed in Baghdad in 2007. Jared spoke at his funeral. Jared signed up to get revenge. To kill the fuckers who killed his brother. He told me that he thought counterinsurgency was bullshit. I asked him what he thought of McChrystal coming down to speak with them tomorrow.

He laughed.

"Fuck McChrystal."

He told me that the men blamed McChrystal and his rules of engagement for Ingram's death. The unit had asked for months to destroy the house that Ingram had been killed in, but they kept getting the permission to do so denied. They were told that they weren't allowed to destroy the home because it would anger the local Afghan population. The soldiers argued that it wasn't a house—it was a fighting position. Nobody lived there. The Taliban just used it to fight and hide bombs.

Pautsch started talking about Ingram. He'd been there when he died.

On April 17, 2010, Arroyo led the squad into the house. Arroyo and Pautsch went one way; Ingram and the unit's medic went the other. An explosion of brown dust. Ingram had stepped on an IED, a small landmine. The military had a new acronym for them, VOIED—victim operated improvised explosive device.

Ingram was bleeding heavily.

It took thirty minutes for the medevac helicopter to arrive. Ingram was "packaged up" and put on the bird, the soldiers said.

In Arroyo's e-mail to McChrystal, he had said Ingram's last words were about McChrystal. I told this to Pautsch.

Pautsch laughed. Arroyo, he said, was taking poetic license.

"More water, more morphine," Pautsch said. "Those were some of his last words."

I told him that Arroyo had written that McChrystal had inspired him.

"Ha, shit, did Arroyo write that? That's funny. Ingram thought all this COIN stuff was bullshit, too. Maybe he did start to look up to McChrystal, but he sure as fuck didn't tell me about it."

Pautsch pulled a small laminated card from his pocket. It was the rules of engagement they'd been given.

"Look at this," he said. It had a list of rules that the soldiers were supposed to follow.

One said: "Patrol only in areas that you are reasonably certain that you will not have to defend yourself with lethal force."

"Does that make any fucking sense?" Pautsch asked me.

It didn't make much sense. Asking infantrymen to patrol where they weren't going to get shot at was like asking cops to patrol in places where there was no crime.

"We should just drop a fucking bomb on this place," Pautsch said. "You sit and ask yourself, What are we doing here?"

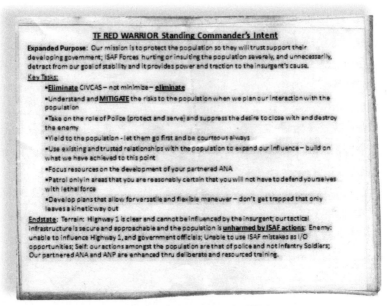

TF RED WARRIOR Standing Commander's Intent

Expanded Purpose: Our mission is to protect the population so they will trust support their developing government; ISAF Forces hurting or insulting the population severely, and unnecessarily, detract from our goal of stability and it provides power and traction to the insurgent's cause.

Key Tasks:

- **Eliminate** CIVCAS – not minimize – **eliminate**
- Understand and **MITIGATE** the risks to the population when we plan our interaction with the population
- Take on the role of Police (protect and serve) and suppress the desire to close with and destroy the enemy
- Yield to the population - let them go first and be courteous always
- Use existing and trusted relationships with the population to expand our influence – build on what we have achieved to this point
- Focus resources on the development of your partnered ANA
- Patrol only in areas that you are reasonably certain that you will not have to defend yourselves with lethal force
- Develop plans that allow for versatile and flexible maneuver – don't get trapped that only leaves a kinetic way out

Endstate: Terrain: Highway 1 is clear and cannot be influenced by the insurgent; our tactical infrastructure is secure and approachable and the population is **unharmed by ISAF actions**; Enemy: unable to influence Highway 1, and government officials; Unable to use ISAF mistakes as I/O opportunities; Self: our actions amongst the population are that of police and not Infantry Soldiers; Our partnered ANA and ANP are enhanced thru deliberate and resourced training.

Rules of Engagement for JFM

Hicks agreed. "My guys keep asking me: What the fuck is the point?"

Hicks explained why he thought the rules of engagement had become so watered down: Because the battalion commander, Andersen, had kept getting his ass chewed out for killing civilians, he'd sent out guidelines that were even more restrictive than what McChrystal had proposed. The guidelines 1st Platoon were given were a way for the higher-ups to cover their asses—to avoid having civilian casualty incidents that could get them in trouble with ISAF HQ in Kabul.

"Ingram was a real fucking success story," Hicks said. Hicks served three combat tours, including two in Ramadi. "He had so much fucking potential. He always made everybody laugh, was willing to learn. He was a good fucking soldier. I mean, this is war, we could get fucking blown up sitting here talking right now, fucking rocket could drop on our fucking heads. Fuck, when I came over here and heard that McChrystal was in charge, I thought we could get our fucking gun on. I get COIN. I get all that. McChrystal comes here, explains it, it makes sense. But then he goes away on his bird, and by the time his directives get passed down to us through Big Army, they're all fucked up either because somebody is trying to cover their ass, or because they just don't understand themselves. But we're fucking losing this thing."

After talking for a few more hours, I headed to my trailer to sleep. Around midnight, there was a loud boom. More outgoing mortar rounds from the mortar pit.

The next morning, I woke up, brushed my teeth with bottled water, and grabbed a coffee.

At around 0830, the gates to JFM opened up again. McChrystal's convoy of MRAPs rolled in. Two Afghan soldiers were in the way. One American soldier threw rocks at them, yelling at them to move. "Those fucking Afghans just walk around faded all the time," the soldier said, meaning they were high.

The plan was for McChrystal to speak with the senior NCOs and officers.

The younger enlisted men smoked cigarettes down by a garbage burning pit.

McChrystal walked by me, flanked by Captain Duke Reim.

"Hey Mike," Reim said. "Lucian, your photographer friend, told me to fucking watch out for you," he said.

McChrystal looked up, a flash of panic on his face as he walked by.

Charlie Flynn jumped out of the MRAP.

"Duncan, Mike, come over here," he said.

Duncan and I walked over to him.

"Tell me what's going on here, how they are feeling," he asked.

"The men are in high spirits," Duncan told him. "They are excited that The Boss is down here."

I was stunned. I wasn't on the staff. It wasn't my job to explain to them what was actually going on. But he'd asked for my opinion. I decided to answer diplomatically.

"Uh, I think they're pretty upset by the rules of engagement," I said. "Frustrated, you know, and they just lost Ingram—"

Duncan interrupted. "I wouldn't say that. They feel like they've had some setbacks, but I wouldn't say they are upset."

Duncan had spoken to the men the night before as well. Was that what he had learned from talking to them? Did the men tell Duncan that because he was on McChrystal's staff? Was Duncan asking the right questions? Or did Duncan know that's what Charlie Flynn wanted to hear, so that's why he told him the lie? Everything's fine, they all love it here. Because of the dozen soldiers I'd interviewed the night before, I knew McChrystal was about to speak in front of a bunch of very angry men who felt like their sacrifices were a complete waste, who thought they were losing, and who weren't shy about expressing that feeling. McChrystal's staff always credited themselves with an ability to face hard truths, yet here the hard truth was being avoided. Or it wasn't understood. Or the bubble was so powerful that they couldn't see what McChrystal was about to walk into.

I told Duncan that Ingram should be called Corporal Ingram, not sergeant, as that's what the men knew him as. It would give McChrystal credibility with them. He passed this information on to Charlie.

Underneath a tent, McChrystal gathered about twenty soldiers.

"I ask you what's going on in your world, and I think it's important for you all to understand the big picture as well," McChrystal started. "How's the company doing? You guys feeling sorry for yourselves? Anybody? Anybody feel like you're losing?"

"Sir, some of the guys here, sir, think we're losing, sir," said Hicks.

McChrystal nodded. He held a black marker in his hand. He had two whiteboards set up behind him.

McChrystal said they weren't losing. He started talking about leadership.

"Strength is when you're not sure. Strength is when you don't feel like you're being strong. Strength is leading when you just don't want to lead.

Sometimes you don't. All of us have those days. You don't want to listen or talk to anyone. You don't want to lead. You're leading by example, everybody is watching you. That's what we do. Particularly when it's really, really hard and it hurts inside."

He spent twenty minutes talking through counterinsurgency, diagramming his concepts and principles on the whiteboard. "We are knee-deep in the decisive year," he told them, insisting the Taliban no longer had the momentum, "but I don't think we do, either." It was similar to what he'd done in Paris and in Berlin, but the soldiers weren't buying it.

"This is the philosophical part that works with think tanks," McChrystal joked. "But doesn't get the same reception from infantry companies."

During the question and answer period, the frustration from the soldiers boiled over. They complained about "catch and release" (insurgents they detained who got freed), about not being able to shoot as freely as they liked, about how they haven't been able to use force.

"We haven't put enough fear into the people," one soldier said. "I don't think we've accomplished much."

"Winning hearts and minds in COIN is a cold-blooded thing," McChrystal said. "But you can't kill your way out of this war. The Russians killed one million Afghans, and that didn't work."

"I'm not saying go out and kill everybody, sir, that's not what I'm saying. You say we've stopped the momentum of the insurgency. I don't believe that's true in this area. I've seen the insurgency gain momentum in this area. The more we pull back, the more we restrain ourselves, the stronger it's getting."

"One, I agree with you," McChrystal says. "In this area, we've not made progress, probably. You have to show strength here, you have to use fire. What I'm telling you is fire costs you. What do you want to do? You want to wipe out the population and resettle it?"

The soldiers felt like they weren't being heard, that he didn't understand. They wanted to be able to fight—like they did in Iraq, like previous units had done in Afghanistan.

"Don't do anything here that you don't want to look at your wife and kid when you get home," McChrystal said. "Don't make any moral judgments that the ends justify the means. At some point, you're going to have to live with everything you've done. Don't get cynical."

"That doesn't bother me as much as my soldier being killed," the soldier who'd been questioning him responded. "We'd rather err on the side of caution. Ninety percent of the people are not friendly. All they want to do is kill us. Everybody else is just watching the way we come in to put in the IEDs."

"We make many more mistakes than you imagine, more mistakes than you think," McChrystal said. "I see the whole thing."

"When they don't have weapons but we know they're insurgents, they become a civilian casualty," the soldier answered.

"That's the way this game is," McChrystal said. "It's complex. I can't just decide: It's shirts versus skins and we'll kill all the shirts. These people have been here doing this long enough. They know the deal. We're not the first people here."

The discussion wound down—there was no real resolution, no clapping, no photos taken with the general.

"I got a note from Sergeant Arroyo inviting me to Corporal Ingram's memorial service," McChrystal said. "That was one of those when it suddenly hits you. It hits you up close. There's no way I can make that easier. No way I can pretend it won't hurt. No way I can tell you not to feel that. Because if you don't feel that, that's not the kind of organization you happen to be in. There's no stronger bond than in a rifle company. I will tell you, you're doing a great job. Don't let the frustration get to you."

Duncan and I stood next to each other. Charlie Flynn came up to us.

"Man, he did great," Charlie said. "He's so good in situations like this."

The convoy of MRAPs rolled out. The soldiers down at the burn pit stared up at us, sullen and smoking. At FOB Wilson, we rushed over to the helicopters. We landed at Kandahar Airfield twenty minutes later. McChrystal had a meeting with the regional commander. I saw him talking to Duncan before he went inside the tactical operations center. I hadn't seen him like this before—he looked worried, shaken.

McChrystal walked past me, stopped, then pulled me aside. Over the past few weeks, he'd been comfortable with allowing almost everything to be out there, transparent and open. He'd never tried to take anything back or personally spin me. Even if his staff thought he'd nailed it, McChrystal knew that what I'd just seen, and what he'd just been through, wasn't good.

"That was a raw wound back there," McChrystal told me. "You've been around, I don't have to tell you."

"Yes, sir, they all seemed pretty frustrated."

He went into his meeting.

Duncan came up next to me, in damage control mode.

"We're a little concerned with what just happened," he said. "We don't want you to write a story saying those soldiers don't get counterinsurgency. That they don't get it."

I said I wouldn't write that, and I wouldn't. The soldiers didn't get counterinsurgency? Jesus. I had the exact opposite view. I felt the soldiers understood exactly what was being asked of them. It was McChrystal and his staff who failed to understand the soldiers—or if they did, they knew they couldn't say so in the words the soldiers wanted to hear. The soldiers, from what I could tell, actually didn't want to hear anything—they just wanted someone to listen. The talk had been an outright disaster. Israel Arroyo, the soldier who'd invited McChrystal down, had been evacuated with another soldier for post-traumatic stress. Mikie Ingram, the soldier he had gone on his well-publicized patrol with, had been killed. The platoon was borderline mutinous. Yet McChrystal and Duncan were worried that I was going to write that the soldiers didn't understand the war.

I tracked down Israel Arroyo by phone a few weeks later. The twenty-five-year-old was back at the base in Fort Carson, Colorado. He was suffering from post-traumatic stress. I asked him about Ingram. I asked him if he remembered Ingram's last words.

"I can't tell you what he said, I can't tell you that," Arroyo told me. "What he said before he died . . . He . . ."

He started talking again. He told me what Ingram had said. He asked me to swear that I would never repeat it.

Before hanging up, Arroyo told me he had bad dreams of "the things I could have done better" to save Ingram's life. But there was nothing he could do, and that was the nightmare.

37 | AN ARMY OF NONE

NOVEMBER 2009 TO PRESENT DAY, KABUL

Lieutenant General William B. Caldwell IV arrives in late 2009 at Camp Eggers to take over what's considered the most crucial mission in the war: training the Afghan army and police. Camp Eggers is home to the NATO Training Mission Afghanistan, Combined Security Transition Command-Afghanistan, known as NTM-A CSTC-A (pronounced *see-stick-uh*). It's an $11.6 billion a year operation. The idea is to create a formidable security force to hand the country over to as the NATO forces withdraw. As the Afghans stand up, the Americans stand down. Or so goes the theory.

Eggers is a crowded complex in downtown Kabul, about six square blocks of space housing some fifteen hundred servicemen and -women. The space is tight, with senior officers bunking often four to a room. It's impossible to throw a brick without smacking a colonel in the face, hard to turn a corner without running into a shoulder of stars.

Caldwell is a three-star general from a military family—his father was a general (like McChrystal's father and Petraeus's father-in-law—to become a general, it helps to have a general for a dad). He's had a fairly undistinguished career. No big mistakes, no great achievements—"a nice guy," says a West Point classmate, "just not much gray matter." He's charming up to a point.

Post–September 11, Caldwell hooks up with Deputy Secretary of Defense Paul Wolfowitz. Wolfowitz is the man who notoriously dismissed estimates that the Iraq War would cost billions, claiming the Iraq "can really finance its own reconstruction." Wolfowitz conspires with others in the Bush administration to fix the intelligence to justify an invasion; he holds meetings with top columnists and media figures before the war to figure out what's the best way to sell it to the American public. After Wolfowitz leaves his post in government, he ends up becoming head of the World Bank. He gets forced out after he promotes his girlfriend to a top job.

Wolfowitz, Caldwell says, is one of his mentors. Under Wolfowitz, Caldwell soaks up how to play the game. "The lessons I've learned by just watching [Wolfowitz] in action and seeing how he makes decisions will be extremely beneficial and useful to me as I continue my career," Caldwell gushes in 2003. In 2006 and 2007, Caldwell serves as the spokesperson for U.S. forces in Iraq, where he regularly makes statements that challenge the truth. As early as the fall of 2006, commanders on the ground in Iraq tell Caldwell Iraq is in a "civil war," a charge he denies from his podium for the duration of his term, even as hundreds of bodies get dumped each morning on the streets.

After Saddam Hussein's botched execution in December 2006, Caldwell says that the United States had no role in the execution— despite the fact that the Americans had brought the Iraqi execution team, including the man who taped the execution on his cell phone, to and from the gallows on Blackhawk helicopters, picking them up and dropping them off in the Green Zone.

Surrounded by a cadre of highly paid media advisors, Caldwell tries his best to convince a skeptical public that the war in Iraq is being won. He renames press briefings "media roundtables," and he ditches the typical podium and microphone in favor of an earpiece and a round wooden table. Cosmetic changes to the format to help convince journalists to buy the message.

Retreating from Baghdad, he spends the next two years as commander of Combined Arms Center at Fort Leavenworth, a training academy, occupying a position that had been held by General David Petraeus. Caldwell needs an issue to make his own: What Petraeus does for counterinsurgency, Caldwell wants to do for "information operations," a military doctrine that focuses on how to influence a potentially hostile foreign audience's perception. Caldwell wants to take information operations and combine it with public affairs, the branch of the military focused on influencing the domestic audience. He calls the combination of the two "information engagement."

One of his concerns is to figure out ways to bypass U.S. media outlets in order to reach Americans directly. He exits Baghdad during a period of violence that leaves more than one hundred thousand dead and is convinced the "good news" just didn't get out. He turns to YouTube to speak directly to the public. "It eliminated the [media] gatekeeper," he says.

("A You-who?" he asks the staffer who brings up the idea. Within six months, Caldwell claims his video "was in the top ten of all YouTube sites visited in the world.")

In 2008, Caldwell sings the merits of information operations—echoing General David Petraeus's assertion that information operations helped turn the tide in Iraq. But he still, at least in public, sticks to a distinction: "Public affairs is there to inform [domestic audiences]," he says in April 2008. "Information operations is there to influence foreign audiences." In 2009, he also tries to rewrite the official doctrine on information operations, though that effort ultimately fails.

Caldwell gets the chance to put his theories to the test. Obama gives him the job to train the Afghan security forces.

Arriving in Afghanistan in November 2009, Caldwell soon realizes he'll need a steroid-sized dose of spin to convince Americans the mission is worth it, and to explain how creating a highly trained Afghan army is an even plausible goal. The truth actually works against him: The Afghan army, in his own words, "just wasn't working." The "entire focus [was on] quantity, not quality," he claims of his predecessors, referring to the types of recruits.

The stats: Only 20 percent of new recruits can read. One out of four deserts the ranks on a regular basis. Child rape is endemic in both the police and Afghan armies; in the south, Afghan soldiers take boys as young as eight or ten years old as lovers, dressing them up as girls at parties. It makes the Western forces very uncomfortable. ("Boys are for pleasure, women are for children" is a popular expression in the country.) It isn't until January 2011 that Afghanistan signs a UN agreement to prevent child soldiers from joining the security forces (though teenagers are still welcome in government-backed militias). An American trainer estimates that 54 percent of the Afghan army and police smoke hash regularly. Another earlier study showed at least 60 percent of police in Helmand province were users.

Worse: The American forces and the Afghan forces don't trust each other. Afghan soldiers have picked up a very bad habit of murdering American soldiers there to train them. NATO orders a study, and the conclusions are hot—there is a "growing systemic threat" that is "provoking a crisis of confidence" between the Afghan and American soldiers. Almost every twelve days there is a murder. In one five-and-a-half-month period, 16 percent of American casualties are caused by the Afghan security forces killing soldiers in the American Army. In a three-year period, at least fifty-eight NATO soldiers have been killed, and around the same number wounded, in what are officially called ANSF-committed fratricide murders, 6 percent of all NATO deaths. ISAF decides they better classify the study, and quick. The study gets classified, but not before it gets leaked to *The Wall Street Journal.*

The American trainers, according to the study, have a list of complaints about the Afghan soldiers: "pervasive illicit drug use, massive thievery, personal instability, dishonesty, no integrity, incompetence, unsafe weapons handling, corrupt officers, no real NCO corps, covert alliances/informal treaties with insurgents, high AWOL rates, bad morale, laziness, repulsive hygiene, and the torture of dogs." The Afghans are cowardly and are ready to run away in battle, the Americans say.

The Afghan soldiers have a list of complaints about the Americans: "extremely arrogant, bullying, unwilling to listen to their advice and lacking concern for civilian and ANSF safety." The Americans are always "urinating in public . . . cursing at and insulting and being rude and vulgar" to Afghans while "unnecessarily shooting animals." The Americans are cowardly, the Afghan soldiers say, hiding behind heavily armored vehicles and close air support in battle.

The study includes anecdotes from the approximately six hundred Afghans and five hundred American soldiers surveyed.

Verbatim quotes from the Afghans: *They take photos from women even when we tell them not to. U.S. soldiers kill many innocent civilians: If ambushed, U.S. soldiers panic, spraying fire in all directions. A U.S. MRAP killed six civilians traveling in a vehicle—it was intentional. We once loaded and charged our weapons because we got tired of U.S. soldiers calling us "motherfuckers." They always shout and yell "motherfucker." They are crazy. They are too arrogant. We try to warn them if the enemy is planning something, they usually fail to listen and get shot up. They treat us like thieves. U.S. soldiers killed a carload of civilians in front of an OP. U.S. soldiers have never been held responsible and sent to prison for any of these crimes. A raid in [redacted] province killed nine students; they were a study group and had no weapons. They pee all over, right in front of civilians, including females. If we tell them not to, they either don't listen or get angry. Two U.S. soldiers even defecated within public view. They peed in front of a house. They don't care if women see them. A U.S. soldier peed in a stream right in front of a woman. This greatly angered us. U.S. soldiers shoot cattle for no reason. They fired on donkeys for no reason. How we treat dogs is no one's business; the Koran is very clear about the low status of dogs. U.S. soldiers often retreat and leave us be-hind during firefights. Often the U.S. lets itself get involved in personal feuds by believing an unreliable source. These people use the U.S. to destroy their personal enemies, not the insurgents. They will break in doors before the peo-ple can answer. They don't care if they cause accidents. For years, U.S. mili-tary convoys sped through the streets of villages, running over small children, while shouting profanities and throwing water bottles at people. Infidels are not allowed inside mosques. They often don't even take off their boots. It's rude for them to wear their sunglasses when meeting with elders. They constantly pass gas in front of ANSF, in public, in front of elders—a very low class peo-ple. If they hand out candy to children, the children are at risk of getting hurt by being too close to the Americans if there is an attack. They put them in danger. The U.S. soldier threw his hand grenade (without pulling the pin) with the candy he was throwing at the children.*

Verbatim quotes from Americans soldiers on Afghans: *They are high as fuck. Their eyes are always bloodshot. One ANA shot himself in the chest twice and leg once. He was high as shit. The ANP were high off their asses. The ANA were always high on hash. A police officer was shot. His tolerance for morphine was astronomically high due to heroin use. We were on patrol and they stopped the patrol so they could start smoking in front of us. They are totally infiltrated by insurgents. You just could not trust them. One of them at a base in Pech got caught working for the Taliban. [They] drew down on U.S. soldiers a few times. [An] ANA locked and loaded on a U.S. civilian contrac-tor because he accidentally bumped into him even though he had apologized right away. A U.S. soldier then locked and loaded against the ANA to em-phasize the point of the apology. We do everything for them. It's like a kid you have to spoon-feed . . . but you have to put on an Afghan face. We even got training at JRTC [with role players] who acted like stupid and lazy ANA. That set us up for what we found there. This is a lazy ass culture; they won't do anything unless they have to. They are constantly showing up for duty or missions late, even thirty minutes late. They make excuses . . . but nothing changes. Their leadership is hot garbage. Many of their soldiers are much bet-*

ter than their leaders. It's like the commercial of the big bulldog and the small yipping dog bouncing around; you take away the big bulldog and the small dog hides its tail and slinks away. Whenever we made contact they would just hide. Others refuse to patrol if it is at all dangerous. If they are afraid, they won't do anything. Theft among [them] is bad; they have local kids steal things for them. [They] are garbage, shit. These guys are not soldiers; they are a ragtag bunch of thugs and civilians dressed in uniforms. I would never like to admit that Iraqis are smarter, but they are Einsteins compared to Afghans. They talk on their cell phones, yell into them on missions. They learned to be helpless and that is partly why they are so fucking bad. They are always on their cell phones during patrols. They are worse than teenage girls. They don't plan ahead for fuel and water. We just give them shit so they stop bothering us. They are completely dependent on the U.S. They are turds. We are better off without them. The "Afghan Face" strategy doesn't work. They fucking stink. We all had to take cover while they were returning fire. They would spray and pray. They listened to local mullahs and were pretty radical. The ANA use culture and religion as a shield to hide their incompetence. We had a big clearing mission during Ramadan. They just lay down and fell asleep. The ABP killed a couple of our dogs. They were strays but we fed them. Slowly they started disappearing. They killed them. We received no training for trainers. We got one part day cultural training. It was crap. We do not socialize outside of operations. I'd just as soon shoot them as work with them. Interaction with ANA was minimal. The only time was to go see what they had stolen. The people don't want us here and we don't like them.

"U.S. soldiers perceived that 50 percent of the ANA were Islamic radicals," the report states. Afghan soldiers "were more likely to think a suicide bomber in Afghanistan would see salvation than a U.S. soldier killed in action."

NATO has already spent more than $30 billion training the Afghan security forces. Police officers regularly accept bribes; it's the least trusted institution in a land of mistrusted institutions. The training courses are completed again and again by the same Afghan soldiers to get a $240 stipend without actually having to fight. And fighting-wise, though the Afghan army is allegedly getting better, they are still years away from being able to "take the lead," says Caldwell.

Caldwell's plan to fix the debacle? To teach the Afghan security forces how to read. Only then, Caldwell believes, can they fight. "You can't expect a soldier to account for his weapon if he can't even read the serial number on his rifle," Caldwell says. In briefing after briefing, he goes on at length about the "literacy problem" in the security forces. He needs to "educate an entire generation of Afghans," he says, for his plan to succeed.

Despite the $11.6 billion allocated to the training program in 2011 year, he doesn't feel that it's enough. He takes to the media to complain. He doesn't have enough trainers (nine hundred short), he doesn't have enough Afghan recruits (he needs to add seventy thousand more), and he doesn't have enough money—he wants $2 billion extra, on top of the billions spent on the training over the previous decade. The $2 billion will put them over the top, he claims. Three times as many Afghan troops drop out as stay—to increase the forces by 56,000, Caldwell explains, he needs to recruit 141,000 Afghans.

To keep retention up, Caldwell will soon start to charter commercial planes for Afghan soldiers and police to go on vacation to their homes in the southern part of the country. Despite his own statements that information operations are for "foreign audiences," he'll assign a team of American information operation specialists to target the U.S. public. IO teams are typically trained in electronic warfare, psychological operations, military deception, among other skill sets, to "influence, disrupt, corrupt, or usurp adversarial human and automated decision making while protecting our own," according to the Department of Defense. This IO team, which had received training in conducting psychological operations, is tasked with convincing visiting senators and other VIPs to give Caldwell more funds. It's unclear if the information operations team's efforts have any effect, but at the end of the year, leading senators will endorse his call for $2 billion more. Serious legal questions are raised by a whistleblower under Caldwell's command about whether he directly violates the law banning the Department of Defense from propagandizing its own citizens, as well as other government rules. However, a subsequent Pentagon investigation into the program, prompted by a story I published in *Rolling Stone*, will find that Caldwell has done nothing wrong. The Afghan training mission continues.

38 | IN THE ARENA

APRIL 30 TO MAY 8, 2010, KABUL

Duncan's office was on the second floor in a building hidden in the back of the headquarters campus. The floor housed the ISAF media center, an open newsroom filled with computers and telephones, where military public affairs pumped out an endless stream of press releases and photographs.

Duncan decorated his office carefully with a pattern of ironic mementos. There was a photo of Hamid Karzai, snapped in a way that made it look like the Afghan president was giving the middle finger to the audience. There was a picture of McChrystal, Photoshopped into the famous Obama "Hope" campaign photo, red and white coloring over the general's face. There was a political cartoon from October 2009, drawn during the lengthy troop review process—it showed McChrystal calling the White House and being put on hold. ("How long have you been on hold?" a soldier asks. "At the top of the hour, it will be about three months," McChrystal says.) An *Onion* headline: U.S. CONTINUES QUAGMIRE BUILDING EFFORT IN AFGHANISTAN. A copy of a book called *Selling War to America* was stacked atop a pile of books on the floor.

The pièce de résistance of the office was a handwritten note on a yellow Post-it. It was a message from a Pentagon spokesperson named Bryan Whitman that had been left for Duncan and Lieutenant Colonel Tadd Sholtis, the public affairs officer Duncan shared his office with. The Pentagon spokesperson had telephoned from Washington, and when no one could take his call, he had an ISAF staffer transcribe his message verbatim:

"I'm calling the bullshit flag on this," the message said. "What the fuck is going on over there? What the fuck is wrong with that public affairs office there? I know exactly what you are doing to me there. Get him to answer my fucking questions. Go get him on the phone."

Duncan and Tadd saved the note for posterity. They didn't really get along with the Pentagon press office, Duncan explained. Sholtis, an aspiring writer turned public affairs officer, had a weirdly subversive streak, too, keeping a personal blog called The Quatto Zone, named after the Martian rebel leader from the movie *Total Recall*. On the blog, he regularly slammed the media for seeing the war through "shit-colored glasses" and complained about press coverage—he said it was a blog for him to "think and write."

I was back at ISAF headquarters to do my final interviews with McChrystal's top advisors. I had a sit-down interview with Sir Graeme Lamb, the British Special Forces commando; General Mike Flynn; Command Sergeant Major Michael Hall, the top-ranking enlisted man in the country; and a few other members of the team.

I met with Lamb in the Italian café and pizza shop within the complex. He looked the part of the wild commando: tanned, well-built, fraying gray hair on a balding head, hairy chest peeking out beneath his olive button-down shirt, top buttons undone. Among the staff, he had a reputation as a mystic, a violence-prone Buddha offering trippy wisdom that started to make sense only after much thought.

They nicknamed him Lambo, like Rambo. He described himself as a "science fiction sort of a guy." He had an old leather jacket like Harrison

Ford, rode a motorcycle, and was inspired by *The Hitchhiker's Guide to the Galaxy*—"just give me an improbability drive," he tells me, "all will be well." If McChrystal's team were the Rolling Stones, he said, "Oh hell, I'd be Keith Richards. About three separate doctors told him what he needed to stop doing. He went to all their funerals."

In McChrystal's command, Lambo's style represented an unprecedented departure from previous U.S. military history—a command made up of elite Special Forces soldiers who'd climbed the ranks through secret operations and daring raids. Generally, they'd been in charge of a few thousand of the most brilliant people in the service, and they were now running an army that numbered in the hundreds of thousands. It was the largest military force Special Forces operators had ever commanded. A drawback: McChrystal and Lamb were used to dealing with the best of the best, high IQs, not the dumbness of the hated Big Army.

"This is crap retirement," he said. He could have been in Chile snowboarding, or riding his motorcycle to a chalet in Switzerland. But it was hard to leave the comradeship behind. "A lot of people say, Graeme, you don't seem to have many friends. I say, that's no surprise. If people don't really like me, I don't really give a shit. But the truth is, I have quite a number of acquaintances. Most people in life are like that. They mistake the word *acquaintance* for *friend*. A friendship that I would understand is companionship, a comrade. That is forged in difficult circumstances where his or her endeavors have given you a chance that otherwise wouldn't have been there, because they believed in what you are doing and who you were. Those sorts of relationships are hard-forged. But those friendships are few and far between."

He started off the interview quoting Kipling and *Apollo 13:* "Savage wars peace," he called the war in Afghanistan, describing the situation as "like *Apollo 13,* heading out to the moon, with a bloody great hole in the side, bleeding oxygen." He talked about McChrystal and his disdain for politicians. "The soldier's lifetime experience is command and leadership. You tend not to be a comedian or a clown. You tend to be a pretty straight shooter. We are not politicians. I think it was General Sherman's brother who wrote him: Will you take up politics? Sherman wrote back: Why would I? He who's not a dollar in debt will never be a politician." We live in politics, he said, we operate around politics—but, he said, if as Clausewitz wrote, war is an extension of politics—"he didn't finish his sentence: To politics you must return."

He said men like himself and McChrystal were never driven by money—like a bloke from Goldman Sachs—but by something "mightier than the self, a great endeavor undertaken by men who knew what it meant to be in the arena."

The arena: It was a favorite concept for men like Lamb, capturing a dangerous and seductive worldview when applied to war. The idea came from Theodore Roosevelt's famous speech, trashing critics and valuing the experience of risk over all else. "It is not the critic who counts . . . The credit belongs to the man who is actually in the arena, whose face is marred by dust and sweat and blood, who strives valiantly, who errs, and who comes up short again and again . . ." I'd heard other generals use the quote in Iraq. What mattered wasn't what the war was about, or what might or might not be accomplished; what mattered was that there was an inherent value in being a man, in going into action, in bleeding. There was little difference in victory or failure. The sacrifice of blood had an almost spiritual value beyond politics, beyond success, beyond good and evil; blood and sweat and pain made up its own ideology, existing within its own moral universe of a very narrowly defined concept of honor and bravery. It was as brave and honorable to take a bullet for the brotherhood as it was to cover up a bullet's mistake. It didn't matter that in Afghanistan, the U.S. military had come up short again and again. What mattered is that they tried. The simple and terrifying reality, forbidden from discussion in America, was that despite spending $600 billion a year on the military, despite having the best fighting force the world had ever known, they were getting their asses kicked by illiterate peasants who made bombs out of manure and wood. The arena acted as a barrier, protecting their sacrifices from the uncomfortable realities of the current war—that it might be a total waste of time and resources that historians would look back on cringing, in the same way we looked back on the Soviets and the British misadventures there.

"I'll be here as long as it takes," he told me. "Just don't tell the wife that. This is high-stakes poker, this is a world-class game here. We're playing for these chips: blood and treasure. The grim reaper is absolutely going to get us all. So why slow down?"

I saw what the guys meant about Lamb—his freewheeling thought process didn't lend itself to sound bites. Lamb kept hitting an idea that McChrystal had first mentioned at the bar in Paris, and then I'd seen it in action at JFM. The loyalty to McChrystal—the desire to make him happy and to please him—often ended with the general getting an inaccurate picture of what was actually taking place. Men like Lamb and McChrystal told themselves they operated within a strict code of honor. A brotherhood and friendship, unique to the warrior brand, trumped all other values. And this is where I saw the flaw. How could they, at the same time, be involved in cover-ups—with Tillman, with torture, with endless allegations of reckless civilian killings? How did those actions fit into the images they had of themselves as honorable men? The answer, I believed, was that they considered the loyalty that they felt for one another as the highest measure of integrity. Any crime or transgression, any acts of immorality they committed or ordered were excused, in their own minds, by the high principles that guided them. Any act of violence, any atrocity, any action they were called upon or felt compelled to do in order to complete the mission and protect their own pack—whether it was leaking to the press or forcing a president down a path he didn't want to take—they saw as acceptable.

The military culture was by nature authoritarian, and it was there they were most comfortable. Even if, as Special Forces operators, they pushed against its rigidness, they still felt more at home among their brothers on the inside than on the outside. In fact, with the Special Forces, the element of separateness, the insulated feeling of superiority was even greater. They could do things that other men couldn't do, and had done them. Good or bad—if it was the mission, then it was permissible. If it was for us against them, it was inherhentyly right. If it took place in the arena, it was sublime. What wasn't permissible was breaking trust, or what they viewed as trust—straying outside the pack. The decade of war had hardened these feelings, creating an almost insurmountable boundary between them and the rest of society. The media just didn't play up this romantic image of warriors; the men held dearly to the romantic image themselves. They were willing to protect one another, to die for one another. That was the value that they cherished. And if you weren't part of the team, your motives were immediately suspect—impure, like the motives of politicians or diplomats. The base reasons that drove others—money and power—were not what drove them, or so they told themselves. They yearned for a pure relationship—it was a kind of love that could only be found in a world they saw reflected in themselves.

I walked back to the headquarters building with Lamb. I waited with Duncan for my last scheduled sit-down interview with Mike Flynn. We took seats next to a tree in the beer garden. Duncan sat in on the interview with me.

"I just want to establish that this is on the record," Duncan said.

"You don't mind if I eat this apple, do you? On the record?" Flynn replied, taking a bite from an apple.

I asked him about the political opposition he received to his plans.

"I spend 80 percent of my day easily fighting our own system," he said.

How about an exit strategy?

"No. I'm looking at long-term, enduring solutions."

"A lot of people dig who you guys are, they dig your plan. But they say, hey, you should have been here six years ago."

"Yeah, we should have left five years ago," Flynn said. "Karzai had been elected in a free and fair election. We should have said, 'Hey, we are ready to get the international community to help develop this country, but you're on your own.' We keep plodding along, and we made huge mistakes. The government got lazy. They got lazy because we were doing too much for them."

I'd wanted to get Flynn to elaborate on his theory of intelligence gathering. Whatever gets reported, he told me, think the opposite.

"What I want people to do is get rid of your biases," Flynn said. "You see something occur, everything was wonderful. What's the opposite of that?"

He paused.

"You came in here and you talk to me and you seem like a friendly guy," he said. "Maybe you're not."

"I'm a friendly guy," I said. "I'm also a reporter, and that's a caveat."

I had a final question: Were there any historical precedents that you look at where a foreign power accomplished something here?

"Genghis Khan," Duncan said.

"He extended himself, he wasn't from here," Flynn said. "When you look at the history of the country, everyone who came here to dominate, they came here for the wrong reasons. Alexander the Great, Genghis Khan, the Russians . . . They failed to understand that the people of Afghanistan didn't want to be dominated. They wanted help."

I didn't bother pointing out that both the Russians and the British also thought they came here for noble reasons. The interview ended.

The beer garden was being taken over by the Europeans. It was Friday. The Dutch were setting up for a party. The soldiers dressed in orange colors, waving orange flags. One Dutch partier had made a burka—the traditional full-cover dress for Muslim females—all in orange. He was running around the beer garden, cheering. I resisted the urge to take a camera phone picture of the Dutchman in an orange burka—that kind of cultural insensitivity and mocking wouldn't have played well on the Internet.

I called my security guard to come pick me up. I ran into Dave Silverman outside the headquarters. He and Duncan were going to go back to

Washington, DC, soon to do advance work. "Breaking some china," as Duncan put it. Karzai and McChrystal had a visit planned there for the next week.

The Dutch party was picking up. I asked him what he thought.

"They're fucking celebrating going home," Dave said.

Over the next few days, I finished up my interviews. No big revelations, except that Command Sergeant Major Michael Hall compared McChrystal to John Paul Vann, an important American military official in the Vietnam War. Vann died in a helicopter crash in 1972. His life story would come to represent the tragedy of that war, plagued by a disturbing personal life and the embrace of ideas he once knew to be flawed. Hall had known McChrystal since the early eighties. I wondered why he would make the comparison, and figured that he didn't really mean it.

39 | "I DIDN'T EVEN KNOW WE WERE FIGHTING THERE"

MAY 10–14, 2010, WASHINGTON, DC

Karzai is staying at the Willard InterContinental Hotel—he's rolling with a big entourage and an even bigger Secret Service detail. The block in the back of the hotel is closed off, lined with black SUVs and crew-cut security guards with earpieces and concealed pistols. The entranceway has a large tent extending from it, a sniper shield, to block the visibility of seeing when Karzai arrives and leaves.

This is Karzai's make-up tour. A month earlier, he'd threatened to join the Taliban after NSC chief James Jones had told reporters publicly that the White House was cracking down on Karzai's corruption. That didn't sit well with Hamid—he throws a fit. The White House backs away—this week, his first visit to the capital since Obama became president, is a way to smooth things over. To mark the new beginning of what Hillary Clinton will call a "long-term partner" and a "friend."

McChrystal's team has packed in a tight schedule for Karzai, and they're getting pushback from the White House. McChrystal wants to bring Karzai to Fort Campbell, Kentucky, where he can visit with troops who are preparing to go to Afghanistan. The White House is uneasy about this; it might make it seem that we're fighting for Karzai—and we know how fucked up Karzai is—rather than for the greater Afghanistan and to defeat terrorists. How about bringing him to Arlington National Cemetery? the White House suggests. Duncan nixes this idea—he doesn't think it's too good a visual to have a Muslim president getting photographed in front of rows of white crosses.

A compromise: Send him to Walter Reed, the medical center in upper Washington, DC, Springs, Maryland, that takes care of wounded American soldiers and Marines.

It's Karzai's second hospital visit in a month—McChrystal had brought him out to the field hospital in Bagram, where he made the rounds, gave a few less than inspirational speeches, and posed for photos with wounded U.S. and Afghan soldiers. At Walter Reed, it's the same pattern—though the reception from Americans is only superficially friendly, according to a wounded soldier at the hospital. ("We fucking hate Karzai," a soldier at Walter Reed will explain to me months later. "He's lucky none of us had guns.") At one point, Karzai talks to three American soldiers who've been wounded in Uruzgan province. He looks up from the bed and shouts to McChrystal, "General, I didn't even know we were fighting in Uruzgan!"

The next day, Karzai visits the White House for a sit-down meeting with Obama, Biden, and their top advisors. Karzai goes on at length, reminiscing about his love for Afghanistan. He also starts defending his brother, Ahmed Wali Karzai. He's a businessman, Karzai explains. "He's innocent," Karzai tells Obama. ("I was with him up until he said *innocent*," McChrystal will tell his staff later. "I think he went a little too far with *innocent*.") McChrystal explains to the president the plan for the upcoming operation in Kandahar. Biden is shocked: "This looks like CT-Plus," he exclaims at the meeting. Counterterrorism plus, the plan that Biden had recommended from the beginning, which called for far fewer troops and no nation-building. White House officials are also confused: What McChrystal is doing in Kandahar doesn't seem to be what he'd promised the White House earlier. He doesn't impress them—and it will be held against him a few weeks later.

After the meeting, Karzai and Obama hold a press conference. The White House press corps fills up the rows of seats, with a few additions. Afghan journalists on the trip to cover Karzai's visit. A female Afghan reporter is excited to be there: She's walking around, taking pictures of herself in the White House. The Washington press corps is not amused—there are a few hisses for her to sit down, to take her seat, she's getting in the way of the camera shots.

There is nothing to shoot yet: Obama and Karzai haven't entered the room.

A reporter from NBC News stands up, staring directly into a camera seven seats away, and delivers an unbroken monologue about what to expect.

Important visit. Mending fences. Rebuilding relationships. The reset button.

McChrystal, Hillary, Mullen, Gates, and Eikenberry come in through the side door and sit down in the front row.

The Afghan journalist is still walking around—she again tries the patience of the American press corps.

"Get down, sit down," cameramen yell at her.

She sits down.

The two men walk in. The room erupts in the clicks and clacks of cameras capturing every step to the two podiums.

Obama—he's gotten older. He's aged. He's graying. He's different from the junior senator I saw four years ago in Baghdad. He was on his first trip to Iraq then. He'd come into the U.S. embassy and had a press conference with reporters stationed in the capital. It was January of 2006, and only a handful of reporters showed up. After the press conference, Obama asks the reporters if we want to stay and have a private chat. We agree; the journalists sit down in a semicircle around him.

"Tell me what's really going on," he says.

A journalist from *The New York Times* tells him that the situation is as bad as we said it is in the newspapers and magazines. He makes a personal connection with us. It works. I got a picture with him after the press conference was over.

The Obama at the podium is changed. It's been a long four years.

Karzai stumbles as he speaks. He hasn't prepared a speech. He thanks everyone for their hospitality and then rambles on with sentence after sentence of platitudes.

Obama gives his remarks.

He points out that he didn't become president to have "civilian casualties," as if his only relationship with the war in Afghanistan is how it relates to his political career, as a writer from *Harper's Magazine* will later note.

"There is no denying progress," he says, "as I saw lights across Kabul when I landed, lights that would not have been visible just a few years earlier."

It's what Donald Rumsfeld and other Republican officials used to say about Baghdad, when that war was going horribly wrong. From a few thousand feet above, the lights are twinkling and everything looks fine. "It was one of our first impressions," one GOP official said in 2006, after landing in Baghdad at the height of the sectarian violence. "So many lights shining brightly." So it is to the language of the Iraq War that the Obama administration has turned—talk of progress, of city lights, of metrics like health care and education. Rhetoric that just a few years ago they would have mocked.

"We are steadily making progress," he says.

Does Obama really believe in the war? McChrystal and his team have their doubts. This press conference is a chore. No passion. One of the reasons he agreed to the escalation in Afghanistan was because he felt he would be politically vulnerable if he didn't—he might look weak on national security, he couldn't overrule his generals. He is allied on this issue mostly with Republicans, people who don't like him and are never going

Inside the W Hotel

to support him anyway. The stresses of power, the push and pull from the Pentagon had forced him, or he forced himself, to abandon his antiwar supporters. Did he really go along with a war he didn't believe we could win so he wouldn't get criticized for losing it?

The press conference ends and Karzai and Obama walk offstage.

McChrystal and his team are working out of the W Hotel, a corner suite on the tenth floor, a block down from where Karzai is staying. Earlier in the week, General Flynn and Jake had discussed the trip so far.

"You want to go meet with the NSC?" Jake asked him.

"No," Flynn groans. "Do I have to? Is it Jones?"

"No, it's not Jones," says Jake.

"Then no, I don't want to."

Flynn leans back in his chair. He's frustrated. Less than seventy-two hours in DC, and no one gets it.

"It's like they don't even know there's a war on," he says.

After the meeting at the White House with Obama and Karzai, McChrystal arrives at the W and takes his seat at the head of the table to confer with his staff. "Okay, guys," McChrystal says, and the meeting begins.

McChrystal reviews a new plan to supply $200 million worth of diesel generators to Kandahar. He says that Holbrooke wants to be at the head of it, but he'd rather have his own military commander in Kandahar handle it. "Let's not get brought into the palace politics on this one," he says. McChrystal talks about the meeting Obama had with Karzai. He spoke for thirty minutes about what it means to be an Afghan, McChrystal says, adding, Obama "hit every talking point they had given him."

"How'd the press conference go?" another staffer asks.

"Obama sounded stronger in the press conference than he's sounded before," McChrystal says.

"Like he's in charge," Jake says.

"Yeah," McChrystal answers.

At least Obama now sounded like he believed in the war, at least compared to West Point, the team thinks. More important, though, despite Obama having said in his speech that he wasn't going to do nation-building, the U.S. policy had shifted to nation-building, of handing out generators in Kandahar, what Secretary Clinton called a long and enduring partnership. A year after taking command, McChrystal has gotten exactly what he wanted from the president. His team had filled the policy vacuum, had sensed hesitancy, and rammed through the strategy they'd dreamed up. One senior military official on McChrystal's staff privately disagrees with the assessment on Karzai and Obama, however. He doesn't think the relationship between the United States and Karzai is stable at all. "This is just a honeymoon period," he tells me. "I doubt if it's going to last two weeks."

40 | THE CONCLUDING CONVERSATIONS WITH DUNCAN BOOTHBY, GENERAL PETRAEUS FACE-PLANTS IN CONGRESS, AND THE STORY BREAKS WHILE I WATCH AMERICAN HELICOPTER PILOTS KILL INSURGENTS

MAY 14 TO JUNE 23, 2010, WASHINGTON, DC; WEST POINT; MILTON, VERMONT; AND KANDAHAR

The plan: Come interview the general. Meet us in Paris.

Volcano. Booze. Bus trip. Yikes.

New plan: Follow us to Berlin. Fuck it, let's do Kandahar and Kabul. Join us in Washington, DC.

The vision: McChrystal on the cover of *Rolling Stone*. McChrystal holding his nunchuks. A close-up of McChrystal's face, half in shadow, half in the light. The life lived in secrets and death etched in wrinkles. McChrystal is a rock star. McChrystal is cool. McChrystal is a warrior poet, a philosopher, a risk taker, a snake eater. McChrystal is badass. McChrystal is wild&crazy&serious&sober. McChrystal drinks hard. McChrystal pays attention. McChrystal's kid has a blue Mohawk. McChrystal is Patton, is MacArthur, is Sherman, is Grant, is Big Man historic. McChrystal is in *Rolling Stone* to speak to the twentysomething lieutenants and captains who are out there fighting his war. How could you not fall in love with him? How could you not see what we see? How could you not swoon? How could you not write a 110 percent blowjob profile that just plainly fucking rocked? Earn it.

I'd spent the week in Washington, interviewing State Department and White House officials and hanging out with McChrystal's staff. The deadline for my story was a week away. I'd picked up another vibe in Washington, DC: Officials in the White House weren't as enamored with McChrystal as those in the Pentagon. They were still pissed about the leak of the strategic assessment and the failure to explain the rationale of the Kandahar offensive to the president and his staff. I had seventy pages of single-spaced notes, over twenty hours of audio recordings, and I was still riding high from the monthlong assignment. I'd rented a car in Washington and planned to drive back home to Vermont, stopping at West Point along the way to look at McChrystal's old yearbooks.

I met with Duncan outside the W Hotel. He was on his way to pick up *New York Times* columnist Tom Friedman. Friedman was a friend of McChrystal's, and the most influential foreign policy columnist in the country. "When I took over the job," McChrystal had told me, "Tom said, 'You're going to hear a lot of criticism. Don't pay attention to the bullshit.'"

As I joined him on the walk to meet Friedman, Duncan said he had a few issues he wanted to raise.

"There's concern that you might write about the night in Paris, any offhand comments they might have made about our allies and, you know, about others in the administration and, you know, the soldiers in Kandahar."

I told him I was going to write about all those things and that he had known that all along.

He chastised me, asking me not to go too hard.

"Remember," he said. "We have a war to win."

Friedman came out of his hotel. I introduced myself to him, and he told me to call him if I wanted any other perspectives on McChrystal.

I picked up a rental car at Union Station and drove five hours to West Point, near Highland Falls, New York. I spent the next day at the West Point library, where I found writings of the young Stanley McChrystal. I couldn't believe the stories he'd written—a weird case of life imitating juvenilia. Over thirty years earlier, he'd written fictional accounts of themes that he'd find playing out in Afghanistan, like that of a young soldier yelling at his commander about the injustice of counterinsurgency. It was a scene that I'd seen replayed at JFM two weeks earlier, yet in the real-life version, McChrystal was the one getting yelled at. He'd also written an editorial about why it was a bad idea for women to be allowed at the academy and published an issue of his literary magazine all in pink to mock the decision. Before leaving, I went to get a look at "the Area," the courtyard where cadets who'd earned demerits had to walk off their punishment. McChrystal and many others had spent hours of their lives pacing this block of concrete. A lone cadet stood there, walking back and forth.

I got home to Vermont. I wrote the first draft of the story in forty-eight hours, sending a rambling fifteen thousand words to my editor, Eric Bates. The draft expressed my conflicting feelings—I'd liked hanging out with McChrystal and his team, yet I hated the war. Everything that I'd seen and heard and knew about the war would not reflect well on them—they were an unchecked force, steamrolling the civilian leadership, flipping them the giant bird along the way. What they told me, I realized, revealed the attitudes behind one of the most brazen assaults on civilian control of the military that the Pentagon's generals had ever attempted. Not that I didn't think all of their complaints were unjustified— if I were in their shoes, I'd probably be pissed if I thought that the civilians who gave the orders didn't actually appear to be committed to the war. On the other hand, McChrystal and other military officials had pushed Obama to get the mission they wanted. In Iraq, the generals could always blame Bush and Rumsfeld for starting the war—they just followed orders. Not so here: Though Obama had pushed fixing the war in Afghanistan during the campaign as a slap at Bush, he wouldn't have gotten much support if he had campaigned on tripling the size of the conflict. Obama resisted doing so, but the military leadership pushed hard and played dirty to get the war in Afghanistan they wanted. It shouldn't have come as much of a shock to McChrystal and his team that after getting politically jujitsued the White House would be less than enthusiastic.

Over the next three weeks, Eric and I went through two more drafts of the story. Under his guidance, the piece took shape. Eric had more than twenty-five years' experience in reporting and editing investigative pieces, earning seven National Magazine awards, the industry's highest honor. I knew McChrystal's team wouldn't be happy with the way the story was shaping up. It was the classic journalist dilemma. Janet Malcolm had famously described journalism as the art of seduction and betrayal. Any reporter who didn't see journalism as "morally indefensible" was either "too stupid" or "too full of himself," she wrote. I disagreed. Without shutting the door on the possibility that I was both stupid and full of myself, I'd never bought into the seduction and betrayal conceit. At most, journalism—particularly when writing about media-hungry public figures—was like the seduction of a prostitute. The relationship was transactional. They weren't talking to me because they liked me or because I impressed them; they were talking to me because they wanted the cover of *Rolling Stone*.

Should I not write it? On a personal level, part of me didn't want to disappoint McChrystal and Dave and Casey and Flynn and Duncan—part of me wanted to write a story that pleased them. Dave had even called me and left a voicemail, asking what I'd been up to. The month I spent with them was exciting, and I'd gotten a privileged view from inside a top military command. If I wrote the story I wanted to write, it would be years before I ever had that view again. The access I'd gotten was unprecedented. But what do you do with it? Bury the story? Write a puff piece to ensure further access? Or write what actually happened?

I knew, too, that McChrystal and his team could play rough with reporters and hadn't hesitated in the past to launch personal smear campaigns against them. Three months earlier, Jerome Starkey, a reporter for *The Times* of London, had broken a story about the killing of two pregnant Afghan women, a teenage girl, and two other men by a Special Forces team. McChrystal's command had tried to cover it up, originally issuing a press release and claiming to CNN that the Taliban had killed the women in an "honor killing." That wasn't true, and the more Starkey dug, the more horrible the story became: The killings happened during a night raid, and the ISAF soldiers even dug bullets out of the bodies of the Afghan women to hide the atrocity. Rather than own up to what had happened, Admiral Gregory Smith and Duncan Boothby called up rival outlets and reporters to "brief" against Starkey, saying he wasn't a credible journalist because he used to write for *The Sun*, a British tabloid. Smith sent out a press release which named Starkey twice, saying his allegations of a "cover-up" incident were "categorically false"; the release also said he "incorrectly quoted" Admiral Smith. Within days, though, Starkey's reporting was confirmed by a UN investigation, an Afghan investigation, and a story in *The New York Times*—there had been an atrocity, there had been a cover-up, and Smith and ISAF had been lying. Sheepishly, Smith released another statement, acknowledging ISAF's responsibility for five deaths. They quietly took the press releases down from the ISAF website.

No one on McChrystal's staff, or anyone in command of the Special Forces unit responsible for the killing, was punished.

It was June 15. I took a break from writing to check the Internet. There was an incredible headline on the Drudge Report about General David Petraeus. I clicked through and watched the clip from C-SPAN.

Petraeus was testifying in Washington at the Dirksen Senate Office Building on Capitol Hill. I'd learn later that he was jet-lagged from a trip to the Middle East. I'd watched him testify half a dozen times before—most memorably when he was the commander of U.S. troops at the height of the Iraq War. I didn't notice anything wrong, but a source close to him would later tell me that Petraeus didn't drink enough water that morning: "No one wants to be sitting there with a full bladder," a senior military official close to Petraeus told me. "Those who ask the questions get to go in and out—but if you're the one sitting there in front of the cameras, you have to stay there the entire time."

Senator John McCain took the floor. McCain wanted Petraeus, the commander of all U.S. forces in the Middle East and Central Asia, to say that the deadline President Obama had set for withdrawing U.S. troops from Afghanistan—July 2011—was a bad idea. Petraeus was no fan of the deadline, but he was too shrewd to be drawn into such an obvious spat with his commander in chief. As he evaded McCain's badgering with an almost Clintonian ease, McCain started to get frustrated.

"Do you believe that we will begin a drawdown of forces in July 2011, given the situation as it exists today?" McCain prodded, rephrasing his question for the third time.

"It's not a given as the *situation* exists today," Petraeus corrected. "It's given as *projections* are for that time."

"You believe we can begin a drawdown in July 2011, under the projected plans we have?" McCain persisted.

"That's the policy, and I support it," Petraeus answered, taking a sip of water.

"I understand you support the policy," McCain snapped. He tried again to press Petraeus for an answer, and even resorted to quoting Vice President Joe Biden: "In July of 2011, you're going to see a whole lot of people moving out—bet on it." But a minute later, the expression on McCain's face suddenly changed from one of exasperation to befuddlement. Petraeus had fainted, slumping forward in his chair. "Oh my God," McCain gasped.

The general regained consciousness a few seconds later. He was escorted out of the hearing room with the help of his aides. He returned under his own power a half hour later. He'd gotten dehydrated, a combination of missing breakfast, jet lag, and, critically, not enough water. But the committee, shaken by the unexpected turn of events, decided to adjourn for the day.

It seemed like a strange omen. A crack in the facade of Petraeus over the most critical issue of the war—the military still bucking Obama's promise to start drawing down American troops.

That week, Duncan called me. He'd been in contact with the fact-checkers from *Rolling Stone*.

I went outside on my porch to smoke a cigarette.

We talked for about forty minutes. I went through the story with him—I told him again I was writing about the night in Paris. I told him I was writing about the tensions between the civilian and military sides.

"That night in Paris," he said. "That was sort of off the record."

Sort of off the record? What did that mean? That was the first time he had said that. It wasn't true, either.

"Come on, man, you had asked that I put it in proper context. I've done that."

"Your story," he said. "It sounds serious. I was expecting it to be fun."

"No, it's pretty serious," I said.

"Should I be worried about it?"

How to answer?

"Well, it's probably going to cause you a headache for a few days, but you guys have been through worse," I said, thinking of the London conference, the *60 Minutes* interview, and the leak of the strategic assessment.

"I'd like to work with you again," he said. "There's another story you could do—about Karzai and the palace."

"Sounds great," I said.

"If, that is, we like your story."

"Yeah, well, it's been good working with you. I appreciate all your help. Hope we can work together again sometime."

He hung up. I hung up. It was business. Everyone involved was a professional. I'd heard from other sources that Duncan was worried about what the story would say—he'd been telling people about the wild times in Paris and Berlin. He'd told a State Department official that the story would "either be fun, or end my career."

Rolling Stone closed the story. It was set for publication next week. Lady Gaga, not Stan McChrystal, was going to be on the cover.

On Saturday, I got back on a plane from the Burlington International Airport to JFK to Dubai, then another Safi Airways flight to Kabul. By Monday morning, I'd taken a C-130 from Kabul to Kandahar Airfield. My next assignment for *Men's Journal* was to embed with a Kiowa helicopter unit.

The Kiowas were small, two-seat scout helicopters that had been around since Vietnam. Lately they were being used like attack helicopters for close-quarters fighting, flying near constant patrols in southern Afghanistan. It was one of the more dangerous jobs in the war—certainly one of the most dangerous aircrafts to pilot. The Kiowas were shot at regularly and had a reputation for crashing—the second-highest crash rate among Army aircraft.

I was staying in a room at the media support center, a two-floor building with a series of dorms on the first floor and a second floor with a public affairs staff. It looked like a metallic barn with a flat roof. It had been a long day. I'd spent it outside on the flight line, getting briefings about the helicopters. I was feeling dehydrated. The temperature had risen to about 120 degrees.

I figured I would have a couple of days on the ground to finish my Kiowa story before the McChrystal story dropped on Thursday. I assumed the story would get some attention in Washington, maybe get in the news for a few hours. But I didn't expect much else. I'd been writing about the wars in Iraq and Afghanistan for the past five years. Usually, most news stories and the wars themselves were ignored. Back in the United States, the media were focused on the Deepwater Horizon explosion and the BP oil spill in the Gulf of Mexico.

I didn't have Internet access, and only had two cell phones with me— one with an international number and another with a local Afghan number.

I was about to go to bed around one A.M. My cell phone buzzed. It was a text message from a friend. It said that the Associated Press was running with a story, quoting my article, saying that McChrystal had felt "betrayed" by Eikenberry over the leak of the cable he'd written to Washington.

Huh. The story had leaked. I shut my phone off and tried to go to sleep. I wasn't very successful. A few hours later, I turned my phone back on. There were about fifteen new text messages.

Lucian Read, the photographer I was on assignment with, was getting his cameras ready.

"Hey, man, looks like my story is getting some pickup," I said.

We had breakfast, then waited for our ride across the base to take us out to the flight lines. We were going to get a demonstration of how the Kiowas worked.

The airfield had undergone a massive expansion in recent months. There were row after row of helicopters parked, separated by stalls made up of blast walls, each parking spot marked with a letter and a number. There were Apache helicopters, Blackhawks, and Kiowas, lined up like rental cars at Hertz. The temperature was already more than 100 degrees.

The metal on the aircraft burned bare skin; an egg could literally be cooked on the concrete runway.

We were hanging out with the pilots and mechanics, climbing in and out of the aircraft.

An Apache pilot and I started chatting.

"Hey, man, have you seen this McChrystal story everyone is talking about?"

"Uh, yeah, I wrote it."

"What? That's fucking crazy!"

I got a call from a friend at *The Washington Post*. Could I send him a copy of the story? I didn't have my own copy of the PDF from *Rolling Stone*, but a contact at CNN had sent a leaked copy to me.

I ran in off the flight line, logged on to a computer, and forwarded him the PDF that had been forwarded to me from CNN.

It was the first time I'd checked my e-mail since I'd arrived in Kandahar. That was unusual, but it had been a hassle finding good Internet connections. There were dozens of e-mails regarding the story. I was surprised by how fast it was spreading. It wasn't up on the website yet, but it seemed dozens of people in the government and the media had copies.

There was also an e-mail from Duncan.

"Michael, read your story. It has certainly created a reaction. What are you planning for promotion? Doing broadcast?"

"D, thanks for the note," I responded. "Yes, a bit surprised. Not sure what RS has planned, but will give you heads up."

There was another e-mail from a McChrystal staffer.

"McChrystal's been called back to Washington," the e-mail said.

I took Lucian aside.

"Dude, McChrystal just got called back to Washington. It looks like I'm going to have to deal with this now."

I spent another few hours with the Kiowa unit, then headed back to the media support center. I had free time until three A.M. the next morning, when the Kiowa unit was going to come pick us up and bring us out on a morning flight. The pilots would wake up at three A.M. to be ready for a six A.M. flight.

I spent the next ten hours on the phone, doing radio and television interviews.

I had a bad sunburn. I was dehydrated and wasn't eating anything. I didn't know which way the story was going to go. I kept getting texts about whether or not McChrystal would be fired.

I didn't think it was possible for him to be fired. No way.

Without good communications and e-mail, I felt vulnerable. I felt like the situation could at any minute spiral out of control.

My phones kept ringing. It was triggering some strange kind of post-traumatic stress. I was in a war zone. I was not in a comfortable place. I felt like I had when I was fifteen and had eaten two tabs of acid and a bag of mushrooms at a warehouse in downtown Montreal. As the skyline had started to collapse, I put on Pink Floyd's *Dark Side of the Moon*, which, in retrospect, had been a mistake.

I was, in the parlance of the times, about to be in the middle of a "media firestorm."

I got another text. McChrystal had issued an apology.

They weren't denying it—which would have been difficult to do anyway because of the tape recordings and notes I had of the interviews. And they weren't personally attacking me yet, either. By apologizing, they had confirmed the validity of the story. I was relieved.

I had to calm down. This was me doing my job. In a media firestorm, I knew I needed to be clearheaded and rational, yet the excitement and adrenaline and fatigue conspired to put me at my least clearheaded and rational. The bigger the wave a story makes, the bigger the receding tide of bullshit is likely to be. McChrystal apologized and he'd been ordered back to Washington, so the media hadn't gotten around to training its fire on me yet.

At around midnight, I hung up the phone after another interview. I'd been on the phone for almost ten hours straight, talking.

Lucian pulled me aside. "Mike, earlier, you sounded good. That time, not so much."

I needed to get out of Kandahar. I kept getting warnings from friends and other colleagues in the media: It's not safe for you there. Someone might try to take you out or attack you. They meant Americans. I thought the fears were overblown, but it added to a sense of insecurity in an already insecure place.

At three A.M., one of the pilots came over to pick Lucian and me up. I drank a Red Bull to stay awake. We picked up the other pilots from their barracks across town and piled into the van.

Captain Stephen Irving got into the van last. He was leading the mission. The temperature had dropped to a bearable 75 degrees. Floodlights and kicked-up dust lent the black sky an eerie pinkish tint, giving the flattened air base the feel of an empty fairground after the carnies have cleared out. The hum of diesel generators and the overflight of jets were a constant background noise.

We crawled along the road. There was a ten-mile-per-hour speed limit on base, and it was well enforced.

I found a certain kind of peace: Focus on the story with the Kiowa pilots.

"You'll get a ticket if you don't have your civilian driver's license from the states on your person," said Chief Warrant Officer Joshua Price, Irving's copilot.

"Oh shit, I forgot my PT belt, too. I wonder if they're going to shoot me," another pilot chimed in. He was talking about the bright orange or yellow reflective belts that U.S. troops are required to wear on base so they don't get hit by vehicles. Like the speed limit, it was one of those strange rules in a war zone—rockets might be landing every night, a Taliban dude with an RPG might be preparing, right now, to blow your tail rotor off, but you can't leave home without a bright orange reflector belt.

"If we get pulled over, you should know we're prepared to throw you under the bus," Officer Price told the pilot who'd forgotten his belt. Price was from Alabama and spoke in an expansive southern drawl. "We should make it our mission in Banshee troop to get so many tickets they run out of fucking paper."

The van arrived at Banshee troop headquarters. There was a plywood porch with a leather couch and a flat-screen television, which opened up into a briefing room with a large table and maps. A line of the pilots' old-school cavalry hats—worn with dress uniforms, like what Robert Duvall wears in *Apocalypse Now*—were hung up along the top of the wall, complete with sets of honorary silver and gold spurs.

"You check out your M4 already?" Irving asked his copilot, looking in the small armory, where the pilots hung their rifles and pistols.

"Got it," said Price, picking up the rifle. "If you ain't Cav, you ain't shit," he said under his breath, the unofficial motto of the unit.

Before the briefings started, the pilots dropped off their gear at their helicopters. The helicopter runway had been built out in recent months, part of an $850 million expansion, taking over land that used to be an old Soviet minefield.

Price and Irving were weighed down by almost thirty pounds of gear: rifle, pistol, ammo, water, night vision goggles, a med kit, PowerBars, body armor, binoculars, and flight helmet. Price had a pair of gloves, the same kind NASCAR drivers used, made by Southwest Motorsports.

They started walking out to their bird.

Irving, a father of two, thirty-four years old. There was a reason he'd been chosen to lead the mission that the reporter and photographer were on. He didn't give any hint of that wild-man culture that Kiowa pilots were known for. What'd he think about the poker game the warrant officers were playing the other night? I don't know anything about that, he told me. (Gambling is against the rules.) How many hours of sleep did you get last night? Ten hours, he said, because that's more or less what the regulations say he has to sleep, even though I find it hard to believe. He has a crew cut and he's on his third combat tour—one in Iraq, two in Afghanistan. When I asked him to tell me a war story, something hairy, something nuts, he did—but it was all very technical, methodical, on-message. He doesn't even swear, which is an incredible feat in this environment where *fucks* and *shits* and *motherfucking cocksuckers* pass for transitional verbs.

They got to the helicopter they were flying. Price nicknamed it Gertrude.

The preflight ritual: Irving cocked his pistol and put it in his side holster. They loaded up their M4s, which were strapped to the dash—not as a last resort in case they wreck, but loaded up with tracers so they could get into rifle range, lean out the door, take aim, and shoot. ("Some of these guys have confirmed kills just shooting the M4 out the aircraft," a helicopter mechanic told me.)

Irving explained that pilots gauge enemy and friendly areas by the reaction of the Afghans they fly over. Friendlies wave and smile. Enemies throw rocks and show the bottoms of the soles of their feet, an insult in the Muslim world.

Price and Irving wrapped up the preflight check.

On the way back for the briefing, Price and Irving talked about an attack last week on a nearby American base. The Kiowas were called in to prevent the base from being overrun.

"They attacked the American base, ran a SVBIED [a car bomb, or Suicide Vehicle–Borne Improvised Explosive Device] through the wall, and tried to send two insurgents through the breach with suicide bombs," Irving said. "But as soon as Josh flew overhead—"

"The bomber paused and looked up. We saw a big explosion. A pink mist," said Price. The suicide bomber had prematurely exploded, killing only himself.

We passed through the tactical operations center on the way to the first briefing. There were two clocks on the wall. One had a sign underneath that said CLARKSVEGAS, set to the local time of their sleepy Tennessee hometown, Clarksville. The other clock next to it had a sign that said HELL. It was set to our local time in Kandahar. It was five A.M.

At 0645, Lieutenant Colonel Hank Taylor arrived at Banshee troop headquarters. He stood in front of a map of the area and explained the mission for today: Two Kiowas would go out and scout for improvised explosive devices along Highway One, and then be on call in case any American or Afghan troops came in contact. Lucian and I were going to be with Taylor in a Blackhawk, following along to be able to observe the Kiowas on their mission. Another Blackhawk was following with what was essentially a well-armed search-and-rescue team inside.

Taylor was about six feet five, thick. He's what folks in the military call a hard charger.

"Do your normal business," he told the eight pilots gathered in the room. "Be safe. This is not just a flight from Bagram or KAF. This is a combat zone out there, and there are people trying to shoot us down every day."

Taylor left and passed the brief over to Irving to get into the specifics. The briefing lasted thirty minutes. Irving compressed years of information and training into a language almost indecipherable to an outsider.

"Twenty-three June, scouts weapons, two, UH-60, 0800 to 1300, QRF at the back end. Risk assessment? You signed? Maps? Primarily one change, call sign Hard Luck Two-Three-One. I have one of the new pilot packs, with new calls signs, briefs, pod locations. Anybody tired? No. TAC charge. No change to that. No change to the EGI bridges, weight point loads, current as two-zero June. NVGS, should have them, spare batters. Camera. PCI on the camera. Data card, battery. Task work, lead scout aircraft nine-nine-six parked on foxtrot one long knife one-two. Config is rocket-rocket. Chuck's in the right seat, Quinn's is the left seat. We're going to match laser codes. One-one-one-seven. Load one is six-three. Alternates one-one. Load two is one-zero-zero-two. Trail Kiowa zero-two-one parked on alpha two long knife two-two. Got fifty cal and rocket. Josh is right seat. I'll be in left seat. Zero-one-five on road two. Mr. Bailey, your configuration today?"

Lucian and the pilots went to go get breakfast. I passed out on the couch on the porch, trying to catch another hour of sleep.

I woke up. The helicopters were ready. Time to fly.

I climbed into a Blackhawk, sitting across from Taylor. Next to me sat the unit's intelligence officer. I was glad they were going to take us up, but I didn't expect much. Originally, I'd wanted to go up in the actual Kiowa, but I wasn't allowed to for safety reasons. They wanted two people who knew how to pilot in the craft at all times. And, with the growing heat of the McChrystal story, it started to look like this assignment might be a total bust.

All of that went out of my mind as the helicopters took off.

Here we go.

The Kiowas flew low along Highway One, checking out a few places along the way where they believed insurgents might be placing possible IEDs. We were a few hundred feet above the birds, watching as they dropped up and down, zipping above telephone poles, following the road, every few minutes hovering to get a closer look at a car or a gathering of people. The doors to the Blackhawk were open, plastering our faces with wind. The Kiowas peeled off to the east, swooping over the red desert, endless blood-colored dunes and steep cliffs. We headed away from the villages, into the mountains, so the Kiowas could make sure their weapons were working. They took turns letting off rounds into the craggy mountainside: rockets and fifty caliber machine guns.

We passed over the city of Kandahar. "It's a bustling city," Taylor said. "When I was first here a few years ago, the place was dead. Now the industry is booming."

We'd been flying around for about an hour and nothing had happened. I was hot and tired. I was beginning to think I was screwed. This story wasn't going to happen, and with the way the things were playing out with McChrystal, I wondered how long it would be until reporting on Kandahar Airfield became impossible. I needed to see combat. I needed to see explosions. I needed to get close to the fighting. I needed to wrap this shit up and get the hell out of southern Afghanistan.

It was the twisted sickness of the war junky: There I was, waiting to witness death and destruction.

I started to fall asleep, doze off. Thinking about how I should get back to Kabul. Thinking about the e-mails I needed to return and the phone call I needed to make to Eric at *Rolling Stone*. I was starting to think that this flight was just a dog and pony show, that I was being kept away from the fighting and it was a total waste of time. I started worrying that my tape recorder and phone were going to fly out the door. (It was a strange fear I always had on helicopters—not about crashes or heat-seeking rockets, but that my laptop or notebook would fall out of the open door.) I searched for the best pocket to store my notebook so it didn't drop out if I fell asleep. I was thinking about keeping up to date with what was happening. Had McChrystal made it back to Washington? Had anyone else released any statements? What was the White House going to say . . .

The Kiowa helicopters buzzed low in the distance. The *thwump* of the Blackhawk blades lulled me to sleep.

My eyes closed. My head started to bob up and down.

"Troops in contact," Taylor yelled over the radio.

I woke up. Like a true professional, I dropped my pen. It rolled back under the Blackhawk seat. The soldier next to me handed me a new pen.

Along Highway One, I saw a convoy of American MRAPs. They'd been ambushed. Price and Irving, flying the tail helicopter, started to head in that direction. They were five minutes away from the firefight. Information about the enemy came in over the radio: They were heavily armed, with heavy machine guns and RPGs.

Already Irving was thinking tactically, he would tell me later. What was the best way to arrive without giving his position away to the enemy (usually flying very low, then popping up at the last second)? Because once the Kiowas showed up, the insurgents often fled. They needed to retain the element of surprise. I watched Irving's Kiowa shoot low across the ground.

Two minutes out, Irving raised the ground troops on the radio. They told him that they'd dismounted from their MRAPs and had pinned down a group of insurgents in an orchard. They were still taking heavy fire. Irving was focused. The adrenaline was racing. He was thinking: Where are all the friendlies? Where is the enemy and what are his capabilities? How can I take them out or suppress them—or, as he would put it, "maximize ballistic effect on the enemy"?

I was thinking tactically, too: Shit, if this is a real shoot-out, then that means I have my story, I have my scene. I can get the fuck out of Kandahar.

The Blackhawks pulled up in the air to give us a view of the battle. Taylor pointed to a puff of red smoke that was rising up.

"Five to eight insurgents, small arms and RPG," Taylor said.

The soldiers on the ground had tossed a can of smoke to mark the position of the insurgents.

Another pop of smoke—this is yellow.

"My position is the yellow smoke," the ground element called up over the radio.

The two Kiowas dove down for a final look over their target. Price picked out where the insurgents were believed to be hiding—the orchard. Irving grabbed the control stick. He moved the yellow button over to the right, switching from rockets to his fifty caliber machine gun.

"Friendlies one o'clock low. Tally friendlies. Turning left. Enemy in sight. Roger in sight. Roger. Clear to engage . . ." Irving said over the radio.

Irving pressed the yellow firing switch, the trigger. The recoil was deafening. The helicopter shook, as did Irving's jaw, as he would later describe the moment to me.

For about five more minutes, the Kiowas stuck around, making sure the American patrol could continue.

"Two insurgents confirmed KIA," Taylor told me, by aircraft fire. "Scout weapons team two engaged, disrupted the enemy."

We returned to base. Two insurgents confirmed killed. That was good enough for me. Two faceless dead guys, the enemy, with all the Americans coming home. A perfect story.

I was wide awake now. Now I could leave Kandahar without feeling guilty.

Back at the base, one of the pilots told me a public affairs officer was looking for me.

I found the public affairs officer. We talked. We agreed it was best if I left Kandahar. I'd become a distraction and I was distracted. More important, I had gotten my story. We agreed on that, too.

It was usually difficult to get on a flight leaving Kandahar. The public affairs officer told me not to worry. There was a seat waiting for me on the next plane out.

I checked my e-mail at the media affairs center. Eric at *Rolling Stone* asked me to write up a blog post. McChrystal had arrived in Washington and they wanted to put something up on the web before he met with Obama.

I typed out a blog post on e-mail.

Right when I was about to hit send, I heard two loud booms.

"Rockets!" someone yelled.

Everyone in the media center dove to the floor. I was flat on my face under a desk.

The all-clear alarm sounded a few minutes later. I went back to my e-mail. The computer screen was dark. The power had gone out. I lost my blog post.

I needed to get to a computer where I could use e-mail. A young public affairs officer told me there wasn't time to waste. I was going to miss my flight. I said okay. I grabbed my gear and they drove me down the road to the passenger terminal. It was another nondescript building, two floors. It was a weird imitation of a normal airport terminal; they even had a security check to scan the bags, despite the fact that the majority of the passengers would be armed with assault rifles.

After I got through security, I asked if I could use a computer to send off my blog post. The public affairs officer showed me a back room where the two Air Force personnel who ran the terminal were sitting in an office.

Both were looking at their computer screens when I came in. They were reading a story called "The Runaway General."

The Air Force woman minimized her copy and let me sit down.

"Have you seen this story?" she asked me.

"Yeah, I wrote it," I said.

"No shit."

She thought it was pretty hilarious. She was a fan of *The Rachel Maddow Show*, which I had been on the night before over the phone. Coincidentally, I had a brand-new Rachel Maddow baseball cap with me, which I gave her.

I finished typing up my blog post and sent it to Eric. By that time, a few other soldiers had printed out copies of the *Rolling Stone* story and asked me to sign it. I joked that it wasn't going to add to any eBay value, feeling less nervous.

I waited on the second floor of the terminal for the flight to arrive. Thirty minutes later, another air force sergeant called out that there was a C-130 flight to Kabul boarding now. Everyone heading to Kabul lined up in a row, slinging their rucksacks on their backs and putting on their body armor and helmets. We walked in single file across an airstrip, the sun just beginning to go down. I carried my computer bag over my shoulder and a Kelty backpack on my back. I walked up the ramp of the C-130 and took a seat near the front of the cabin, strapping myself in with the metal clasps, sitting on the sagging red canvas jump seats.

I looked around the cabin of the plane. Three other soldiers were reading printout copies of the *Rolling Stone* story.

The plane was delayed.

"Why are we waiting?" a soldier asked.

"We're waiting for a one-star," the soldier next to him responded.

"Shit, he might be running this thing soon enough," a third soldier said.

I tilted my helmet down over my head. I'd never seen a story take off so quickly around an American military base overseas. The soldiers seemed to be reacting pretty positively to the story, too. The general sense that the war was totally fucked was so widespread, not many disagreed with the thesis. (A poll would later find that one out of three veterans of the wars in Iraq and Afghanistan would say the wars weren't worth fighting.) But I had the feeling that inside the cabin wasn't the best time for me to identify myself. I fell asleep. The flight to Kabul took forty-five minutes. My security guard picked me up and took me back to the CNN bureau.

E-mail was working. My phones were working.

The news broke.

President Barack Obama had accepted Stanley McChrystal's resignation.

He'd been fired.

Obama named General David Petraeus as his replacement.

There were thirty-eight missed calls on my phone.

PART IV
THE GRACEFUL EXIT

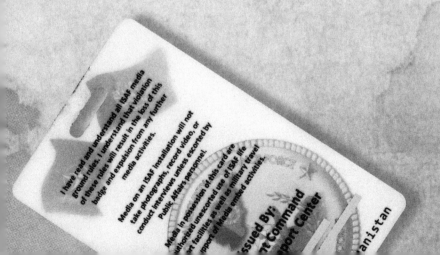

41 | "VERY, VERY BAD"

JUNE 22–23, 2010, KABUL AND WASHINGTON, DC

At two thirty A.M. on June 22, 2010, a close aide to General Stanley McChrystal walks up the stairs to the general's hooch above the situational awareness room. It's Spartan quarters, a single cot with a few wooden bookshelves and industrial-strength green carpets with a treadmill outside to work out on. The staffer knocks on the door and wakes up the general. The *Rolling Stone* story is out, the staffer tells him. "It's very, very bad," the aide says, according to an account in *The Washington Post.*

The A.P. is already running with the story, the aide explains—quoting him saying that the Eikenberry memo left him feeling "betrayed."

That's just the beginning of it. Biden—"bite me." Making fun of the French, making fun of Ambassador Holbrooke. And then the troops: The scene down south with the soldiers looks like they are in near mutiny. It doesn't look good. The night in Paris—"totally shit-faced."

He did have that fucking tape recorder running all the time. Can we attack him? It's going to be hard to deny the Paris night. Duncan had been telling the story to everyone who would listen.

McChrystal gets on the phone. He calls Bob Gates. He apologizes. What's the best way to handle it?

Preempt it. This too shall pass.

Holbrooke's phone rings. He's staying at the U.S. embassy across town in Kabul. He's half-asleep. He's had a brutal twenty-four hours; his helicopter had been fired upon while he was flying across Helmand. He's pissed that he's been woken up, not really understanding why. McChrystal tells him there's a *Rolling Stone* story coming out, and that he's said some embarrassing things in it. McChrystal apologizes to him.

"Stan, don't worry about it," Holbrooke tells him.

"I've submitted my resignation to Bob Gates."

"What?"

Holbrooke is wide awake now. He hangs up the phone. He dials Hillary.

"Stan McChrystal has submitted his resignation to Bob Gates."

"What?" Hillary says.

McChrystal continues to make phone calls. He gets through to Vice President Biden. Biden is on Air Force Two. It's around five thirty P.M. in the United States.

"Sir, I failed the mission," he tells Biden.

It's a quick call. Biden doesn't know what he's talking about. Hell, Biden has said a few things in his time to reporters that caused him trouble.

Biden asks his aide to get him a copy of the story. Biden reads the story. Biden is furious.

At the White House, Tommy Vietor, Obama's press aide, gets a copy forwarded to him from another government official. The PDF of the story is bouncing around the Internet on e-mail—it's not posted publicly yet. Vietor e-mails it around to others in the press and national security team. They can't read it on their BlackBerrys, so he prints out copies for the national security staff to read. He gives a copy to Robert Gibbs, the president's press secretary, with passages highlighted, as recounted in

Politico. The president has already gone to the second floor of the residence, working from his office in the Treaty Room. Gibbs walks a copy in.

"Joe Biden called me," Obama would later tell *Rolling Stone.* "He was the first one to hear about it." Obama spends five minutes on the phone calming him down. Obama reads the story. Stan McChrystal has to go. It's not certain yet, but the national security team, which stays at work until around ten thirty that night, is thinking the same thing. Okay, there are the stupid things they said—there's the "bite me," and the "clown," and slamming Holbrooke. All that is bad—it's bad, too, that they think we're wimps, a White House insider will tell me. But what's most troubling to a few of the members of the national security team, according to White House officials, is an aspect that doesn't get much attention in the press: The scene where the troops are in near revolt against McChrystal.

It's morning in Kabul now. McChrystal's staff gathers in the planning room.

Dave Silverman wants to kill that fucking guy. I'd just called him, a week before, left a funny voicemail on his answering machine. I can't believe he did this. Dave Silverman wants to *fucking kill that guy.* Dave Silverman expresses this out loud. A military official who works with Admiral Mullen tells him to shut the fuck up: You've done enough damage.

Another U.S. State Department official asks the Flynns: What were the ground rules when he interviewed you? They say they don't know what the ground rules were. The official is horrified—this is basic press handling 101. You protect the principal.

McChrystal spends the morning working on his apology. Holbrooke's staff helps him draft it. He gets called back to Washington for a meeting. He asks that the meeting be held over VTC. The White House tells him: Get your ass back to Washington.

McChrystal releases an apology. The apology reads:

"I extend my sincerest apology for this profile. It was a mistake reflecting poor judgment and should never have happened. Throughout my career, I have lived by the principles of personal honor and professional integrity. What is reflected in this article falls far short of that standard. I have enormous respect and admiration for President Obama and his national security team, and for the civilian leaders and troops fighting this war, and I remain committed to ensuring its successful outcome."

Apologize, repent, move on. He's done it before. Gates has got his back. And Gates has the president's ear, right?

Holbrooke has dinner with Eikenberry that night at the embassy, with a host of Afghan and UN officials. Eikenberry had just gotten back from a meeting with Karzai. Karzai wants McChrystal to stay—both Karzai and his half brother Ahmed Wali Karzai, like McChrystal and think he's good for Afghanistan. They convey this message to Obama.

At dinner, Eikenberry is relaxed, he's chatting away, very charming. Holbrooke is tense, jet-lagged, tired. He looks withdrawn and pale, birdlike. He's worried his job might be on the line. Hillary wants to keep Stan. Mullen wants to keep Stan. Gates wants to keep Stan. That wouldn't be good for him—if he stays, it means the four-star got away with dissing him with no consequence. That doesn't look good in the Beltway. How is this going to play out?

Holbrooke's phone rings—he excuses himself from the table. It's his wife. His phone rings again—it's the White House. There's going to be a meeting on Wednesday, and he's asked to be in it over the video teleconference.

Duncan Boothby blames himself. Running around the world, breaking china, pushing hard, at the center of things. Who could have anticipated the result?

There is plenty of blame to go around—command climate and all that. It was McChrystal himself who started making fun of Biden. (Biden will consult with six four-star generals, and all tell him the same thing: McChrystal has to go.)

Duncan tries to contain the damage; if he takes the fall, maybe that will save the rest of them. Spin it as a PR fuckup, that's all. He offers his resignation—McChrystal accepts. CNN blasts the headline: PRESS ADVI-SOR FOR MCCHRYSTAL DUNCAN BOOTHBY RESIGNS.

That week, Duncan Boothby heads over to the *New York Times* Kabul bureau for dinner. It's a sad affair—everyone there feels pity for Duncan. They liked him. He's a good source and a good friend to one of the reporters. Who the fuck is this Hastings guy? Duncan tells a guest that there was a "gentleman's agreement," and Hastings broke it. Dexter Filkins—who, Duncan notes, has never paid for a beer in all the time he's known him—and John Burns, the *New York Times* London bureau chief, file stories slanted toward McChrystal keeping his job, saying he's the most hardworking general they've ever met. They take to the airways, slamming the story. Filkins makes excuses—they were stressed out, they have a tough job, they were venting steam, they are young guys. Filkins tells Charlie Rose that he'd never heard any kind of talk like this. "To what extent can we change the way we behave in such a way that this sort of thing doesn't happen again?" Burns later says on PBS, while telling a right-wing talk-show host that the story "will impact so adversely on what had been pretty good military/media relations."

On Fox News, Geraldo Rivera takes the same tack. He compares the *Rolling Stone* story to Al-Qaeda's attack on Ahmad Shah Massoud, an assassination that occurred on September 9, 2001, two days before the September 11 attacks. A few days later, a CBS News reporter Lara Logan will say, "Michael Hastings never served his country the way McChrystal has."

In Washington, Bob Gates calls National Security advisor Jim Jones. Gates is suggesting that McChrystal should stay. Jones isn't so sure—Jones got tagged as a "clown" by one of McChrystal's closest aides, a guy "stuck in 1985."

Jones sends a clear message to Gates: McChrystal is going down. This isn't the time to stand in the way.

On the plane to Washington, McChrystal gets e-mails of support from friends. One is from Greg Mortenson, the author of the best-selling

Three Cups of Tea. The humanitarian worker and the general have become friendly over the past year. Mortenson offers him his backing. McChrystal e-mails back: "Will move through this and if I'm not involved in the years ahead, will take tremendous comfort in knowing people like you are helping Afghans build a future."

On June 23, McChrystal arrives at the Pentagon to meet with Gates. He runs into NBC News Pentagon correspondent Jim Miklaszewski. Miklaszewski is a legendary reporter—his voice has carried Americans through the past decade of turmoil, starting on September 11, 2001, when he was reporting live from the Pentagon when it got hit. Jim is the most well-respected of newsmen, and, naturally, he happens to be in the right place at the right time—the moment Stan arrives at the Pentagon.

"Have you already submitted your resignation?" he asks him.

"You know better than that," McChrystal says, rushing up the steps. "No!"

The White House is watching: They do not see remorse in that clip. Stan doesn't seem to get it.

No one knows whether McChrystal will keep his job. NATO officials have prepared two press releases—one for if the general stays, another for if he is fired. Even the military's top brass is kept out of the loop: Pentagon spokesperson Geoff Morrell, viewed as particularly untrustworthy by the Obama administration, is frantically calling Brussels to find out what's happening across the Potomac at the White House.

At the White House, they start discussing names, possible replacements. Reasons for him to stay, reasons for him to go. The biggest reason for him to stay, White House officials think, is that it won't disrupt the mission. But the comments in the story reflect a direct attack on civilian control of the military—and the frat boy–like banter doesn't look very good.

Petraeus's name comes up—that solves a bunch of problems.

After meeting with Gates, McChrystal gets driven in a black SUV from the Pentagon to the White House.

His meeting with Obama lasts twenty minutes. McChrystal apologizes. Explains that it won't happen again. Obama is unmoved. "You've done a good job, but—" he tells McChrystal, and accepts his resignation. McChrystal leaves through the back door and ducks into his SUV to return to his Fort Myer home.

Around that time, Petraeus arrives at the White House. Petraeus is following the McChrystal thing closely, but he more or less expects a slap on the wrist. He's "surprised" by the comments McChrystal made, and "disappointed," according to a source close to him. If Obama wants a replacement, Petraeus is thinking, maybe General James Mattis, the Marine general currently running the United States Joint Forces Command. What Petraeus doesn't expect is that he'll be going into a National Security meeting that will radically alter his life. "No one's crystal ball is that good," says a senior military official close to Petraeus. "He had no indication whatsoever that he was about to be offered the job."

At eleven A.M., Obama's National Security Council convenes. It's just the principals—the support staff has been left out of this one. "I've accepted Stan McChrystal's resignation," Obama tells those gathered in the room, according to a senior administration official who attended the session. There is a shocked silence. Secretary of State Hillary Clinton, Defense Secretary Bob Gates, and Admiral Mike Mullen of the Joint Chiefs of Staff had all lobbied hard to keep McChrystal on board. But Obama didn't do that—he listened to Biden. He listened to Jones. He listened to his gut, which told him, on a fundamental level, McChrystal had to go.

Obama's next meeting is with General Petraeus. Petraeus is waiting down in the White House basement. Two military officers are chatting. A White House aide looks into the office, according to an account in *Newsweek*. "Does anyone know where General Petraeus is?" "I'm right here," Petraeus says, raising his hand. "They want you in the Oval, sir." He walks up the narrow staircase into the Oval Office, passing Leon Panetta, Gates, and Clinton, who "avoided eye contact, like physicians about to give a grim diagnosis," as *Newsweek* put it. Obama greets him and offers him a seat near the fireplace. "As your president and com-

mander in chief, I'm asking you to take over command in Afghanistan."
Petraeus is surprised, to put it mildly. He knows he can't say no. He's not
built to say no, anyway. It's another one of those moments. It was like
the Baghdad job: He got the call on the California interstate, sitting in
the passenger seat of a rental car, plowing through e-mail as his wife
drove the three-star and their son to visit his elderly father. He thought
he was going to end up in Europe, and he got Baghdad—that moment
turned him into the most famous and celebrated general of his generation. And here, the country and the president have turned to him again.
Patraeus had only one way to answer. "Yes, sir," he answers the president.

He signs up for a thirteen-month tour.

Obama and Petraeus meet for forty minutes. They schedule a press
conference in the Rose Garden for Obama to break the news. But the
announcement couldn't be made public until Obama allows the general
to fulfill one simple request.

"Before we announce this," Petraeus tells the president, "I better call
my wife."

Obama walks out to the Rose Garden. He reads from a prepared
statement. Mullen, Gates, Biden, and Petraeus stand behind him.

"Today I accepted General Stanley McChrystal's resignation as commander of the International Security Assistance Force in Afghanistan. I
did so with considerable regret, but also with certainty that it is the right
thing for our mission in Afghanistan, for our military, and for our country," he says. "But war is bigger than any one man or woman, whether a
private, a general, or a president. And as difficult as it is to lose General
McChrystal, I believe that it is the right decision for our national security."

For White House officials watching, it's one of Obama's strongest moments as commander in chief. It's cruel irony for McChrystal and his
staff—their complaint about the president had been his weakness, his
unwillingness to make tough decisions, his hesitancy. They tested him on
it, they called him out publicly, and Obama stood firm. McChrystal's

intended targets—Holbrooke, the vice president, and Jim Jones—were not the folks who went down, though. McChrystal did. "It was incredible seeing Obama like that," says a senior U.S. official intimately involved in Afghanistan policy. "The way he spoke about the war—it was a forcefulness that we hadn't heard before." At another meeting around that time, when remembering a visit he'd made to Walter Reed where he'd spoken to a teenage triple amputee, Obama would say, "We have a lot of kids on the ground acting like adults and we have a lot of adults in this room acting like kids."

Petraeus's critics are few, but he wants to "prove them wrong," a source close to him tells me. What his critics say is that he shouldn't get all the credit for Iraq. That he got lucky. That it was a fluke. That violence in Iraq died down for reasons beyond his control. But now, after engineering a face-saving withdrawal from that nightmarish war, he's going back to another active war zone, with all the responsibility on his shoulders. The president said it: This is Petraeus's plan too. He helped "design and lead our new strategy." Obama doesn't mention he had worked along with Gates and Mullen to "box in" the president in the decision to escalate the war.

The White House knows that if they are going to sack McChrystal, they can't put some no-name in his place. If Petraeus can't do it, no one can, or so the thinking goes.

Petraeus stays in Washington for his confirmation hearings. It's speedy and it's relatively painless. He drinks enough water this time. He already knows what he needs to focus on: getting more time on the clock and downplaying the next review of the strategy, which is supposed to be due in December. He needs to change the headlines, get the struggles in Kandahar off the front pages and get the soldiers off his back about rules of engagement, the issue that had damned McChrystal in the troops' eyes.

On June 25, Petraeus calls for a review of the rules of engagement. He points out that not all the troops are in place—very quietly, the much ballyhooed Kandahar offensive slips from public view. He points out that

July 2011 will mark the beginning of a process, not the date when the United States will "head for the exits and turn off the lights."

Petraeus flies down to Tampa to get his things ready. He'll be leaving CENTCOM, his home for almost two years. At his headquarters there, he gives a farewell speech. "He sounds psyched, looks like a man on a mission," according to a source close to Petraeus. One June 29, Petraeus has dinner with Biden, who has come down to Tampa to see the general off before he goes to Kabul. It's Biden, Petraeus's wife, Holly, and a few other close advisors and military officials. Biden wants to show they are on the same page; Biden wants to show that despite the disrespect McChrystal showed him, he's not going to be cowed. He's demonstrating that he is the vice president, and to cross him is to tempt fate. There will be no more jabs or jokes about Biden coming out of Kabul. He'll later recall that he took McChrystal's trash-talking as a compliment—"I mean, it was clear that I was the only guy they worried about," he tells a reporter.

Petraeus arrives in Kabul on July 3, 2010. He's the third new commanding general to take over in less than a year and a half, a turnover in commanders matched perhaps only by Abe Lincoln's repeated sacking of generals in the Civil War. After a rough two weeks at ISAF HQ—where grown men walked around with tears in their eyes and "heartbroken" thanks to the McChrystal firing—Petraeus's arrival is a boost to morale. Petraeus is a winner; the troops like a winner.

At the U.S. embassy, Petraeus gives his welcoming address in front of a huge American flag. It's no accident that he's speaking there—it's a way to visually reaffirm the civilian and military partnership. Eikenberry gives him a badge to the embassy, then sits off stage, next to his wife, Ching, wearing a summery hat. The next day at another ceremony, a reporter for the NATO channel describes Petraeus as "cool and confident" upon his arrival. He tells the crowd, "We are engaged in a tough fight. We have arrived at a critical moment."

An Afghan general talks to a reporter: "There is no difference to us between General McChrystal and General Petraeus. Unfortunately, sometimes politics get much stronger than the professionalism of a soldier."

Petraeus won't have that problem—*Petraeus is politics.*

42 | THE PENTAGON INVESTIGATES McCHRYSTAL

JUNE 28 TO AUGUST 2010, NEW YORK, MILTON, AND WASHINGTON, DC

Stephen Colbert pushed a shot of whiskey across his desk. He wanted me to take a shot of booze before we started the interview.

The cameras were rolling. We were in his studio on 54th Street, taping a segment for his Comedy Central show, *The Colbert Report*.

Within forty-eight hours, I'd gone from the insanity of Afghanistan to sitting for an interview on a cable show.

I pushed the shot back across the desk, telling him no thanks, and that I didn't drink. The studio audience laughed awkwardly. Colbert took the shots and the bottle and moved them under his desk.

I didn't want to fall off the wagon (again) on national television. I figured I would have ended up vomiting if I took a whiskey shot cold, which would have made a disastrous, if amusing, YouTube video.

The media attention on the story was dying down. After a week of flood-the-zone coverage on McChrystal, most of it supporting our story, the national agenda shifted back to the BP oil spill and other news. There was more blowback to come, however. A few of my colleagues in the media eventually got around to attacking *Rolling Stone*. At the time, it didn't really sink in as to why. That would become clearer over the next few months.

It started with a story in *The Washington Post*. The story, citing anonymous sources, claimed that I had violated ground rules. This wasn't true, and the quotes about me that the anonymous sources gave the *Post* were total fabrications, imagining a scene where some unnamed person had told me to leave the bar the night in Paris. I'd worked for *The Washington Post* before, filling in at their Baghdad bureau a few months earlier. The editors had been happy with my work at the time, and one of my stories made the front page. The *Post* had mentioned my work for them in their earlier McChrystal coverage, but failed to point out that they'd recently employed me in the story criticizing my reporting.

McChrystal's defenders would launch another round of pushback in the press, claiming that my quotes came only from "junior staff," men who "make tea, keep the principal on time, and carry bags," as another unnamed official put it. This wasn't true, either: McChrystal had got the Biden insults rolling, made fun of Holbrooke's email, and told me Eikenberry had betrayed him. Jake and Duncan were McChrystal's top civilian advisors; Charlie Flynn was his executive officer; and it would be a stretch to call Lt. Commander Dave Silverman a junior staffer. The anonymous officials quoted in the critical stories, I would learn, were under investigation for insubordination. The stories didn't mention that. Ironically, I was also criticized for my use of unnamed sources—in articles citing unnamed sources. It was the beginning of a whisper campaign from McChrystal and his allies that would continue throughout the next year.

I returned to Vermont in July to finish my piece on the Kiowa helicopter pilots for *Men's Journal*.

On July 13, I received an e-mail from the Army inspector general's office. The e-mail informed me that the Army had launched an investigation "to determine the facts and circumstances related to the article" published in *Rolling Stone*. Two days later, the inspector general's office sent a list of questions for me to answer, noting "under the provisions of 10

USC 3583 the Army takes matters of insubordination very seriously and accordingly have interviewed all personnel we have been able to identify based on Mr. Hastings' article." The questions included: "Do you believe your article accurately portrays the culture/atmosphere/thinking of the commander's staff members?" and "Would you say that there's a general climate of insubordination?" The e-mail claimed to have "identified the personnel who made the derogatory comments about high ranking officials."

There was no way I would cooperate with an investigation, particularly if I was being asked to name sources. (Even though I wouldn't be breaking any agreement with them by naming them, I felt it was a bad precedent to set.)

Rolling Stone agreed with me. It was better to risk getting threatened with a subpoena than to roll over for the government. On a more fundamental level, I didn't think it was my job to assist the Pentagon in its investigation—the story, I believed, spoke for itself.

Two weeks later, I was asked to give a talk in New York to a group of magazine editors. At one point, a media blogger in the audience asked me how my relationship was with the military. I told him it was good, at least so I thought. I had another embed lined up to go on in the fall, I said.

The media blogger reported that the next day on his blog. Within twenty-four hours of the blog post, I received a letter from ISAF headquarters. They hadn't realized that I had another embed already approved until I said it publicly. In a one-page letter from Colonel Wayne Shanks, chief of public affairs, I was informed that I no longer had an embed. Among other reasons, the letter said this was due to the "political fallout" of the story about McChrystal. The letter stated that if I wanted to return for an embed, I would need to provide sworn statements from commanders on the ground, as well as a sworn statement of my own attesting to "the scope and intent of your proposed coverage." It was an unprecedented restriction to put on a reporter, and effectively banned me from embedding in the future.

The ban was in clear violation of ISAF's own policy—to not punish reporters for publishing "embarrassing" information. It was strange. Other journalists, including Geraldo Rivera, had been kicked off embeds for revealing troop movements, a serious violation that put lives at risk. Yet they'd never gotten permanently banned. It was clearly retribution. Failing to find factual fault in my story about General McChrystal and my follow-up story on Kiowa helicopters, the ISAF command decided to get their revenge by not allowing me to embed.

The Department of Defense wasn't satisfied with the Army's investigation, either. The Army investigation had pointed the finger at the individuals they believed made insubordinate comments. Not coincidentally, the Army investigation concluded that no one in the Army was at fault. The Army's investigation blamed the Navy (Dave Silverman) and the civilian advisors surrounding McChrystal. In September, the Pentagon decided to launch a second investigation. They would spend eight months looking for answers, when all they really had to do was reread the story.

To me, both the investigations seemed absurd. My story had never claimed McChrystal and his staff violated any laws, yet the press coverage of the investigation made it appear as if the men were all being exonerated. Exonerated from what? From looking like jerks? For being illegally, rather than casually, insubordinate? The stories missed the bigger picture: the name calling—and the later attempts by the Pentagon investigators to rewrite history—represented an unapologetic contempt toward the White House. Pentagon officials would privately tell journalists that the intent of the investigation wasn't even to find wrongdoing; it was to "damage" my credibility.

43 | THE MEDIA-MILITARY-INDUSTRIAL COMPLEX

OCTOBER TO NOVEMBER 2010, WASHINGTON, DC

I walked into Café Milano in Georgetown to meet a few friends. It was a DC restaurant known for its power-dining scene. Darkly lit, loud, patrons trying for stylish. It was cool for DC, meaning it wasn't cool at all. Congressional staffers and lobbyists and State Department officials and other bureaucrats gathered around the bar, knocking back drinks, swapping the latest gossip.

In October, I'd moved down to Washington for the year, renting a fully furnished studio in Foggy Bottom, the neighborhood where the State Department was located. I hated Washington. I hated it the last time I had lived there during the 2008 election campaign, and I hated it this time around, too. There's a saying: Washington is Hollywood for ugly people. That's being unfair to Hollywood. In Hollywood, at least they're making a product that people actually want.

Ambassador Richard Holbrooke was sitting at a table in the back. He was finishing up dinner with a movie producer, a White House official, and a well-known billionaire.

He came up to the bar. A friend introduced us. He nodded. He said he liked my story and the criticisms about him didn't bother him.

I apologized for what I was wearing: a hoodie and jeans. I told him if I knew he was going to be there, I would have worn a much nicer hoodie. He stepped in next to me and pulled me aside.

"You can fuck with a general," he said. "But you do not fuck with my team."

I nodded. Pretty hilarious, I thought.

That was Washington for me. I'd run into politicians and government officials and they'd all tell me they liked my reporting. Maybe they were lying, or trying to bullshit me, I didn't know. While living in Vermont, I hadn't understood the exact nature of the official Washington freak-out. But once I arrived in DC and started going to the cocktail parties and hitting the bars, I saw how the political and media class had completely misinterpreted my piece. The story had terrified them, striking deep-seated fears in the Washington psyche. It demonstrated just how tenuous one's own position could be—careers could flame out overnight. And the political and media class saw the story as a threat to their schmoozy relationship—their very existence and social life. If you can't get wasted with a journalist who's writing a profile of you and piss all over the president who appointed you, what's the world coming to?

A number of famous journalists would say they heard these kinds of things all the time, but never reported them. It didn't matter to them that I was on assignment to write a profile—I didn't go to France and Kandahar on a social engagement. It didn't seem to make a difference that I hadn't violated any agreement with McChrystal. The unwritten rule I'd broken was a simple one: You really weren't supposed to write honestly about people in power. Especially those the media deemed untouchable. Trash Sarah Palin all you want, but tread carefully when writing about the sacred cows like McChrystal and Petraeus. You're supposed to keep the myths going. I'd fucked up—I wasn't to be trusted because I tried to tell the truth. At one event, a prominent Republican senator pulled me aside and said, "You know, your story was a good thing. Got everybody focused back on Afghanistan."

Strangely, as I continued to report on the politics behind the scenes of the war, I ended up on pretty good terms with a number of military officials, White House officials, and State Department officials. It was the other journalists who covered the military and politics that I clashed with most often. A number of reporters had paid side gigs at defense-industry-funded think tanks, essentially getting financial support from the very same people they were supposed to be covering. They seemed to take my criticism of the military-industrial complex personally. It might as well be called, I thought, the media-military-industrial complex.

I could understand why the government officials would be pissed; I was telling them their whole strategy was a waste of time. But the reaction from a number of journalists on the national security beat seemed pretty twisted. Thankfully, I didn't have to endure Washington much longer. In December, I returned to Afghanistan to find out what General David Petraeus had been up to.

44 | I'D RATHER BE EATING A BURGER

AUGUST TO DECEMBER 2010, ARLINGTON AND WEST POINT

It's a late summer morning in Washington, and Bob Gates is outside his office in the hallway of the Pentagon. A military aide is standing in the doorway, poking his head outside, keeping an eye on him. Gates is due over at the White House, and the military aide's job is to make sure he gets there on time. Lately, Gates has been silently resisting, dragging his feet at these visits. Gates, the aide says, has a tendency for passive resistance—to get a haircut, or to pick up a burger at Burger King, anything to delay crossing the Potomac to have another frustrating tête-à-tête.

Publicly, the president and the secretary of defense regularly express admiration for each other—and journalists ponder the strange historical circumstance of how a sixty-seven-year-old white Republican dude and a forty-nine-year-old African-American Democrat have been joined at the hip to oversee two American wars. Privately, though, as Washington has a way of doing, the initial luster of their relationship has been worn down by eighteen months' worth of policy battles that left the president feeling, at times, duped and betrayed by the Pentagon.

Gates is tired, too. Tired of Washington, mainly. He took the secretary of defense job in 2006, appointed by President Bush to take the place of Rumsfeld. He planned to leave after Bush left office, carrying a small little clock in his briefcase, counting down the days, hours, and seconds to January 20, 2009, Obama's inauguration. But Obama asks him to stay—it gives him cover on national security, and he likes the guy.

No one in Washington has a bad word to say about Bob Gates—nowadays, at least.

It's been a brutal four years. In that time, he gets credit for reversing the tide of the war in Iraq and oversees the drawdown from a hundred and fifty thousand troops to the approximately fifty thousand left there now. He tamps down on reckless calls for a war in Iran. He gives the impression of reluctantly endorsing a tripling of the scope of the war in Afghanistan, leftover skepticism from his experience watching the Soviets falter there during the eighties. Over twenty-eight hundred American servicemen and -women will die on his watch, a toll that his friends say he's taken personally.

He's living alone in Washington, in a military-supplied house. His wife hates DC and has stayed at their house in Washington State. According to one magazine profile, Gates does his own laundry, cooks for himself, and waters his own flowers. He spends his nights writing personal letters to the families of soldiers who've been killed in Iraq and Afghanistan. He relaxes drinking Belvedere martinis and smoking cigars, watching fun action flicks like *Wolverine* and *Transformers*, avoiding the usual Beltway bullshit cocktail parties. He is a former Eagle Scout, joins the CIA in 1966 as an analyst, and climbs the ranks to run the company in 1991—the only entry-level employee to do so. He's got his scars—he was dinged in the Iran-Contra affair. He learns his lesson and tones down his rhetoric, arriving at the Department of Defense fifteen years later with a persona of humility and self-deprecating humor. (His humor: The jokes are sometimes so bad, his speechwriters complain. Corny as hell, and they can cut too close to home. His joke about DC: The first six months in Washington, you wonder how you got here; the next six months, you wonder how everyone else got here; the next six months you spend trying to get out of here.)

The buttoned-up Gates is, at times, strangely subversive. He marches in a protest against Nixon's bombing of Cambodia in 1970, during his first years at the CIA—Bob Gates in an antiwar rally! In his memoir, he reprints a flyer he's found on a college campus, calling him a war criminal: WANTED: ROBERT GATES, FOR VIOLATION OF INTERNATIONAL LAW NND HUMAN RIGHTS VIOLATIONS. He likes to take digs at the general officers who flaunt around the Pentagon with bloated staffs—"brass creep," he calls it. He tells folks that if you want to really know what he's thinking, do what he did as a Soviet analyst: dissect his speeches. He is seriously, or at least as seriously as possible for a secretary of defense, going after the military's own trillion-dollar-a-year defense budget—rare in Washington for someone to actually say, hey, we have too much power, take it away.

The White House, though, is sending signals—they've felt burned by the Pentagon. They are turning inward. Tom Donilon, a friend of Vice President Biden's, is taking over as the national security advisor, a choice that Gates told Woodward would be a "disaster." (Gates is the man Woodward talks to last, says a Pentagon official, which just shows how much power Gates truly has.) It's a sign, subtly, of the feelings that Obama's team has been burned by relying on outsiders, and by hiring Donilon they show they aren't planning on making the same mistake again.

The McChrystal thing—that burns Gates up. In the days following McChrystal's firing, he has to make calls to allied defense ministers, making nice, explaining no harm meant. He tells one NATO minister, "A journalist did in one day what the Taliban had failed to do." It's not a fair assessment, of course, but another sign of his frustration. Gates fires people all the time, for infractions of varying scale. He tosses McKiernan without a word of remorse. And at McChrystal's retirement ceremony in July, Gates will bemoan the fact that Americans have lost a hero, someone whose record of service is unmatched. (Forget Tillman, forget Camp Nama, forget the negative command climate . . .)

Gates will later say that he defended McChrystal so strongly because he thought doing otherwise would interrupt the flow of the mission—"the lightbulb went on—yes, [Petraeus] will work." But more important, and what stings, is that McChrystal was *his* and Mullen's recommendation to the president, and though he won't say it publicly, on some level, it made him look bad. (The behavior in the story made Mullen "nearly sick," the admiral will admit.)

Gates's reservations about the war are privately surfacing—he's focusing in on how to get out. Those qualms he had when looking at Afghanistan a year earlier—from the perspective of an analyst who followed the jihadists' secret war against the Soviets there in the eighties—bubble up. That summer, the Defense Department commissions a report from U.S. military officials and diplomatic advisors to look at "end states"—in short, what the country will look like when we leave. A U.S. official who was asked for input on the document says it was "an attempt to get the withdrawal strategies." But despite its "stay the course" rhetoric, even the Pentagon fears the war isn't going well. One paper in the report provided to me describes a plan to split Afghanistan into seven regions, each centered around a major city, and to include both "insurgents" and "local strongmen" in the new regional governments. "This is not to sanction warlordism," the paper explains, "but an acknowledgement that local strongmen have a part to play in the initial stage of rebalancing the state." At a meeting in October, Gates is presented with the paper, according to Pentagon sources—they say that he reacts "positively" to the plan.

He keeps saying he's leaving the office, but the date keeps getting pushed back. He's finishing up his DoD bucket list. In December, he visits Afghanistan, flying around with General Petraeus. He hands out three silver stars. He consoles a unit that has just lost six men—maybe it doesn't make a difference, maybe it does, just for the men to know that someone somewhere out there gives a shit. He hears an assessment from a commander in the east: The fighting is heavy. Thirty-eight hundred insurgents killed or captured. Eight hundred and fifty bombs dropped. "Every single day in this valley, we are either dropping bombs or shooting Hellfire missiles, because this is a very, very kinetic fight," a commander there tells him. He gives a speech to the soldiers: "I'm actually the guy that signs the orders and sends you over here, and I consider my highest priority to get you what you need to do the job, to complete your mission, and to come home safely," he says. "I feel a personal responsibility for each and every one of you since I sent you here. I feel the sacrifice and hardship and losses more than you will ever imagine." He'll return home on the flight with soldiers finishing up their tours, something he'd been wanting to do before leaving office. He says what he's seen has convinced him that the strategy "is working" and making "progress."

But however the defense secretary describes what's happening in Afghanistan publicly, every other independent assessment—by the Red Cross, the United Nations, an independent group of experts—says violence is at its worst.

In February, Gates makes one of his final trips to West Point. He is speaking to an audience of cadets, many who will be deploying to finish off the wars in Iraq and Afghanistan. Gates the Sovietologist spent days and nights in the seventies and eighties analyzing the Soviet leaders' speeches, looking for clues, for signs—to divine the true mind-set of the leadership by reading between the lines. And what does Gates say in this speech? Gates, the man who has designed and overseen the last four years of the military fighting machine, the man who calls himself Secretary of War? "Any future secretary of defense who advises the president to again send a big American land army into the Middle East or Africa," he tells the cadets, "should have their head examined."

45 | ONCE UPON A TIME IN KANDAHAR

DECEMBER 2010, KANDAHAR

The motel in Kandahar was like a foreign language version of a Days Inn. It was called the Continental Guest House, its courtyard hidden behind a white and blue wall along one of the city's busiest streets. I had a small room with one single bed, an old IBM desktop computer that didn't work, and two space heaters. The shower and bathroom drain and toilet melded into one small porcelain cube. The motel provided rubber slippers to bathe in.

I felt like I was stuck in a limited release David Lynch movie—an atmosphere too strange and surreal for audiences to comprehend. A few doors down, three Filipino construction workers passed the days hanging laundry, waiting for work to start on the new American base they'd been hired to build outside the city. My Afghan bodyguard, Razzi, stayed in the room next to mine. He didn't speak much English, but had a range of facial expressions to indicate who I shouldn't trust. We ate each meal in a large dining room. The lighting was poor. I could barely see the food on the plate—bread, stew, rice, and cans of Diet Coke. At the meals, none of the guests talked much, all staring down at their plates, except for an older Afghan man, an engineer.

The old man never gave me his name or his e-mail. He'd survived in Afghanistan since 1985 by giving his name to as few people as possible. In the early seventies, he'd attended a university in Florida. He hid the fact that he spoke English from most of his friends. He was in Kandahar to advise on another American construction project. He knew the score, and outlined the network of corruption during our first dinner. It all led to the local gangster in chief, Ahmed Wali Karzai—Hamid Karzai's half brother—who lorded over Kandahar from his position as head of the provincial council.

Ahmed Wali, he explained, was a key player in the provinces' booming drug network. Afghanistan was producing about four billion dollars of opium a year, and the industry was increasingly concentrated in the south of the country. There were all sorts of allegations, ranging from black tar heroin to hashish to opium to targeted assassinations. American military and diplomatic officials were well aware of Karzai's business activities. They gave him a three-letter acronym, an honor given to foreigners who end up in lots of government reports. (OBL for Osama Bin Laden, AMZ for Abu Musab al-Zarqawi, AWK for Ahmed Wali Karzai.) AWK was also on the CIA's payroll. "My friend's fourteen-year-old son was kidnapped," the old man told me. "He went to see Ahmed Wali to get his son released. Ahmed Wali told him, I can't help, but I can get the ransom lowered."

Afghans I'd spoken to in Kabul believed Ahmed Wali had a hand in a string of assassinations. Finding evidence of that was difficult. However, Ahmed Wali was so blatantly corrupt that for a few months beginning in 2010, the Americans were actually thinking of arresting him or killing him. When AWK visited General Mike Flynn at ISAF headquarters, AWK "was really nervous, he thought he was going to get arrested," Flynn told me. U.S. officials convened a series of meetings to figure out what to do with AWK and a few others like him. Arrest them? Bring charges against him? Give him a slap on the wrist?

In the end, the Americans did nothing. Actually, that's not quite accurate. They did do something—they fully embraced AWK and his cronies. After Petraeus took charge, he turned to a network of warlords, drug runners, and thieves known as the Afghan government to implement his strategy. Within weeks of assuming command, Petraeus had pushed through an ambitious program to create hundreds of local militias—essentially a neighborhood watch armed with AK-47s. Petraeus expanded the militia program from eighteen districts to more than sixty, and planned to ramp it up from ten thousand men to thirty thousand.

In Afghanistan, however, arming local militias meant, by definition, placing guns in the hands of some of the country's most ruthless thugs, who ruled their territories with impunity. In the north, Petraeus relied on Atta Mohammed Noor, a notorious warlord-turned-governor considered to be one of the most powerful men in Afghanistan, to prepare militias for a long fight with the Taliban. Smaller militias in the region—which had been likened to an L.A. "gang" by their own American advisors—were also getting U.S. training. In the east, where violence had significantly increased, efforts to back local strongmen had already resulted in intertribal violence. And in Kandahar, Petraeus had given near-unconditional support to Ahmed Wali Karzai.

"The Americans have backed so many warlords in so many ways, it's very hard to see how you unscramble the egg now," John Matisonn, a former top UN official who left Kabul in June 2010, told me. "There has never been a strategy to get rid of the warlords, who are the key problem. The average Afghan hates them, whether they're backed by the Taliban or the Americans. They see them as criminals. They know that the warlords are fundamentally undermining the rule of law."

That was the reason I decided to go back to Kandahar: to try to get a sense of who those militia leaders were. What kind of men were we cutting deals with here? In Iraq, Petraeus had found weakened Sunni insurgent leaders, gave them hundreds of millions of dollars, and pretended they were allies. What type of allies would he find in Afghanistan?

Before leaving Kabul a few days earlier, my security advisors warned me that whatever I did in Kandahar, I should stay within the city limits. I should certainly stay out of Arghandab, a district bordering the city where there was heavy fighting. After spending twenty-four hours in Kandahar, however, my translator, Fareed Ahmad, told me he'd arranged an interview with a militia in Arghandab.

Did I want to go?

"Yes," I said. "If it's safe."

"It's safe, it's no problem. It is on the main road."

"Okay," I said. "Let's do it then."

My Afghan bodyguard, Razzi, didn't like the plan.

"Mike," he said, taking me aside. "Do you know this translator?"

"No," I said. "But he's highly recommended from a friend."

"You trust him?"

"Trust is a strong word."

My translator shook his head.

"He say it is safe," Razzi told me. "It is very danger. He's doing this for—" and Razzi made the international symbol for money, rubbing his thumb and middle finger together. (Ahmad would get twice as much per day if he traveled with me outside the city.)

"Fuck it, man, I know what you're saying, but this is what I'm here for."

I had reservations about going. I knew my security advisors wouldn't be happy that within one day I was already ignoring their advice. I knew that the risks weren't worth the payoff. But I felt the pressure to get a good story and I'd traveled down to this shithole of a city. I wasn't just going to stay in my hotel, self-aware enough to know I was behaving in the classic war junkie fashion.

And so I found myself driving along a road from Kandahar to Herat in a white Toyota Corolla, thinking, You never put yourself in these situations, but you always seem to find yourself in them. Thinking of it as something out of my control decreased the blame—and there is plenty of blame if things go wrong, and it's all blame on me. I know it's a risk, I know it's a rush, I know it's not a healthy lifestyle. I know it's an addiction; I know it's the wrong week to quit sniffing glue. As the old Afghan contractor had said—and I knew this without his saying it—if something goes wrong, if I get kidnapped, it's my Afghan driver, translator, and bodyguard who will be immediately killed. They're not worth the trouble of a ransom. As an American journalist, however, I was more or less a walking dollar sign.

I dressed up like a native, with a salwar kameez—which look to Westerners like pajamas—and a small cap on my head. I purchased a messenger bag from a local store to carry my notebook and recorder in. I didn't carry any identification with me. I'd fail any close inspection, but there were enough mixed bloodlines in Afghanistan that even with blue eyes and brown hair, I didn't necessarily scream American. More likely Turkish, or perhaps from another part of Central Asia.

"There are the most suicide bombers and IEDs around here," Ahmad told me as we passed a stretch of road about ten minutes outside the city. These were the kinds of details Ahmad regularly provided, like the narration of a tour guide whose ass-backwards goal was to get the visitor to call off the tour and flee the country for his life. An IED went off there, a targeted killing here, a particularly corrupt checkpoint up ahead.

Two American convoys passed us, ten giant MRAPs in total, lumbering along the other way. A series of new checkpoints had been set up to provide security, around thirty in all around the city, manned by Afghans lounging about on concrete barriers. The checkpoints were part of the massive U.S. offensive that had been under way since the summer.

The meeting is with a militia leader named Mohammed Nabi, a man the mayor of Kandahar would later describe to me as a "warlord." Nabi was officially part of Petraeus's new program to start arming and training Afghan Local Police, or ALP.

We took a right off the main road, entering a quiet countryside, dust and stone paths between brown and dried-up grape fields. Without the hectic activity of the main road to give us a false sense of safety in numbers, it dawned on us—me, my driver, my translator, and my Afghan bodyguard—that we were out there now on our own, beyond the narrow bounds of government or Coalition control. I realized that I might have made a horrible fucking mistake.

It was one thing to hear the president of the United States proclaim there was progress in Kandahar; it was another to be putting that progress to the test sitting in a shitty white Toyota waiting for a stranger to arrive to take us to a warlord's hangout.

A boy about sixteen years old drove up to us on a motorcycle. He was our contact. It immediately became clear to everyone else in the car that we might be walking into a kidnapping. Things might or might not soon go terribly wrong. I should have heeded the warnings from our security company, I thought—whatever you do, do not go to Arghandab, they had told me. I had made the decision to go, and once you start this kind of thing, it becomes almost impossible to stop. The truly important decision is to go or not to go—once you go, you're gone, no backing out, no turning back. We've come this far, we're almost there, I've spent $400 dollars on a car and bodyguard for the day. Dice rolled, fates tempted. Two possible outcomes: You're fucked or not fucked. Scrape by, I'm a hero. Don't scrape by, I'm a beheaded fuckup.

The motorcycle took off down a one-lane road, with a drainage ditch to the left, an eight-foot-high mud wall to the right. It was a road where we could be easily ambushed, with no way to turn around or escape. Were we about to meet the Taliban or the militia? Or was the militia Taliban? How greedy were they? How desperate for cash? Would they risk snatching me? It felt funny, a tight spot, a jolt of fear and adrenaline— and I thought, If this ends in a kidnapping, which I'm putting at about a 20 percent probability at that moment, I'm going to feel, among other things, pretty stupid.

We pulled into a dirt lot next to a grape field behind another small wall. A group of ten men sat cradling their AK-47s. There were about eight motorcycles and a green Ford Ranger truck parked there as well. My translator introduced me to the leader, Mohammed Nabi.

Nabi was sitting cross-legged on a carpet spread out over the dirt. His silver AK-47, decorated with green and silver on the grip, was resting up against the wall. It didn't take much prompting before he started bitching about the Afghan government, the Canadians, and the Taliban.

First, the Taliban tried to kill him, he said, by blowing up a suicide bomber at his cousin's wedding. It was in retaliation for the militia he had formed with U.S. backing. Over a thousand members of Mohammed Nabi's tribe had gathered in a field to celebrate the event last summer. Mohammed said he saw the bomber slip past the guards, pull the pin on the suicide vest, and detonate. "Blood everywhere," he said, the bomber killing eighty and injuring three hundred. On a late September evening, the Taliban tried again—this time Nabi heard the shooting, called up one of his guards on his cell phone, then rushed over to join the fight. He claimed a victory that night: thirteen Talibs dead, while only losing three of his own.

Nabi wanted to go on the offensive against the Taliban, but he was, at least temporarily, prevented from doing so. That was why he was so pissed at the Canadians.

"The Canadians stopped us when we would try to go on operations in other villages," he told me. "Two or three times they stopped us, and we could have made this entire area secure." The outpost where we were sitting was one of twelve checkpoints he commanded over seven villages. Tribal elders from other villages also didn't appreciate his incursions and claimed he was overstepping his bounds. Nabi had ninety members in his militia and said with the proper funding he could easily increase that number to three or four hundred. He'd been paying his men out of his own pocket, seven thousand afghani a man, and wished the Afghan government would soon start chipping in. The youngest member was a fourteen-year-old, who I watched walk around the outpost, cleaning up and serving tea.

Thankfully, Nabi said, two months ago the U.S. Special Forces came to offer him more support. His advisors—who go by the names Chip and Rob, he said—gave him eight new AK-47s. They provided his militiamen with government identification for the ALP—the ID has an Afghan flag and an American flag with a picture and serial number on it. The Special Forces soldiers have promised to pay him regular visits. He also received the new Ford Ranger, because the new police chief of Kandahar is from his tribe.

Razzi paced back and forth around the perimeter, making chitchat with the militiamen. He gave me a thumbs-up and a smile—his sign saying that it was all clear, for now. I would have liked to have stayed longer, but after twenty minutes, I figured it was time to go. I took pictures with the militia members, made sure I hadn't dropped my cigarettes or recorder, and as casually as possible got back in the car.

We pulled out on the dirt road. Everyone in the car was quiet. We took a left on the other dirt road. We arrived back at the main road.

Everyone in the car started laughing hysterically.

Ahmad turned around in his seat.

"I admit, after I saw that motorcycle, I thought we were in trouble," he said.

"On the main fucking road my ass," I said.

"We are not doing that again," Razzi said definitively. I agreed.

"Those are not good people," my translator explained. "They are not people who good Afghans want their children and teenagers to be around." The militias, Ahmad explained, have a reputation for having teenage boys around to have sex with. Like the fourteen-year-old who was hanging out there, Ahmad said.

"Glad to see we're putting our faith in these guys," I said.

46 | KING DAVID'S WAR

JULY 2010 TO JANUARY 2011, KABUL

Dave Petraeus takes over the morning briefings. It's his war now. He asks more questions than McChrystal, according to a senior military official who sits in on over a dozen briefings that summer. McChrystal was quieter—Petraeus interrupts, peppers the briefer with questions.

Almost every morning he lasers in on one of his favorite topic: information operations. How to spin the Afghans and how to spin the Taliban. How to convince them that we're actually winning this thing—that they can trust us, that we're on their side. It worked in Iraq, he has said: "We amplified [the insurgents'] atrocities and broadcast them and saturated the media throughout Baghdad, using TV, radio, billboards, Internet, you name it."

In August, he gets a briefing that "makes him almost giggly," according to a senior military official who attended the briefing. The Taliban have written a book about how to treat the local population—a book whose principles they violate pretty regularly. It's the Taliban who kill the majority of Afghan civilians—usually a breakdown of about 20 percent killed by NATO, 80 percent killed by the Taliban. Sure, the Taliban are doing operations in areas because NATO is there, but the theory still holds—the Taliban are abusing their own worse than the international community, which may or may not matter.

Petraeus thinks it matters. An enterprising colonel has developed what Petraeus thinks is a clever response. It's called "Throw the Book at Them," a presentation which compares the Taliban's alleged principles to their alleged deeds.

This, Petraeus exclaims, is what we need more of. This guy gets it! ("If you say the wrong thing, you're skunked," says a senior military official. "He hit it off, thought it was a great idea, asked the officer to send him his résumé.")

Petraeus goes on a tour of the country. In July, he stops by the IJC to say hello to Rod, Lieutenant General David Rodriguez. Rod is a McChrystal holdover, a boots-and-mud kind of general, who in private has the habit of stringing multiple *fucks* and *fuckers* together. Petraeus works the room. He asks the Dutch soldiers to stand. He mentions his Dutch ancestry. Then he says, poorly but a nice try, *thank you* in Dutch: *dank u wel.*

Petraeus, according to those who work with him, has received something of a shock in Afghanistan. It's not Iraq. He knows it's not Iraq, he has said it's not Iraq, but regardless, his experience is forged in Baghdad; his entire framework is hard to shake. "He brings up Iraq every five minutes," says an Afghan official. Earlier in the year, he was on a plane with Holbrooke coming back from a ROC drill to discuss plans for Kandahar. In one conversation, according to a senior U.S. administration official, "He must have said Iraq twenty-one times in fifteen minutes." Iraq is on the brain. It's in Iraq where Petraeus made his name—mostly good, a little bit of bad, depending on who you ask.

Petraeus was born in Cornwall, New York, a town on the Hudson near West Point. His father is a Dutch merchant marine. His first nickname is Peaches—easier to pronounce than Petraeus. He goes to West Point, class of '74. He gets set up on a blind date with the superintendent's daughter—he bluffs his way into a football game. It's love, but the haters will hate on him for that, too, noting that it's quite convenient for him to have married into a general's family. He excels at West Point and excels at everything that follows—ranking in the top of his class at Ranger School, an incredibly difficult feat.

He doesn't get his war, though. Petraeus misses Vietnam. He deals only in Vietnam's ghosts. He writes his dissertation in Princeton about it: "The American Military and the Lessons of Vietnam."

He misses almost everything big. In the Gulf War, he is a major, a staff aide to a top general—he "looked more concerned with keeping the two VIP generals on schedule for their next celebrity visit in the desert" than an upcoming attack that seemed "a distant possibility," according to one account from an officer who was his contemporary. A superior of his, Admiral William Fallon, reportedly puts it less delicately: He's an "ass-kissing little chicken shit." He comes close to losing his life in a training accident in 1991—shot through the chest, ignores the doctor's orders and does push-ups just days after. He breaks his pelvis jumping out of a plane in 2000.

The invasion of Iraq launches his public career. He seizes the moment. He gets to lead the 101st Airborne and he's accompanied by historian Rick Atkinson. He serves up a quote that will define his legacy there: "Tell me how this ends."

Brilliant—like he can already see the upcoming debacle. He'll set himself up to answer that question five years later. *Tell Me How This Ends* becomes the title of one of the first biographies written about him—he'll later bring the journalist/biographer to work for him as a senior advisor down at CENTCOM.

He arrives in Baghdad in 2003 and runs into an old friend from West Point. "Can you believe it took us thirty years to get our Combat Infantry Badges?" Petraeus tells him. It took him a long time to get his war. He gets awarded a Bronze Star for valor—though his critics will raise questions about whether he should have gotten a Bronze Star for meritorious service instead of valor, claiming he didn't appear to have done anything valorous while under fire. This sounds like nitpicking, but it also might fit a pattern. "Petraeus was handing out Bronze Stars to all his boys," a military official tells me.

He earns the nickname King David while up in Mosul, ruling over the ancient Iraqi city. Within months of his leaving Mosul, the city collapses—not his fault, he explains, things were great when he was there. His next gig is heading the organization that trains and equips the Iraqi security forces, both army and police, called MNSTCI.

He gets a different nickname this time. He's taking over from General Paul Eaton. Petraeus arrives in Baghdad on a day that Eaton happens to be up at the Kirkush Military Training Base. Eaton has a nice office in Saddam's Republican Palace—the palace, like most of Saddam's architecture, resembles a McMansion dipped in gold. It's Petraeus's office now. Without Eaton's permission, according to military officials who were at the embassy, Petraeus sends his men in to move all of Eaton's stuff into a broom closet–sized office down the hall. U.S. military officials working at the palace are stunned when they see Eaton sitting in there—why is Eaton in a tiny office? Eaton, says one military official, "was incensed." (When I ask Eaton about the incident, he declines to comment, though he insists he had a "very positive" transfer of power with Petraeus.)

It's Petraeus marking his territory. Petraeus looks out the window of the palace and sees a trailer, where some poor schmuck soldier is living. He says he wants that one—the Joe gets his ass booted out within hours. "Petraeus," Lieutenant General John Vines will confide to colleagues, "leaves the dead dog on your doorstep. Every time." Another U.S. military official explains, "He has the ability to make anyone who comes before him look like a total fuckup." The U.S. military officials say it's this kind of behavior that earned him the nickname General Betray-Us years before the Moveon.org ad campaign.

Petraeus is getting attention in his new role, which brings out envy, those close to him will say. In August of 2004, he posed for the cover of

Newsweek—CAN THIS MAN SAVE IRAQ? This does not go over well with his colleagues in the military. He is showboating, he is drawing attention to himself. It will be years before he does another photo shoot like he did for that *Newsweek* story.

In the summer of 2004, at the height of the presidential election between John Kerry and George W. Bush, Petraeus writes an op-ed for *The Washington Post*, saying that the Americans were making progress in Iraq. It certainly didn't hurt his relationship with President Bush, despite the fact that there is absolutely no progress being made. Under his watch, one hundred thousand weapons supplied to the Iraqi army and police go missing. More disturbingly, the army and police units he trains go on to become the death squads in Iraq's brutal civil war—it's men "dressed like army and police" who rampage through Baghdad, killing tens of thousands, kidnapping men in the middle of the night, and, as we will learn later, running a system of secret prisons and torture dungeons. Yes, it's the Iraqi security forces trained and equipped by Petraeus who do these horrible things, who set the stage for the sectarian war in Baghdad. "After he leaves a legacy of shit behind because of the long-term effects of the choices he's made, he's never held to account," explains a U.S. military official in Baghdad. "No one calls him out."

After a stint running Leavenworth, where he oversees the rewriting of the counterinsurgency manual, he's given the chance to put his theories to work. He returns to Iraq in February 2007. He gets his surge of more than twenty thousand troops.

In September 2007, he cements his legacy: He testifies on Capitol Hill. The morning of his testimony, he gets attacked in a way he has never been attacked. A full-page advertisement in *The New York Times* calling him General Betray-Us, paid for by MoveOn.org. This one stings—this one, according to those close to him, shocks him. Before having said a word, to have his integrity, honor, and patriotism questioned? He's shocked that *The New York Times* even printed it. It says that he's been constantly "at war with the facts" and "cooking the books" for the White House.

The ad backfires, though—MoveOn.org overplays its hand. You don't question generals like that, at least not yet. The congressional testimony makes "him the face of the war in Iraq," a military official close to him tells me, adding, "he didn't enjoy that." President Bush from there on out will repeatedly defer to General Petraeus, hanging what's going on in Iraq around his neck.

The mainstream press worships him, treats what he did in Iraq as an almost Mother Teresa–like accomplishment. PETRAEUS'S MIRACLE touts a headline in *The Washington Post*; Petraeus is a "near miracle worker," *Newsweek* will say. Petraeus convinces the Beltway that we won in Iraq. He's a star, a historical figure. Autographed copies of Petraeus memorabilia command up to $825 on eBay. Those who know him say privately that he would never have run for president in 2012, but that hasn't stopped speculation that he'll be in the mix in 2016. He has joked about running for president at the American Enterprise Institute, a right-wing think tank, and PETRAEUS FOR PRESIDENT T-shirts are already available online.

In 2009, he flips the coin before the opening kickoff at the Super Bowl. Two years later, he has the chance to watch the Super Bowl from Kabul, where he'll help arrange the delivery of seven thousand pizzas from the United States for troops stationed there. Heads or tails? Win or lose? Can Petraeus repeat his "miracle" in Afghanistan?

47 | "TOURISM, NOT TERRORISM"

DECEMBER 2010, KANDAHAR

I was supposed to be convinced that we were making progress in Kandahar. The mayor of the city, Ghulam Hayder Hamidi, was supposed to do the convincing. I had an interview with him in the afternoon.

Back in the white Toyota Corolla, we made our way across town to the mayor's office.

"In November and October, I didn't leave my house," Ahmad said. "Now it is okay."

Okay is a relative word. In the past five days, there had been two assassinations and one major bombing. An improvement, Ahmad said.

Ahmad holed up for two months, fearing he'd be another victim in the widespread campaign of assassination that had paralyzed the city. Anyone who worked for the government or for a nongovernmental organization was a target. Afghan journalists, too. While the U.S. offensive in Kandahar reached its peak, there was at least one high-level assassination a day, an astonishing and unprecedented leap in violence. A source gave me a list of the names of 515 tribal elders and religious figures who'd been assassinated over the past nine years, gutting the ranks of the Afghans who Americans hoped to rely on.

No one knew how long the relative lull in violence would last. Everybody had a theory. Afghan officials said the Taliban had fled to Pakistan. American officials said they'd killed so many Taliban, the insurgency in Kandahar was permanently damaged. The Taliban admitted that the NATO offensive had taken its toll, but promised to be back in force once the winter was over. Sources in the Taliban told me that many insurgents had just left the countryside to hide in the city until the NATO operation was over.

The mayor's office was in a poorly lit, dark and dank building, one of those office complexes in conflict zones that seem to be permanently under construction, with cheap building materials scattered haphazardly about beneath random coils of wires. Security there was shockingly lax, considering that insurgents had already tried to kill the mayor once this past year; they failed, killing two of his deputy mayors instead. Our car sailed through the checkpoints without even a cursory search, and any one of the people I brought with me could have easily carried in a weapon or suicide vest.

"This has been the worst year," the mayor told me as we sat down to talk. The mayor was a short man with glasses and trimmed gray hair, the look of a beleaguered college professor who keeps hoping against hope that he'll get tenure one day. His deputy mayor was gunned down in the spring while praying in a mosque and his successor was gunned down in October on his way home from work. Nearly a third of his staff of seventy-six quit. (He also had to fire ten other staff members after a series of corruption investigations.) He had no luck filling the vacant slots— partly, he said, because he can only pay his employees thirty-five hundred afghani a month, or eighty dollars, half of what Mohammed Nabi's militiamen get.

The government in Kabul, he said, had promised to give his staff raises, but it's been months and he hasn't seen the extra funds. Kabul has also been slow to help get his police force in order, he said, not providing adequate funds for them, either. It was this kind of talk that prompted a U.S. official to tell me, "There's talk of transition next year. But in Kandahar, there's not going to be anything to transition to in a year."

I asked the mayor what he thought of the corruption accusations against Ahmed Wali Karzai, his friend. He responded indignantly, saying that AWK was being unfairly singled out, and that the real corruption was elsewhere—with other Afghan officials and Western reconstruction agencies. "Gul Agha Sherzai, why are you not writing that he is corrupt?" he asked me, naming the former Kandahar governor who now runs Nangarhar province.

He rattled off a few other names of corrupt government officials. "There are killers, enemies of society, sitting in our peace jirga," he said, referring to the conference to discuss peace that was recently held in Kandahar.

He had few kind words for the $250 million in reconstruction funding being poured into the city. He accused a Canadian firm of blowing $1.9 million on a solar panel system that didn't work, and a large development firm, IRD, of wasting millions on a program to harvest grapes.

"Why has the Taliban become angry? Why are they fighting? Because of weak and corrupt government, because of the deals made with warlords and power brokers," he said. But warlords and corruption are in the eye of the beholder—the mayor sees Abdul Razzik, a notorious human rights abuser and drug smuggler, as a "hero" and AWK as a victim of "propaganda." (Another of AWK's top associates, a powerful tribal elder and provincial council member named Hajji Agha Lalai, explains AWK's bad reputation like so: "People involved in drugs and drug dealing come to [Ahmed Wali's] house to visit and stay over at his house," he told me, "which has given the wrong impression.")

The mayor was of two minds regarding the prospects of success in Afghanistan. The enemy, he said, "hasn't lost their power." On the other hand, his public spiritedness prompted him to say that this summer will be more peaceful than the last. He told me he wanted to promote a new slogan for Kandahar: "Tourism, not terrorism."

Back at the motel, I met with one of the mayor's media advisors, a twenty-six-year-old named Berkazai. Besides advising the mayor on media, he published a newspaper and did reporting for a radio station. I asked him if things were getting better. "Better? I didn't say better. I said there have been only two targeted killings this week. This calm will not last forever. We have had military operations again and again, and this is not a solution to the problem."

48 | PETRAEUS DOES BODY COUNTS

OCTOBER 2010 TO AUGUST 2011, KABUL AND WASHINGTON, DC

In late October, Petraeus meets with President Karzai in a room at his palace. A dozen U.S. officials, including Ambassador Eikenberry, are there with him, sitting around a glass-topped, U-shaped table, according to one reported account of the meeting. Karzai has been pushing to ban security companies—the Americans don't want the ban to take place. Petraeus lectures Karzai for an hour. Karzai gets frustrated. Take your troops and go home, he says. Karzai tells Petraeus he has "three main enemies": the United States, the Taliban, and the international community. An Afghan official familiar with the meeting tells me, "He didn't care if Petraeus took his projects or his troops home."

Karzai will lash out publicly two weeks later: "The time has come to reduce the presence of, you know, boots in Afghanistan," he says. He says he might be a partner of America, but he's no "stooge."

Karzai doesn't want Petraeus's counterinsurgency plan. Petraeus isn't having much luck figuring him out. Petraeus tried to stand up to him, according to White House officials, and is standing up to him. He pushes through the controversial initiative to arm local militias, a plan that Karzai had been trying to block. It's his first run-in with the man in the funny hat. "Petraeus is big enough," says a senior U.S. official." When Karzai pushes, he pushes back."

In November, Petraeus flies to Lisbon, Portugal, for a conference with the NATO allies. Karzai refuses to go on the plane with him, but he does allow the speech he's going to give to get cleared by the Americans. Obama is going to be there as well, and Petraeus isn't supposed to steal the spotlight—he doesn't do any press conferences over the three days, a rarity for the general when he's surrounded by reporters at an international event.

In February, there's a civilian casualty incident in the eastern province of Konar. Karzai is claiming fifty civilians are dead. Karzai wants an apology. NATO pushes back: They say the Afghan governor is lying, or the Taliban is lying. Karzai insists on an apology. Petraeus is back in the palace for another meeting. Petraeus does not apologize. He accuses the Afghans of burning their own children to make it look like civilian casualties. Karzai and his staff are horrified. "I was dizzy. My head was spinning," one Afghan at the meeting told the *Post*. "This was shocking. Would any father do this to his children? This is really absurd." Says another Afghan official, "Killing sixty people, and then blaming the killing on those same people, rather than apologizing for any deaths? This is inhuman." Another source familiar with the meeting will tell me, "I'd never heard Karzai's people get so upset. They were truly offended."

As for President Obama, Petraeus's relationship is starting to get better, according to White House officials. He's reportedly more deferential to Petraeus's opinion.

That's personality stuff—on the policy stuff, it's a constant battle. The next strategic review is due in December. Petraeus will clash again in "daily battles with the White House," according to a U.S. official. Staffers at the National Security Council in Washington and at ISAF headquarters in Kabul are pulling fourteen-hour days to put together a document they could agree on. Problem is, they can't agree.

Petraeus and his staff are squaring off against a handful of key players in the White House—"the optimists versus the pessimists," as one U.S. official who worked on the review puts it. The metrics used to judge progress in Afghanistan are classified, U.S. officials familiar with the review say. Petraeus is focusing on a few key statistics to make his case: the growing number of Taliban commanders being killed and captured, the drop in average age of a typical Taliban commander (meaning they were killing more of them), evidence that the local population is becoming more receptive to U.S. troops, and signs that more Taliban fighters are joining the government. Military commanders in Afghanistan also stress what they see as security gains in Kandahar and Helmand provinces.

The intelligence community isn't buying Petraeus's spin about progress, and its new national intelligence estimate (NIE)—a document that distills the insights of the nation's seventeen intelligence agencies—threatens to repeat the "grim" assessment it had offered two years earlier to General David McKiernan. So the general sets out to remake the NIE to his liking. "Petraeus and his staff completely rewrote it," says a U.S. official with direct knowledge of the assessment, which remains classified. Every time the CIA or the NSC cited something negative, Petraeus pushed to include something positive. "There was much more back and forth between the military and the intelligence community than usual," says another official who has read the NIE. "The draft I saw reflected this debate."

Petraeus wants more time. He continues to walk back from the July 2011 deadline. Petraeus says it's not a "sure thing" that the war would be over by 2014.

Petraeus steps up the violence. He drastically ups the number of airstrikes, launching more than 3,450 between July and November, the most since the invasion in 2001. He introduces U.S. tanks into the battle, unleashes Apache and Kiowa attack helicopters, and triples the number of night raids by Special Forces, killing and capturing thousands of insurgents. At the briefings every morning, Al-Qaeda, says one senior military official, is almost never mentioned. More shockingly, Petraeus signs off on the total leveling of a small town in southern Afghanistan, Tarok Kolache. Commanders on the ground will claim that it is "Taliban infested" and that it required forty-nine thousand and two hundred pounds of bombs to level it. They say there were no civilian casualties, as all the residents had been cleared before the explosives went off. They say they are going to rebuild the town immediately. The pictures of the village reveal a before and after like the war has never seen, a mini–shock and awe. An entire village wiped out, and then given one million taxpayer dollars to rebuild it. A blogger who accompanies the unit will dismiss one Afghan man's complaints about the destruction of his house as a "fit of theatrics." This blogger is a Petraeus protégé and is also working on a biography about him.

Petraeus is looking to find his groove on the diplomatic side. He's not getting much help from Eikenberry. Eikenberry tells his staff in December that he's on his way out. Eikenberry is extremely unpopular within the military and within the embassy, and has been almost totally ineffective. He's been a constant critic of Petraeus's plan, and U.S. officials familiar with the relationship between the general and the ambassador describe it as "lukewarm" and "so-so." Eikenberry is in a downward slide that began after two top secret cables were published in January 2009 in *The New York Times*, followed by the release of WikiLeaks cables later in the year in which he criticizes Karzai, as well as calling Karzai "off his meds" and a possible manic depressive in Woodward's book. One State Department official in Kabul describes the atmosphere at the U.S. embassy as "rudderless," with many of Eikenberry's top deputies operating in a "micromanaged culture of fear."

Even Eikenberry's own people have been telling the White House he's useless. In October, a senior official from the embassy met in Washington with General Doug Lute, a top player at the National Security Council, and told him that Eikenberry's relationship with Karzai is "completely destroyed." U.S. officials describe Eikenberry's tenure as one of the great tragedies of the war—that a man widely respected for his knowledge of Afghanistan was unable to stop a military strategy he knew was destined to fail.

In Kabul, rumors of Eikenberry's imminent departure abound; a former U.S. ambassador came just short of publicly calling for his resignation, a sentiment that Afghan officials express privately. Petraeus needs a diplomatic partner he can work with, like he did with Ambassador Ryan Crocker in Baghdad. Petraeus needs someone to act as counterweight. He once joked that Holbrooke was his "wingman." Holbrooke found this amusing, but thought it was also misguided: "Since when did a diplomat become the general's wingman?" he said to his friends. "It should be the other way around."

On December 16, President Obama gives a speech about the review. The final report, in fact, says almost nothing. We are making progress, but that progress is fragile and reversible. We have broken the momentum of the Taliban, but there will still be heavy fighting with the Taliban next year. The troops are going to start coming home soon, but they aren't going to start coming home soon. We aren't "nation-building," the president says, though we're committed to be in Afghanistan past 2014 to build its nation. It was, in the end, a nonreview review, which suits Petraeus just fine, giving him more time to shape the outcome not just in Kabul and Kandahar, but in Washington. Petraeus will tell an interviewer, he's not looking for "a graceful exit."

At another meeting in the fall, one of Petraeus's top generals briefs on anticorruption in the Yellow Building at ISAF headquarters. Billions of dollars in cash, the country dominated by a "criminal oligarchy of politically connected businessman," according to one study.

(The latest: Kabul Bank, once a highlight of progress, turns out to be one of the largest scams going, reaching the highest levels of government. The Americans know all about the scandal. They have the wiretaps and electronic intercepts of the Afghan players, "acting all like the Godfather," says one U.S. official who is familiar with the intelligence, "talking about payoffs and how they're going to fuck the other partners.")

One participant in the meeting suggests the White House has a different view of the corruption problem. "The White House doesn't always understand the reality on the ground," Petraeus explains to those gathered at the briefing.

Yes, only Petraeus understands the reality on the ground. It's his reality. He wants to repeat his success in Iraq. That was a success made out of shaping the narrative as much as any tactical success. Or, as one U.S. military official put it to me, "If anyone can spin their way out of this war, it's Petraeus."

Petraeus keeps claiming progress, despite the fact that violence keeps going up. In 2011, February, April, May, and June all have record levels of violence. Petraeus explains that violence is going up because that's what happens when you send soldiers to fight in areas that they weren't in before. This is true, but it provides a convenient win-win situation: If violence goes up, it's progress. If violence goes down, it's progress. So sayeth Petraeus.

Petraeus is tired. How can he not be tired? How can he not feel the stress and the pressure of the grueling days? "Petraeus hates Afghanistan," says an Afghan official who has worked with him. Petraeus is already looking for his out. He talks with Bob Gates about becoming the head of the CIA. He can get out of his uniform and get into Washington. He can be at the heart of the intelligence community; he can make the transformation of the CIA from an intelligence gathering unit to a DoD-like paramilitary organization complete. In April, President Obama announces Petraeus will become his next CIA chief. In June, he returns home, his tour in Afghanistan complete. In August, a retirement ceremony is held for him. No top White House officials attend. By nearly all accounts, Petraeus has exited gracefully.

49 | THE NEW AFGHANISTAN

DECEMBER 17, 2010, SPIN BOLDAK

We'd left early in the morning to get to the interview. It was a ninety-minute drive from Kandahar, heading toward the Pakistan border. I'd hired two cars for the trip—one that I'd be in, and the other to drive ahead to look out for any problems. If one car broke down, we'd have a backup, too. The two-lane road was nicely paved with very few potholes. It was the nicest road I'd ever seen in Afghanistan. My translator and bodyguard argued over the reasons for it.

"The Americans built this road," my bodyguard, Kazzi, said, "so they can invade Pakistan."

"The Americans built this road," Fareed Ahmad countered, "so Pakistan can invade Afghanistan."

We arrived in the town of Spin Boldak and pulled off into a walled compound. Originally, I had wanted to see Ahmed Wali Karzai, the president's half brother, but he was in Dubai for the week, unsurprisingly. Instead, we'd lined up a meeting with the young warlord Abdul Razzik. An American spy balloon hovered to the east, keeping watch on the border. The United States was building a new base in the area, and there was another small outpost that my translator mysteriously referred to as the Blackwater base, though I couldn't figure out why—it seemed like it was just another compound for a military contracting business. Afghan guards waved us through a set of Hesco barriers and we were brought into an office to wait for Razzik to arrive. He got there fifteen minutes later.

"General Petraeus and I have very similar opinions," Razzik said, taking a seat in his office along the wall. "I want to kill the Taliban, he wants to kill the Taliban." At just under five feet nine, the thirty-four-year-old—turning thirty-five soon, he said—was a bundle of charisma and charm. A beard, a sly smile, camouflage desert fatigues with a head of hat hair, all vibe and innate confidence and uncanny warmth. A picture of Afghan president Hamid Karzai hung above a desk empty of papers, and there was a black desktop Dell computer that was switched off—Razzik didn't know how to read anyway, so paper and the Internet would just get in the way of his work, which was basically kicking Taliban ass by any means necessary. From most accounts, he'd been doing a pretty bang-up job of it lately, leading a series of operations around the country's most dangerous province. "We don't take prisoners—if they are trying to kill me, I will try to kill them. That's how I order my men," he tells me. He paused, perhaps his recent American public relations training kicking in. "If they submit, and say they made a mistake, then yes, we will take them prisoner."

Razzik ran Spin Boldak, the Afghan border town, which also happened to be one of the most lucrative spots to make a buck—an estimated three hundred thousand dollars passed through each day, easy money to skim for an ambitious border chief, which Razzik most certainly was. Since Petraeus took over command, his influence had expanded well beyond his hometown into Afghanistan's second largest city, Kandahar. He's one of the reasons for the lull in violence I keep hearing about, according to U.S. and Afghan officials. I'd scheduled an interview with him because of his skyrocketing star status, topped off with a visit this past fall from Petraeus himself. The two men got along swimmingly, according to Razzik's account, meeting for an hour and a half and exchanging ideas on both the security situation and the lack of potential for peace in Afghanistan. ("How can we have peace talks while the Taliban are still killing tribal elders and women and children?" Razzik tells me, another point on which he says Petraeus agreed.) It was the second time he'd met Petraeus—the first was when Petraeus was "just a three-star," he says—and now, despite his official rank of colonel, Razzik calls himself a general, too.

Razzik is the on-steroids version of the Afghan Local Police, the name for the militia program that Mohammed Nabi is a part of. If you were going to make a movie of Colonel Razzik's life—which actually is incredibly cinematic—you could call it *Afghanistan Gangster*, attaching Ridley Scott as the director. Razzik would be in the Denzel Washington role—maybe Petraeus or one of Razzik's Special Forces buddies could get Russell Crowe to stand in for him. As the men's two life stories intertwine, connected by a war that shaped their existence, giving each a rise to fame and fortune, the audience would be left pondering the differences and similarities between the two men.

The film would open with the major trauma of Razzik's life: In 1995, his uncle was killed fighting the Taliban, and his eleven-year-old brother was taken prisoner. While many of the anti-Taliban forces fled to Pakistan, Razzik decided to stay in the country and fight, hiding in the sandy mountains south of town, taken in and hidden by shepherds of his own tribe. He then snuck up to Kabul, where he fought for a few months alongside Afghan hero Ahmad Shah Massoud before leaving town to fight in Herat against the Taliban, in western Afghanistan. In Herat, his leaders also decided to turn tail—they fled to Iran. Again, Razzik refused to leave his own country. ("Iran and Pakistan are our enemies; why would I go there?" he tells me.) He returned home in a white Toyota Corolla, which the Taliban took from him just a few miles outside Spin Boldak. He had to walk another two kilometers before a rickshaw picked him up and took him the rest of the way to his relatives. He swore then to pick up arms and fight against the Taliban if he ever had the chance—the U.S. invasion after September 11 would give him that. It's here where the official version of his story gets a bit blurry: How did a twentysomething Afghan become one of the most powerful figures in the province?

In 2002, he was named chief of the border police in Spin Boldak, thanks in part to his tribal connections. The Achekizai tribe had run the border for decades and had allied themselves with the Soviets during the eighties. With Hamid Karzai—and Ahmed Wali Karzai, provincial chief of Kandahar, and Gul Agha Sherzai, then governor—as his patrons, he consolidated his power, creating one of the most stable districts in Afghanistan. It was a vital district as well, as NATO supplies and other goods from Pakistan come across the border daily. (As Razzik points out, not a single NATO serviceman has been killed in Spin Boldak.) U.S. military and diplomatic officials started to believe that he had become a central figure in a large-scale drug ring, shipping illegal narcotics over the border. More disturbing reports filtered up the chain of command, concerning executions and "indiscriminate tactics against men, women, children," as one human rights official put it.

His reputation as a killer grew during an offensive in 2006, where he terrorized the population of a rival tribe. "People began to say he was here to kill every Noorzai he could find," according to one eyewitness. The aggressive tactics backfired, however. "In our area, the Taliban went from forty to four hundred in days," said another eyewitness. Other stories started to circulate: According to local reports, Razzik's men stopped sixteen civilians on their way to a New Year's celebration and summarily executed them. Razzik was briefly suspended while his men were investigated, but the results of the inquiry were never made public. As he took a leading role in operations around Kandahar in 2010, more human rights abuses were reported, though local Afghans were too afraid of retribution to go on the record. A Human Rights Watch report came to the same conclusion about Razzik: "In Afghanistan an ordinary person can't do anything," an Afghan was quoted as saying. "But a government person can do what he wants—killing, stealing, anything."

The swirling allegations did give NATO a temporary pause. On February 4, 2010, deputy to U.S. ambassador to Afghanistan Karl Eikenberry met with the then intelligence chief, Major General Michael Flynn, along with a number of other American officials supposedly involved in stopping corruption. The meeting was intended to figure out how to handle the "prominent Afghan malign actors" or "corrupt/criminal Afghan officials," according to a leaked State Department cable describing the meeting. Three Afghan officials were specifically named and discussed at the meeting based on information from the "intel and law enforcement files" that had been gathered on them: Ahmed Wali Karzai, a police chief and, yes, Abdul Razzik. By embracing Razzik, U.S. officials acknowledged in another cable, they were undercutting any chance for legitimate governance: "by ascribing unaccountable authority to Razzik, the Coalition unintentionally reinforces his position through its direct and near-exclusive dealings with him on all major issues in Spin Boldak."

American officials briefly considered ways to sideline Razzik and his partners in crime, like Ahmed Wali Karzai. Take them out? Capture them? Bring corruption charges or legal cases against them? At minimum, U.S. officials thought, they could at least try to give them a slap on the wrist—by (1) having "no public meetings with the official (and no photos), and no high-profile public visits from CODELs [congressional delegations] and other dignitaries; (2) no giving or receiving of gifts; and (3) restrictions on opportunities for corrupt officials to participate in U.S.-funded training, travel, and speaking engagements," according to a leaked cable. The cable concluded that "Applying minimum COAs [courses of action] is designed to help change perceptions held by parts of the Afghan public that the U.S. supports, explicitly or implicitly, known corrupt officials." Over the past year, even those modest goals were abandoned, much to the dismay of local Afghans. "Americans are always choosing stupid friends here," says Izatullah Wasifi, a former governor in Herat. "Razzik has killed hundreds of people. Karzai and the rest are all crooked, and they are ruling now. They're seeking a weak and fragmented state for their own self-interest. We are heading to another civil war. To get stuck in this shit? That's a shame."

After Petraeus assumed command, any pretense of even the most minimal punishment became a joke. If the Afghan government was a criminal syndicate, it was a syndicate we embraced. We both implicitly and explicitly supported corrupt officials that U.S. officials had fretted about months earlier. Ambassador Eikenberry posed for a photo op with Razzik in November. In August, Razzik received even more funding and direct ISAF military support, officially getting welcomed to run operations around Kandahar; and he's been given the gift of a dedicated Special Forces team to personally advise him and a force of three thousand Afghans under his command. "Sometimes I travel in the American helicopters, sometimes in my own trucks and Humvees, sometimes even in the Corollas," he says.

It still wasn't a relationship that everyone in the government was comfortable with, but perceived expediency had clearly won out over any chickenshit moral qualms. "On one side, you have State, DEA, FBI saying, hey, this guy is a smuggler, a criminal, he's letting drugs in over the border," a U.S. official in Kabul tells me. "On the other side there's the CIA and the military, who are saying, this guy is giving us good intel in Panjway or Zabul, or wherever else." (In fact, by supporting Razzik, Petraeus and the U.S. military were pushing up against American law: A condition in the supplemental bill passed last year to fund the war stated that no U.S. money could go to units where there was "credible" evidence of human rights violations. In the fall of 2011, a journalist for *The Atlantic* will publish photos of Razzik's torture victims.)

To me, Razzik represented just how warped our role in Afghanistan had become. He was getting the Extreme Makeover, Afghan Edition. As in Iraq, insurgents and criminals of yesterday became the heroes and patriots of tomorrow. His military and Special Forces advisor had gone into overdrive to refurbish his image. Another State Department cable suggested offering Razzik an "information operations" team to rehabilitate his image by getting "stories in the international press." Nine months later, his senior American military advisor told *The Washington Post* that he was like "Robin Hood," while Major General Nick Carter endorsed him as "Afghan good enough," a play off the most condescending and colonial phrase imported from Iraq. (*Iraq good enough* basically meaning a high-grade level of shit.) In November, his Special Forces mentor gushed to *The Wall Street Journal* that he was a "folk hero," bragging about his recent exploits, like when his men accidentally ran a truck into a tree and a suicide bomber popped out, blowing up. As one Afghan contractor told me, "The difference between Abdul Razzik and others in government: When Abdul Razzik sees a Taliban, he kills them. Karzai and the rest are part Talib, part government."

Not all of the coverage has been positive, however. Razzik almost didn't do the interview with me, he told my translator, because he doesn't feel like his recent portrayals in the press have been fair, blaming the "journalists in Kabul" for biased coverage. (Usually, news stories about Razzik mention that he's been accused of human rights abuses, graft, and drug smuggling.) In a magazine profile from last year, he was tagged as a drug lord—that story, Razzik says, was because the author was associated with the Pakistani intelligence service, the ISI. "It's a democracy, so sometimes the press you get is bad and sometimes it is good," he says rather diplomatically when I ask about all the accusations. "But I think the press should act responsibly and not spread rumors and suspicions to target a man's character with no proof."

Once we begin to leave Afghanistan, it will be warlords like Abdul Razzik who'll take over. And if we aren't engaged in "nation-building," then it doesn't really matter what kind of government we leave behind in Kabul, as long as the Afghans let us use their country as a base for killing Al-Qaeda. Robert Grenier, a former CIA station chief in Islamabad, called for just that—balancing a "small but capable Afghan army" with "local militia forces . . . sometimes disparaged as warlords" to provide "a platform for U.S. lead counterterror operations." In the end, despite all of the counterinsurgency doctrine's emphasis on good governance, the desire for stability trumps the fight for human rights. The face of Afghanistan after ten years of America's war is that of a thirty-four-year-old drug lord.

Sitting in the office at Razzik's base, I was reminded of something that Berkazai, the mayor's media advisor, told me. "The world promised us, America promised us democracy and human rights," he said. "If America is fighting for that, they should stay. If they are not, if they are going to leave behind militias and warlords, then they should leave now."

That would suit Colonel Abdul Razzik just fine. I finished up my interview with him. I posed for a picture with him. I noticed his watch—I showed him mine, a Breitling Super Ocean. He showed me his, a diamond-encrusted black Concord. "Nice watch," I said, and he returned the compliment. We strolled outside to take a look around his base. He had a parking lot full of Humvees and armored SUVs, all provided by the Americans. He pointed out a fort on top of the small rocky hill behind his headquarters. "That's an old British castle," he says. "It's about ninety years old." I asked him what his plans for the future were. "It is the happiest time in my life," he says. "I am the police chief around here, and I am in my own country."

He asked if I needed security for the trip back. I politely declined, thanking him for his time. As we drove back to Kandahar, my translator noticed that we were being followed by two green Ford Rangers, courtesy of Colonel Razzik. He wanted to be sure his guests left safely.

50 | JOE BIDEN IS RIGHT

DECEMBER 10, 2010, TO JUNE 2011,
WASHINGTON, DC, AND KABUL

On December 10, 2010, Ambassador Richard Holbrooke walks into Secretary of State Hillary Clinton's office in Foggy Bottom. He turns pale; he puts his hands over his eyes and tells the secretary of state that he's not feeling right. She picks up the phone and calls an ambulance—she wants him brought to George Washington University Hospital a few blocks away. Holbrooke, being Holbrooke, argues that he'd rather be taken to Sibley Hospital. Hillary wins this battle.

The doctors diagnose him with a torn aorta. It requires lengthy surgery.

On December 13, it's the night of the annual Christmas party at the State Department. About three hundred people gather in the eighth-floor ballroom, most of the foreign emissaries in the city. Clinton takes Holbrooke's staff of about thirty into a private room and tells them how much his staff means to Holbrooke, calling him "a true fighter." Obama joins the private gathering, offering his support to Holbrooke's wife, Kati, and the ambassador's two sons. Out in the main ballroom, the singer Marvin Hamlisch entertains the crowd with Christmas carols, singing "Deck the Halls" and "Frosty the Snowman," a surreal moment, officials on Holbrooke's staff will later recall, listening to the festive tunes while their boss was on life support at the hospital only a few blocks away. Obama gives a speech to the assembled crowd, calling Holbrooke a "titan" of diplomacy.

Before the president's speech, Holbrooke's family leaves for the hospital. Soon after, his son Anthony would take the elevator down to the hospital lobby. He has tears in his eyes. "He's gone," he says to a friend. They smoke a cigarette outside. Clinton arrives in the lobby next. She'd rushed over from the ballroom within five minutes after learning of Holbrooke's death. Along with her assistant, Huma Abedin, and her security detail, they sit, wiped out in the Starbucks connected to the lobby of George Washington Univeristy hospital. Holbrooke's other close friends start to arrive—senators, journalists, and the dearest members of his staff—trickling in over the next hour. As the mourners gather, Clinton takes command. "We need an Irish wake for Richard," she tells his family and friends, saying they would plan a tribute for him. But right now, she observes, everybody needs a drink. "Where's the nearest bar?" she asks.

Hillary and Holbrooke's staff go to the Ritz Carleton on M and 22nd. They drink and share stories, an impromptu wake. Hillary consoles his staff members—she was a close friend of Richard's as well. The crowd begins to split up into smaller groups, with a few friends heading to Holbrooke's Georgetown apartment to be with the ambassador's family, where they order Thai food and talk late into the night. It starts to snow outside. His son Antony leaves, and walks back to a member of Holbrooke's staff's apartment in Foggy Bottom, where he's crashing on the couch, a symbol of just how close the ambassador was to the people who both loved him and worked for him.

The Pakistanis send dozens of flowers, which Holbrooke's friends joke should be "swept for listening devices." There's a gathering in Holbrooke's wife's Central Park West apartment in New York City on Friday, December 17, which draws celebrities and political leaders—Bill and Hillary are there, Chelsea Clinton, Al Gore. "You know, if Dad were here today, he'd be pretty proud that you all came out here for him—he loved this sort of stuff, being at the center of attention," Holbrooke's other son, David, tells the room. "But he'd also think you're crazy to be here talking about him when the Heat are in town playing the Knicks right now."

On January 14, 2011, there's a memorial for him at the Kennedy Center. Two presidents speak, Clinton and Obama. His friends notice a distance during Obama's remarks ("You could tell Obama just didn't know him," says one State Department official, comparing Obama's remarks to Clinton's), which to them symbolizes something larger: Obama's failure to embrace and listen to Holbrooke represented a larger failure to get control of the war in Afghanistan.

Holbrooke's replacement is named, Ambassador Marc Grossman. As special envoy to Pakistan and Afghanistan, Holbrooke had an odd role, where he had to fight for his own diplomatic turf. He did so by the force of his personality, which poses a problem for Grossman: He's got a lower profile. It's a signal, according to State Department officials, that the White House is trying to shut down Holbrooke's operation, putting an end to the special envoy slot. It's the White House quietly "strangling" the position that Holbrooke held, says one State Department official.

It marks the shift to unmake Afghanistan as an issue.

In January, Vice President Biden travels to Afghanistan and meets with Petraeus. "It's a little uncomfortable with those two," says a White House official. "Petraeus views him as the competition." During one of his meetings, Biden listens to Petraeus's reports on progress. Biden sees the larger game ahead: The military is making its case for why it needs to stay longer, testing out the arguments they'll make to avoid the planned drawdown in July 2011. "He could tell they were going to try to stay as long as possible," says a White House official. At another stop along the trip, an American civilian talked to Biden about a well they were building. "Why do they need a well?" Biden says, sensing "mission creep."

Over the next few months, Biden quietly presses the president to change the mission in Afghanistan, to get as far as possible away from the decade-long nation-building commitment that Petraeus wants and to the counterterrorism proposal he'd advocated for two years earlier. White House officials start to make the case: The surge worked, let's declare victory and go home.

There's an increasing confidence within the White House. They help to rehabilitate Stanley McChrystal's image, appointing him to lead a high-profile initiative supporting military families—no need to have a potential voice criticizing the administration in the upcoming election, either. McChrystal spends his first fall out of the United States military teaching at Yale University in New Haven, Connecticut. The students love him. One morning, as he gets off the train, he bumps into a professor who's jogging. The professor recognizes him. "General McChrystal," the professor says. "Don't call me general. I'm Stan, I got fired," McChrystal jokes. There is a controversy when a screening of a documentary about Pat Tillman is scheduled to air; the Yale College Democrats back away from endorsing it. He starts up a consulting company, the McChrystal Group. He names Dave Silverman as his cofounder and CEO. He signs up with a speaker's bureau, and he's reportedly getting $60,000 a speaking engagement. He gets a slot on the board of JetBlue. He allows another profile of him to be written by a *Yale Daily News* reporter, giving her full access to his classroom. The profile opens with McChrystal arriving at the classroom an hour and twenty minutes early, now as fully dedicated to his new teaching gig as he was to the missions he commanded in war.

In February, he gives a speech with Greg Mortenson at Yale. In March, he gives another speech at the prestigious TED conference in Long Beach, California. He talks about leadership and the Middle East. He gets a standing ovation.

On April 8, the Defense Department investigation into McChrystal and his staff is completed. The investigators didn't talk to McChrystal or

Rolling Stone. The investigation reads comically—no one the investigators spoke to admits to saying what they said, but they also don't admit to the quotes not having been said. It also contradicts the findings of the earlier Army investigation. "In some instances, we found no witness who acknowledged making or hearing the comments as reported. In other instances, we confirmed that the general substance of the incident at issue occurred, but not in the exact context described in the article," the report states. McChrystal says he doesn't remember hearing the "bite me" response (though he laughed when he heard it). Jake McFerren doesn't admit to saying it. Witnesses deny that McChrystal shared his private interactions with Obama, offering that McChrystal considered the "contents of his discussions [with the president] sacrosanct." (Though I had witnessed him share the contents of those discussions with his staff, and he'd shared them with me as well.) Charlie Flynn wouldn't admit to McChrystal having given him the middle finger, though if he had, "it would not have been a failure by GEN McChrystal to treat his executive officer with dignity or respect," the report says. Dave Silverman wouldn't admit to calling the French "fucking gay," though the report concludes "witnesses testified the comment was not directed toward any French official, or toward French government or military." The report found "insufficient evidence" that they called themselves "Team America." (Though Dave, Casey, Duncan, and a few others on his staff had called themselves that.) In a section of the report titled "Conduct at Kitty O'Shea's," the report concludes: "Our analysis of witness testimony led us to conclude that the behavior of GEN McChrystal and his staff at Kitty O'Shea's, while celebratory, was not drunken, disorderly, disgraceful, or offensive."

It is the last whitewash of McChrystal's military career.

Two days after the report is finished, the White House announces that President Obama appointed McChrystal as an unpaid advisor to military families. Mary Tillman, Pat Tillman's mother, is outraged. "It's a slap in the face to all soldiers," she says of the choice. "He deliberately helped cover up Pat's death. And he has never adequately apologized to us." In the following months, McChrystal will sit down and give off-the-record interviews to a number of high-profile journalists. He'll tell one television pundit that the generals in the Pentagon don't trust the White House. In another talk, he'll say that if he were Obama, he'd have fired himself "several times," while describing Afghanistan as stuck "in some kind of post-apocalyptic nightmare." In the fall of 2011, on the tenth anniversary of the war, he tells the Council on Foreign Relations the war is just "a little better than 50 percent" done. General Michael Flynn takes a job in intelligence analysis back at the Pentagon, and gets his third star. His brother Charlie gets a promotion to general, too. Duncan Boothby moves to DC, determined to continue his career. The family of Sergeant Michael Ingram will set up a foundation in his honor called Mikie's Minutes, which donates calling cards to troops serving in Afghanistan.

In Afghanistan, both the UN and International Red Cross say that violence is the worst it has been in nine years, and security across the country is deteriorating. A group of highly respected academics and Afghanistan experts publish an open letter to President Obama, saying that negotiating, not an increase in military operations, is the only way out. "We are losing the battle for hearts and minds," the experts write. "What was supposed to be a population centered strategy is now a full-scale military campaign causing civilian casualties and destruction of property."

On July 12, Ahmed Wali Karzai is assassinated. Military officials try to put a positive spin on it, saying now a "more constructive local leadership" can take his place. Fifteen days later, Mayor Ghulam Hamidi, who I had interviewed months before in Kandahar, is also killed.

In Washington, political pressure to get out is building. According to the latest poll, 64 percent of Americans—a record level—don't think the war is worth fighting. On Capitol Hill, 204 congressmen voted against funding for the war last year, up from 109 in 2010. A host of think tanks express serious doubts: The left-leaning Center for American Progress is calling for an "accelerated withdrawal," and the bipartisan Council on

Foreign Relations has concluded that "at best, the margin for U.S. victory is likely to be slim."

In late February, President Obama meets with his national security team in the White House room. Hillary is there, Doug Lute is there, Tom Donilon, Bob Gates, Admiral Mullen. The topic of discussion: negotiations with the Taliban. They want to start with secret, high-level talks as quickly as possible. Lute says that the current strategy is no longer tenable. They discuss possible places to negotiate: Turkey and Saudi Arabia are the two biggest contenders. They can't make the missteps of the past summer, when they were duped into giving millions to a Taliban impostor. It signals a significant change—finally, after years of expensive and fruitless fighting, plans to negotiate. At the meeting, Vice President Joe Biden comes in with about five minutes left, according to sources familiar with the meeting. He's exuding confidence, White House officials tell me, sure that he's been proven right by history. The plan Biden had called for a year earlier is the plan that the Pentagon is going to be forced to adopt.

It only took an additional 711 American lives and 2,777 Afghan lives for the White House to arrive at this conclusion.

July 2011 is approaching. That's the date Obama promised to start bringing troops home. In June, he holds a series of meeting with Petraeus. Obama tells Gates and Mullen to warn Petraeus—no leaks this time, no getting fucked by the press. No repeat of the "Seven Days in May dynamic" of 2009, says one national security official to a reporter— a reference to the film about American military generals staging a coup against the president. Petraeus is playing nice. Obama meets with Petraeus three times—he wants options for the drawdown. Petraeus suggests keeping the thirty thousand troops until the end of 2012. Petraeus wants to move the troops to eastern Afghanistan, where the fighting has gotten worse. Obama shuts the door on the plan. He says he's going to bring ten thousand home by the end of the year, and twenty thousand more home by the end of the summer of 2012. Petraeus's allies complain to the press, and the next general in charge of the war, General John Allen, will go on the record to say that the president isn't following the military's advice. What the president decided, says Allen, "was a more aggressive [drawdown] option than which was presented," and "was not" what Petraeus had recommended.

This time, though, the charges don't stick. Obama has regained control of his policy from the Pentagon. The war is too unpopular, the myth of progress too obviously a lie.

Obama gives a speech on June 24, 2011, announcing his decision to start the drawdown. "The tide of war is receding," he says. "It's time to focus on nation-building here at home."

EPILOGUE:
SOMEDAY, THIS WAR'S
GONNA END

MAY 1, 2011, WASHINGTON, DC

The car horns sounded like victory. I could hear them blaring from my apartment. Osama Bin Laden was dead. We'd killed him.

I sent a message to a friend in the intelligence community who'd been working on finding Bin Laden for the last five years. "God Bless America and God bless those who kept up the vigil," he replied. A former soldier who'd lost both his feet in Iraq texted me: "We got Bin Laden!" I went on Twitter and sent my congratulations to the president and his staff who'd pulled off the operation. A few blocks from my apartment, crowds gathered in front of the White House to cheer. I didn't join them.

The details of Bin Laden's killing would trickle out over the days ahead. The White House would lift its curtain to provide reporters with the dramatic scenes of bureaucratic decision making. On Sunday morning, Obama plays only nine holes of golf, nervous about the mission he ordered the previous night. In the afternoon, he gathered in the situation room at the White House with his national security team. Biden played with a rosary ring he had in his pocket; Admiral Mullen had his own. Hillary put her hands up over her mouth as the White House photographer took pictures—her face is an expression of terror, what she later claimed was allergies. After they had been watching the video feed for forty minutes, the Navy SEAL team sent back the word for success: Geronimo. Obama turned to his team: "We got him."

I was in New York City on September 11, 2001, a senior in college. After the towers collapsed, I walked ninety-five blocks to get as close to Ground Zero as possible so I could see firsthand the destruction that would define our future. By the time I got to Baghdad four years later, very few Americans believed that the people we were fighting in Iraq posed a threat to the United States. Even the military press didn't bother lying about it anymore, referring to our enemies as "insurgents" rather than "terrorists." A woman I loved was killed in Baghdad in January 2007—Al-Qaeda in Iraq took credit for it—and my younger brother fought for fifteen months as an infantry platoon leader, earning a Bronze Star. Other friends—both Americans and Iraqis—suffered their own losses, living without limbs, loved ones, and in exile without homes.

By the fall of 2008, when I had moved on to Afghanistan, Bin Laden and Al-Qaeda were barely footnotes to what we were doing there. "It's not about Bin Laden," a military intelligence official told me. "It's about fixing the mess." If it wasn't about Bin Laden, then what the fuck was it about? Why were we fighting wars that took us no closer to the man responsible for unleashing the horror of September 11? When I traveled with McChrystal, I was shocked when General Michael Flynn had told me that he didn't think we'd ever get Bin Laden. Yet each time our presidents and generals told us why we were still fighting in Iraq and Afghanistan, they always used Bin Laden and September 11 as an excuse. As long as they insisted on fighting these wars we didn't need to fight, the wound to the American psyche wasn't allowed to heal.

Right from the start, the idea of the War on Terror was a fuzzy one at best. We were promised there would be no "battlefields or beachheads," as President George W. Bush put it. It would be a secret war, conducted mostly in the dark, no holds barred. And that's how it might have played had we gotten Bin Laden early on, dead or alive. But that's not what happened. Instead, we went on a rampage in the full light of day. We got our battlefields and beachheads after all. Kabul, Kandahar, Baghdad, Fallujah, Ramadi, Najaf, Mosul, Kirkuk, Basra, Kabul and Kandahar again—the list went on and on. We couldn't find Bin Laden, so we went after anyone who looked like him.

Bin Laden's death revealed the biggest lie of the war, the "safe haven" myth, Afghanistan's version of WMDs. The concept of waging an extremely expensive and bloody counterinsurgency campaign to prevent safe havens never truly made sense. Terrorists didn't need countries. Bin Laden had been killed in Pakistan, an American ally and recipient of $20 billion in foreign aid since 2001. He had lived out in the open in a suburb of Islamabad, a five-minute walk from a Pakistani military training academy. The majority of terrorist attacks against the West had been planned over the past decade not from Afghanistan, but from other countries and our own—Yemen, Nigeria, Somalia, Indonesia, Pakistan, Connecticut, Texas, and London. Worse, rather than decreasing the threat of terrorism, our large-scale troop interventions spawned an unprecedented level of suicide bombers—there were more than twenty times more suicide bombings in the past ten years than there had been in the previous three decades. We'd been fighting the wrong war, in the wrong way, in the wrong country.

Nearly three thousand Americans were killed on September 11. Since then, 6,000 American servicemen and -women have been killed in Iraq and Afghanistan, and over forty-two thousand have been wounded. More than three thousand allied soldiers have died, along with nearly twelve hundred private contractors, aid workers, and journalists. Since Obama became president, a thousand soldiers were killed in Afghanistan, more than double the total in the years under Bush. Most of the killing didn't take place in battles—it was in the dirty metrics of suicide bombs, death squads, checkpoint killings, torture chambers, and improvised explosive devices. Civilians on their way to work or soldiers driving around in circles, looking for an enemy they could seldom find. We may never know how many innocent civilians were killed in Iraq, Afghanistan, and Pakistan, but estimates suggest that more than a hundred and sixty thousand have died so far. Al-Qaeda, by contrast, has lost very few operatives in the worldwide conflagration—perhaps only "scores," as Obama would say. Maybe there weren't that many to begin with.

That night, I thought of all the dead, and what adding Bin Laden's name to the list actually meant. I thought of Ingram, and I thought of Arroyo, who would never sleep peacefully again. I thought of the thumbs I'd seen hanging off barbed wire, the pools of blood, like oil on concrete, in small outposts I could barely remember. The memorial services with grown men crying over empty boots. The memorial service with me crying over an empty coffin. The explosions in hotels and government office buildings. I thought of the operators, all of us who'd made our careers off Bin Laden's horror show: McChrystal, Petraeus, Duncan, Dave, the Flynns, Lamb, Starkey, Hoh, Hicks, the twenty-three Navy SEALs who killed him, and even the president himself, who'd ridden to power on an antiwar tide. I thought of the harsh judgment history was going to one day render on us all.

Strangely, Bin Laden's death would have little impact on the actual war—the war in Afghanistan hadn't been about capturing Bin Laden for many years. But it would have an impact on how Washington thought about the war. It would give Obama the political cover he needed to give his speech in June where we declared the war in Afghanistan was coming to an end, or at least the beginning of the beginning of the end.

SOURCE NOTES

This book is based primarily on my reporting collected during four trips to Afghanistan between 2008 and 2010, as well as interviews conducted with State Department, White House, and Pentagon officials in Washington, DC, from 2008 to 2011. During my time with General McChrystal, I recorded over twenty hours' worth of interviews and scenes with him and his staff. I also documented the journey contemporaneously with a half-dozen notebooks, a camera phone, and about seventy pages of single-spaced typed notes. Three other book-length inside accounts of the Obama administration's decision making in Afghanistan were particularly helpful: Jonathan Alter's *The Promise*, Richard Wolffe's *Revival*, and Bob Woodward's *Obama's Wars*. For the history of the war correspondent, Phillip Knightley's classic *The First Casualty* remains the definitive and most excellent account. For the chapter on counterinsurgency, I was greatly aided by Anne Marlowe's writings on David Galula (though I interpreted her work in my own fashion). Both Noah Schactman's and Spencer Ackerman's work on Robert Gates, the Pentagon, and counterinsurgency were also invaluable (again, the interpretation is my own). As always, I'm indebted to the daily journalism produced by the folks in the Kabul bureaus at *The Washington Post*, *The New York Times*, *The Wall Street Journal*, the Associated Press, and the *Financial Times*, among other publications. A few chapters contain material that has been previously published in *Rolling Stone*. The description of the suicide bombing in "Interlude: Dubai" was first reported in *GQ*. It was one of the more horrible things I've witnessed covering war, and I also referred to it in the afterword of my previous book. I have done my best to credit in these notes all the work that aided my writing of this story. Any oversights are unintentional and due mostly to the desire to see this book published in a timely manner. I've refrained from naming the two journalists mentioned in Chapter 7, "On the X," one for legal reasons, and the other because Duncan asked me not to. In Chapter 11, "Totally Shit-Faced," I refer to the British Special Forces commando as C. in order to protect his identity, as he's still involved in ongoing operations. Kerina is not the real name of the woman we encountered in the Berlin Ritz-Carlton. Nor are real names used for the Afghan translators and the security guards I employed. A version of the Epilogue was originally published as an essay in *Rolling Stone*.

CHAPTER 1. DELTA BRAVO

Page 3: *"Hello, Duncan?"*: Author interview with Duncan Boothby, April 7, 2010.
Page 4: *Hamid Karzai . . . had threatened to join*: A. Shaw and C. Bodden, "Lawmakers: Afghan Leader Threatens to Join the Taliban," Associated Press, April 5, 2010.

CHAPTER 2. IT'S NOT SWITZERLAND

Page 6: *A handful of staffers are watching television*: Author interview with military officials, ISAF HQ, October 2008.
Page 7: *"Sounds like someone's running for prom queen"*: Author interview with military officials, ISAF HQ, October 2008.
Page 7: *He pissed off Don Rumsfeld*: B. Graham, *By His Own Rules: The Ambition Successes and Ultimate Failures of Donald Rumsfeld* (New York: PublicAffairs, 2009), p. 408.
Page 7: *. . . McKiernan had testified to defend the Crusader*: K. Peraino, "Low-Key Leader," *Newsweek*, March 19, 2003.
Page 7: *After seeing McKiernan in Iraq*: B. Graham, *By His Own Rules: The Ambition Successes and Ultimate Failures of Donald Rumsfeld* (New York: PublicAffairs, 2009), p. 408.
Page 7: *His promotion to fourth star gets held up*: Ibid., p. 409; author interview with military officials, ISAF HQ, October 2008.
Page 8: *He gets dubbed the Quiet Commander*: Ibid. R. Neuman and E. Grossman, "The Quiet Commander," *U.S. News & World Report*, March 31, 2003.
Page 8: *Even in the midst of an invasion, "he is rarely known to swear"*: Ibid.

Page 8: *"In any type of a chaotic situation"*: Ibid.

Page 8: *His best friend growing up says*: Samieh Shalash, "WM Grad Makes *Time*'s Top 100 List," *Daily Press*, Newport News, Virginia, May 7, 2009.

Page 8: *He hates PowerPoint*: R. Neuman and E. Grossman, "The Quiet Commander," *U.S. News & World Report*, March 31, 2003.

Page 8: *. . . an autographed picture of himself*: W. Stern, "The General Motors," *Runner's World*, December 3, 2007.

Page 8: *. . . seem to treat war "like summer camp"*: Anne Scott Tyson, "Commander in Afghanistan Wants More Troops," *The Washington Post*, October 2, 2008.

Page 9: *This time, the staff gathers to watch the vice presidential debate*: Author interview with military officials, October 2008.

Page 9: *. . . NATO to pony up the reserves*: Rajiv Chandrasekaran, "Pentagon Worries Led to Command Change; McKiernan's Ouster Reflected New Realities in Afghanistan," *The Washington Post*, August 17, 2009.

Page 9: *Palin keeps calling him "McClellan"*: CQ Transcriptions, Sen. Joseph R. Biden Jr. and Gov. Sarah Palin Participate in a Vice Presidential Campaign Debate, October 2, 2008.

Page 9: *The staff breaks out laughing*: Author interview with military officials, October 2008.

Page 9: *"The reason we don't read about Afghanistan"*: CQ Transcriptions, Sen. Joseph R. Biden Jr. and Gov. Sarah Palin Participate in a Vice Presidential Campaign Debate, October 2, 2008.

Page 9: *"It's not a quagmire"*: Department of Defense transcript, Secretary Donald Rumsfeld Remarks, outside of ABC TV Studio, Washington, DC, October 28, 2001.

Page 9: *In 2003, the commanding general*: S. Tanner, *Afghanistan: A Military History of Afghanistan from Alexander the Great to the War Against the Taliban* (New York: Da Capo Press, 2009), p. 330.

Page 9: *. . . says the Taliban "is increasingly ineffective"*: Statement by General John P. Abizaid to Senate Armed Services Committee, March 1, 2005.

Page 9: *In 2005, the Taliban is "collapsing"*: "U.S. Commander Sees Near-Collapse of Taliban Within Year, Terrorists Could Still Strike," Associated Press, April 17, 2005.

Page 9: *. . . "prevailing against the effects of prolonged war"*: Department of Defense transcript, News Briefing with Maj. Gen. Robert Durbin and Minister Abdul Hadir Khalid from the Pentagon, January 9, 2007.

Page 9: *. . . "my successor will find"*: Interview with Top ISAF Commander McNeill, "More Than Promises Needed in Afghanistan," *Der Spiegel* online, March 31, 2008.

Page 9: . . . *"very successful counterinsurgency"*: Statement by Secretary Robert Gates to Senate Armed Services Committee, April 10, 2008.

Page 10: . . . *"larger western footprint"*: John J. Kruzel, "Three Combat Brigades Available for Afghanistan by Summer, Gates Says," American Forces Press Service, September 23, 2008.

Page 10: . . . *there are over thirty thousand troops*: Amy Belasco, "Troop Levels in the Afghan and Iraq Wars, FY2001–FY2012: Cost and Other Potential Issues," Congressional Research Service, July 2, 2009.

Page 10: . . . *violence has spiked dramatically* : "NATO Figures Show Surge in Afghanistan Violence," guardian.co.uk, January 31, 2009.

Page 10: *American and NATO soldiers are getting killed*: Operation Enduring Freedom statistics at http://icasualties.org/oef/.

Page 10: *Civilian casualties have tripled*: Kenneth Katzman, "Security Policy and Force Capacity Building; Afghanistan: Post-Taliban Governance, Security, and U.S. Policy," Congressional Research Service (CRS) Reports and Issue Briefs, March 1, 2010; Human Rights Watch, "Troops in Contact: Air Strikes and Civilian Deaths in Afghanistan," September 2008.

Page 10: . . . *saying the prognosis is "grim"*: Brian Ross, "'Grim' Afghanistan Report to Be Kept Secret by U.S.," ABC News, September 23, 2008.

Page 10: *A White House staffer nicknames Lute*: Author interview with White House official, October 2010.

Page 10: *He didn't want to surge in Iraq*: Hearing of Senate Armed Services Committee, Nomination of Lieutenant General Douglas Lute to be Assistant to the President and Deputy National Security Advisor for Iraq and Afghanistan, Capitol Hill, Washington, DC, June 7, 2007.

Page 10: *He tells McKiernan*: Author interview with military officials, September 2010.

Page 10: *McKiernan is impressed when he meets Obama that summer*: Author interview with General David McKiernan, October 30, 2008.

Page 10: *McKiernan . . . is pulling for Obama*: Author interview with senior military official, October 2008.

Page 11: *McKiernan is suspicious of McCain, too*: Author interview with military official, October 2008.

Page 11: . . . *three strategic reviews are going on*: Author interview with military officials; Karen De Young, "U.S. Urgently Reviews Policy on Afghanistan," *The Washington Post*, October 9, 2008.

Page 11: *"There's no way this place is going to be the next Switzerland"*: Author interview with General David McKiernan, October 30, 2008.

CHAPTER 3. LADY GAGA

Page 12: *The hotel* Rolling Stone *put me up in sucked*: Author notes, April 15, 2010.

Page 15: *"If we don't get Zarqawi, we will be failures"*: Author interview with military official, April 2010.

Page 16: . . . *enough of a fingerprint*: Department of Defense, Press Availability with Secretary Rumsfeld en Route from Brussels to Washington, DC, June 8, 2006.

Page 16: *President George W. Bush publicly thanked McChrystal*: Federal News Service, Joint Media Availability with President George W. Bush and Danish Prime Minister Anders Rasmussen, Camp David, Maryland, June 9, 2006.

Page 16: *"Michael is writing the article for* Rolling Stone*"*: Author notes, April 2010.

CHAPTER 4. "INTIMIDATED BY THE CROWD"

Page 18: . . . *"the highly classified conversations"*: Author phone interview with military official, Washington, DC, April 2010.

Page 18: . . . *"coming to kiss the ring"*: Ibid.

Page 18: . . . *"intimidated by the crowd"*: Author interview with senior military official, April 2010.

Page 19: . . . *"like a Democrat who thinks he's walking into a room full of Republicans"*: Ibid.

Page 19: *A CBS sports announcer*: "Golf Analyst Feherty Sorry for Pelosi Joke in Dallas Magazine," Associated Press, May 10, 2009.

Page 20: . . . *pushing a story that Obama snubbed*: Ron Claiborne, "Anatomy of an Attack: How McCain Hit Obama," ABC News, July 27, 2008.

Page 20: *At the embassy, he gives a talk*: Abigail Hauslohner, "Obama's Trip: Substance or Drive-By?" *Time*, July 21, 2008.

Page 20: *"He didn't want to take pictures with any more soldiers"*: Author interview with State Department officials, U.S. Embassy Baghdad, January 2010.

Page 21: *Truman can't run for reelection*: David McCullough, *Truman* (New York: Simon & Schuster, 1993), p. 913.

Page 22: . . . *Obama orders up his own review*: David Ignatius, "Shaping a War on Two Fronts," *The Washington Post*, February 22, 2009.

Page 22: *He says he's sending seventeen thousand troops*: Helene Cooper, "Putting Stamp on Afghan War, Obama Will Send 17,000 Troops," *The New York Times*, February 17, 2009.

Page 22: . . . *upping the number of drone strikes*: New America Foundation, "Year of the Drone," http://counterterrorism.newamerica.net/drones.

Page 22: *He doesn't think Afghanistan can support too many more American troops*: Federal News Service, "Special Defense Department Briefing, General David McKiernan, Commander, U.S. Forces Afghanistan and NATO's International Security Assistance Force," Pentagon Briefing Room, Arlington, Virginia, February 18, 2009.

Page 23: *McKiernan . . . is not going to press*: Author interview with military officials, Washington, DC, October 2010.

CHAPTER 5. ARC DE TRIOMPHE

Page 24: *"We'll follow them"*: Author notes, April 2010.

Page 25: . . . *a few wouldn't fight after a snowfall*: Kenneth Katzman, "Afghanistan: Post-Taliban Governance, Security, and U.S. Policy," Congressional Research Service, September 22, 2011.

Page 27: *He was of Irish descent*: Author interview with General Michael Flynn, May 2010.

Page 28: . . . *spending $4.7 billion in a single year*: "Pentagon Sets Sights on Public Opinion," Associated Press, February 5, 2009.

Page 29: . . . *a bunch of "crazy monkeys"*: Michael Yon Facebook posting, April 15, 2010, 4:14 P.M.

Page 30: *"Let's do it"*: Author interview with General Stanley McChrystal, Paris, April 15, 2010.

CHAPTER 6. "A VIOLENT ACT"

Page 33: *In January, General David McKiernan receives an e-mail from the White House*: Author interview with U.S. military official, Washington, DC, March 2011.

Page 33: . . . *poppy eradication*: Fisnik Abrashi, "Afghanistan Will Break Opium Growth Record, U.S. Ambassador Says," Associated Press, July 17, 2007.

Page 33: . . . *engaging in "deviant actions"*: Project for Government Oversight, Letter to Hillary Clinton, September 1, 2009.

Page 33: . . . *vodka butt shots*: Ibid.; D. Schulman, "Animal House in Afghanistan," *Mother Jones*, September 1, 2009.

Page 34: *Eikenberry is a three-star general*: Political Transcript Wire, Sen. John

Kerry Holds a Hearing on the Nomination of Karl Eikenberry to be Ambassador to Afghanistan, March 30, 2009.

Page 34: . . . *almost killed him, he recalls*: James Gonser, "Reinforced Glass May Have Saved Ex-Hawai'i General," *Honolulu Advertiser*, September 20, 2001.

Page 34: . . . *with master's degrees*: Karl Eikenberry biography on webpage of the Freeman Spogli Institute for International Studies at Stanford University.

Page 35: . . . *McKiernan speaks to Obama only twice*: Author interview with senior military official, March 2011.

Page 35: . . . *briefs . . . Mullen . . . and Gates in a video teleconference*: Ibid.

Page 36: *Gates takes the decision to the White House in April*: Rajiv Chandrasekaran, "Pentagon Worries Led to Command Change; McKiernan's Ouster Reflected New Realities in Afghanistan," *The Washington Post*, August 17, 2009.

Page 37: . . . *Gates is asked at a press conference*: CQ Transcriptions, Secretary of Defense Robert M. Gates Holds a Defense Department News Briefing, May 11, 2009.

Page 38: *"McKiernan was on the wrong team"*: Author interview with senior military official, May 2009.

Page 39: *Privately, McKiernan will tell*: Author interview with senior military official, March 2011.

Page 39: . . . *"of course that's what Petraeus would say"*: Author interview with Pentagon official, April 2010.

Page 39: . . . *a "dirty" move*: Author interview with military official, May 2009.

Page 39: . . . *a chance to "reset"*: Author interview with military official, April 2010.

Page 39: *"Gates was the mastermind"*: Author interview with military official, April 2010.

CHAPTER 7. ON THE *X*

Page 40: . . . *handle the Sync Matrix*: Author interview with Lieutenant Commander Dave Silverman, April 2010.

CHAPTER 8. THE A-TEAM

Page 45: . . . *Charlie Flynn is sitting at his desk*: Author interview with Colonel Charles Flynn, April 16, 2010.

Page 47: . . . *Casey Welch walks into his grandmother's house*: Author interview with Major Casey Welch, April 17, 2010.

Page 48: *It's crazy, says Pitta*: Author interview with Lieutenant Commander John Pitna, May 2010.

Page 48: *"Cardinal Richelieu"*: S. Weinberger, "McChrystal Gaffe Spotlights New Breed of Media Advisor," Aol News, June 23, 2010. http://www.aolnews.com/2010/06/23/mcchrystal-gaffe-spotlights-new-breed-of-media-adviser.

Page 49: . . . *"one of the general's old army drinking buddies"*: G. Porter, "Switch to Petraeus Betrays War Crisis," *Asia Times* online, June 25, 2010.

Page 49: *"I've always seen myself as a bit of a martini"*: Author interview with Sir Graeme Lamb, May 2010.

CHAPTER 9. "BITE ME"

Page 52: *The staff gathered in room 314*: Author notes, April 16, 2010.

CHAPTER 10. THE PHOTO OP

Page 55: *At four thirty P.M. on May 19, 2009*: "The POTUS Tracker," *The Washington Post* online, Obama Meets with Secretary of Defense Robert Gates, May 19, 2009, 4:30 P.M., Oval Office, White House.

Page 55: . . . *Stan McChrystal walks into the Oval Office*: "Obama to Meet with New U.S. Commander for Afghanistan," *The New York Times* Caucus Blog, May 18, 2009.

Page 55: *When the music stops in Washington, it's McChrystal*: Author interview with General Stanley McChrystal, April 18, 2010.

Page 56: *That's what he'd told the National Security Council*: Author interview with military officials, April 2010.

Page 56: *McChrystal's team knows that detainee abuse is going to come up*: Author interview with military officials, April 2010.

Page 56: *A Human Rights Watch report*: Human Rights Watch, "'No Blood, No Foul': Soldiers' Accounts of Detainee Abuse in Iraq," *Human Rights Watch*, July 2006.

Page 56: The New York Times *reported that soldiers there*: Eric Schmitt and Carolyn Marshall, "In Secret Unit's 'Black Room,' a Grim Portrait of U.S. Abuse," *The New York Times*, March 19, 2006.

Page 56: *An investigation by Vice Admiral Lowell Jacoby*: Human Rights Watch, "'No Blood, No Foul': Soldiers' Accounts of Detainee Abuse in Iraq," *Human Rights Watch*, July 2006.

Page 57: *An interrogator who was there*: Ibid.

Page 57: *McChrystal's team has a preemptive strike*: Spencer Ackerman, "McChrystal Paints Bleak Picture of Afghanistan War," *The Washington Independent*, June 2, 2009.

Page 57: *The Tillman thing . . .* : Jake Tapper, "Pat Tillman's Mom Wants General Stanley McChrystal Removed from Chairing White House Initiative," ABC News, April 14, 2011.

Page 57: *His mother, Mary Tillman, sends a letter*: Mary Tillman, "Pat Tillman's Mother on Army Gen. Stanley McChrystal: I Told You So," *Los Angeles Times*, August 8, 2010.

Page 57: *. . . participated in a "falsified homicide investigation"*: http://articles.nydailynews.com/2010-06-24/news/27067978_1_pat-tillman-mary-tillman-friendly-fire.

Page 57: *One of the interrogators from Iraq won't shut up*: Spencer Ackerman, "Former Interrogator Presses for McChrystal's Stance on Abuse," *The Washington Independent*, June 2, 2009.

Page 58: *He gets only one question about Camp Nama—from Senator Carl Levin*: Transcript of U.S. Senate Committee on Armed Services Hearing, Washington, DC, June 2, 2009.

Page 58: *He's got a line prepared on Tillman*: Ibid.

Page 58: *The headlines from the confirmation*: Anne Mulrine, "McChrystal Not Sure If More U.S. Forces Needed in Afghanistan," *U.S. News & World Report*, June 2, 2009.

Page 58: *McChrystal gets unanimous confirmation*: "Full Senate Approves McChrystal's Confirmation," Associated Press, June 10, 2009.

CHAPTER 11. TOTALLY SHIT-FACED

Page 59: *A man I'll call C.*: Author notes, April 16, 2010.

Page 63: *After dinner, the gang headed to Kitty O'Shea's*: Author notes, April 16, 2010.

CHAPTER 12. "DEAD SILENCE"

Page 67: *On June 12, Charlie Flynn takes a bus*: Author interview with Colonel Charles Flynn, April 16, 2010.

Page 67: . . . *Casey is at the headquarters*: Author interview with Major Casey Welch, April 17, 2010.

Page 68: *There's some Italian guy with an office*: Ibid.

Page 69: *A NATO bomb kills seventy Afghan civilians*: "Afghan Alcohol Ban after NATO Staff Were 'Too Hungover' to Give Explanation for Air Strike That Killed 70 Civilians," *Daily Mail*, September 9, 2009.

Page 70: *"We must avoid the trap"*: ISAF Revised Tactical Directive, July 6, 2009.

Page 70: *The previous general . . . had a set of tactical directives*: ISAF Revised Tactical Directive, September 2, 2008.

Page 71: *"What we're doing is moving to a more classic counterinsurgency"*: Eric Schmitt, "U.S. General Maps New Tactic to Pursue Taliban and Al-Qaeda," *The New York Times*, February 18, 2004.

CHAPTER 13. THE HORROR, THE HORROR

Page 73: *One hundred thousand flights were canceled*: Omar R. Valdimarsson, "Icelandic Volcano Lava Flow Stops, Ash Eruptions Diminish, University Says," Bloomberg, May 22, 2010.

Page 73: *The airlines were estimated to lose $1.7 billion*: Ibid.

Page 73: *Seven hundred fifty tons of ash had spewed into the air*: Stuart Biggs and Jeremy van Loon, "Icelandic Volcano Unlikely to Change the Weather," Bloomberg, April 19, 2010.

Page 73: *It was the first time the volcano had erupted since 1821*: Henry Fountain, "Eruption Wasn't That Powerful, but Effects May Linger," *The New York Times*, April 15, 2010.

Page 73: *A reporter for* The New York Times *spent a few days in Kabul with him*: Dexter Filkins, "Stanley McChrystal's Long War," *The New York Times*, October 14, 2009.

Page 74: *A writer from* The Atlantic *had enjoyed a good stay*: Robert Kaplan, "Man Versus Afghanistan," *The Atlantic*, April 2010.

Page 74: Time *magazine had put him as runner-up for Person of the Year*: Joe Klein, "Person of the Year: General Stanley McChrystal," *Time*, December 16, 2009.

Page 74: 60 Minutes *spent the most personal time with him*: "McChrystal's Frank Talk on Afghanistan," CBS News, September 24, 2009.

Page 74: . . . *a "Jedi Knight," as* Newsweek *called him*: Michael Hirsh and John Barry, "The Hidden General: Stan McChrystal Runs 'Black Ops.' Don't Pass It On," *Newsweek*, June 26, 2006.

Page 75: *"First, I wondered why"*: Author interview with State Department official, State Department, May 2010.

Page 75: *"It's not going to look like a win, smell like a win, or taste like a win"*: Author interview with General Bill Mayville, Paris, April 18, 2010.

Page 75: *"The main thing I learned"*: "The Surprising Lessons of Vietnam," *Newsweek*, November 6, 2009.

Page 76: . . . *McChrystal watched a man on a video feed in his headquarters for seventeen days*: Dexter Filkins, "Stanley McChrystal's Long War," *The New York Times*, October 14, 2009.

Page 77: *Or the president himself, who had visited the front only once*: Alissa Rubin and Helene Cooper, "In Afghan Trip, Obama Presses Karzai on Graft," *The New York Times*, March 28, 2010.

CHAPTER 14. WE'RE ACTUALLY LOSING

Page 78: *On June 26, Gates asks McChrystal*: Nancy A. Youssef, "McChrystal Says He Won't Pull Punches on Afghan Proposals," McClatchy Newspapers, July 12, 2009.

Page 78: *"I was back to save the war"*: Author interview with Andrew Exum, May 2010.

Page 79: *He's planned a vacation at the Basin Harbor Club*: Author interview with Steven Biddle, April 2010.

Page 79: . . . *"scare the hell out of them"*: Author interview with Andrew Exum, May 2010.

Page 80: *"It hurt," one soldier lamented*: Alissa Rubin, "U.S. Forces Close Post in Afghan 'Valley of Death,'" *The New York Times*, April 14, 2010.

Page 80: *"It confuses me why it took so long"*: Ibid.

Page 81: . . . *they've stocked up on influential reporters*: Tara McKelvey, "Too Close for Comfort?" *Columbia Journalism Review*, September/October 2009.

Page 81: . . . *"it jeopardizes the mission"*: Author interview with Stephen Biddle, April 2010.

Page 81: . . . *"out of my sandbox"*: Interview with White House official, October 2010.

Page 82: *"We were just for show"*: Interview with assessment team member, May 2010.

Page 82: *Jones has a message from the White House*: Bob Woodward, "U.S. Says Key to Success Is Economy, Not Military," *The Washington Post*, July 1, 2009.

Page 82: . . . *Whiskey Tango Foxtrot*: Ibid.

Page 82: *"My strong view"*: Jon Meacham, "A Highly Logical Approach," interview with President Obama, *Newsweek*, May 15, 2009.

Page 83: *"retired general time"*: Richard Wolffe, *Revival* (New York: Crown, 2011), p. 244.

Page 83: *"Is this a modern Crusade?"*: Author interview with Major Casey Welch, April 17, 2010.

CHAPTER 15. PETRAEUS CAN'T DO AFGHANISTAN, AND WE AREN'T GOING TO GET BIN LADEN

Page 85: *Ocean 11 wasn't allowed to leave France*: Author notes, April 18, 2010.

Page 89: . . . *adding that he felt "betrayed"*: Author interview with General Stanley McChrystal, April 18, 2010.

CHAPTER 16. THE ELECTIONS, PART I

Page 95: *"I don't know how much sense"*: Author interview with U.S. official, May 2010.

Page 95: *The election will cost about $300 million*: Jon Boone, "The Great Afghan Election Swindle," *The Guardian*, October 20, 2009.

Page 96: *Matthew Hoh works for the State Department*: Author interview with Matthew Hoh, November 2010.

CHAPTER 17. TEXTS TO BERLIN

Page 100: *"How is your trip progressing"*: Author's text messages, April 18–19, 2010.

CHAPTER 18. THE ELECTIONS, PART II

Page 102: . . . *Holbrooke offers him a job*: Author interview with Ambassador Peter Galbraith, February 17, 2011.

Page 103: . . . *he tells Galbraith to knock it off*: Ibid.

Page 103: . . . *it's clear to those UN officials gathered*: Author interview with UN officials, January 2011.

Page 105: . . . *"those who are out to get you are out to get me"*: Document obtained by author, The United Nations Dispute Tribunal, Galbraith V. Secretary General of the United Nations, April 23, 2010.

Page 105: *At two thirty* A.M., *Galbraith gets a text message from Eide*: Ibid.

Page 106: *You might as well resign; you've lost the faith of the president*: Author interviews with White House and State Department officials, January 2011.

Page 106: *"Richard Holbrooke expected everyone in the White House"*: Author interview with White House official, May 2011.

Page 107: . . . *armed gunmen storm a guesthouse in Kabul*: Jon Boone, "U.N. Workers Killed in Afghanistan Attack," *The Guardian*, October 28, 2009.

Page 107: . . . *an e-mail getting bounced around among Afghan elites*: E-mail obtained by author, November 2009.

Page 107: . . . *"Elections: What's the Point?"*: State Department, Kabul, October 2009, Wikileaks.org.

Page 107: *"The people do not want change"*: Ibid.

CHAPTER 19. TEAM AMERICA ROLLS THE RITZ

Page 108: *The lobby of the Ritz-Carlton*: Author notes, April 20, 2010.

Page 109: . . . *"networked security"* and *"humanitarian action"*: Gale A. Mattox, "Germany and Elections: Dodging the Afghanistan Bullet," American Institute for Contemporary German Studies.

CHAPTER 20. ON PRINCIPLE

Page 116: *Matt Hoh has seen enough*: Author interview with Matthew Hoh, November 2010.

CHAPTER 21. SPIES LIKE US

Page 127: *"Nothing new could ever be expected"*: Philip K. Dick, *A Scanner Darkly* (New York: Penguin Press, 2008), p. 64.

Page 128: . . . *"To resign oneself to monotony"*: Richard Zenith and Fernando Pessoa, "Masquerades," *Harper's Magazine*, December 2009.

CHAPTER 22. "I'M PRESIDENT. I DON'T GIVE A SHIT WHAT THEY SAY"

Page 130: . . . *on the verge of "mission failure"*: Bob Woodward, "McChrystal: More Forces or 'Mission Failure,'" *The Washington Post*, September 21, 2009.

Page 130: . . . *"Hey, maybe it's better that it's out there"*: Author interview with Major Casey Welch, April 17, 2010.

Page 130: . . . *the leak undercuts the strategic impact of the twenty-one thousand troops already sent*: Author interview with White House official, May 2010.

Page 131: *"they may change their minds and crush me someday"*: John F. Burns, "McChrystal Rejects Scaling Down Afghan Military Aims," *The New York Times*, October 1, 2009.

Page 131: . . . *"letting just half the building burn down"*: Evan Thomas, "McChrystal's War," *Newsweek*, September 25, 2009.

Page 131: . . . *Petraeus calls a* Washington Post *columnist*: Michael Gerson, "U.S. Has Reasons to Hope in Afghanistan," *The Washington Post*, September 4, 2009.

Page 132: *Stephen Biddle writes an essay supporting*: Stephen Biddle, "Is It Worth It?" *The American Interest*, July/August 2009.

Page 132: *The Kagans do the same*: Fred Kagan, Kimberly Kagan, and James M. Dubik, "While Afghan Forces Are Trained, U.S. Forces Must Stay," *The Washington Post*, September 13, 2009.

Page 132: *As does Anthony Cordesman*: Anthony Cordesman, "A Chance to Avoid Defeat in Afghanistan," *The Washington Post*, August 31, 2009.

Page 132: *Exum fails to disclose*: Andrew Alexander, "Undisclosed Conflict in a Review of Jon Krakauer's Book on Pat Tillman," *The Washington Post*, November 15, 2009.

Page 132: *The same book is also reviewed in* The New York Times: Dexter Filkins, "The Good Soldier," *The News York Times*, September 8, 2009.

Page 132: . . . *publishes a glowing* New York Times Magazine *cover story*: Dexter Filkins, "Stanley McChrystal's Long War," *The New York Times Magazine*, October 14, 2009.

Page 132: *For guidance, the guys in the White House*: Peter Spiegel and Jonathan Wiesman, "Behind Afghan War Debate, a Battle of Two Books Rages," *The Wall Street Journal*, October 9, 2009.

Page 132: . . . *all Eikenberry does is "whine"*: Author interview with White House official, October 2010.

Page 134: . . . *Senator Lindsey Graham has to remind*: Bob Woodward, *Obama's Wars* (New York: Simon & Schuster, 2010), p. 155.

Page 135: *Press reports quote other unnamed*: Nancy A. Youssef, "Military Growing Impatient with Obama on Afghanistan," McClatchy Newspapers, September 18, 2009.

Page 135: . . . *want "to sandbag his old colleagues"*: Jonathan Alter, *The Promise* (New York: Simon & Schuster, 2010), p. 381.

Page 136: *"I'm president. I don't give a shit"*: Ibid., p. 392.

CHAPTER 23. THE STRATEGY

Page 137: *On the mezzanine level of the Ritz-Carlton*: Author notes, April 21, 2010.

Page 138: *I made copies of his sketches in my notebook*: As noted in the text, sketches included are my renditions of McChrystal's whiteboard diagrams, recreated from my original notebook pages for publication in this book.

CHAPTER 24. "LET ME BE CLEAR"

Page 149: *"Let me be clear"*: Barack Obama, "Address to the Nation on the Way Forward in Afghanistan and Pakistan" (speech), December 1, 2009, transcript from whitehouse.gov.

Page 150: *"It was clearly a political decision*: Author interview with Pentagon official, April 2011.

Page 151: *McChrystal prepares for his testimony*: Author interview with Colonel Richard Gross, May 2010.

Page 152: *"So we will start bringing troops home"*: Congressional testimony of Representative Ted Poe before House Armed Services Committee, December 8, 2009.

CHAPTER 25. WORSHIPPING THE GODS OF BEER

Page 153: *I walked back to the Ritz*: Author notes, April 21, 2010.

Page 157: *"The more you know"*: Author interview with former U.S. official, April 2011.

CHAPTER 26. WHO IS STANLEY McCHRYSTAL? PART I, 1954–1976

Page 158: *He writes a series of provocative articles and stories for the school's literary magazine*: Michael Hastings, "The Runaway General," *Rolling Stone*, June 2010.

Page 159: *Barno recalls having eggs thrown at him*: Author interview with General Dave Barno, May 2010.

Page 160: *"I remember going down to the Area*: Author interview with Jake Mc-Ferren, April 2010.

Page 161: *There are famous Goats—like George Armstrong Custer and George E. Pickett*: James S. Robbins, *Last in Their Class: Custer, Pickett, and the Goats of West Point* (New York: Encounter Books, 2006).

Page 161: *The Goat excels in "mischief"*: Ibid.

Page 162 *One story, written in November 1975, titled "Brinkman's Note"*: Stanley McChrystal, "Brinkman's Note," *The Pointer*, 1975 (copy obtained by author).

Page 162: *In a story called "The Journal of Captain Litton," the main character is a British officer*: Stanley McChrystal, "The Journal of Captain Litton," *The Pointer* (copy obtained by author).

Page 163: *Another story, "In the Line of Duty"*: Ibid.

Page 163: *"The bombs are in place and in minutes vengeance will be mine," the story opens*: Ibid.

CHAPTER 27. "THE JERK IN GREEN"

Page 165: *. . . I checked out the local papers*: Author notes, April 22, 2010.

CHAPTER 28. WHO IS STANLEY McCHRYSTAL? PART II, 1976–PRESENT DAY

Page 171: *. . . introduces mixed martial arts, like jujitsu, to the hand-to-hand combat training*: Author interview with Sergeant Major Michael Hall, May 2010.

Page 174: *"We are soldiers, God, agents of correction"*: Dick Cheney, *In My Time: A Personal and Political Memoir* (New York: Simon & Schuster, 2011), p. 464.

Page 174: . . . *"the mortally wounded Zarqawi pulled"*: Donald Rumsfeld, *Known and Unknown: A Memoir* (New York: Sentinel, 2011), p. 694.

CHAPTER 29. REALITY CHECKS IN

Page 176: *The Afghan embassy was in an upscale neighborhood on the city's west side*: Author notes, April 22, 2010.

INTERLUDE: DUBAI

Page 185: *"There is danger here! A dry brown vibrating hum or frequency in the air"*: William S. Burroughs, *Interzone* (New York: Viking, 1989), pp. 65, 75.

Page 186: *I headed off to my hotel in the city*: I spent the first two nights in Dubai at Le Royal Meridien and my last night at Atlantis: The Palm. For the sake of the narrative, I've spared the reader events that took place at the Meridien and jumped ahead to the Palm, which was the only hotel worth writing about anyway.

Page 186: . . . *the Emirates had a gross domestic product of some $261 billion*: World Bank Development indicators, via Google.

Page 188: *He first appeared in the Crimean War in 1854*: Phillip Knightley, *The First Casualty* (New York: Harcourt Brace Jovanovich, 1975), p. 20.

Page 188: *"Exaggeration, outright lies, puffery, slander," wrote one historian on the quality of Civil War coverage*: Ibid., p. 21.

Page 189: . . . *"Why, once Jakes went out to cover a revolution"*: Evelyn Waugh, *Scoop* (New York: Little, Brown, 1937), p. 92.

Page 189: *"Fuck my shit," he said privately, using a dropped expression picked up from GIs*: William Prochnau, *Once Upon a Distant War* (New York: Crown, 1995), p. 345.

Page 190: *"Ernie got it," he heard*: Robert Capa, *Slightly Out of Focus* (New York: Henry Holt, 1947), p. 230.

Page 190: *"There's absolutely no reason for me to get up"*: Ibid., p. 30.

Page 190: *"I would say the war correspondent gets more drinks, more girls, better pay"*: Alex Kershaw, *Blood and Champagne: The Life and Times of Robert Capa* (New York: Thomas Dunne Books, 2003), p. 20.

Page 193: *In October of 2008, I'm in Afghanistan for the first time*: Author notes, originally published in "Obama's War," *GQ*, May 2009.

Page 197: *Two hours later, I stumbled through airport security*: Author notes, April 27, 2010.

CHAPTER 30. A SHORT HISTORY OF A HORRIBLE IDEA

Page 201: . . . *that Arabs have a "notorious inability to organize"*: David Galula, *Pacification in Algeria, 1956–1958* (Santa Monica, CA: RAND Corporation, 2006), p. 18.

Page 201: *"I sound no doubt terribly colonialist"*: Ibid.

Page 202: *In 1960, Galula takes a position at the Armed Forces Staff College in Norfolk, Virginia*: Ann Marlowe, *David Galula: His Life and Intellectual Context* (Charleston, SC: CreateSpace, 2010).

Page 202: *In 1962, Vietnam War architect General William Westmoreland*: Ibid.

Page 202: *tries to help him get a job at Mobil Oil company*: Ibid.

Page 203: . . . *and the controversial Phoenix Program*: Ibid.

Page 203: *COIN had been "overblown and oversold"*: Ibid.

Page 203: *Caspar Weinberger pens what is seen as official repudiation*: Andrew Bacevich, *The Limits of Power: The End of American Exceptionalism* (New York: Macmillan, 2009), p. 129.

Page 203: . . . *definitively replaced by a new fad of the moment*: Andrew Bacevich, *Washington Rules* (New York: Macmillan, 2010), p. 178.

Page 203: *"Never Send a Man When You Can Send a Bullet"*: Colonel David H. Petraeus, Major Damian P. Carr, and Captain John C. Abercrombie, "Why We Need FISTS: Never Send a Man When You Can Send a Bullet," July 1997.

Page 204: *Kilcullen, too, views the decision to invade Iraq as "fucking stupid"*: Spencer Ackerman, "A Counterinsurgency Guide for Politicos," *The Washington Independent*, July 27, 2008.

Page 205: . . . *explicitly points out that the best way to defeat terrorist networks*: Seth Jones "How Terrorist Groups End," RAND Corporation, 2008.

Page 206: . . . *that "JSOC was a killing machine"*: Author interview with General Bill Mayville, April 2010.

Page 206: . . . *he would have "worked with the devil" to beat Al-Qaeda*: Lieutenant Colonel Daniel L. Davis, "The Spark, the Oxygen and the Fuel," *Armed Forces Journal*, September 2010.

Page 206: . . . *about $360 million spent in just one year*: Erica Goode, "U.S. Military Will Transfer Control of Sunni Citizen Patrols to Iraqi Government," *The New York Times*, September 1, 2008.

Page 207: *"They are true Iraqi patriots"*: Author interview with senior military official, Baghdad, January 2011.

Page 207: . . . *"graduate level of war"*: FM 3-24: Counterinsurgency, December 2006.

Page 207: . . . *the key is "perception"*: Major David Petraeus, "American Lessons in Vietnam," *Parameters*, 1987.

Page 208: *COIN strategy is a fraud perpetuated*: Author interview with Douglas Macgregor, May 2010.

Page 208: *It's all very cynical, politically*: Author interview with Marc Sageman, former CIA analyst, May 2010.

Page 208: *"Losing wars is really expensive"*: Tara McKelvey, "The Cult of Counterinsurgency," *The American Prospect*, November 2008.

Page 208: *"The intellectual construct for the War on Terror"*: Hearing of the Military Construction, Veterans Affairs, and Related Agencies Subcommittee of the House Appropriations Committee, witness General David Petraeus, Commander, U.S. Central Command, Washington, DC, April 24, 2009.

Page 209: . . . *examined eighty-nine insurgencies and pointed out*: Ben Connable and Martin Libicki, *How Insurgencies End* (Santa Monica, CA: RAND Corporation, 2010), pp. 2–11.

Page 209: . . . *"I keep Galula by my bedside"*: Author notes, April 2010, from a talk at the École Militaire.

CHAPTER 31. BAD ROMANCE

Page 212: . . . *$206 billion in private contracts*: Congressional Research Services Report, Department of Defense Contractors in Iraq and Afghanistan, May 13, 2011.

Page 213: *A number of the security companies had connections to the insurgency*: Aram Roston, "How the U.S. Funds the Taliban," *The Nation*, November 30, 2009.

Page 213: . . . *from 2002 to 2009 found at least $18 billion unaccounted for*: Billions in Afghanistan Aid unaccounted for, AFP, October 28, 2010.

Page 213: *Karzai had talked about banning the mercenaries*: Joshua Partlow, "Karzai Wants Private Security Firms Out," *The Washington Post*, August 17, 2010.

Page 215: *"It's not going to work"*: Author interview with Hekmatullah Rahmini, April 27, 2010.

Page 217: . . . *ran into the hotel, detonated a suicide bomb, and killed seven*: "Attack on Luxury Hotel Kills Seven," Associated Press, January 15, 2008.

Page 225: The Washington Post *would describe the video's "powerful poignancy"*: Sarah Kaufman, "U.S. Soldiers in Afghanistan Make a Telephone Connection with Hit Video Remake," *The Washington Post*, May 1, 2010.

CHAPTER 32. PRESIDENT KARZAI HAS A COLD

Page 227: *"We have to be careful not to believe our own bullshit"*: Richard Wolffe, *Revival* (New York: Crown, 2011), p. 294.

Page 227: . . . *there's a ninety-minute window to make the decision*: Author interviews with senior military officials. April 2010.

Page 228: *"They are like 'Inshallah'"*: Author interview with Colonel Charles Flynn, April 2010.

Page 228: . . . *the "chicest man on the planet"*: Judy Hevrdejs, "Hamid Karzai: The World's Most Stylish Man," *Chicago Tribune*, January 31, 2002.

Page 228: . . . *"the Gray Wolf's Vagina"*: Author notes, April 2010.

Page 229: *Karzai looks back on fondly as the "Golden Age"*: U.S. State Department cable, July 16, 2009.

Page 229: *That changes when Obama takes over*: Ahmed Rashid, "How Obama Lost Karzai," *Foreign Policy*, March/April 2011.

Page 231: . . . *describe it as "a bleeding ulcer"*: Dion Nissenbaum, "McChrystal Calls Marjah 'Bleeding Ulcer,'" McClatchy Newspapers, May 24, 2010.

CHAPTER 33. AN E-MAIL EXCHANGE: COME WALK IN OUR BOOTS

Page 232: *On February 27, 2010, at 6:27 P.M.*: E-mails obtained by author.

CHAPTER 34. A BOY BORN IN 1987

Page 235: *One night this month, he calls home*: Author interview with Julie Ingram, June 2011.

Page 239: *I was asked to see if you would attend a memorial*: E-mail obtained by author.

CHAPTER 35. WHERE IS ISRAEL ARROYO?

Page 240: *My Afghan security guard dropped me off*: Author notes, April 28, 2010.

CHAPTER 36. INGRAM'S HOUSE

Page 254: *The twenty-two-ton MRAP bounced up and down along*: Author notes, April 28, 2010.

CHAPTER 37. AN ARMY OF NONE

Page 267: . . . *arrives in late 2009 at Camp Eggers*: "New NATO Command in Kabul Focuses on Afghan Training," American Forces Press Service, November 23, 2009.

Page 267: *It's an $11.6 billion a year operation*: Michael Hastings, "Another Runaway General," *Rolling Stone*, February 2010.

Page 267: *Caldwell is a three-star general from a military family*: Gregg K. Kalesako, "Caldwells and Army Go Back a Long Way," *Honolulu Star-Bulletin*, September 9, 2001.

Page 268: . . . *"a nice guy"*: Author interview with a military official, Washington, DC, February 2011.

Page 268: . . . *"can really finance its own reconstruction"*: Transcript of House Committee on Appropriations: Subcommittee on Defense Hearing on FY 2004 Defense Appropriations, March 27, 2003.

Page 268: . . . *he holds meetings with top columnists*: Julie Bosman, "Secret Meeting Included Journalists," *The New York Times*, October 9, 2006.

Page 268: *"The lessons I've learned by just watching [Wolfowitz]"*: American Forces Press Service, July 22, 2003.

Page 268: . . . *commanders on the ground in Iraq tell Caldwell Iraq is in a "civil war"*: Author interview with senior military official, February 2011.

Page 268: . . . *says that the United States had no role in the execution*: Press conference attended by author in Baghdad, Iraq, January 3, 2007.

Page 268: *He renames press briefings "media roundtables"*: Scott Johnson with Michael Hastings, "We're Losing the Infowars," *Newsweek*, January 14, 2007.

Page 269: . . . *"information engagement"*: Department of Defense Bloggers Roundtable with Lieutenant General William Caldwell, Commanding General, U.S. Army Combined Arms Center and Fort Leavenworth, February 26, 2008.

Page 269: *In 2009, he also tried to rewrite*: Michael Hastings, "Another Runaway General," *Rolling Stone,* February 2010.

Page 269: *"It eliminated the [media] gate keeper"*: "Iraq Social Media Experience Sparks Training for Leaders," U.S. Department of Defense, American Forces Press Service, July 30, 2009.

Page 269: *"A You-who?" he asks the staffer who brings up the idea*: Ibid.

Page 269: . . . *"was in the top 10 of all YouTube sites"*: Ibid.

Page 269: *"Public affairs is there to inform"*: Department of Defense Bloggers Roundtable with Lieutenant General William Caldwell, Commanding General, U.S. Army Combined Arms Center and Fort Leavenworth, February 26, 2008.

Page 270: . . . *"just wasn't working"*: "Fixing the Unfixable," *The Economist,* August 19, 2010.

Page 270: *Only 20 percent of new recruits can read*: Transcript of Lieutenant General William Caldwell, NATO Training Mission-Afghanistan and Combined Security Transition Command-Afghanistan Commanding General, News Briefing, August 23, 2010.

Page 270: *One out of four deserts*: Gareth Porter, "Afghan Army Turnover Rate Threatens U.S. Plans," *IPS,* November 24, 2009.

Page 270: *It isn't until January 2011*: Rod Norland, "Afghans Plan to Stop Recruiting Children as Police," *The New York Times,* January 29, 2011.

Page 270: . . . *estimates that 54 percent of the Afghan army and police smoke hash regularly*: "Afghan Army's Hashish-Smoking Troops," *The Huffington Post,* December 22, 2009.

Page 270: . . . *at least 60 percent of police in Helmand province were users*: Robert M. Perito, "United States Institute of Peace Special Report on Afghan Police," August 2009.

Page 270: *Almost every twelve days there is a murder*: "A Crisis of Trust and Cultural Incompatibility: A Red Team Study of Mutual Perceptions of Afghan National Security Force Personnel and U.S. Soldiers in Understanding and Mitigating the Phenomena of ANSF-Committed Fratricide Murders," May 12, 2011, p. 4.

Page 270: *In one five-and-a-half-month period*: Ibid.

Page 270: . . . *at least fifty-eight NATO soldiers have been killed*: Ibid.

Page 270: . . . *leaked to* The Wall Street Journal: Dion Nissenbaum, "Report Sees Danger in Local Allies," *The Wall Street Journal,* June 17, 2011.

Page 270–271: . . . *a list of complaints about the Afghan soldiers*: "A Crisis of Trust and Cultural Incompatibility: A Red Team Study of Mutual Perceptions of Afghan National Security Force Personnel and U.S. Soldiers in Understanding and Mitigating the Phenomena of ANSF-Committed Fratricide Murders," May 12, 2011, p. 3.

Page 271: *The Afghan soldiers have a list of complaints*: A Crisis of Trust and Cultural Incompatibility: A Red Team Study of Mutual Perceptions of Afghan National Security Force Personnel and U.S. Soldiers in Understanding and Mitigating the Phenomena of ANSF-Committed Fratricide Murders, May 12, 2011, pp. 3 and 36.

Page 273: *NATO has already spent more than $30 billion training the Afghan security forces*: Special Inspector General for Afghanistan Reconstruction (SIGAR) Quarterly Report to Congress, April 30, 2011, p. 53.

Page 274: . . . *"take the lead"*: Transcript of Lieutenant General William Caldwell, NATO Training Mission-Afghanistan and Combined Security Transition Command-Afghanistan Commanding General, Defense Department News Briefing Via Teleconference, September 26, 2011.

Page 274: *"You can't expect a soldier to account for his weapon"*: Michael Evans, "Local Recruits Vanish," *The Australian*, August 25, 2010.

Page 274: . . . *"educate an entire generation of Afghans"*: Transcript of Lieutenant General William Caldwell, NATO Training Mission-Afghanistan and Combined Security Transition Command-Afghanistan Commanding General, News Briefing, August 23, 2010.

Page 274: . . . *(nine hundred short)*: Transcript of Lieutenant General William Caldwell, NATO Training Mission-Afghanistan and Combined Security Transition Command-Afghanistan Commanding General Teleconference from Afghanistan, November 9, 2010.

Page 274: . . . *(he needs to add seventy thousand more)*: Michael Hastings, "Another Runaway General," *Rolling Stone*, February 2010.

Page 274: . . . *$2 billion extra*: Michael Hastings, "Another Runaway General," *Rolling Stone*, February 2010.

Page 274: . . . *billions*: Special Inspector General for Afghanistan Reconstruction (SIGAR) Quarterly Report to Congress, April 30, 2011, p. 53.

Page 274: . . . *to increase the forces by 56,000*: Transcript of Lieutenant General William Caldwell, NATO Training Mission-Afghanistan and Combined Security Transition Command-Afghanistan Commanding General, News Briefing, August 23, 2010.

Page 274: . . . *he'll assign a team*: Michael Hastings, "Another Runaway General," *Rolling Stone*, February 2010.

CHAPTER 38. IN THE ARENA

Page 276: *Duncan's office was on the second floor*: Author notes, April–May 2010.

Page 278: *"like* Apollo 13, *heading out to the moon, with a bloody great hole"*: Author interview with Sir Graeme Lamb, May 2010.

Page 281: *"You don't mind if I eat this apple, do you?"*: Author interview with General Michael Flynn.

CHAPTER 39. "I DIDN'T EVEN KNOW WE WERE FIGHTING THERE"

Page 284: *Karzai is staying at the Willard InterContinental Hotel*: Author notes, May 2010.

Page 284: . . . *"long-term partner"*: Remarks with Afghan President Hamid Karzai in a moderated conversation, U.S. Institute of Peace, May 13, 2010.

Page 284: . . . *"friend"*: Remarks by Secretary of State Hillary Rodham Clinton at reception in honor of Afghan President Hamid Karzai, State Department, May 11, 2010.

Page 286: *He'd come into the U.S. embassy*: Barack Obama, *The Audacity of Hope* (New York: Random House, 2006), p. 352.

Page 287: . . . *he didn't become president to have "civilian casualties"*: White House Office of the Press Secretary, Remarks by President Obama and President Karzai of Afghanistan in Joint Press Availability, May 12, 2010.

Page 287: . . . *as a writer from* Harper's Magazine: David Samuels, "Barack and Hamid's Excellent Adventure," *Harper's Magazine*, August 2010.

Page 289: . . . *"hit every talking point they had given him"*: Author notes from W Hotel, May 12, 2010.

CHAPTER 40. THE CONCLUDING CONVERSATIONS WITH DUNCAN BOOTHBY, GENERAL PETRAEUS FACE-PLANTS IN CONGRESS, AND THE STORY BREAKS WHILE I WATCH AMERICAN HELICOPTER PILOTS KILL INSURGENTS

Page 291: *I'd spent the week in Washington*: Author notes, May 2010.

Page 294: *Jerome Starkey, a reporter for* The Times *of London*: Author interview with Jerome Starkey.

Page 295: *"No one wants to be sitting there with a full bladder"*: Author interview with senior military official, February 2011.

Page 295: *"Do you believe that we will begin a drawdown?"*: Senate testimony of Senator John McCain, June 15, 2010.

Page 297: *The Kiowas were small, two-seat scout helicopters*: Author notes, June 2010.

Page 299: *"Michael, read your story"*: Author e-mail from Duncan Boothby.

Page 302: *Irving, a father of two, thirty-four years old*: Author interview with Captain Stephen Irving, June 2010.

CHAPTER 41. "VERY, VERY BAD"

Page 313: *At two thirty A.M. on June 22, 2010, a close aide to General Stanley McChrystal*: Karen DeYoung and Rajiv Chandrasekaran, "Gen. McChrystal Allies, *Rolling Stone* Disagree over Article's Ground Rules," *The Washington Post*, June 26, 2010.

Page 313: *"It's very, very bad"*: Ibid.

Page 313: *He did have that fucking tape recorder running all the time*: Author interview with U.S. officials, June 2010.

Page 314: *Holbrooke's phone rings*: Author interview with senior State Department officials, November 2010.

Page 314: *. . . his helicopter had been fired upon*: Miguel Marquez, "Taliban Attack Ambassador Richard Holbrooke's Plane in Marja," ABC News, June 21, 2010.

Page 314: *They can't read it on their BlackBerrys, so he prints out copies*: Mike Allen, "The Tick-Tock: How President Obama Took Command of the McChrystal Situation," *Politico*, June 24, 2010.

Page 315: *"Joe Biden called me"*: Jann S.Wenner, "Obama in Command: The *Rolling Stone* Interview," *Rolling Stone*, September 28, 2010.

Page 315: *Obama spends five minutes on the phone*: Author interview with U.S. officials, January 2011.

Page 315: *You've done enough damage*: Author interview with Pentagon and State Department officials, June 2010.

Page 315: *Another U.S. State Department official asks the Flynns*: Author interview with U.S. State Department official, June 2010.

Page 315: *"I extend my sincerest apology for this profile"*: Noah Shachtman, "McChrystal Apologizes for Incendiary Article," *Danger Room* blog, Wired .com, June 21, 2010.

Page 316: *Holbrooke has dinner with Eikenberry that night at the embassy*: Author interview with UN and U.S. officials, February 2011.

Page 316: *Biden will consult with six four-star generals*: Transcript of *This Week*, ABC News, July 11, 2010.

Page 316–317: *He offers his resignation—McChrystal accepts*: "Top Aide to General McChrystal Resigns," Reuters, June 22, 2010.

Page 317: *Filkins tells Charlie Rose*: Transcript of "A Look at Gen. Stanley McChrystal and Afghanistan," *The Charlie Rose Show*, June 23, 2010.

Page 317: *"To what extent can we change the way we behave in such a way that this sort of thing doesn't happen again?"*: Transcript of John Burns, the *New York Times* London bureau chief, *PBS News Hour*, July 8, 2010.

Page 317: . . . *"will impact so adversely"*: Transcript of John Burns speaking about the McChrystal/Petraeus change in Afghanistan, *The Hugh Hewitt Show*, July 6, 2010.

Page 317: *On Fox News, Geraldo Rivera takes the same tack*: Colby Hall, "Geraldo Rivera Likens *Rolling Stone* Writer to Al Qaeda. Seriously," *Mediaite*, June 25, 2010.

Page 317: *"Michael Hastings never served his country"*: Transcript of interview with Lara Logan, *Reliable Sources*, CNN, June 27, 2010.

Page 317: *In Washington, Bob Gates calls National Security advisor Jim Jones*: Bob Woodward, *Obama's Wars* (New York: Simon & Schuster, 2010), pp. 371–372.

Page 317: *One is from Greg Mortenson*: Elisabeth Bumiller, "Unlikely Tutor Giving Military Afghan Advice," *The New York Times*, July 17, 2010.

Page 318: *"Have you already submitted your resignation?"*: Mike Allen, "The Tick-Tock: How President Obama Took Command of the McChrystal Situation," *Politico*, June 24, 2010.

Page 318: *They do not see remorse in that clip*: Ibid.

Page 318: *Geoff Morrell, viewed as particularly untrustworthy*: Author interview with White House officials, November 2010.

Page 319: *"You've done a good job, but—"*: Author interview with U.S. officials, November 2010.

Page 319: *Petraeus is waiting down in the White House basement*: John Barry, "Petraeus's Next Battle," *Newsweek*, July 17, 2011.

Page 320: *It was like the Baghdad job*: Thomas Ricks, *The Gamble* (New York: Penguin, 2006), p. 127.

Page 320: *"Before we announce this," Petraeus tells the president*: Author interviews with White House and military officials, January 2011.

Page 320: *"Today I accepted General Stanley McChrystal's resignation"*: White House Office of the Press Secretary, Statement by the President in the Rose Garden, June 23, 2010.

Page 321: *"It was incredible seeing Obama like that"*: Author interview with senior U.S. official, January 2011.

Page 321: *"We have a lot of kids on the ground"*: Peter Baker, "For Obama, Steep Learning Curve as Chief in War," *The New York Times*, August 28, 2010.

Page 321: . . . *"design and lead our new strategy"*: White House Office of the Press Secretary, Statement by the President in the Rose Garden, June 23, 2010.

Page 322: . . . *"head for the exits and turn off the lights"*: Jen Dimascio, "Gen. David Petraeus Defends Afghan Exit Date," *Politico*, June 30, 2010.

Page 322: *"He sounds psyched, looks like a man on a mission"*: Author interview with U.S. official, January 2011.

Page 322: *It's Biden, Petraeus's wife, Holly*: Josh Rogin, "Inside the Biden–Petraeus Dinner." *The Cable* blog, *Foreign Policy* online, June 30, 2010. http://thecable .foreignpolicy.com/posts/2010/06/30/inside_the_biden_petraeus_dinner).

Page 322: *"I mean, it was clear that I was the only guy"*: Mark Bowden, "The Salesman," *The Atlantic*, October 2010.

Page 322: *Petraeus arrives in Kabul:* Laura King, "Petraeus Stresses Unity in First Appearance in Kabul," *Los Angeles Times*, July 3, 2010.

Page 322: . . . *with tears in their eyes and "heartbroken"*: Karen DeYoung and Rajiv Chandrasekaran, "Gen. McChrystal Allies, *Rolling Stone* Disagree over Article's Ground Rules," *The Washington Post*, June 26, 2010.

Page 322: *Petraeus gives his welcoming address:* U.S. Embassy Kabul Public Diplomacy Flickr account, photographs of July 3 Independence Day event.

Page 323: *"There is no difference to us between General McChrystal and General Petraeus"*: "General David Petraeus Takes Command," NATOChannel123, YouTube video, July 4, 2010. http://www.youtube.com/watch?v=l3bFnBfxTA8.

CHAPTER 42. THE PENTAGON INVESTIGATES McCHRYSTAL

Page 325: *On July 13, I received an e-mail from the army inspector general's office*: Author e-mail.

Page 326: . . . *the "political fallout" of the story*: Letter to the author from Colonel Wayne Shanks, July 30, 2010.

Page 327: . . . *for publishing "embarrassing" information*: International Security Assistance Force media regulations.

CHAPTER 43. THE MEDIA-MILITARY-INDUSTRIAL COMPLEX

Page 328: *I walked into Café Milano in Georgetown*: Author notes, October 2010.

CHAPTER 44. I'D RATHER BE EATING A BURGER

Page 331: *Lately, Gates has been silently resisting, dragging his feet at these visits*: Author interview with Pentagon officials, March 2011.

Page 332: *Tired of Washington, mainly*: Noah Shachtman, "Take Back the Pentagon," *Wired*, October 2009.

Page 332: *He's living alone in Washington, in a military-supplied house*: John Barry and Evan Thomas, "A War Within," *Newsweek*, September 20, 2010.

Page 332: *He relaxes drinking Belvedere martinis and smoking cigars*: Noah Shachtman, "Take Back the Pentagon," *Wired*, October 2009.

Page 332: *The jokes are sometimes so bad*: Greg Jaffe, "Defense Secretary Robert Gates Leaves 'Em Laughing—as His Staff Cringes," The *Washington Post*, September 18, 2010.

Page 332: *His joke about DC*: Gordon Lubold, "Afghanistan War Decision: How Robert Gates Thinks," *The Christian Science Monitor*, November 8, 2009.

Page 333: *Nixon's bombing of Cambodia*: Ibid.

Page 333: *WANTED: ROBERT GATES*: Bob Gates, *From the Shadows: The Ultimate Insider's Story of Five Presidents and How They Won the Cold War* (New York: Simon & Schuster, 1996).

Page 333: . . . *"brass creep," he calls it*: John Barry and Evan Thomas, "A War Within," *Newsweek*, September 20, 2010.

Page 333: . . . *what he did as a Soviet analyst*: Ibid.

Page 333: . . . would be a *"disaster"*: Bob Woodward, Obama's Wars (New York: Simon & Schuster, 2010), p. 343.

Page 333: . . . *Gates is the man Woodward talks to last*: Transcript of *CNN Newsroom*, September 24, 2010.

Page 333: *"A journalist did in one day"*: Author interview with NATO official.

Page 333: *Gates will bemoan*: Department of Defense news transcript, Remarks by Secretary Gates, General Casey, and General McChrystal at Fort McNair, Washington, DC, July 23, 2010.

Page 334: . . . *"the lightbulb went on"*: Peter Baker, "For Obama, Steep Learning Curve as Chief of War," *The New York Times*, August 28, 2010.

Page 334: *One paper in the report provided to me*: Draft paper obtained by author.

Page 334: *He's finishing up his DoD bucket list*: Jim Garamone, "Gates Visits Littoral Combat Ship USS Independence," American Forces Press Service, May 7, 2011.

Page 334: *In December, he visits Afghanistan*: James Kitfield, "Robert Gates, David Petraeus: Partners in War," *National Journal*, December 9, 2010.

Page 335: *"I'm actually the guy that signs the orders and sends you over here"*: Ibid.

Page 335: . . . *violence is at its worst*: Michael Hastings, "King David's War," *Rolling Stone*, February 2, 2011.

Page 335: *Secretary of War*: Noah Shachtman, "Take Back the Pentagon," *Wired*, October 2009.

Page 335: . . . *"should have their head examined"*: Remarks delivered by Secretary of Defense Robert M. Gates, West Point, NY, Friday, February 25, 2011.

CHAPTER 45. ONCE UPON A TIME IN KANDAHAR

Page 336: *The motel in Kandahar was like a foreign language version of a Days Inn*: Author's notes, Kandahar, Afghanistan, December 2010.

Page 337: . . . *four billion dollars of opium a year*: G. Peters, *Seeds of Terror: How Heroin Is Bankrolling* (New York: Thomas Dunne Books, 2009), pp. 11, 319.

Page 337: *AWK was also on the CIA's payroll*: Dexter Filkins, Mark Mazzetti, and James Risen, "Brother of Afghan Leader Said to Be Paid by C.I.A.," *The New York Times*, October 27, 2009.

Page 337: . . . *"was really nervous, he thought he was going to get arrested"*: Author interview with General Michael Flynn, ISAF Headquarters, Kabul, Afghanistan, April 30, 2011.

Page 338: . . . *from eighteen districts to more than sixty*: Michael Hastings, "King David's War," *Rolling Stone*, February 2, 2011.

Page 338: . . . *"unscramble the egg"*: Ibid.

Page 339: *"It's safe"*: Author notes, Kabul, Afghanistan, December 2010.

CHAPTER 46. KING DAVID'S WAR

Page 344: . . . *asks more questions*: Author interview with senior military official, February 2011.

Page 344: . . . *"makes him almost giggly"*: Ibid.

Page 345: *"If you say the wrong thing"*: Ibid.

Page 345: *"He brings up Iraq"*: Author interview with Afghan official, Kabul, Afghanistan, December 2010.

Page 345: . . . *"twenty-one times in fifteen minutes"*: Author interview with senior U.S. administration official, Kabul, Afghanistan, December 2010.

Page 345: *Petraeus was born in Cornwall, New York*: Alexa James, "Gen. Petraeus Pays Visit to His Old High School in Cornwall," *Times Herald-Record*, September 9, 2009.

Page 346: . . . *"looked more concerned"*: D. McGregor, *Warrior's Rage: The Great Tank Battle of '73* (Annapolis, MD: Naval Institute Press, 2009), p. 21.

Page 346: . . . *senior advisor*: L. Robinson, "How Afghanistan Ends," *Small Wars Journal*, December 2, 2010.

Page 346: *"Can you believe it took us thirty years to get our Combat Infantry Badges?"*: Author interview with military official.

Page 347: *Without Eaton's permission . . . Petraeus sends his men in to move all of Eaton's stuff*: Ibid.

Page 347: . . . *earned him the nickname General Betray-Us*: Author interview with military officials.

Page 348: *Petraeus writes an op-ed for* The Washington Post: David Petraeus, "Battling for Iraq," *The Washington Post*, September 26, 2004.

Page 348: . . . *more than twenty thousand troops*: President George W. Bush's Address to the Nation, White House, January 10, 2007.

Page 348: *A full-page advertisement in* The New York Times *calling him General Betray-Us*: Clark Hoyt, "Betraying Its Own Best Interests," *The New York Times*, September 23, 2007.

Page 349: . . . *"the face of the war in Iraq"*: Interview with a military official, Washington, DC, January 2011.

Page 349: *PETRAEUS'S MIRACLE*: David Ignatius, "Petraeus's Miracle," *The Washington Post*, September 17, 2008.

Page 349: . . . *"near miracle worker"*: John Berry and Evan Thomas, "Obama's Vietnam," *Newsweek*, February 9, 2009.

Page 349: . . . *up to $825 on eBay*: Michael Hastings, "King David's War," *Rolling Stone*, February 2, 2011.

Page 349: . . . *seven thousand pizzas*: Eileen O. Daday, "Soldiers to Get 'a Slice of Home' for Super Bowl," *Chicago Daily Herald*, January 31, 2011.

CHAPTER 47. TOURISM, NOT TERRORISM

Page 350: *"In November and October, I didn't leave my house"*: Author notes.

Page 350: . . . *at least one high-level assassination*: Michael Hastings, "King David's War," *Rolling Stone*, February 2, 2011.

Page 351: *The Taliban admitted that the NATO offensive*: Ibid.

Page 351: *Sources in the Taliban told me that many insurgents had just left*: Ibid.

Page 351: *"This has been the worst year"*: Author interview with Ghulam Hayder Hamidi, Kandahar, Afghanistan, December 2010.

Page 352: *"There's talk of transition"*: Michael Hastings, "King David's War," *Rolling Stone*, February 2, 2011.

Page 352: *"Gul Agha Sherzai, why are you not writing that he is corrupt?"*: Author interview with Ghulam Hayder Hamidi, Kandahar, Afghanistan, December 2010.

Page 352: *"People involved in drugs and drug dealing"*: Author interview with Hajji Agha Lalai, Afghanistan, December 2010.

Page 352: . . . *"hasn't lost their power"*: Author interview with Ghulam Hayder Hamidi, Kandahar, Afghanistan, December 2010.

Page 353: *"Better? I didn't say better"*: Author interview with Ahmad Berkazai, Kandahar, Afghanistan, December 2010.

CHAPTER 48. PETRAEUS DOES BODY COUNTS

Page 354: *In late October, Petraeus meets with President Karzai*: Rajiv Chandrasekaran, "As U.S. Assesses Mission, Karzai Is a Question Mark," *The Washington Post*, December 13, 2010.

Page 354: *"The time has come"*: Excerpts from Afghan President Hamid Karzai's interview with *The Washington Post*, November 14, 2011.

Page 355: *"Karzai pushes, he pushes back"*: Author interview with White House official.

Page 355: *Karzai refuses to go on the plane with him*: Michael Hastings, "King David's War," *Rolling Stone*, February 2, 2011.

Page 355: *In February, there's a civilian casualty incident*: Joshua Partlow, "Petraeus's Comments on Coalition Attack Reportedly Offend Karzai Government," *The Washington Post*, February 22, 2011.

Page 355: *NATO pushes back*: Joshua Partlow and Habib Zahori, "Afghan Officials

Allege That 65 Civilians Were Killed in U.S. Military Operation," *The Washington Post*, February 20, 2011.

Page 355: *"I was dizzy"*: Joshua Partlow, "Petraeus's Comments on Coalition Attack Reportedly Offend Karzai Government," *The Washington Post*, February 22, 2011.

Page 356: *Petraeus says it's not a "sure thing"*: Kate McCarty, "Exclusive: Gen. Petraeus Not 'Sure' Victory in Afghanistan by 2014," ABC News, December 6, 2010.

Page 356: *He drastically ups the number of airstrikes*: Michael Hastings, "King David's War," *Rolling Stone*, February 2, 2011.

Page 356: *He . . . triples the number of night raids*: Ibid.

Page 357: *Petraeus signs off on the total leveling*: Tom Ricks, "Travels with Paula (I): A Time to Build," Foreign Policy's The Best Defense blog, January 13, 2011.

Page 357: *"Taliban infested"*: Ibid.

Page 357: . . . *"fit of theatrics"*: Ibid.

Page 358: . . . *a former U.S. ambassador came just short*: Joshua Miller, "Former Top Diplomat Says Eikenberry Must Go," ABC News, December 5, 2010.

Page 358: *"Since when did a diplomat"*: Jonathan Alter and Christopher Dickey, "Richard Holbrooke's Lonely Mission: The Late Diplomat Never Lost His Passion for Peacemaking, But It Turned Out That Some of His Toughest Adversaries Were on His Own Side," *Newsweek*, January 24, 2011.

Page 358: *On December 16, President Obama gives a speech*: Statement by President Barack Obama on the Afghanistan-Pakistan Annual Review, White House, December 16, 2010.

Page 358: *We aren't "nation-building"*: Ibid.

Page 358: . . . *"a graceful exit"*: Dexter Filkins, "Petraeus Opposes a Rapid Pullout in Afghanistan," *The New York Times*, August 15, 2010.

Page 358: . . . *"criminal oligarchy of politically connected businessman"*: International Crisis Group Report, The Insurgency in Afghanistan's Heartland, June 27, 2011, p. 1.

Page 359: *Petraeus explains that violence*: Matthew Green, interview transcript: "Gen. David Petraeus," *Financial Times*, February 7, 2011.

CHAPTER 49. THE NEW AFGHANISTAN

Page 360: *"The Americans built this road"*: Author notes, December 9, 2010.

Page 360: *An American spy balloon*: Ibid.

Page 361: *"General Petraeus and I have very similar opinions"*: Author interview with Abdul Razzik, Spin Boldak, Afghanistan, December 9, 2010.

Page 361: *"We don't take prisoners"*: Ibid.

Page 362: *"How can we have peace talks*: Ibid.

Page 362: . . . *"just a three-star"*: Ibid.

Page 362: *In 1995, his uncle was killed*: Ibid.

Page 362: *"Iran and Pakistan are our enemies"*: Ibid.

Page 363: *In 2002, he was named chief of the border police*: Ibid.

Page 363: *"People began to say he was here to kill"*: Anand Gopal, New America Foundation Counterterrorism Strategy Initiative Policy Paper, The Battle for Afghanistan: Militancy and Conflict in Kandahar, November 2010.

Page 363: *Razzik's men stopped sixteen civilians*: Michael Hastings, "King David's War," *Rolling Stone*, February 2, 2011.

Page 363: *Razzik was briefly suspended*: Ibid.

Page 363: *"In Afghanistan an ordinary person"*: Human Rights Watch, "NATO/Afghanistan: Abusive Partners Undermine Transition Plan," November 18, 2010.

Page 364: *On February 4, 2010*: Wikileaks State Department cable, "New Civ-Mil Effort to Influence Behavior of Criminal and Corrupt Afghan Officials," February 17, 2010.

Page 364–365: *"Americans are always choosing stupid friends here"*: Author interview with Izzatullah Wasifi, Kabul, Afghanistan, December 2010.

Page 365: *Ambassador Eikenberry posed for a photo op*: Michael Hastings, "King David's War," *Rolling Stone*, February 2, 2011.

Page 365: *In August, Razzik received even more funding*: Ibid.

Page 365: *"Sometimes I travel in the American helicopters"*: Author interview with Abdul Razzik, Spin Boldak, Afghanistan, December 9, 2010.

Page 365: *"On one side, you have State, DEA, FBI"*: Author interview with U.S. official, Kabul, Afghanistan, December 2010.

Page 365: *A condition in the supplemental bill passed last year*: Michael Hastings, "King David's War," *Rolling Stone*, February 2, 2011.

Page 365: . . . *a journalist for* The Atlantic: M. Aikins, "Our Man in Kandahar," *The Atlantic*, November 2011.

Page 366: *Another State Department cable suggested*: Wikileaks State Department cable, "Kandahar: Corruption Reforms by the Master of Spin?" February 17, 2010.

Page 366: . . . *like "Robin Hood"*: Rajiv Chandrasekaran, "The Afghan Robin Hood," *The Washington Post*, October 4, 2010.

Page 366: *"Afghan good enough"*: Michael Hastings, "King David's War," *Rolling Stone*, February 2, 2011.

Page 366: . . . *"folk hero"*: Yaroslav Trofimov and Matthew Rosenberg, "In Afghanistan, U.S. Turns 'Malignant Actor' Into Ally," *The Wall Street Journal*, November 18, 2011.

Page 366: *"The difference between Abdul Razzik"*: Author interview with Afghan contractor, Kandahar, Afghanistan, December 2010.

Page 366: *"It's a democracy"*: Author interview with Abdul Razzik, Spin Boldak, Afghanistan, December 9, 2010.

Page 367: . . . *"small but capable Afghan army"*: Michael Hastings, "King David's War," *Rolling Stone*, February 2, 2011.

Page 367: *"The world promised us"*: Author interview with Ahmad Berkazai, Kandahar, Afghanistan, December 2010.

Page 367: *"That's an old British castle"*: Author interview with Abdul Razzik, Spin Boldak, Afghanistan, December 9, 2010.

CHAPTER 50. JOE BIDEN IS RIGHT

Page 368: *On December 10, 2010, Ambassador Richard Holbrooke walks into*: Jonathan Alter and Christoper Dickey, "Richard Holbrooke's Lonely Mission: The Late Diplomat Never Lost His Passion for Peacemaking, But It Turned Out That Some of His Toughest Adversaries Were on His Own Side," *Newsweek*, January 24, 2011.

Page 370: . . . *"strangling" the position that Holbrooke held*: Author interview with State Department official, February 2011.

Page 370: *"It's a little uncomfortable with those two"*: Ibid.

Page 370: *"He could tell they were going to try"*: Ibid.

Page 370: *"Why do they need a well?"*: Mark Landler, "Obama's Growing Trust in Biden Is Reflected in His Call on Troops," *The New York Times*, June 25, 2011.

Page 371: *They help to rehabilitate Stanley McChrystal's image*: Thom Shanker, "McChrystal to Lead Program for Military Families," *The New York Times*, April 10, 2011.

Page 371: *There is a controversy when a screening of a documentary*: Esther Zuckerman, "Yale Dems Pull Support for War Documentary," *Yale Daily News*, September 2, 2010.

Page 371: *He starts up a consulting company*: Katherine Skiba, "Ex-General Joins First Lady's Effort to Assist Troops: Stanley McChrystal Will Be an Unpaid Advisor to Her New National Campaign," *Los Angeles Times*, April 12, 2011.

Page 371: *He signs up with a speaker's bureau*: PR Newswire, "General Stanley McChrystal Signs With Leading Authorities, Inc., for Exclusive Lecture Representation," August 18, 2010.

Page 371: *$60,000 a speaking engagement*: Ben Smith, "McChrystal's Fee," *Politico*, August 30, 2010.

Page 371: *He gets a slot on the board of JetBlue*: PR Newswire, "JetBlue Airways Names General Stanley McChrystal to Its Board of Directors," November 9, 2010.

Page 371: *He allows another profile*: Emily Foxhall, "Professor McChrystal," *Yale Daily News*, January 18, 2011.

Page 371: *In February, he gives a speech with Greg Mortenson*: "McChrystal, Mortenson Talk Leadership," *Yale Daily News*, February 17, 2011.

Page 371: *In March, he gives another speech*: "Listen, Learn . . . Then Lead: Stanley McChrystal on TED.com," TED2011, March 2011.

Page 371: *On April 8, the Defense Department investigation*: Memorandum for the Inspector General, Department of the Army Subject; Review of Army Inspector General Agency Report of Investigation (Case 10-024), stamped April 8, 2011.

Page 372: *"In some instances"*: Ibid., p. 2.

Page 372: *. . . the "bite me" response*: Ibid., p. 3.

Page 372: *Witnesses deny*: Ibid., p. 4.

Page 372: *. . . "it would not have been a failure"*: Ibid., pp. 1–2.

Page 372: *. . . "witnesses testified the comment"*: Ibid., p. 4.

Page 372: *The report found "insufficient evidence"*: Ibid.

Page 372: *"Our analysis of witness testimony"*: Ibid., pp. 4–5.

Page 372: *Two days after the report is finished*: Thom Shanker, "McChrystal to Lead Program for Military Families," *The New York Times*, April 10, 2011.

Page 372: *"It's a slap in the face"*: "Army Mom Takes on White House; Wants General Removed from Post," ABC News, April 14, 2011.

Page 373: *. . . give off-the-record interviews*: Steve Clemons, "Biden's Burden: Last One Standing in Afghanistan Policy Wars," *Atlantic.com*, July 21, 2011.

Page 373: *"a little better than 50 percent" done*: Federal News Service, Council on Foreign Relations HBO History Makers Series Speaker: Stanley McChrystal, New York, NY, October 6, 2011.

Page 373: *General Michael Flynn takes a job in intelligence analysis*: Kimberly Dozier, "Officer Who Vowed to Fix Intel Now Troubleshooter," Associated Press, October 7, 2011.

Page 373: *His brother Charlie*: Melissa Bower, "Flynn Promoted to Brigadier General," *Fort Leavenworth Lamp*, September 08, 2011.

Page 373: . . . *violence is the worst it has been in nine years*: Michael Hastings, "King David's War," *Rolling Stone*, February 2, 2011.

Page 373: *"We are losing the battle for hearts and minds"*: "An Open Letter to President Obama," www.afghanistancalltoreason.com, December 2010.

Page 373: . . . *"more constructive local leadership"*: Josh Partlow, "Ahmed Wali Karzai, Half Brother of Afghan President, Killed by Trusted Confidant," *The Washington Post*, July 12, 2011.

Page 373: . . . *64 percent of Americans*: Scott Wilson and Jon Cohen, "Poll: Nearly Two-Thirds of Americans Say Afghan War Isn't Worth Fighting," *The Washington Post*, March 15, 2011.

Page 373: *On Capitol Hill, 204 congressmen voted against*: Eugene Mulero, "House Passes Defense Bill After Close Vote on Afghanistan Withdrawal," *Congressional Quarterly Today*, May 26, 2011.

Page 374: *"Seven Days in May dynamic"*: Marc Ambinder, "How the White House Played Petraeus," *National Journal*, June 23, 2011.

Page 374: *Obama meets with Petraeus*: Andrea Terkel, "Petraeus Backs Obama's Afghanistan Plan But Says Drawdown Is More 'Aggressive' Than Military Wanted," *Huffington Post*, June 23, 2011.

Page 375: . . . *"was a more aggressive [drawdown] option"*: Mark Landler and Helene Cooper, "Obama Will Speed Military Pullout from Afghan War," *The New York Times*, June 23, 2011.

EPILOGUE: SOMEDAY, THIS WAR'S GONNA END

Page 376: *Obama plays only nine holes of golf*: Christopher Dickey, Ron Moreau, and Sami Yousafzai, "A Decade on the Lam," *Newsweek*, May 6, 2011.

Page 376: *Biden played with a rosary ring*: Mark Mazzetti, Helene Cooper, and Peter Baker, "Behind the Hunt for Bin Laden," *The New York Times*, May 3, 2011.

Page 376: *Admiral Mullen had his own*: Mark Landler, "Obama's Growing Trust in Biden Is Reflected in His Call on Troops," *The New York Times*, June 25, 2011.

Page 376: *Hillary put her hands up*: Barry Moody, "Clinton: Allergy, Not Anguish in My Bin Laden Photo," Reuters, May 5, 2011.

Page 377: . . . *for forty minutes*: Federal News Service, White House Press Briefing by Press Secretary Jay Carney, Washington, DC, May 3, 2011.

Page 377: *Obama turned to his team*: N. Schmidle, "Getting Bin Laden," *The New Yorker*, August 8, 2011.

Page 378: . . . *more than double the total*: http://www.icasualties.org., October 17, 2011.

Page 379: . . . *the twenty-three Navy SEALs who killed him*: N. Schmidle, "Getting Bin Laden," *The New Yorker*, August 8, 2011.

An index for this book is available at
www.penguin.com/theoperatorsextras.